Trading Post to Metropolis

Milwaukee County's First 150 Years

The Courthouse, seat of Milwaukee County Government.

Trading Post to Metropolis

Milwaukee County's First 150 Years

Ralph M. Aderman, Editor

Milwaukee County Historical Society

ISBN 0-938076-08-6

Library of Congress Card No. 87-061340

Copyright 1987

Milwaukee County Historical Society
910 North Old World Third Street
Milwaukee, Wisconsin 53203

Printed in the United States of America
C. W. Brown Printing Co.
Oconomowoc, Wisconsin

Table of Contents

Introduction

During its existence of more than one hundred fifty years Milwaukee County has grown from a fur-trading center to an urban metropolis, comprising Wisconsin's largest city and eighteen suburban communities. The history of this development has never been told in a unified way. Most historians dealing with the area have focused on the City of Milwaukee, with County involved only incidentally in the narrative. The present volume attempts to redress that imbalance and deal with issues and developments from a Countywide perspective. In this respect it is a pioneering effort.

When it was proposed that a history of Milwaukee County would be an appropriate outgrowth of the County's Sesquicentennial observance in 1985, the Milwaukee County Historical Society readily agreed to explore the possibility of coordinating the preparation of such a study and serving as its publisher. The result was a series of meetings between representatives of the County and the Historical Society at which the suggestion was discussed and a plan for the project formulated.

Out of these discussions came a proposal for preparing a history of Milwaukee County which took into account the geographical nature of the County and its growth and development as a governmental entity. Although Milwaukee County is the oldest continuous form of representative government in southeastern Wisconsin (it was originally created as a part of Michigan Territory in 1834 and formally organized a year later), the nature and scope of its services and functions have materially changed in recent decades. Almost from the very beginning of its existence it provided basic governmental and judicial services for its citizens. In the twentieth century its responsibilities have been substantially enlarged, particularly in the areas of public welfare and health, parks and recreation, and such modern aspects of transportation as expressways, airports, and operation of a Countywide bus system. This ever-increasing range of public services merits historical analysis. Moreover, it was determined that the historical treatment of these topics should be scholarly rather than popular, using the original research of professional historians and specialists into the archives and files of various County agencies to provide fresh, accurate data for this new look at the County's evolution to the present day.

The areas to be treated in this volume include 1) a study of the towns and villages of the County in their shift from a rural to an urban setting; 2) the treatment of the governance and administration of the County; 3) an analysis of County judicial services; 4) a description of the evolution of the health and social services needed in an urban environment growing in complexity; 5) a study of the parks and recreational services and facilities provided by the County; and 6) an examination of the changing patterns of transportation and their effects upon the social and economic development of the County. While these large areas do not encompass all aspects of County life and concerns, they provide an overview and background against which more specific topics and concerns may be placed. From these discussions and from the listings of sources used in them, interested readers are provided with the means of pursuing topics in greater detail. Indeed, one of the hopes of the sponsors of this history is that it will spur interested scholars and students to explore other aspects of County history and development.

The task of directing and coordinating the project was given to a special committee consisting of Dr. Carla H. Hay, Professor of History, Marquette University; Dr. F. Paul Prucha, S.J., Professor of History, Marquette University; Dr. Frederick I. Olson, Professor Emeritus of History, University of Wisconsin-Milwaukee; Mr. Harry H. Anderson, Executive Director of the Milwaukee County Historical Society; and Dr. Ralph M. Aderman, Professor Emeritus of English, University of Wisconsin-Milwaukee. This committee formulated the guidelines, recruited the investigators, examined the outlines for the various chapters, made suggestions concerning them, and read the drafts of the chapters as they were written. Because of the ongoing commitments of some of the authors and the necessity of doing considerable original research in archives and materials not previously used, the writing has taken somewhat longer than was originally contemplated. The end product, however, is a fresh look at the various facets of the enduring and lively entity we call Milwaukee County.

Such a venture as this involves the efforts and interest of many people in addition to the authors and persons who helped them. We particularly wish to thank County Board Chairman F. Thomas Ament, who originally suggested the history as a permanent reminder of the 1985 Sesquicentennial observance, and also County Executive William F. O'Donnell, who gave the project his welcome endorsement and support. Essential financing was provided through the County Executive's budget, subsequently adopted by the County Board of Supervisors. Valuable cooperation was forthcoming from County department heads and their staffs. In special areas assistance was provided by Mackie Westbrook, who served as a useful liaison with the County Board; Judith A. Simonsen, who has helped with proofreading, picture selection, and the layout of the chapters; Kathleen O'Hara, for editorial assistance; Charles Cooney, who provided access to the resources of the library and archival materials in the Milwaukee County Historical Society; Robert Cassidy, whose expertise in the area of design was called upon; Richard Hyrnewicki for photographic services; Erika Metzger for typing and clerical assistance; Darlene E. Waterstreet for compiling the index; and the staff of C.W. Brown Printing Company for their assistance in seeing the book through the press.

Ralph M. Aderman
April 1987

City Expansion and Suburban Spread: Settlements and Governments in Milwaukee County

by Frederick I. Olson⎯⎯⎯⎯⎯⎯⎯⎯⎯⎯⎯⎯⎯⎯⎯⎯⎯⎯⎯

In 1986 Milwaukee County comprises 240 square miles which serve as home for nearly a million people. It is the third smallest of the state's seventy-two counties (only Ozaukee and Pepin are smaller, and by a narrow margin), but by far the most populous, indeed, roughly equal to the next four combined (Dane, Waukesha, Brown, and Racine). It forms the major component in the nation's twenty-fourth largest urban population cluster as defined by the U.S. Bureau of the Census, a Standard Metropolitan Statistical Area which also includes the adjacent counties of Ozaukee, Washington, and Waukesha. In a broader context the SMSA which includes Milwaukee County is the second largest population concentration in an almost unbroken urban ribbon of cities and suburbs which stretches from the greater Chicago area in Michigan, Indiana, and Illinois, at the foot of Lake Michigan, northward along the west shore of Lake Michigan to the Wisconsin-Michigan border north of Green Bay.

It is the purpose of this essay to describe how a tiny portion of the earth's surface was defined geographically and politically as Milwaukee County, how it was peopled and thus shaped into a set of complex economic, social, and cultural entities, and how these people reshaped their original simple political structure into a congeries of governing units responding to their changing needs.

From Indian Occupancy to Land Sales

What is now Milwaukee was inhabited for thousands of years by a variety of American Indians before a sudden influx of European and American settlers a century and a half ago deprived the Indians of their prehistoric claims. The first recorded European discoveries and explorations occurred in Wisconsin in the seventeenth century. The first known French visitors came as early as the 1630s, and in much greater numbers and to more precise purposes in the 1670s. Father Jacques Marquette ascended the Milwaukee River and camped there in 1674, as part of the aggressive drive of Jesuit missionaries into the interior of North

America via the water routes lying along the present U.S.-Canadian boundaries. Here the Jesuits were challenged by hundreds of thousands of pagan Indians in the interior of North America; and their almost unbelievable exertions on behalf of Indian conversions in the latter seventeenth century, as set forth in the *Jesuit Relations*, evoke the greatest admiration.

But the official French objectives in North America, as elsewhere in the world where they competed with Europe's other great colonizing powers, had less to do with souls than with the greater glory of the French monarch and the French nation, with a mercantilist philosophy, with a rapidly changing and expanding economy, and with the spirit of human adventure in the post-Renaissance world. By the early eighteenth century the French focus on the acquisition of fish and furs in the New World had narrowed, after a series of Indian wars in Wisconsin, to the establishment and maintenance of a stable fur trade system that utilized the western Great Lakes Indians as primary hunters and trappers supplying more easterly French trading posts.

This French fur system was mildly threatened by the aggressive Spanish competition from the south via the Mississippi and Ohio Rivers. It was doomed by the approach from the east of the British, who defeated the French at Quebec in 1759 and in 1763 confirmed their conquest of New France, or Canada, in the Treaty of Paris. The British fur trade system differed in detail from that of the French, but it was similarly founded on the extraordinary European demand for furs at the time and on the use of Indians as the major source of manpower for the trade in the interior. After 1763 the British fur traders moved aggressively north and west from their earlier posts south of the Great Lakes, but much of the fur trade, including Indian contacts in the interior, remained in French hands until after the end of the War of 1812. Thus French names such as Mirandeau, Vieau, Juneau, La Croix, La Framboise, and Le Claire appear just before and after 1800 in the Milwaukee trade. And this is despite a second change of sovereignty for the Milwaukee area which occurred in the 1783 treaty between Britain and the newly independent United States at the end of the Revolutionary War.

Nonetheless, however similar, British and French policy and practice in the New World differed sharply on several counts. By 1763 France, despite valiant efforts, had succeeded in producing only a small farming colony in the St. Lawrence Valley, without local governance or a significant urban society. The English, on the other hand, had many seaboard colonies of surprising population and great political, economic, and social sophistication. Their colonial charters forecast, indeed promised, that settlement would sooner or later move westward across the Allegheny-Appalachian chain into the area south of the Great Lakes and along the Ohio River Valley. After 1763, however, government policy from London restricted such population movements as long as these areas were occupied by the Indians. Colonial grievances over the slowness with which the West was opened served as a major source of revolutionary sentiment. In the long run the transfer of Canada to the British in 1763 and the resulting freedom of the British and the British colonials to move into the western Great Lakes area ensured that settlers, not fur traders, would soon become dominant there.

British motives in the cession of the western country to the United States in the treaty concluded in 1783 remain in dispute even today, but the consequences of the decision were enormous. The new nation was not only partially relieved of a potential political and diplomatic headache (though resulting complications in Anglo-American relations persisted until 1815), but it also acquired a vast expanse of land for which the Confederation Congress was responsible. Cessions by several states of their western lands gave the Confederation (and later the new government under the Constitution) a chunk of real estate from whose sale the government could realize revenues which would stabilize its financial status for decades to come; and it ensured uniform policies for the governance of this vast area.

The policies by which the Confederation Congress arranged for distribution of the public domain and for its self-government evolved between 1781 and 1787 and, with modifications, were directly applicable to the settlement of what is now the State of Wisconsin, including Milwaukee County. Following the British lead, the U.S. government undertook to negotiate a series of Indian treaties with each tribe occupying lands of the public domain lying in the path of the westward-moving settler. Army officers doubled as Indian agents and American negotiators and dealt with tribes and putative tribal leaders that could be crudely identified with substantial parcels of Indian-occupied land.

The American government never really conceded either absolute land ownership or total sovereignty to the Indians. The use of the term "treaty" did not suggest direct arms-length negotiations with a sovereign nation like England or France; and after the Civil War the House of Representatives ended the "treaty" myth by insisting upon a role in the implementation of any such agreement with an Indian tribe. American jurisprudence has been hard pressed to assimilate relations with Indian tribes ever since. John Marshall defined them as "dependent domestic nations," and today federal courts and the U.S. Congress are still wrestling with the legal consequences of the treaty era. As a practical matter, since the federal government ordinarily had the superior force, the Indians were negotiating the best deal they could in the extinguishing of Indian occupation rights to lands lying in the path of European settlement.

Treaties directly bearing on Indian occupancy of Wisconsin were begun in 1801 and continued spasmodically for more than half a century. The federal government was firmly opposed to the opening of lands to settlement, that is, to public sale of lands at a land office, until a treaty had been concluded and the tribe had vacated the land voluntarily or by force. The land comprising the present Milwaukee County was ceded by the occupying tribes in the late 1820s and early 1830s, and substantial removal of tribes took place quite promptly, in any case by 1838 or 1839 for Milwaukee. Black Hawk's effort to lead bands of Sac and Fox Indians back into their ceded lands in the Rock River Valley in 1832 is a well-known exception to the general peace which accompanied the process of extinguishing Indian titles in Wisconsin. The brutal pursuit and hunting down of Black Hawk's less than warlike followers by militia in federal service was an exceptional case for this time, but it illustrated the determination of the federal government and the settlers to be done with the problem, and it was followed in less than two years by the opening of some Wisconsin lands for sale.

As was the case in the Milwaukee area, tribal agreements made in the period immediately following 1825 were premised on the belief that the various tribes could be moved beyond a permanent Indian frontier extending into the trans-Mississippi West, an area which contemporary Americans did not then openly covet for permanent settlement. While tribes usually moved as a body in accordance with treaties, individual Indians or small bands could and often did remain, although they thus lost some corporate advantages accruing from the treaties. The Menomonee Valley near downtown Milwaukee, as well as other outlying areas of Milwaukee County, probably had scattered Indian residents into the post-Civil War era. Their status under state and federal law was then anomalous, for they were not normally considered citizens nor were they accorded constitutional protections. That individual Indians remained in the vicinity of Milwaukee as late as the Civil War is demonstrated by the unwarranted Indian scare which permeated counties to the north of Milwaukee in the fall of 1862 concurrent with the Sioux uprisings in Minnesota.

According to federal policy, removal of the Indians was to be followed by survey of the lands to be sold by the government. The survey of the Milwaukee area followed closely the actions regarding Indian titles. One can only imagine the physical obstacles encountered by the individual surveyors in traversing almost every inch of even so level and attractive a piece of real estate as primeval Milwaukee County. Rivers, creeks, valleys, swamps, woods, underbrush could make even so benign a landscape formidable. Present-day Milwaukee County, except for Jones Island, Lincoln Memorial Drive, and the historic downtown west from the lake to the North-South Freeway, has not been massively altered in the last century and a half, and many portions of the newer, outlying suburbs which were used for farming may not have been changed very much at all. But the surveyor's task was an exacting one, and the wonder is not that the prior federal survey conducted throughout the old Northwest Territory — Ohio, Indiana, Illinois, Michigan and Wisconsin — required some minor corrections, but that it was possible to do it at all.

The rectilinear survey system prescribed by Congress in the Land Ordinance of 1785 virtually guaranteed the integrity of land titles as well as facilitating the government land sales. It was in sharp contrast to the "indiscriminate locations" permitted in Virginia and other original colonies, a practice which was carried across the mountains to Kentucky and Tennessee, resulting inevitably in endless land litigation. It improved upon New England precedents for controlling settlement in hitherto unoccupied lands.

The system itself used an east-west base line crossed at six-mile intervals by meridians, the whole originating at a base line running due west from the point where the Ohio River crossed the western border of Pennsylvania. The land lying between each meridian constituted a range of townships six miles by six miles, or thirty-six square miles, and each section within the township was one square mile in size and was numbered consecutively from one to thirty-six beginning at the northeast corner of the township and running horizontally to the southeast corner. Each section of 640 acres could in turn be subdivided into a half section (320 acres) and a quarter section (160 acres) and so on.

Through numbering of the components in this system an extremely accurate description of land was possible, no matter the topography or the way in which the land was subdivided. As the case proved in Milwaukee County, the rectilinear survey also provided the boundaries defining the seven towns which were later formed as local civil governments in the county, identical to the township boundaries. And the section and township lines formed the basis for major streets in the urban grid systems and for county highways in the rural areas.

Prior survey was, of course, a prelude to land sales in what was then Michigan Territory, soon to become the Territory of Wisconsin in 1836, and a state twelve years later. Land offices opened at Mineral Point and Green Bay for Wisconsin land sales in 1834; some Milwaukee area land became available the next year, and by 1839 there was a land office in the Village of Milwaukee. The first two years of Wisconsin land sales coincided with the peak of the public land sale boom nationally during the Jackson administration, a frenzy of speculation fueled not only by runaway public psychology but also by easy credit from the state banks favored by Jackson's fiscal policies. The President brought the boom to a sudden halt in

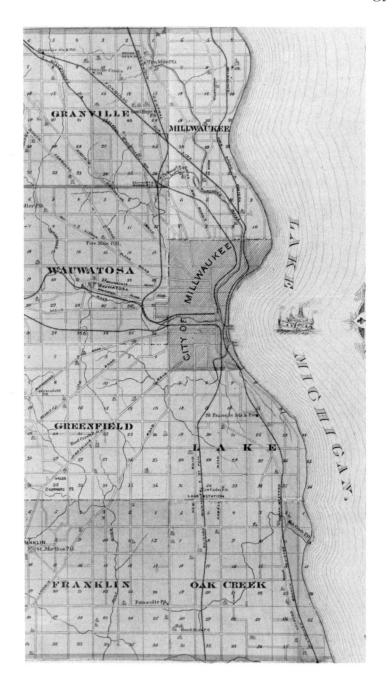

A sectional map from H. Belden and Co.'s Illustrated Historical Atlas of Milwaukee Co. 1876.

**FORMATION OF THE ORIGINAL SEVEN
TOWNS IN MILWAUKEE COUNTY
AS SHOWN ON THE MAP
FROM THE 1876 HISTORICAL ATLAS**

Date of Territorial Legislative Approval	Name	Future Entities Included in Area	Approximate Size in 1876
January 2, 1838	Town of Lake	Towns of Franklin, Greenfield, and Oak Creek	23.5 sq. mi.
January 2, 1838	Town of Milwaukee	Towns of Granville and Wauwatosa and Village of Milwaukee	24 sq. mi.
March 8, 1839	Town of Kinniken-nick (renamed in 1841 Town of Greenfield)	Town of Franklin	36 sq. mi.
December 20, 1839	Town of Franklin		36 sq. mi.
January 13, 1840	Town of Granville		36 sq. mi.
April 30, 1840	Town of Wauwatosa		36 sq. mi. (less 1,000 acres)
August 13, 1840	Town of Oak Creek		28.5 sq. mi.

1837 by the Specie Circular, which stipulated that most purchases would require hard money rather than paper bank notes. Sales of land in Milwaukee and Wisconsin nosedived, as they did nationally, in 1837 and for the next half dozen years, but by the early 1840s recovery was apparent and all of Milwaukee county lands were soon patented.

Initially the federal government had hoped to sell the public domain in wholesale lots, but it soon became instead a retailer. The nearly fifty years of federal experience as real estate agent had witnessed several changes in the terms of government sale — the minimum price per acre, the minimum acres per sale, cash versus installment buying, the rights of squatters — but the basic premise remained of open auction sales to the highest bidder at a minimum price. In 1834 that meant eighty acres at a minimum price of $1.25, or $100 in cash. The insistent demand of squatters periodically led Congress to provide for preemptive rights to 160 acres at the minimum price, restricted to the area then being opened up for sale, and Congress legislated preemption for Wisconsin lands almost immediately. In 1841 a general and permanent preemption act was adopted; and in the 1862 Homestead Act Congress extended the preemption principle to an outright gift, but with a few strings attached.

The increasingly liberal, populist provisions of federal land sales did not, however, entirely satisfy the public appetite for cheap land in the 1830s, at the time Wisconsin lands were opened; and in Milwaukee in 1836 and 1837, as elsewhere at that time, a claims association was organized in advance of the auction to protect small claimants against the vagaries of an auction in which large-scale speculators with ample resources might bid up prices. Hostility to land speculators was intense among those newcomers who were very poor and feared that the best lands would elude them; but the evidence is not clear that at this time large eastern investors were actually able to identify the best farm lands and outbid the average settler. Indeed, land speculation was widespread, but eastern investors were often represented by local agents and it is probable that the agents were at times incompetent and at other times devious in their stewardship.

It is evident that the evolving federal land sales terms reflected a bias toward farming as the normal American pursuit. But most of the very earliest settlers were attracted to Milwaukee County because of the confluence of three rivers and its potential as the site of a city. Not all who arrived prior to the auction sale for this land could be accommodated by preemptive rights for 160 acres in a very constricted area. A provision in the law allowed competing preemptive claimants to be reimbursed for part of their unrealizable claim with a "floating right" to other lands, a sort of secondary preemption. Hence what was expected to be the most valuable real estate in a city planned along either side of the Milwaukee and Menomonee Rivers in the downtown area was assembled by the three chief townsite promoters through the purchase of floating rights, apparently at a price very close to the minimum of $1.25 per acre. The adaptability of the federal system in the hands of ingenious and determined city promoters was substantial. Of course, the use of floating rights was applicable for only a short period in 1834 and 1835, and then for a limited portion of downtown Milwaukee. Lands in the rest of Milwaukee County were viewed with varying degrees of enthusiasm by early settlers — for example, there was a preference as always for lands adjacent to rivers and creeks such as Deer Creek and Oak Creek on the south side, and for some wooded areas — but most of them were soon sold according to traditional values for farming.

No sooner had townsite titles devolved in the middle 1830s on the major assemblers — Solomon Juneau on the east side of the Milwaukee River and Byron Kilbourn on the west — than plats were laid out and lots were offered for sale. The secondary market for Milwaukee lots was, if anything, more feverish than the scramble for original patents from the federal government. It is said that the speculative craze occasionally brought more than one trade to a piece of property in the same day. Juneau, Kilbourn, and George Walker, after he perfected his title to the near south side in 1849, used a variety of promotional devices to sell their own land holdings and to improve the attractiveness of their portion of the city-to-be, laying out streets, grading lots, donating land for public use, making other improvements, and attracting buyer attention to their property.

Primary and secondary land sales in the Milwaukee area closely resembled similar activities in other parts of Wisconsin Territory, especially along the west shore of Lake Michigan. But early Milwaukee experienced the impact of a unique event on its early growth, the effort of Byron Kilbourn and his associates on the west side of the Milwaukee River to construct between 1838 and 1842 a canal from the Milwaukee River to the Rock River in Jefferson County. This was an era of intense enthusiasm for canal construction as the most effective means of economic development, following the model of the highly successful Erie Canal, which opened in 1825 and almost immediately confirmed New York City's place as the nation's commercial center.

Canals were conceived as manmade connectors of important natural waterways, in this case, Lake Michigan and the Mississippi River. The same idea had occurred to Chicago and northern Illinois developers who succeeded with the Michigan-Illinois Canal. Similarly, but with only partial success, the Fox-Wisconsin River promoters worked to connect Green Bay to Prairie du Chien by water. The grandiose scheme to connect Milwaukee to the Mississippi through a series of improvements between rivers, even crossing a subcontinental divide, momentarily captured the public imagination, and led the Territorial Legislature to charter a canal corporation and Congress to grant the Territory, in trust, 140,000 acres of land in alternate sections for ten miles along the proposed canal course. Political opposition soon arose, along with engineering problems, the promoters' diversion of some receipts from the sale of the lands, and public hostility to the special $2.50 minimum per acre sale price and to economic uncertainty created by the withdrawal from normal sales of so many acres within the Milwaukee area.

When the canal project collapsed in 1842, the only tangible results were a Milwaukee River dam at North Avenue and a canal stub running southwesterly therefrom which long provided water power access for several Milwaukee industries (the stub, now paved, is Commerce Street). The flawed and failed canal project thus impinged directly for four years on the conventional land sales method for an important part of Milwaukee's real estate; and many abstracts for Milwaukee real estate holdings reflect this temporary aberration of the federal system. Subsequently, beginning in 1850, the Congress improved on this style of grant of the public domain for advancing the construction of the newer transportation mania, the railroad, through a series of land grants to major railroad developers.

Real estate speculation in the 1830s at the mouth of the Milwaukee River was predicated on traditional expectations of westward-bound settlers that townsite promotion could be very lucrative. Simultaneously, or soon after, similar speculations occurred all along Wisconsin's Lake Michigan shore, from Racine and Kenosha to the south and at Port Washington, Sheboygan, Manitowoc, and Two Rivers northward to Green Bay, wherever it might be expected that a lake harbor or fishing facilities could be developed to serve the hinterland. In this event those who bet on Milwaukee's location were the most successful in Wisconsin, although competitors to the north and south did not readily give up. For several decades, in fact, until it became evident that Chicago's strategic location at the foot of Lake Michigan gave it an impregnable position as the hub of the nation's eastern trunk lines and western transcontinental railroads, many Milwaukee promotors and some outside observers saw a Milwaukee advantage over Chicago's location in that Milwaukee was ninety miles closer for Lake Michigan ships coming from the north and east.

Townsite and County Formation

Identification of a promising townsite, well in advance of actual economic development, had been a commonplace of westward migration through the Great Lakes and in the Ohio Valley. Fur trading with the Indians at Milwaukee played no real role in these commercial expectations. Jacques Vieau and Jean Baptiste Mirandeau had traded with the Indians in the Menomonee Valley on behalf of the Northwest Company as early as 1795, and Antoine Le Claire had a fur station on the Milwaukee River five years later. But French-Canadian Solomon Juneau, Vieau's son-in-law, did not arrive in Milwaukee on behalf of John Jacob Astor's American Fur Company until 1818, he did not erect a frame structure there for six more years, and he probably was not a regular resident there until 1831.

By this time the once highly lucrative international fur trade was entering an era of sharp decline, especially east of the Mississippi River. The European demand, based upon military use and popular fashion, was abating. The federal government's persisting program of Indian removal westward eliminated a significant part of the manpower involved in the traditional fur trade, perhaps coincidental with a decline in the availability of the fur-bearing animals in an area such as Wisconsin which had been heavily hunted over for a century or more.

Most importantly, the federal government's land distribution policy was a response to the feverish demand of eastern Americans for access to western lands as permanent settlers, not as momentary links in an international fur trade. Astor, perhaps sensing the decline, sold the American Fur Company to Ramsay Crooks in 1834, and the latter in turn bailed out in 1841. The company's Milwaukee and Prairie du Chien representatives, Juneau and Hercules Dousman, followed Astor's lead, the former by becoming a townsite promoter, the latter by entering general trade, lumbering, and transportation, in order to exploit the new era of settlement.

In the aftermath of the War of 1812, the federal government's rational sequence of actions leading to permanent settlement of Wisconsin — extinguishing Indian titles, prior rectilinear survey, and retail land sales — moved too slowly to accommodate pent-up demand for western lands. To deal with the Indians and to police the frontier, three army forts were established along the Fox-Wisconsin River route, at Green Bay, Portage, and Prairie du Chien. To serve their needs a variety of civilians and civilian services appeared.

By the 1820s Ohio and Mississippi Valley settlers had already pressed west and north through the Galena and Fever River lead region of Illinois and spilled over into southwestern Wisconsin. Although federal law could forestall legal occupancy of lead-bearing lands, it countenanced extraction of minerals through a royalty system, and inevitably the miners became farmers as well, before they could claim a patent to their land at the Mineral Point land office beginning in 1834. This southwestern Wisconsin mining frontier was at first oriented toward the water routes — the Mississippi and Ohio — whence the miners had come, but it suggested that an overland route eastward to Lake Michigan would develop sooner or later and thus it encouraged promotion of townsites at a transportation break, as at Milwaukee.

But the strongest pressure for opening Wisconsin lands in the 1830s came first from the eastern Americans and very shortly thereafter from western Europeans. As early as the 1790s New Englanders despaired of wresting a living from some of the rock-strewn hilly regions, and they migrated to New York as its western, upstate regions were opened to settlement. Subsequently they removed to the easternmost portion of the Northwest Territory and contributed to the admission to the Union of the states of Ohio (1803), Indiana (1816), Illinois (1818), and Michigan (1837). These Yankee-Yorker settlers, beguiled by the constantly renewed opportunity to purchase cheap farm land just over the next horizon, moved frequently but retained the political, economic, and social outlook of their origins; and when they reached Milwaukee and Wisconsin in the first waves of land seekers in the 1830s, they reproduced their institutions and practices on the frontier.

The Yankee-Yorker westward migration was primarily responsible for a tenfold population growth in Wisconsin Territory in the decade of the 1830s and specifically for the origins of a village at the confluence of the three rivers between 1834 and 1837. But their zeal for Wisconsin's cheap land was only a part of their peopling of the Middle West at this time, and Wisconsin land sales were only a part of the national frenzy for land that reached its climax in 1836-37. Federal revenues from land sales vastly exceeded federal expenditures, and surplus funds were deposited in state-chartered banks of issue, which in turn lent money freely for further land speculation. The Panic of 1837, precipitated by the President's Specie Circular curbing paper money land sales, not only sharply curtailed land speculation in Wisconsin and elsewhere but also brought about a general economic depression lasting into the early 1840s.

The resumption of Yankee-Yorker migration to Milwaukee and Wisconsin, as the effects of the panic wore out, was paralleled by a new flood of settlers from the British Isles and continental Europe as well. Revolutionary economic, social, and political conditions affected a great many Europeans, especially farm and rural folk, and caused them to look favorably upon a trans-Atlantic migration to a land increasingly advertised among them as a place of opportunity. The resumption of European migration to the New World in the 1830s, after a long interruption during the American Revolution and the Napoleonic wars and their aftermath, coincided with the beginning of improvements in ocean travel, though the hardships of the immigrant voyage remained very severe throughout the century.

The push-pull aspect of European migrations meant that the opening up of Milwaukee and Wisconsin to settlement in the middle 1830s made those lands the special focus of the European unrest of Ireland and the German states at this time, as well as of Norwegians and central Europeans such as the Bohemians. Thus on the eve of the Civil War Milwaukee's population of 45,246 was evenly divided between native and foreign born, and of the latter 70 percent were of German origins and 14 percent Irish. But ten years earlier, with only 20,061 residents, the new city had been 38 percent German, and 14 percent Irish, thus being predominantly foreign born (64 percent). The Milwaukee area, both city and county, continued to receive substantial foreign immigrants right up until the First World War, but the percentage of foreign born necessarily shrank with the even more rapid growth of a native-born second and third generation population.

The flood of newcomers was lured west not alone by the promise of economic opportunity, primarily based on cheap land but by the expectation of self-government and an open society. The Confederation Congress in 1787 followed up on its liberal land distribution program by providing in the Northwest Ordinance for the same political status for the new western lands as was held by the original states which comprised the

Confederation, and the Constitution drafted at Philadelphia that same year confirmed the equality of any new states with the old. The Ordinance, by specifying the conditions under which a probationary period — territorial status — could be followed at the appropriate time by admission into the Union, avoided the creation of a subservient empire of colonies in the west, smacking of the inferiority and humiliation the colonies had felt during their recent constitutional arguments with the British king and Parliament in the 1770s.

Foreign-born as well as American immigrants to Wisconsin and Milwaukee in the 1830s and after could thus look forward to a self-governing status through which the residents of Ohio, Indiana, and Illinois had already passed. Wisconsin, the last of the five states to be created under the terms of the Northwest Ordinance, had been attached for administration to the Territory of Michigan upon the latter's organization in 1818. And when Michigan in turn prepared for statehood in 1836, Congress organized the Territory of Wisconsin and for convenience assigned to it the temporary administration of Iowa and portions of the future state of Minnesota across the Mississippi River.

Territorial status assigned to the President the designation of a territorial governor and of many other federal officers whose role, in the absence of other local officials, was obviously paramount. The federal troops based at three army posts were a major force in many aspects of territorial life, not the least as representatives of federal police authority. And Congress retained considerable direct legislative power over territories, a function which lapsed upon the achievement of statehood. Wisconsin voters were entitled to send a delegate to Congress, who, though not able to vote, could represent the Territory's point of view. But the Territorial legislature, even with a presidential appointee as governor, could exercise considerable authority, selecting a capitol site, chartering corporations, and creating by the time of statehood twenty-nine counties. Indeed, the old Michigan Territorial legislature had already provided for six counties in what is present-day Wisconsin: Chippewa and Michilimackinac in the far north and northwest, Crawford and Iowa to the west, and Brown and Milwaukee on the east.

The Milwaukee County which was prescribed by the Michigan Territorial legislature on September 6, 1834, was considerably larger than today's county. On December 7, 1836, the new Wisconsin Territorial legislature lopped off areas which now basically form Racine and Kenosha to the south, Walworth, Rock, and an easterly strip of Green to the southwest, Jefferson and Dane to the west, Columbia (then named Portage), Dodge, and Washington to the northwest, and Ozaukee to the north. Thus "Old" Milwaukee county, as its historian John Goadby Gregory dubbed it, comprised roughly the southeastern corner of the present state lying south and east from the portage of the Fox to the Wisconsin River. It was more a legislative fiction than a governmental reality.

The 1836 shrinkage of Milwaukee County was not the product of an anti-Milwaukee political conspiracy, for few could have foreseen in 1836 the growth in population and political power which would later conjure up out-state fears of the big city at the mouth of the three rivers. Rather, the Territorial legislature was not only acting wholly within its assigned rights but was also actually launching a long-term county line redrafting process which had produced twenty-nine counties by 1848 and seventy-one by 1901.

The legislative zeal for the continual rearrangement of county lines was premised on the services which counties were expected to offer and the political role assigned to them. Derived from English experience, the county in New England and in those western territories such as Wisconsin which New Englanders originally settled was a subordinate unit of government. It was an instrumentality of the territorial and later the state government. Article VI, Section 4, of the original state constitution of 1848 required biennial election of so-called "constitutional" officers, a sheriff, coronor, register of deeds, and district attorney, in every county. These four "constitutional" officers were responsible for a free citizen's most basic relationships to his government and his society. The paramount role of the sheriff in contemporary law enforcement was represented by the special rules pertaining to his tenure; and the general importance to the state of the four was revealed in the governor's power to remove them.

Equally revealing of the importance of counties to popular local government on the frontier were Sections 23 and 22 of Article IV of the 1848 constitution:

> The legislature shall establish but one system of town and county government, which shall be as nearly uniform as practicable.

> The legislature may confer upon the board of supervisors of the several counties of the state such powers of a local, legislative, and administrative character as they shall from time to time prescribe.

In the course of time the legislature recognized that its much larger population and its urban character required that Milwaukee's Board of Supervisors be chosen differently from those of the rest of the counties which were predominantly farm and small town, and an amendment to Section 23 in 1962 authorized the legislature to provide Milwaukee County with a county executive.

In the second third of the nineteenth century a frontier community like Wisconsin, lacking modern means of transportation and communication, thus devolved upon relatively small geographic units (Wisconsin's present seventy-two counties range from 231 square miles — Pepin, to 1,559 — Marathon) responsibility for providing its people with local self-government under state guidance. Further constitutional provisions recognized the sensitivity of people to county government by invoking the use of a popular referendum for removal of a county seat and the division of any county of 900 square miles or less. Thus the county was clearly an instrumentality of the state, but the powers of the 1848 constitution meant to limit the legislature's discretionary authority with regard to the one form of local government prescribed universally in the state.

If there was no malice in the sharp reduction in the size of Milwaukee County in 1836, one can perceive a foretaste of the outlying hostility to the frontier community's urbanizing area in legislation adopted January 31, 1846. Residents of the county's sixteen western townships were then detached to form a new county named Waukesha, and they alone were entitled to vote in a referendum on this action in April. Surprisingly, this secession was not unanimously embraced, winning by about a two to one margin, and the legislative action, though it removed nearly 70 percent of Milwaukee County's land area and over 46 percent of its population, may have been part of a deal to which Milwaukee legislators were a party. In February 1845, the legislature had transferred the county seat to Prairieville (now Waukesha), only temporarily as it turned out, but a harbinger of trouble despite Milwaukee's legislative numbers. Moreover, it is likely that Milwaukeeans logrolled for support for their real legislative priority, a charter for the city to replace the loose village federation of three wards which had evolved between 1837 and 1845. Thus January 31, 1846, marks the birthday of municipal government for Milwaukee and the final determination of county boundaries.

The density of the city's population growth in the next quarter century led to a move by some Milwaukeeans to achieve city-county consolidation in 1870 through legislation, but opponents in the county's seven towns turned the effort on its head by obtaining a referendum to isolate the city by detaching the towns and making them a part of Waukesha County. City voters alone defeated this move, but residents of the seven towns demonstrated their nearly unanimous support for such detachment. Serious proposals for city-county consolidation were made in 1882, 1908, 1910, 1917, and thereafter almost annually until the issue was converted in the 1920s and 1930s into a debate on how to achieve more effective government in a rapidly urbanizing county.

The creation of Milwaukee County in 1834 was soon followed by organization of its legislative, administrative, and judicial functions in the 1830s and 1840s, according to rules set forth by the Territorial and State legislatures and, after 1848, in accordance with the guidelines in the State constitution. The incorporation of the City of Milwaukee by the legislature on January 31, 1846, created for county residents in the 7.3 square miles lying between 27th Street and the lake, and from Walnut Street and North Avenue to Greenfield Avenue, a new and more responsive local government, which gradually was able to provide services felt necessary or desirable in an urbanized area.

Towns, the Farming Hinterland

The rest of the County — more than 230 square miles — had already been divided into seven towns between 1838 and 1841, and these seven towns, or fragments of them, remained in existence until the 1950s, when a spate of village and city incorporations and of annexations to existing municipalities wiped them out. At first the County was divided only into the Towns of Milwaukee and Lake from east to west on the township line which is now Greenfield Avenue. The "towns" (really villages) which were shaped into wards between 1839 and 1845 and became the City of Milwaukee the following year were carved from the Town of Milwaukee east of 27th Street, the range line as it is even now called in its northern extension from Mill Road to the Ozaukee County line. We now differentiate very clearly an incorporated from an unincorporated village, and even more so a town from a village, especially an incorporated village. But during the formative, frontier period in Wisconsin such nomenclature was not always honored.

Nevertheless the constitution of 1848 provided for such municipal corporations as cities and villages, as well as a uniform system of town government. By mandating town units as subdivisions of a county the legislature guaranteed to all residents of the territory and state a means of managing on a democratic basis those very local governmental activities of a housekeeping nature as would be inappropriately dealt with by the county or the state — the building of roads and bridges, the maintenance of order through a system of constables and justices of the peace, the assessing of property and collection of taxes by an assessor and a treasurer, and the conduct of elections and keeping of records by a clerk.

Democracy in towns was exercised through the town meeting, held at least once a year for all qualified voters, and with authority to legislate and spend money for all town residents. This reflection of the most basic democracy in an American political system which had built in many checks and balances on populist rule at the state and national level was probably romanticized by nineteenth-century observers of the American scene, but it surely accorded with the instinct of self-government on a

largely farm and rural frontier. The nominal executive, the town chairman, was popularly elected and originally, but not after 1885 in Milwaukee County, served as a member of the county board of supervisors.
With two elected side supervisors, the town chairman formed a town board
with jurisdiction between town meetings.

The town concept had been authorized as early as 1827 by the Michigan Territorial legislature, but not until the frenzied land sales of the
middle 1830s was the Milwaukee County area divided up between the
north — the Town of Milwaukee — and the south — the Town of Lake, and
these two towns were subdivided before town government actually began,
in most cases by 1842. The southeastern portions of the original Town of
Milwaukee evolved into the City of Milwaukee, 1838-46, whilst the area
west of Twenty-Seventh Street was divided in 1840 along township lines
into two equal towns of thirty-six square miles, the one to the north being
named Granville for a New York community whence some of its original
settlers had come, and that to the south becoming Wauwatosa, a mis-
spelling of the transliteration of the Indian word for firefly.

In 1839 and 1840 the Town of Lake was reduced to twenty-seven
square miles. Two towns identical to the thirty-six square mile surveyor's
townships were carved out in two steps. A new town to the west of 27th
Street, the range line, was originally named Kinnickinnic, but its northern half was then soon renamed Greenfield, a name also assigned to the
avenue running from the lakefront westward across the County and
forming the northern boundary of the Towns of Lake and Greenfield. The
southern half was named for Benjamin Franklin. The final town, lying
east of 27th Street and south of the present College Avenue was Oak
Creek, named for a small but surprisingly lengthy part of the area's
drainage system whose confluence with Lake Michigan had attracted
early settlers near the route of the Chicago Road.

The County's four western towns, like many other Wisconsin towns
created by the legislature, conformed to the lines of the surveyor's township and were therefore six miles square. But the three eastern towns all
contained a smaller land area because they abutted the irregular line of
the lake to the east. Largest of the three at thirty-four square miles was
Oak Creek, which uniquely extended in its far southeastern corner into
Range 23 East of Township 5 North. The legislature has always had
absolute discretion in the creation of towns (one, Menominee, is currently
coterminous with its county) but was inclined, especially in the earlier
years, to make them identical to the surveyor's township whenever feasible, and hence common usage was to make the terms town and township
synonymous. From the beginning, however, the Wisconsin legislature
explicitly adopted the term "town" for the unit of civil government as

distinct from the township and in contrast to both law and practice in many eastern and southern states.

The rudiments of local self-government provided for in the 1840s by the subdivision of the County into seven towns and the City of Milwaukee were extremely important to contemporary Milwaukeeans and for some time to come. Only slowly, and never according to a master plan, did the county, state, and federal governments expand their roles and impinge upon the relatively simple and somewhat isolated lives of the residents of Milwaukee County's seven towns. By tradition almost all Americans were inclined before the Civil War to begrudge the taxes necessary for additional government services. The residents of cities such as Milwaukee only gradually accepted their special fiscal needs for such expensive government projects as a public water supply, street lighting, ongoing fire and police protection, and waste disposal. The city slowly expanded its boundaries by annexation of land in the adjacent towns — Milwaukee, Wauwatosa and Lake — as pressure of population and economic growth required and as city services and taxes correspondingly grew. This in turn served as a warning to the farm and rural folk in the towns to maintain their simple nonurban ways.

The centrifugal force of the central city's physical growth throughout the remainder of the nineteenth century and the first half of the twentieth century and the related conversions of some parts of the towns into incorporated villages and cities beginning in 1879 were not sufficient to destroy the towns as instruments of local government in Milwaukee County until the mid-1950s. Then, very suddenly, in a flurry of annexation and incorporation, all seven died at very much the same time. The reasons for their collapse differed in each case, but the overall conclusion must be that in a metropolitan area such as Milwaukee's the town form of government was no longer adequate for meeting contemporary political, economic, and social needs. The simple nineteenth-century economy and isolated society that was satisfied with the least possible government had totally disappeared.

The settlement of Milwaukee County and its political organization coincided with the spread of democratic sentiment in the United States and with the acceptance of the concept of free public elementary education. Territorial laws only vaguely supported these new directions. Prior to statehood in 1848 towns were authorized to create schools and tax for their support, as well as to obtain additional support from other sources such as a county tax. The constitution, however, responded to the agitation of such advocates of free public schools as Michael Frank of Racine, and it spelled out the obligation of towns and cities to tax for the benefit of free district schools and created additional resources through a school fund derived from the public lands. The City of Milwaukee was obliged to operate under a separate system of ward school commissioners which ultimately evolved into its present superintendent and school board governance.

Outside the city, however, the state legislation of 1848 and 1849 continued a strongly decentralized educational philosophy, giving little authority over schools to the state superintendent and much to an annually elected town superintendent possessing no obligatory educational training. The towns could create common school districts as needed, each governed by its own board. The quality and availability of elementary school education outside of the City of Milwaukee therefore flowed from the lure of the annual school fund allocation, which had to be matched by a town levy, and from the strength of the zeal, or lack of it, of school district residents for education.

Some improvement resulted in 1861, when the legislature created the office of an elected county superintendent whose authority replaced that of the town superintendents. This step removed the towns from direct public school governance and gave a county official reporting to the state superintendent some authority over fiercely independent common school district boards. Subsequent legislation regarding teacher training and state certification undoubtedly improved instruction in the district schools in the unincorporated areas of Milwaukee County, but the major change came soon after the end of World War II, when the towns disappeared and their remaining school districts were swallowed up in city and combined districts everywhere.

Only slowly did the movement for free public elementary schools extend to the high school level. The earliest high schools in Wisconsin emerged in city school systems, under authority granted to all levels of local government by legislation in 1856 and 1875. Thus Milwaukee, after a false start a decade earlier, founded its first high school in 1868. Three years later, before there was an incorporated village of Wauwatosa, that community built the first high school in any town within Milwaukee County, and the first truly rural high school appeared in the Oakwood district of the Town of Franklin in 1883. The formation of eight urban villages and cities in the County between 1892 and 1906 and their ultimate creation of their own school districts led to the proliferation of outlying high schools, to some degree obviating the need for high schools in the still sparsely settled towns lying even farther from the City of Milwaukee. Up until the demise of the seven towns in the middle 1950s, it had been possible and quite common for town residents who had no high school available to their sons and daughters to make them tuition students elsewhere in the County.

More than a generation has passed since the termination of the Milwaukee County school system, and it is not easy to appraise its educational contribution during its roughly 125 years of existence. The common schools it nurtured were probably the chief focus and the pride of local self-government. Until well into the twentieth century most such schools were held in one room with a single teacher. The century-old little white frame schoolhouse in Brown Deer exemplifies the type, though many others in the County were of brick and stone. The brick and stone Hawley Road School, built in 1905 for Town of Wauwatosa elementary school children and still in use, suggests a very high level of educational aspiration, equal to the City of Milwaukee's standard. County schools were probably always inferior in teacher preparation and facilities to the City of Milwaukee's but better than county schools in the rest of the state.

The provision in the decade of statehood for a minimal local governmental unit, the town, and a related school district meant that the public needs of the nonurbanized portions of Milwaukee County were generally well satisfied. Land purchases — both original patents from the United State Land Office and subsequent acquisitions — were premised primarily on the conversion of the pleasantly rolling countryside of Milwaukee County into farms. The outlying farming towns of the County blended imperceptibly with the three farm counties which abutted Milwaukee County on three sides, Ozaukee, Waukesha and Racine. The farming potential of the original seven towns was, however, far from identical. The best and most durable agriculture was probably in Granville, which raised more wheat, as well as other cereals and grains, than any other portion of

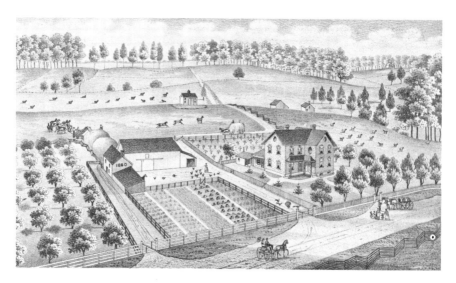

A Town of Granville farm from the 1876 atlas; the house is still occupied. Granville was the most productive agricultural town in the County.

the County, and which retained much of its farm quality until 1956, when it was swallowed up by the City of Milwaukee's strong northwestern thrust and the incorporation of the Village of Brown Deer. The least promising land was in Oak Creek, which was substantially covered with timber or strewn with boulders and rocks, and was also somewhat isolated from downtown Milwaukee. Franklin had prime land for raising crops, and Greenfield, Milwaukee, and Wauwatosa were also favored, while Lake's agricultural potential was more limited. The maps, lithographs, and residential data in H. Belden & Co.'s *Illustrated Historical Atlas of Milwaukee County, Wisconsin* graphically reveal the farm nature of the seven towns forty years after the first settlers patented their Milwaukee County lands. By that date the County's farmers were already turning from wheat and other grains to fruits and vegetables and other cash crops which could be sold in the City of Milwaukee, as well as to the raising of pigs, cows, chickens, horses, and other farm animals. The conversion of Wisconsin farming in the last quarter of the nineteenth and early twentieth century from wheat-raising to dairying was only in part reflected in Milwaukee County, for the latter was never a major producer of wheat or milk but rather engaged in retail cash-crop agriculture oriented toward the nearby urban market.

People, Industry, and Institutional Sprawl

The agricultural emphasis in the seven towns conveyed by Belden's 1876 *Illustrated Historical Atlas* did not conceal the incipient urbanization and industrialization found in every town by that early date. Unincorporated communities like Wauwatosa, Humboldt, Schwartzburg, St. Martins, Oak Creek, and Hales Corners suggested the existence of schools and churches, flour-, grist-, and saw-mills, cement-mills, post offices, highway and railroad intersections, and farmers markets, as well as clusters of nonfarm residents living nearby. But the real urban story was found in the rapid growth of the City of Milwaukee, whose 1840 population of 1,712 leaped dramatically to 45,246 on the eve of the Civil War, to 115,587 twenty years later, and to 285,315 at the turn of the century. Expansion of city boundaries, while substantial, was not so dramatic during that sixty years, for it was not until 1890 that electrification and consolidation of the private street railway system began to extend a Milwaukeean's residential and worksite options, and not until well into the next century that his mobility was extended by the automobile.

Nevertheless by 1892 the city had reached Edgewood Avenue to the north, which was destined to remain as its permanent northern border east of the Milwaukee River, and west to 35th Street as far south as Canal

Street; while the southern boundary extended to Cleveland Avenue from Layton to Howell, and to Oklahoma from there to the lake. Physical expansion of the city since 1846 had been primarily into the Towns of Milwaukee and Lake to the north and south, and in terms of density of residential population, that physical spread had been wholly inadequate. During the first half of the new century the city, not surprisingly, aggressively sought to annex major portions of the Towns of Greenfield, Wauwatosa, and Granville as well as parts of the Towns of Milwaukee, Lake, and even a small piece of Oak Creek. Milwaukee's twentieth-century philosophy was that it had to grow or it would die. It ultimately reached ninety-five square miles.

The phenomenal population growth of Milwaukee in the nineteenth century is easily accounted for. Its location at the confluence of three rivers with Lake Michigan forecast a rosy future as a port for the potential immigrant — from the east or abroad. While initial expectations for the lead trade never really materialized, wheat from Wisconsin's farms reached boom proportions by the Civil War, for shipment to Europe as well as the urbanizing east. Shipments of meat, especially pork, and of lumber came through the city by water and rail, and soon the city developed the capacity to mill flour, pack meat, and tan leather, so that its commercial emphasis was supported by its industrial base.

 The rise of E. P. Allis' Reliance Works not only as a purveyor of French burr millstones but as a maker of steam engines, saw- and flour-mill equipment, and other iron and steel products, and the rise of the Milwaukee Iron Company's rolling mills of Eber Brock Ward, producing iron and steel for the metal trades, forecast a great future for the city as a heavy goods center. Milwaukee's breweries were among the first in the nation to use bottles as well as kegs and to ship outside of the city, entering the national market via Chicago. Milwaukee's dynamic growth in manufacturing, extending for a time to an extraordinary number of consumer products for a local and regional market as well, continued into the twentieth century and through two World Wars.

Such growth was timed to attract migrants — from the east, from Germany and eastern Europe, and from Ireland and Britain — both before and after the Civil War. Milwaukee's Irish remained dominant for a time on the city's lower east side. Germans continued to find Milwaukee attractive as the area west of the Milwaukee River and north of the Menomonee Valley became a re-creation of the culture of their homeland. German immigrants immediately felt at home in a city which spoke their language, taught it in its public and parochial schools, and perpetuated the social and cultural institutions of the fatherland. On the south side of Milwaukee, beyond a tier of Germans and some Irish immediately south of the Menomonee Valley, there grew up a correspondingly intact Polish community beginning in the late 1860s, never as numerous and never as powerful as the Germans in politics, business, or social life, but equally intent on reproducing and maintaining its language, its religion, and its other social and cultural institutions, and in carving out in its enclave some political power.

Before the turn of the century new but considerably smaller ethnic groups made their presence felt, usually in the older downtown or near-downtown neighborhoods — Italians, Greeks, eastern European Jews, and lesser numbers of almost every eastern and southern European national-ity. The Yankee-Yorker founders of Milwaukee had inevitably yielded political control, especially to the Germans and Poles by the turn of the century, and had accepted the newcomers, especially the Germans, into their social, cultural, and economic power structures. The census of 1900 suggested that Milwaukee's population was perhaps the most diversely foreign in the nation.

But geographical location and the timing of European immigrant outflows before and after the Civil War cannot alone account for Mil-waukee's success. Some credit must go to the relentless pursuit of economic growth for the city, initiated by its original Yankee-Yorker leadership and embraced by the newer ethnic leadership. Significant contributions were made by projects which combined private and public funds and efforts, such as the completion of the "straight cut" in 1857 for better shipping access from Lake Michigan to an inner harbor formed by the Milwaukee and Menomonee Rivers, and consequent Menomonee "improvements" which made that river valley the heart of industrial Milwaukee through a series of canals and slips, and the institution of a "harbor of refuge" on the lakefront with the construction of the first portion of a breakwater in the 1880s. Critical to the health of its growing population and expanding borders and to some manufacturing processes was the city's modern water system, its first major public works project, built between 1869 and 1874 to draw water from the lake and distribute it throughout the city.

Civic pride dictated a corresponding attention to cultural and rec-reational activities with the building of an exposition hall and art gallery and the launching of a public library, a natural history museum, and a park system within an eleven-year span from 1878 to 1889. The "Cream City of the Lakes" attracted regional and national attention by hosting the national GAR encampments in 1880 and 1889, an international Saenger-fest in 1886, and many other social and business meetings.

But the strength of the city's expansion is best illustrated by its business leadership. An immigrant Scot, Alexander Mitchell, dominated the local business community by making his Wisconsin Marine and Fire Insurance Company Bank into the soundest in the midwest; he put together the components of the Milwaukee and St. Paul Railroad in 1863 and eleven years later connected the Milwaukee Road to Chicago, the rail hub of the nation; and he was the major local investor in Ward's Milwaukee Iron Company in 1868.

The biggest risk-taker, probably the truest entrepreneur, was Edward Phelps Allis, who won the contract for making the pipe for Milwaukee's water works without owning a pipe foundry and went on with borrowed money to make flour- and saw-mill equipment and steam engines. With the deaths of Mitchell in 1887 and Allis two years later, business leadership passed to Fred Pabst, head of the world's largest lager beer brewery and also owner of a local theater, hotel, skyscraper office building, and suburban resort. But also laying sound foundations for the city's business future were John Plankinton in meat packing, Henry Harnischfeger in cranes, Warren Johnson in heat controls, Guido Pfister in leather tanning, George Burnham in brick making, J.B.S. Kern in flour milling, and Henry Clay Payne in utilities.

The dynamic growth of the City of Milwaukee in the last third of the nineteenth century inevitably extended beyond its own borders, even as those were periodically moved out to the north, west, and south. The City's immediate hinterland was the County's seven towns, where a ripple effect occurred. Coincident with central city population growth came a demand for the fruits and vegetables, the livestock and dairy products of the County's farmers. These were brought in by farm wagons to several farmers markets in downtown Milwaukee and ultimately to a commission row on Broadway. The craze for plank roads in the 1840s died down when the receipts from tolls were eaten up in maintenance costs, but the routes remain to this day as city streets and county and state highways radiating out of the downtown area. Many such farm and rural arteries took their names from their destinations — Green Bay, Fond du Lac, Lisbon, Watertown, Mukwonago, Beloit, Janesville, Loomis, and Chicago.

Local railroad construction began in 1847 with a route from downtown Milwaukee through Wauwatosa reaching Waukesha in 1851. By 1874 Milwaukee was connected to Chicago by both the Milwaukee Road and the Chicago and North Western passing through the Towns of Oak Creek and Lake; and the Milwaukee Road, in addition to its original western tracks through Wauwatosa, had northwestern routes passing through the Towns of Milwaukee and Granville not far from the two affiliates of the Chicago and North Western heading for Fond du Lac and Green Bay. Roads accommodating farm wagons and carriages, however crude, facilitated the passage of goods and people between the inner city and the towns, as did many of the freight and passenger trains. Facilities to support such basic means of transportation soon appeared — in particular stagecoach inns such as the Layton House, still standing on Forest Home Avenue at 25th Street, and railroad stations. Junctions of railroads and intersections of

*A rare portrait of the founder of Wauwa-
tosa, Charles Hart, as a young man in the
1830s. The settlement was originally called
"Hart's Mills."*

roads with each other or with a railroad route might generate the beginnings of a settlement, which in turn might justify the location of a federal
post office for local mail pickup and distribution.

The availability of transportation for goods also encouraged the siting
of grist- and saw-mills, Hart's in Wauwatosa appearing as early as 1837, or
the working of limestone quarries for their lime and their stone. And the
combination of transportation, farms, nonfarm residents, and incipient
industry would soon require retail establishments, saloons, schools, and
churches. To service such small crossroads communities, various craftsmen and other workers settled in the towns, especially carpenters, joiners,
blacksmiths, masons, coopers, physicians, painters, cigarmakers, and
brewers; and many farmers acknowledged that their talents extended to a
second livelihood as sailor, preacher, teacher, or merchant. Most of these
settlements remained small and simple, and their residents felt no urge to
organize a municipality which would only tax them and regulate their
lives.

Very early in their history Milwaukeeans saw additional nonfarm
possibilities for the land lying beyond City boundaries. In 1852 the County
Board purchased a farm south of the Watertown Plank Road in the
southwestern portion of the Town of Wauwatosa, the first step in the
acquisition of enough property to house almost all of the County's health
and social services facilities today. At one time or another the County
Institutions grounds, between 85th and 108th Streets and north of Wis-

The National Soldiers Home near Milwaukee. Clockwise from top left, flower beds & green house, main building, lake & boats, residence of Generals Knox & Moore, dining room, hospital, home store, and General Sharp's residence, as depicted in an 1889 album.

consin Avenue to the Menomonee River and crossed by the Zoo Freeway as well as the Plank Road, have housed the County farm, an old peoples and an orphan home, an insane asylum, a tuberculosis sanitorium, a hospital and nurses training school, a potter's field, the County Agricultural School, the Children's Court, Froedtert Memorial Hospital, the Medical College of Wisconsin, a County garage, and Extension Services offices.

At the end of the Civil War Milwaukeeans raised enough money to successfully petition the federal government for the location near the city of one of three National Homes for Disabled Volunteer Soldiers. In 1867 the first domiciliary building designed by local architect E. Townsend Mix, using Milwaukee cream brick with a Wauwatosa limestone foundation, was opened, this time in the southeast corner of the Town of Wauwatosa. The La Crosse division of the Milwaukee Road passed through the site, and National Avenue lay on its southern border. And when the City's electrified main east-west streetcar line was extended west to serve the new cities of Wauwatosa and West Allis at the turn of the century, one branch served the Home. The pastoral landscaping of the grounds, with lakes, fountains, flowers, a bandstand and curvilinear streets, attracted many city residents on holidays and summer afternoons during the years when the city had at best a limited system of parks.

The recreational or retreat potential of the County's farm and rural towns appealed to affluent Milwaukeeans in many other ways. Some of them purchased farms and lots away from the central city as a refuge from the city's crowding, and some, of course, chose to make their town residences their only ones, a foretaste of the vogue for suburbanization and exurbanization which ultimately destroyed one gold coast after another in the central city. Summer homes along the Milwaukee River north of the city in the Town of Milwaukee or along the Lake Michigan shore to the east were particularly sought after. The Best Brewery acquired 180 acres west of 60th Street near the center of the Town of Wauwatosa before 1876; this land became a hops farm for the brewery and a rural retreat for Fred Pabst and his family until it was subdivided into the Washington Highlands at the end of World War I. But by far the best known and grandest country estate was "Meadowmere." At one time banker Alexander Mitchell and his son John owned 480 rural acres, including a pond and racetrack, and on this property John erected in 1884 a brick Queen Anne residence of fourteen bedrooms, still standing south of Lincoln Avenue at 53rd Street. Here John, less a businessman or politician than he was an art lover and intellectual, hosted many of the nation's literary and artistic figures as they visited the city. In the 1870 census John called himself "farmer."

The impulse to locate outside of the city limits is represented by other enterprises. In 1850 the vestry of St. Paul Episcopal Church obtained a charter for Forest Home Cemetery from the state legislature. The 115-acre site they selected was then a mile south of the city limits, south of Lincoln Avenue and east of Layton Boulevard. Their choice may have been dictated simply by the availability of a large plot of rolling ground covered with a virgin forest and with excellent soil and drainage, an area once the meeting place of various Indian tribes. But additional considerations may have been the escape from city rules and regulations and the lesser likelihood of the building pressures which had already disturbed earlier local burying grounds. In the post-Civil War period two race courses were located in the southeast corner of the Town of Wauwatosa, the Cold Spring track and that of George Stevens. In 1892 the state decided on permanent siting of the annual State Fair on the Stevens property, north of Greenfield Avenue between 76th and 84th Streets. The earlier, temporary use of near downtown land north of Wisconsin Avenue at 13th Street for the Fair was obviously no longer feasible.

A quite different escape from the city, but a very significant one, occurred when Roman Catholic Bishop John Martin Henni ordered the construction of a seminary for the training of German-speaking priests in 1855. The site he selected and which he already owned had been occupied

The City of St. Francis took its name from the Roman Catholic Seminary of that name established there in the 1850s to train German-speaking priests.

by the Brothers and Sisters of St. Francis since their arrival in 1849, and was situated on the lakefront in the Town of Lake in what is now the northernmost section of the City of St. Francis. It is not clear why the site was chosen — because Henni already owned it; because of the failure of previous efforts, some downtown, to mount a seminary building program and even to locate a suitable site; because of the recent cholera plagues which afflicted the infant city; or, perhaps, because of the anti-Catholic and especially anti-priest sentiment which Henni sensed in the city. The isolated location some miles from the city presented special difficulties during construction (300,000 bricks were fired from the clay of nearby Deer Creek) and continuing inconveniences of access, but the Seminary fulfilled its primary purpose and became something of a center of German-Catholic theology in support of a fiercely German diocese. Additional Catholic educational institutions clustered around it, but it did not spark a boom for the settlement of adjacent areas. Indeed its very existence on a large institutional plot may have blocked the city's expansion south from Bay View along the lake and provided the opportunity for Patrick Cudahy to buy up more southerly land for his industrial suburb in the 1890s.

Yet, in the long run, the availability of large pieces of undeveloped, or underdeveloped, land in the surrounding towns meant most to those

The Werner Trimborn farm, bought in Greenfield in 1850, became an important lime production site due to the rich vein of limestone underground. The property is presently owned by the Department of Parks, Recreation and Culture.

Milwaukeeans who were seeking industrial sites. The seven towns, in fact, had never been totally devoted to trade and agriculture. By the mid-1870s there were flour- and saw-mills in Wauwatosa and Granville, the Miller and Gettelman breweries on the Watertown Plank Road, distilleries in both Wauwatosa and Lake, stone quarries, lime kilns, and a cement company in Wauwatosa, Milwaukee, and Greenfield, several nurseries and florists, dairies, and at least one pickle factory, one brick manufacturer, a glue factory, and a pottery manufacturer outside the central city. Such a conglomeration of business activities scattered throughout the seven towns suggested neither a pattern nor a trend.

Suburbanization: The Bay View and Residential Models

But a most significant development occurred in 1868. A Detroit ship's captain and iron and steel maker named Eber Brock Ward persuaded local investors led by banker Alexander Mitchell to finance the erection of an iron and steel mill under the name Milwaukee Iron Company just south of the city limits on the lake front. The company rolled its first rails in 1869 and the following year introduced the then novel Bessemer process of steel-making. Ward exploited the lakefront location by dredging his own harbor access, and he developed the site by building houses for his workers, many recruited from the British Isles. Ward's death and the panic of 1873 led to closing of the mills in 1876, but reorganization under the North Chicago Rolling Mills Company succeeded in reviving what was by this time the city's bellwether for industrial growth. In 1901 U.S. Steel acquired the mills and at the onset of the depression of 1929 closed them down permanently. But for over sixty years the company was an integral part of Milwaukee's heavy goods economy.

What was a forecast of the future for Milwaukee County was Ward's decision to acquire an isolated piece of land outside the city in the Town of Lake south of the entrance to the inner harbor of Milwaukee, build a plant which by its isolation required that a residential community grow up around it, and himself contribute to this development by building workers' houses. By 1885, a decade after Ward's death, the company payroll was 1,500 men, and not far away other heavy goods manufacturing plants, attracted by Ward's example, had located. As early as 1879 it became evident that the governance of such an industrial community could not be left to the town form of government. Not only were the 2,592 residents of the mills area a majority of the town's total population; they were occupying less than one and one-half square miles of the town's total of twenty-three and one-half. Moreover, their needs and those of the mill differed markedly from the rest of the townsfolk and did not square with the powers which town government could exercise under state law.

On April 28, 1879, the residents petitioned the circuit court for village status, and Judge David W. Small accepted their pleas, subject to confirmation in a referendum. Thus on June 5, 1879, the Village of Bay View became the first suburb to be carved out of town jurisdictions in Milwaukee County. The community's historian, Bernhard C. Korn, does not state that the mill's owners instigated the incorporation; but since the company helped fund incorporation costs and its officers and employees were prominent village officials throughout the village's brief existence, one may safely conclude that at the least the company was not opposed to the move. For a time the company performed services for the village such as fighting fires and drafting plats without charge.

Lacking precedents, village officials in Bay View moved cautiously. Most of their business was urban housekeeping, relating to such mundane matters as the opening of streets and alleys and the removal of dead animals, the latter a standard concern of town boards. It is evident that the incorporators were unclear as to their new relationship to the Town of Lake, for they sought (and got) financial help from the Town and claimed the right to continue to vote in Town elections until quashed by the district attorney. As the village struggled to identify its role in the 1880s, the City of Milwaukee continued its interest in moving southward by annexing Bay View, an interest which had originally contributed in the pre-incorporation era to the movement for a separate village. Now, however, the appeal of consolidation with Milwaukee became more attractive. The village trustees realized that the cost of the improvements their citizens desired — better fire and police protection, better street lighting and access to city water and sewers, better schools and more library books, earlier street openings — could be spread among City of Milwaukee taxpayers. A debate over annexation began early in 1886, culminating in trustee approval on September 1, followed soon by Common Council and legislative approval. The referendum on March 3, 1887, was adopted, 262 to 147, thus ending an eight-year experiment in separatism. Over 4,000 persons thus became the City's Seventeenth, and most heavily industrial, Ward, and they soon clamored for all the city improvements they had hitherto denied themselves.

Bay View's eight-year experiment as the County's first suburb was hardly a success, though the precedent of incorporation and of the industrial suburb was to transform the politics and alter the boundaries of six of the seven towns in less than twenty years. Even Bay View survived its political capitulation, and a century later its residents believe that somehow they are different from everyone else, certainly apart from the rest of Milwaukee's citizenry. They prefer to be referred to as Bay Viewites. They recall that they were once an independent municipality housing the Milwaukee area's foremost iron- and steel-mill. They remember that the most spectacular confrontation in state labor history occurred at the mills on May 5, 1886, when the National Guard faced an angry mob of 1,500 during the eight-hour-day agitation, killing five and wounding a half dozen. The inadequacy of a village government in dealing with a near riot may have contributed to a sentiment for consolidation with Milwaukee.

Above all, residents of the area have always felt isolated from downtown Milwaukee, lacking until the recent construction of the Daniel W. Hoan bridge on the Lake Freeway direct access across Jones Island and the Milwaukee River mouth. Bay Viewites devoured John Gurda's (1979) and Korn's (1980) histories of their community and in the latter year organized a unique local affiliate of the State Historical Society, one that represented a city neighborhood and a long dead political entity. To many Milwaukeeans, Bay View did indeed survive.

A lithograph printed about 1870 by the Milwaukee firm of J. Knauber of the "Bay View Iron Works" captures this early industrial site with the city in the background.

Milwaukee's dynamic growth since the Civil War made it by the 1890s one of the nation's major machine shops. Its capacity to ship by rail and water had peaked. The energy of its citizens found expression, despite the panic of 1893 which hit the city's banks particularly hard, in a building boom. Skyscrapers, office buildings, theaters, hotels, department stores, and restaurants made downtown Milwaukee a metropolis. The City erected a new city hall suggesting its north European origins and a neoclassical library-museum, and the federal government contributed a handsome Richardsonian Romanesque post office. Both railroads serving the city had modern stations, and consolidation and electrification of the street railway system by the electric power company serving Milwaukee was a national model.

Just as the vitality of the central city seemed greatest and its continued spatial expansion outward seemed most assured, forces were at work which dramatically altered this concept and ultimately created political counterforces in the County. The first was the revision of laws relating to the incorporation of villages and cities and the annexation to cities. The legislation of 1889, amended in 1893 and 1895, initially provided for a general incorporation procedure to replace the special charters heretofore required. Such incorporation and annexation laws were frequently amended and subject to conflicting interpretation, especially on the application of general incorporation provisions to existing special charters, but the consequence of the 1889 statute was highly encouraging to would-be municipalities in Milwaukee County, eight of which incorporated between 1892 and 1906.

A second force, with clear precedent if not such great success in the case of Bay View, was the impulse of industrial companies and their owners and managers to locate or relocate their plants outside of the Milwaukee City limits and to encourage their workers to follow them to these suburban sites. It is defensible to refer to as many as five of Milwaukee County's new, turn-of-the-century suburbs as industrial, that is, that their main or precipitating reason for existing as an incorporated community was the location or relocation of one or more industrial firms. But such a term is somewhat misleading because each suburb had its own origins and history, and the differences among them proved as important as the similarities.

Typology is even more difficult for the remaining three suburbs which could not be described as truly industrial. One, Wauwatosa, originated as a crossroads community at almost exactly the same time as the original Village of Milwaukee was authorized by the legislature and might be said simply to have developed more slowly into an independent, not exactly a suburban, entity. The two earliest North Shore suburbs had recreational origins and became typically residential or even dormitory suburbs, but even their histories are unique and instructive. In any case suburbs as well as the central city subsequently grew in area and population and in doing so changed their mix.

Wauwatosa, the most persistent suburban expansionist over the years, but by no means the largest in area or numerous in population today, tripled its land area in its final annexation binge in 1952 to become a major commercial, office-building, and industrial suburb, while retaining, more by chance than design, a high proportion of public open space — parks, parkways, golf courses, institutional grounds. As we shall see in examining the origins and growth of the first group of suburbs, and the two later incorporation spasms, 1926-1938 and 1949-1956, the reasons for incorporating are many and complex, and so are the reasons which have led eighteen of the twenty suburbs chartered in the County since 1879 to retain their independence to this day.

The essential ingredient for municipal incorporation — aside from a facilitating state law or an aggressive industrial developer — was the clustering of town residents at a crossroads. The building of transportation routes radiating out of downtown Milwaukee, the location of such social amenities as inns, schools, and churches, the development of retail stores and other modest business enterprises, the allocation of a post office — all of these encouraged the increase of settlers dependent on the nearby agriculture but not themselves farmers. By the 1890s such settlements were found everywhere in Milwaukee County. No doubt the proximity of one of the nation's largest cities, highly industrialized, politically strong, culturally and socially developed, exerted a powerful influence on these communities, but they also shared some of their traditions and their outlook with similar communities in Wisconsin's outlying farm and rural areas, especially in the state's southeastern quadrant.

The most highly developed of such unincorporated communities was Wauwatosa, located just south of the center point of the six-mile-square Town of Wauwatosa. There the Menomonee River had provided the power for a flour- and grist-mill, and a mill pond had been formed. The Watertown Plank Road passed through on its way west from downtown Milwaukee into the heart of Waukesha County, where it merged with the Blue Mound Road on its way to Madison. What later became Harwood Avenue was the United States Road. The state's first railroad line steamed through there en route to Waukesha, Prairie du Chien, and St. Paul. To the east along the Plank Road and the river's route lay two breweries, a distillery, and several limestone quarries; and the village area had mills, a pickle factory, a general store, a nursery, an electric generating station and a street car line under construction, and a variety of craftsmen and professional people. Congregational, Baptist, Methodist, Episcopal, and Lutheran churches served the strongly religious bent of the dominant New England and German residents, while their education needs were already nourished by public and parochial elementary schools, a high school, and a library. Other amenities of a relatively sophisticated community included a road system, a hotel, a cemetery, a commons (reflecting the community's New England origins), many handsome Italianate and Victorian mansions, and an area that might accurately have been described as a business district. As of 1892 no other settlement in the seven towns approached the urban character of Wauwatosa; and, though lacking the dynamism and the employment potential of a Milwaukee Iron Company, Wauwatosa was more of a city than the Village of Bay View had ever been.

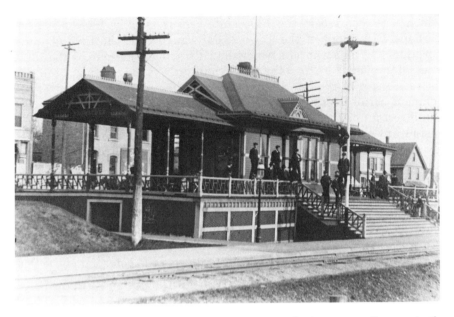

The Victorian depot in Wauwatosa was a familiar stop on this important railway route; the first train from Milwaukee passed through Wauwatosa to Waukesha in 1851.

A small portion of the Town of Wauwatosa assumed village status in 1892 with only 1,150 of the Town's 11,000 or so residents, but this status was exchanged for that of fourth class city in 1897, when its Assemblyman (and first mayor) Emerson D. Hoyt won new incorporation legislation. The 1900 census showed a 2,842 population in an area lying west of 60th Street north and south of the Menomonee River between Blue Mound Road and Center Street. A disastrous fire of 1895 which burned out most of the wood structures of the business area had revealed the need for a stronger charter. Important public and private improvements of this era included a public library building (enlarged with a Carnegie grant in 1905), the city's first artesian well and a steam turbine pumping station, a paid, though still part-time, fire department, improved schools, private facilities for the elderly, orphans, and the mentally ill, and a modern hotel. The *Wauwatosa News*, launched in March 1899, succeeded as a weekly newspaper where four short-lived predecessors beginning in 1885 had failed. Lefeber's, the community's landmark general store, erected a handsome red brick building in 1906, and the next year a national bank inaugurated local banking services.

Also incorporated as a village in 1892, Whitefish Bay contrasted sharply with Wauwatosa in its origins and development. Its population, which was reported in the 1895 state census as only 464, constituted perhaps 10 percent of the Town of Milwaukee's at the time of incorporation. The adjacent lake waters had attracted fisherman by the 1860s and, later, picnickers from the city. Tradition says the platting of the area for residences in the late 1880s led to an interest in a more convenient common school location and thence to the move for incorporation. In 1888 the directors of the Phillip Best Brewing Company decided to build a restaurant and pavilion on the lakefront at the foot of Henry Clay Street. By the next year, when the resort opened, the brewery had been renamed and brought under the complete control of Fred Pabst. For the next quarter century, until the company directors decided to raze the building and plat the land for residences, the Whitefish Bay Resort with its large landscaped park was a popular summer attraction for Milwaukeeans, by land and by water. It not only served to advertise the flamboyant captain's beer, as did the other hotels and restaurants the captain and the company owned locally and nationally, but it drew attention to the potential of the fledgling village.

For a quarter of a century after 1888, the popular Pabst Whitefish Bay Resort drew crowds; many would travel by boat to the site located on Lake Michigan at Henry Clay Street.

Steam and later electrified street railways, together with Lake Drive for private vehicles along the North Shore bluff, connected Whitefish Bay from the beginning of its suburban growth with downtown Milwaukee. The village name was drawn from the lovely and graceful indentation of the shoreline above North Point, which resembled Milwaukee Bay on a more modest scale but lacked the river mouth potential as a lake port. From its incorporation Whitefish Bay was intended as a residential community, and so it has remained to the present, accommodating only a modest retail development along Silver Spring in the 1930s and after.

Early promotion of Whitefish Bay real estate, including the paving of streets and sidewalks, was thwarted by the Panic of 1893 and its aftermath, and population growth was slow for a quarter century. The 1930 census recorded only 882 residents. To become a successful dormitory suburb, Whitefish Bay probably was assisted after World War I by the proliferation of automobiles, a growing middle class, and the decline of Milwaukee's east side Gold Coast. Or perhaps the distance from Milwaukee was initially too great, and the village required some infill of population in the lake shore area lying between itself and the city's northern limits. The impetus for this development was provided in 1900 by the incorporation as the Village of East Milwaukee of the land lying north of the city and east of the Milwaukee River. This step was clearly taken to free the area to spend its local tax money on its own improvements and not those chosen by the Town of Milwaukee. The Town fought the move in court, alleging that the population of the area, shown in the 1905 state census as 473, did not then (1900) meet the state minimum requirements of 300.

If the incorporation of Whitefish Bay eight years earlier proved premature, that of East Milwaukee, renamed Shorewood in 1917, was overdue, though its first decade of population growth to 707 was slow. On the other hand, the community already had a rich history. In the mid-1830s, coincidental with the sale of the land at the federal land office, a dam and saw-mills were erected on the Milwaukee River near the present Capitol Drive bridge and one Daniel Bigelow actually platted a village of Mechanicsville there and sold residential lots in 1836. The Panic of 1837 and another dam downstream destroyed the dreams of the speculators, and the earliest settlers became farmers. Another abortive effort to create a community, this time on the west side of the river, was made by Milwaukeeans in the 1850s and 1860s.

More significant events for the area occurred in 1872 with the establishment of a popular resort, Lueddemann's-on-the-River, at what is now Hubbard Park. The next year tracks for a unit of the Chicago and North Western Railroad were laid parallel to the east side of the river. And in 1875-76 the Milwaukee Cement Company built along the river the first of four area mills for grinding limestone into cement. Organization of the Whitefish Bay Railway Company in 1886 and its ten-year operation of a steam railway until superseded by an electric streetcar to the Bay in 1898 was intended to benefit the neighboring community to the north. It

The Milwaukee Cement Company, established in Shorewood's present Estabrook Park in 1876, expanded to the west side of the Milwaukee River in 1888 and became popularly known as "Cementville."

incidentally also served the southern portion of the Town of Milwaukee, north of Edgewood, through which it passed.

The so-called "Dummy" line and its electrified successor thus opened up the attractive recreational and residential possibilities of the land lying between river and lake, and made possible the conversion of Zwietusch's Mineral Springs Park, as Lueddemann's was now called, into a full-fledged amusement park called Coney Island in 1900. Real success eluded this enterprise as well as its successors, Wonderland and Ravenna Parks, and the adjacent Milwaukee Motordrome built in 1913. Before these properties were converted to Electric Company car barns, a city park, and residential lots in 1916, they helped build the village which was then renamed Shorewood. By that time the village had water service and sewers, paved streets and cement sidewalks, and street signs.

Industrial Suburbs Spread Rapidly

A fourth municipality carved from two towns in the northern half of the County in this period was North Milwaukee, which became a village in 1897 and showed 1,049 residents in the 1900 census. Its origins lay in the early identification of the southeasterly corner of the Town of Granville as the unincorporated German farm community of Schwartzburg, where four rail lines came together on their north and northwest passage through the Town. This North Milwaukee Junction became a shipping point for farm produce, especially sugar beets, but it also acquired industry at the turn of the century, notably the American Bicycle Company, employing 1,000 workers at the height of the pre-automobile cycling craze. Platting of lots in the 1880s was followed by the establishment of Lutheran, Methodist, and Catholic churches, and a public school system. The village, extending west from 27th Street both north and south of Hampton Avenue and thus including the northeastern corner of the Town of Wauwatosa as well, became a city of the fourth class in 1918 and reached a population of 3,047 in the 1920 enumeration.

North Milwaukee Village Hall and Fire Station (left) on 35th Street in the early twentieth century. The view looks north from the roof of the Meiselbach Bicycle Factory, south of the intersection with Villard Avenue.

By 1922 the City of Milwaukee's aggressive annexation program with its strong northwesterly thrust led to a contiguous boundary with North Milwaukee. During the next half dozen years unrelenting pressure from the City of Milwaukee, the transparent unwillingness of the North Milwaukee city administration to provide high quality services and facilities, and the unlikelihood that the tiny suburb could expand its 1.4 square-mile area led to the inevitable consolidation. The referendum vote in the suburb was roughly two to one in favor, and in the City of Milwaukee, twelve to one.

On December 31, 1928, the City of North Milwaukee ceased to exist, as the Village of Bay View had in 1887. But there were differences. Before the residents of the former North Milwaukee could claim the spoils of consolidation in the form of large public works expenditures by the City of Milwaukee, the Depression of 1929 had struck and the City lengthened out the infrastructure rebuilding process which it had promised. References to North Milwaukee are still occasionally heard, and there has been talk of writing a history of the city that once existed for a third of a century in the Hampton-Villard area. But no one is likely to be able to recreate there the fierce parochialism of present-day Bay View, and the only reminder may soon be the former North Milwaukee High School which the city school board renamed for an early settler of the area, Harvey Custer.

While the origins of the Village of North Milwaukee were a mixture of farming, railroading, and industry, four south and west side suburbs of this era were more clearly industrial. Typical of this group was Cudahy. An unincorporated community named Buckhorn appeared on maps in the 1870s and 1880s, but it was a simple cluster of wood houses, an inn, and a general store adjacent to the Chicago and North Western route. The area was suddenly transformed by the decision of Patrick Cudahy, an Irish immigrant meatpacker, to move his operation out of the City of Milwaukee.

The Cudahy packing operation had distinguished lineage. As Plankinton and Armour, it was dissolved in 1884 and reorganized as John Plankinton and Company with Patrick Cudahy as a partner. Upon Plankinton's retirement in 1888, Patrick and his brother John took over as lessors of Plankinton's plant and in 1893 incorporated as Cudahy Brothers Company with Patrick as president. The move that year to a 700-acre site in the Town of Lake was intended to escape a proposed city ordinance which would have defined a packing plant as an objectionable municipal nuisance. The ordinance was never adopted, and other meat packers remained in the city jurisdiction under continuing threat to this day of public protests, if not of common council action.

Relocation of the plant under Patrick Cudahy's leadership soon led to worker relocation in the vicinity, for the plant lay six miles south and east of the existing city, and electric street railways were only then reaching the contiguous settled areas of the city's south side. In 1895 the settlement became an incorporated village of 771 residents, and in 1906, with a population of 2,556, it became a fourth class city. Before Cudahy's death in 1919 this truly industrial suburb had attracted seven other major manufacturing plants, and in the 1920 census showed 6,725 residents. More

The Milwaukee Board of Real Estate issued a booklet of 100 photogravures of the Milwaukee area in 1892, including this bird's eye view of Cudahy showing the stock yards and Cudahy packing houses.

recently it has employed more workers than live in the city. Originally its blue-collar population had been predominantly German and Irish, but later increases changed this until by 1940 over half of its people were of Eastern European descent.

Patrick Cudahy interested himself directly in the development of the community which bore his name. He laid out streets, guided zoning, supplied water from his own operation, in short, promoted everything short of making Cudahy a one-company town. In mid-century two major annexations, one to the south and the other to the west, increased its size from 1.9 to 4.7 square miles, lying between the suburbs of St. Francis and South Milwaukee and east from General Mitchell Field to the lake.

To the south of present-day Cudahy in the former Town of Oak Creek lies South Milwaukee. Its origins lay along Oak Creek, where a typical rural settlement existed as early as the 1840s. Mills, a general store, a post office, a school, and a church served a few residents for several decades, little disturbed even by the building in 1854 of the Chicago and North Western tracks nearby. Brick-making and a lake pier alone suggested an industrial potential. Then in 1890 real estate promoters organized as the South Milwaukee Company began to sell lots and succeeded in inducing eight manufacturers to relocate in the area.

Most prominent of these industrial firms was the Bucyrus Steam Shovel and Dredge Company, whose removal from Bucyrus, Ohio, was critical to local growth. The promoters spent money, $1,200,000 apparently, on streets, sidewalks, and harbor improvements and even persuaded the North Western to add a spur track to the lakefront. This mushroom growth led to incorporation as a village in 1892, with an unbelievable population growth from 512 to 3,392 in less than eight years. In 1897, like Wauwatosa, it changed its classification to that of a fourth class city. Like its northern neighbor Cudahy, it became an industrial suburb with a predominance of production workers, and today it also employs more workers than it houses. Its population is heavily of German and Polish descent.

Although served from the start by the North Western Railway, South Milwaukee remained relatively isolated from the major population growth of the City of Milwaukee outward, which was essentially to the north and west, and from other suburban developments. It never expanded from its original 4.8 square mile northeastern segment of the old Town of Oak Creek, and until after the Second World War, even the substantial part that was left of the original Town of Oak Creek to the south and west had only a few semi-suburban clusters of residents, such as the unincorporated industrial community of Carrollville.

The developers of South Milwaukee had enticed Bucyrus to relocate in 1891 with the classic inducements: fifteen acres of land, over half for a plant site adjacent to the railroad, a third for building lots, and two acres as a dock area on the lakefront connected to the plant by a beltline railway; and $50,000 toward plant construction. Thus at virtually no additional cost, the company achieved a much improved plant on a site with some locational advantages. But there were some locational disadvantages as well. As the company's official historians note:

> Most of the Bucyrus men who came to South Milwaukee in the spring of 1893 to set up the machinery and equipment returned to Ohio discouraged by the inadequate housing in the new town, the cold, damp climate, the unpaved streets hub-deep in mud, the lack of community life, and the generally unsettled conditions.

In addition to largely absentee management and the need to train a new labor force, the company suffered from a series of annual operating losses, some product design and performance deficiencies, a worsening capital shortage, and finally, a year after relocating, the threat of bankruptcy. Between 1895 and 1897 Bucyrus went through receivership and reorganization. Dramatic improvement in sales and profits followed in the next four years, but then in mid-1901 the machinists went out on strike. The company obtained an injunction against picketing, and, with support from the mayor, who was also company secretary, soon restored production. Five years later Bucyrus weathered a molders' strike in its foundries by contracting out the work and training new workers. While the company then became totally non-union, it simultaneously began to improve its labor and community relations.

At this critical juncture in its history the company was making shovels for the excavation of the Panama Canal, which provided competitive experience, good profits, and enormous publicity. Wide distribution of a photograph of President Teddy Roosevelt, immaculate in a white suit and hat and sitting on a 95-ton shovel during a 1908 canal inspection trip, was priceless in advertising value for the company and its host community. The company thus survived its first trying decade or so in South Milwaukee, but one may conclude that the South Milwaukee Company, not Bucyrus, got the better of their bargain. Bucyrus, later Bucyrus-Erie, is now a division of a national conglomerate of Becor Western, whose corporate headquarters remain in South Milwakee.

The last two of the eight turn-of-the-century municipal incorporations were much more centrally in the path of Milwaukee's westward thrust. The smaller of these was the Village of West Milwaukee, incorporated in 1906. This area of farms astride the boundary between the Towns of Wauwatosa and Greenfield first came to general notice with the location of the National Soldiers Home on 400 acres to its north in 1867. A old Indian trail running west from Milwaukee's near south side, variously called the Janesville Territorial Road, Mukwonago Plank Road, Waukesha Plank Road, and Elizabeth Avenue, was now renamed National Avenue as it inclined in a southerly direction beyond 27th Street and touched the south boundary of the Soldiers Home. Beyond the city limits this broad route attracted summer homes and estates for prominent Milwaukeeans — Andrew Dickson, Fred Bues, Peter McGeoch, and John L. Mitchell. Only a few gravel pits disturbed the rural and pastoral character of the area before the platting of home lots began in 1891, coincidental with the extension of the National Avenue street railway line to Soldiers Home.

More significant was the linkage in 1901 of the Milwaukee Road to the north and the North Western to the south, and the removal to the area in 1903 of the growing Pawling and Harnischfeger Company. The two company founders had opened a machine shop on Florida Street in Milwaukee in 1884 and had gradually converted to the manufacture of electric motor-driven overhead cranes, which revolutionized the handling of materials in heavy-goods industries in the United States and the world. The opening in 1905 of the P & H foundry, machine and forge shops, and office on the former William Wells estate diverted the area from its residential to an industrial emphasis.

The next year, with 909 residents, the Village of West Milwaukee

The Pawling and Harnischfeger company relocated from the city to Thirty-eighth and National Avenues in 1905 and transformed the character of West Milwaukee from residential to industrial.

came into being. It was only slightly larger in area than the original neighboring Soldiers Home, and far less populous. Additional estates and farms were now converted to manufacturing plant sites — a candy maker, Robert A. Johnston Company, several malt and milling companies, two major bottlers, several metal-treating and metal-working firms, and two units of General Electric. Some had originally located in the village; others moved there because of its hospitality to industry. A small annexation in 1931 and two large ones in 1950 and 1951 brought the village to approximately two square miles, then as now the smallest of all County municipalities. The population peaked in 1960 at 5,043; subsequent declines parallel population losses in most other Milwaukee municipalities, and the razing of residential properties for freeway construction also reduced the number of inhabitants.

With its heavy industrial emphasis and its modest population, West Milwaukee became known as a tax island under a state tax system which shared corporate income taxes with the host municipality. At times the village largely escaped local property levies, but recent changes in the law have reduced this advantage considerably. Like Cudahy and South Milwaukee, it has long been a net employer. Milwaukee abuts the Village on three sides and West Allis on the fourth, with little to distinguish the Village from its neighbors physically except its density of industry. Residents are fiercely independent, however, and they do not foresee consolidation of municipal services or government with other neighbors. Consolidation of the village schools, two elementary and one high school, with those of West Allis occurred in 1957, following a recommendation of the Milwaukee County School Committee, but village residents fought the action to the end, finally by seeking in vain an alternative school consolidation.

To the west of West Milwaukee lies West Allis, since the census of 1910 the most populous of the County's suburbs. The older portion of West Allis, incorporated as a village in 1902 and raised to a fourth-class city four years later, was carved out of the north central portion of the Town of Greenfield. The town, settled as early as the late 1830s, seemed to be a classic farm and rural portion of Milwaukee County. Four major diagonal roads passed through it on their southwesterly route into Waukesha County. Root River and Honey Creek, its major tributary, drain much of the original town. Post offices were assigned very early to Hales Corners in the southwest corner, Root Creek in the center, and Greenfield in the northwest. Laying of an east-west track of the Chicago and North Western in 1880, followed by a similar and parallel project of the Milwaukee Road to the north, gave the first hint of an industrial potential for the area.

The laying out of lots and subdivisions in an area known as North Greenfield in 1887 and the extension of an electric interurban and the newly electrified street railway to the State Fair to the north after the latter's opening in 1892 suggested rapid residential development. Two major industrial plants had, however, already located in the area — Kearney and Trecker and Rosenthal Cornhusker Company — before the decision of the Edward P. Allis Company to relocate in 1900 to North Greenfield. Since the death of its founder in 1889, Allis had been undergoing management and ownership changes and product adjustments which led in 1901 to a fourway merger as the Allis-Chalmers Company. Abandonment of its Reliance Works at Clinton and Florida Streets near the Milwaukee River mouth was a major move for the company, which for the last third of the nineteenth century had developed under its founder into the area's most important manufacturer and largest employer. On a hundred acres north and east from the intersection of Greenfield Avenue and 70th Street the company built a totally new plant, almost four miles due west from the famous Reliance Works. From its origins in 1860 the Allis operation had involved multiple products, often quite unrelated — iron pipe, mill stones, flour- and saw-mill equipment, and steam engines. For nearly half a century company expansion and product changes occurred around the new site, as the reorganized company moved into new fields, especially related to mining, the generation and distribution of electric power, and agricultural implements. Somewhat reminiscent of the Bucyrus firm experience after its move to South Milwaukee, the new

Allis-Chalmers had difficulty digesting its merger and went through a decade of receivership and reorganization before emerging under the leadership of General Otto H. Falk as president, 1913-32, and chairman of the board, 1932-40.

The relocation of the Allis works precipitated the incorporation of a surrounding village in 1902 and a city four years later. The name West Allis was chosen, though not without a struggle, but in the long run the nomenclature was felicitous, for the company was clearly a prize catch for an ambitious suburb. The company and the city became synonymous as both grew rapidly, the one to be the state's largest private employer, the other the County's most populous suburb. Impressive as had been the achievements before the 1905 plant openings in West Allis, the next half-century saw the Allis-Chalmers Manufacturing Company become a competitor of General Electric and Westinghouse in the electrical energy field, a major farm tractor producer, and a critical manufacturer of war goods in both World Wars.

A solidarity parade staged by union workers at the Allis-Chalmers plant in West Allis during the 1941 strike which resulted in a seventy-six day production standstill.

Dominant as was Allis-Chalmers, the City of West Allis was much more. It developed a large residential area, especially for the production workers of its many industrial plants, and substantial commercial and financial operations serving its own community. The traction era ushered into metropolitan Milwaukee in the 1890s by the development of the Milwaukee Electric Railway and Light Company, familiarly known as TMER&L, served West Allis admirably by east-west routes on Greenfield and National Avenues and a southern branch from the dominant Wells-Farwell streetcar line. Nearby State Fair Park, later annexed to West Allis, became a part of its economy and its social life. Much more than the other turn-of-the-century industrial suburbs, West Allis favored growth through annexation to its original 2.9 square miles, and by the end of the 1950s it had reached 11.6 square miles by assisting in the carving up of the Towns of Greenfield and Wauwatosa, especially to its west. Such growth was predominantly residential and commercial and gave much better economic and social balance to a community that had suffered severely in the Depression of the 1930s from its heavy industrial emphasis. Such expansion also better prepared the city for the corporate turmoil and decline in production and employment which beset Allis-Chalmers in the 1970s and 1980s. Once (1960) the state's fourth largest city, West Allis peaked at 71,649 residents in 1970, and slipped to sixth place in 1980 as its decline was sharper than other second class cities in the state.

Early Twentieth-Century Changes in Milwaukee County

For two decades after the first municipal incorporation binge ended in 1906, the emphasis was on annexation by the City of Milwaukee, relatively slow population and spatial growth for the suburbs, and surprising stability for the County's outlying rural and farm areas. The major instrument of change, becoming far more important in the decade of the 1920s than in the first two decades of the twentieth century, was the private automobile. It made the wealthy and the professional and business middle class immensely more mobile. Residential suburbs of the North Shore and Wauwatosa to the west, especially with the opening of the Pabst's Washington Highlands subdivision at the end of the First World War, became far more accessible in a society which still looked to the Downtown for almost all government offices, the best retail shopping, major cultural institutions, recreation, entertainment, and fine dining, professional and banking services, and, above all, employment. The possibilities of suburbanization — having the best of both worlds — were only dimly perceived by most people, but Milwaukee's Gold Coasts — Wisconsin Avenue and Highland and Washington Boulevards to the west and Prospect, Terrace, and Wahl Avenues and Lake Drive to the north — were already peaking in the First World War and 1920s.

The impact of the automobile was expressed in the improvement of city streets, in the coordination at the beginning of the war of state and federal efforts at financing state and interstate highways, and in the early 1920s of Milwaukee County creating a highway department which became the County's principal vehicle for planning. Even without the rapid spread of the automobile, however, the first quarter of the twentieth century would have seen much greater spatial mobility for Milwaukeeans. This was the era of the streetcar, which radiated out of the downtown into the city's important decentralized shopping districts, many of them created by transfer points on the streetcar system, and even into most of the suburbs. Access to the farther reaches of the County and into all adjacent counties and beyond was also available through the Electric Company's interurban system with its car barns in the Public Service Building at 3rd and Michigan. This dream of the local traction magnate John I. Beggs proposed to serve almost all population centers lying north, south, and west of the city within a radius of up to fifty miles. It peaked in the 1920s, when public preference shifted sharply to the private automobile and thus supported major public street and highway construction.

One of the consequences of the rise of the automobile was the continuing shift of agriculture in the County away from feed crops and dairying to truck gardens, orchards, nurseries, and florists serving the metropolitan market. Commission Row on Broadway, the near northside Haymarket, and public farmers markets such as at 29th and Center and in West Allis provided ready outlets. Another consequence of the auto age was in the provision of park facilities. Near downtown breathing spaces, private parks, and the more elaborate City parks such as Lake on the east and Washington on the west were gradually superseded by the County Park Commission's efforts after 1907. These latter included parkways, a special interest of Charles B. Whitnall, a florist turned park planner, who proposed them for virtually every major water course in the County. They also included large land acquisitions of farmland in the still open town areas, along the south lake front and in Oak Creek, Franklin, and Granville. The County also provided the first of its many public or municipal golf courses in 1919 in Grant Park, following the lead of the two most prestigious private country clubs, Milwaukee and Blue Mound, which first built in Shorewood and Wauwatosa early in this century, and then relocated farther out in the 1920s. Inevitably also the mushrooming of private golf and country clubs during the prosperous 1920s occurred entirely outside the City of Milwaukee and even later outside the County limits.

Suburbanization did not immediately fragment the metropolitan economy, despite the increasingly large proportion of the area's manufacturing which gravitated toward major industrial suburbs such as Cudahy, South Milwaukee, West Milwaukee, West Allis, and even North Milwaukee. Despite suburban siting of major industrial plants and even more common suburban residence of business leaders, the broader metropolitan view continued to prevail. Downtown was still where the action was and where business leaders met. There was the financial center — the brokerage houses, the insurance companies, and particularly the major banks which had evolved by merger and internal growth into the First Wisconsin National Bank, the Marshall and Ilsley, and the Marine National Exchange by the 1930s.

Critical political decisions affecting the metropolitan economy still faced the scrutiny of the private power structure, whether its members were suburban or not — the conversion of the private inner harbor downtown into a public outer harbor on Jones Island, the construction of a sewage treatment plant there and the postponement of a water filtration plant to 1937, and the reshaping of the City's lakefront through the construction of Lincoln Memorial Drive on land reclaimed from the lake. In other cases the City acquiesced in the gravitation of metropolitan functions toward the County — the building of a commercial airport in 1926 on a private flying field on the south side, the interlocking of the City's sewerage commission (1913) with a metropolitan body in 1921, and the merging of the City's into the County's park system by 1937. Some of the City's key downtown institutions — the library, the museum, the auditorium, and the Milwaukee Art Institute and its neighbor the Layton Art Gallery — remained clearly within City jurisdiction.

The evidence of the City's acquiescence in some gravitation toward County power is more than offset by the City's alarm during this period over the swallowing up of unincorporated town land by the suburbs. The City's counterattack was a vigorous program of annexation. Milwaukee's spatial growth had never before been systematic or sustained. Flurries of activity between 1852 and 1857 and again from 1887 to 1891 left the City less than three times its 1846 size but with over ten times the population. Fifteen individual increments between 1900 and 1923 added about 27 percent, over half of it in the tumultuous Socialist Party years which covered 1910 to 1913. Intensive annexation pressure, spearheaded by a City Division of Annexation, produced a two-thirds increase between 1923 and 1932, but this included the consolidation with North Milwaukee.

The City's annexation weapon was its promise to provide the high level of public improvements which already characterized its own neighborhoods, and its major threat was the withholding of access to Milwaukee's cheap, abundant, and good-tasting water supply. The City's water system, originally constructed just after the Civil War and periodically expanded and extended, drew on an inexhaustible supply of Lake Michigan water, while many suburban and town areas lacked direct access to the lake and were either unable or unwilling to commit the funds to build their own systems. Unincorporated rural and farm areas continued to use individual wells, while a suburb such as Wauwatosa had built its own artesian well and distribution system as early as 1897.

Until 1893 the City annexed through specific acts of the state legislature. Thereafter until 1950 the annexation process involved the filing with the Common Council of a petition by a majority of the taxpayers and property owners in an area, followed by a council ordinance approving the annexation. The creation of a division to advance annexation was an effort to make the process more systematic and efficient in practice as well as to overcome the apathy of the residents involved. But as persuasive was the evidence in the 1920 census that Milwaukee was second only to New York City in density of population and the accompanying civic viewpoint that the City must either grow spatially or die. Further supporting such annexation was the outlook of the City's mayor Daniel W. Hoan and the Socialist Party of which he was necessarily the titular head in local affairs. Hoan was a reformer rather than a Marxist revolutionary, and in the Progressive Era he had imbibed the dream of the city beautiful and the city as a focal point in American democracy. In the 1920s he sounded very much like Sinclair Lewis' civic boosters at the same time that his sometimes revolutionary rhetoric outraged the local business men. His well-organized local party support was also more reform than revolutionary, and of all American manifestations of organized socialism, it was conceivably the most successful in politics, that is, in winning elections. The Socialists had elected a mayor and a Common Council and County Board majority in 1910, only to lose almost everything in 1912. Hoan, Socialist city attorney from 1910 to 1916, was elected mayor seven times between 1916 and 1940, but only twice, briefly in the early 1920s and again in 1932, could he command a working majority in the council. The Socialist party disappeared as a local power after Hoan's defeat in 1940, but an openly avowed party member, Frank P. Zeidler, again served as mayor from 1948 to 1960.

The Socialists realized that their electoral strength lay in the city proper, not in the unincorporated areas, though they had scattered members there, nor in the suburbs, though a Socialist, Marvin V. Baxter, was elected mayor of West Allis in 1932. If the Socialists could not win in a countywide vote nor in the various suburban municipalities, their best hope for power lay in an expanded City of Milwaukee, they reasoned. Therefore they favored annexation and consolidation and, conversely, generally opposed the piecemeal transfer of functions from the City of Milwaukee to the County or to a separate metropolitan authority. The strong support for annexation by Hoan and his party almost certainly contributed to hostility toward annexation by political conservatives everywhere, and Hoan and his non-Socialist as well as his Socialist successors as mayor raised the volume level in their arguments against the alleged iron ring of suburbs.

Despite the City's annexation program, or perhaps because of it, there were three municipal incorporations between 1926 and 1938, but none was contiguous to the city or even an early or likely candidate for annexation. All were distinctly residential in character. The first was Fox Point in 1926. This was in a north lake shore area of bluffs and wooded ravines lying beyond Whitefish Bay. Dutch farm settlers had appeared there very early in the 1840s, but subsequently the major occupants were summer residents. Only 1.8 square miles in size, the new village had only 464 residents by 1930, and grew very slowly thereafter, due in part to stringent zoning of lots and the preference for single family residences. A substantial jump in population between 1950 and 1960, from 2,585 to 7,315, reflected three developments; opening of an area for retail shopping, the postwar housing boom, and the annexation of about a square mile. In the 1960s zoning was relaxed to permit multi-unit housing, but in many respects Fox Point still epitomizes the north shore's dominant mode of single-family residential or dormitory suburb.

To the west of Fox Point lies River Hills, a relatively large — now 5.4 square miles — but sparsely settled village which was incorporated in 1930. Lying largely along the first five miles of the Milwaukee River as it enters Milwaukee from Ozaukee County, River Hills may properly be said to be the only suburb in the County consisting of large estates. These are protected by zoning even more carefully than in Fox Point, generally by a five-acre-lot requirement. The area, once called Riverdale, became attractive in the 1920s to wealthy Milwaukeeans who chose to bypass the older lake shore suburbs in favor of the upper Milwaukee River in their retreat from the city. Slow population growth from 439 in 1930 to 1,642 in 1980 reflects the stringent zoning. The flavor of the community is suggested by its origins — the movement to incorporate as a village was launched at the 1929 annual meeting of the members of Milwaukee Country Club, which lies along the Milwaukee River in the southwest corner of the village.

The third village incorporation, also residential rather than industrial, occurred in 1938, but in the south central portion of the Town of Greenfield and more than a dozen miles from downtown Milwaukee. Among the County's suburbs its origins are unique, for it began as one of the Federal Resettlement Administration Greenbelt towns, an experiment launched for the New Deal in 1935 by Rexford Guy Tugwell of the Department of Agriculture. The concept involved conscious community planning of 633 rental units surrounded by farmland and wooded areas and providing curvilinear streets, parks and playgrounds, a shopping center, and community facilities. This garden living was deliberately meant to take inner city residents out into the country. A sense of community cooperation was to be fostered, leading to charges of collectivism. So remote was Greendale that a streetcar spur had to be laid from downtown Milwaukee to provide construction workers access to their jobs, as well as to serve the tenants later on.

Rentals in this federal project were in great demand, but a certain unease developed among the renters, for the units were managed according to Washington guidelines by a federal official on the project. Some occupants claimed the village government was therefore undemocratic. Increases in the value of the rental units and the loss of Washington zeal for the project led to a decision to offer the homes for sale to the occupants in 1952. Subsequently the substantial expansion of the village area and its active promotion for large and semi-luxury home sites altered dramatically the character of the village and its residents. Also significant in providing an adequate tax base for this former housing and planning experiment was the opening of an industrial park in 1958 and the 1970 development of Southridge, one of two mammoth shopping centers in

This postcard view publicized the "Greenbelt" community planned and built by the Federal government as Greendale in the late 1930s. The project provided jobs and became available as low-income rental housing.

metropolitan Milwaukee, largely located in the Village of Greendale. From 2,527 residents in 1940, soon after incorporation, Greendale had grown to 16,928 by 1980.

Any observer of the incorporation of Milwaukee suburbs between 1892 and 1938 must be struck by their diversity in size and population, density of population, economic and social makeup, and growth patterns. Impulses common to their original incorporation and to their continuing survival may be discerned, but equally cogent reasons may be perceived for some of them to consolidate with each other or even with the City of Milwaukee. Yet the Bay View and North Milwaukee precedents for consolidation, forty-one years apart, have had no emulators. Most political observers of the Milwaukee scene have concluded that neither style of consolidation — with each other or with the City of Milwaukee — lies in the near future. More likely would be transfer of specific city functions and facilities to the County, as in the case of the parks in 1937, and after the Second World War several instances of this occurred. But it should be noted that two failed consolidation efforts were made in 1928, one in Wauwatosa and the other in Whitefish Bay, and there was talk of consolidation that same year in Shorewood and West Milwaukee. In the two serious efforts there were many and conflicting views and confusing issues, but three conclusions may be drawn: the suburb's water needs and the likely high cost of meeting them were important; suburban growth and expansion would cost money and, in the manner of North Milwaukee's view, the costs could be borne by others under consolidation; and suburban officials would generally oppose their own elimination. Behind both consolidation proposals lay City of Milwaukee efforts, as well as *Milwaukee Journal* editorial sympathy if not support. Consolidation appealed to some as the inevitable rationalization of fragmented local government, just as in earlier decades and before the first wave of incorporation the political leaders of the City of Milwaukee took for granted a slow but persisting and irresistible outward expansion of the city.

The severe housing shortages at the end of the First World War had been gradually alleviated by a home and apartment building boom during the 1920s in the Milwaukee area. The Garden Homes development on the City's northwest border produced more than 100 low-cost dwellings as a demonstration of the economies of mass production and the potential of the cooperative system, but the sponsors — city and county governments and components of the housing industry — withdrew in haste as a rising real estate market led the occupants to demand the right to buy their units. Individual home construction predominated in subdivisions platted through much of the County's remaining farmland and even into Waukesha County. Rising construction costs had slowed the home building boom even before the depression of 1929 brought almost all area home construction to a halt in the 1930s; some outlying subdivisions, replete with street signs and curbs and gutters, became overgrown with weeds, not to be revived until the next building boom following the Second World War. Thus suburbanization of housing, the most conspicuous demographic fact of the 1920s, ground to a temporary halt after 1929.

It is significant that the only suburban incorporation of the depression 1930s was federally inspired. In truth, the general economic conditions in the County were very grim in the 1930s and the politics were turbulent, especially in the City. While there was a delay in production cutbacks in Milwaukee's heavy-goods industries and therefore in the rise in her unemployment rate, by 1931 all the evidence of the nation's worst depression had appeared — heavy job losses, rising public assistance rolls, sharp increases in tax delinquencies and mortgage foreclosures, bank closings, and low public morale.

The New Deal programs alleviated personal suffering and substituted some public for private employment. They also provided the funds for permanent improvements in the parks and other public facilities, a long-needed city water filtration plant on the lakefront, another south side high school, a model public housing project on the city's northwest side, and bridge and road construction. Moreover, modest job relief was provided by the return of beer and the reopening of Milwaukee's breweries following modification of the Volstead Act and repeal of the Prohibition amendment. But only the defense plant work under the threat of war and the Second World War itself restored employment and general prosperity to the pre-depression levels in metropolitan Milwaukee.

Suburbanization and Milwaukee's Downtown

The depression had a particularly severe impact on Milwaukee's downtown. Never clearly defined, this central business district had finally emerged by the 1920s as an east-west ribbon extending a few blocks north and south from Wisconsin Street on the east side of the Milwaukee River and Grand Avenue on the west side (these became East and West Wisconsin Avenues in 1926). The lake precluded expansion east, while the Menomonee and Milwaukee Rivers limited a southward movement through an area of light manufacturing, warehousing, and wholesaling served by the city's two major rail systems and river and lake transport. To the west and north the area merged into an increasingly residential mix with commerce and light industry.

Still anchoring the downtown in the 1920s were the characteristics Americans had associated with downtowns historically — major governmental buildings, intercity railroad stations, all the area's major financial institutions, its utility headquarters, its cultural institutions, its leading professional practitioners, and the social clubs, hotels, and restaurants for the well-to-do. Since the early 1890s improved technology and a rapidly rising real estate market had combined to spawn skyscrapers such as the Pabst Building and the Wells Building, but of a more modest height than elsewhere, severely constrained in height for a long time by a city ordinance because of the tamarack swamp underlying much of the Milwaukee River flood plain. Commercial and office space had expanded during the downtown building boom from the 1890s to the First World War, a period which also saw the evolution of the new retailing mode, the department store — T.A. Chapman's, a Milwaukee tradition since 1857, serving the carriage trade on the east side of the river, and Gimbels, Boston Store, and

Espenhain's on the west. Supporting this downtown development was an efficient and inexpensive electrified street railway system radiating out of the area after 1890 toward every residential neighborhood and into several close-in suburbs.

The prosperity of the 1920s reinforced the central role of the downtown with the construction there of sumptuous movie palaces and the film industry's distribution of "first runs" therein. Later in the decade, but before the depression of 1929 struck, a series of major new buildings reconstructed Wisconsin Avenue — the Mariner Tower, the Schroeder Hotel, the Kresge Building, the Warner Theatre Building, the Empire Building (housing the Riverside Theater), the Bankers Building, and the Milwaukee Gas Light Company Building. Some of these were not fully occupied, or even completed, before the great depression struck, and the perception of an overbuilt downtown virtually foreclosed new office construction in the main downtown corridor not only through the depressed 1930s and the Second World War years but for another decade and a half. A parallel hiatus in major downtown construction occurred in many American cities, such as Chicago, as a result of the depression and the war. Construction of the twenty-two-story Marine Plaza, the city's "first major glass curtain wall skyscraper," ended a thirty-year downtown building drought and began the area's renaissance in 1960-61.

Additional evidence of at least a temporary slowdown in the regional hegemony of the downtown is found in the survival of Milwaukee's many neighborhood shopping areas. The most conspicuous of these was along Third Street for three miles north of downtown, so varied and exciting in merchandise and services as to be called Milwaukee's Baghdad by one observer who long frequented it. Its most important intersection was with North Avenue, and nearby was the flagship of Schuster's, Milwaukee's most conspicuous department store. Schuster's — together with Goldmann's and a major Sears store in later years — also contributed to the southside's premier shopping strip along West Mitchell Street. Significant commercial districts scattered throughout the city, especially at transfer points on the electric street railway, and parallel districts in many suburbs — Wauwatosa alone had three — held down the retail trade in the downtown area.

Moreover, Milwaukee consumers who already felt comfortable with the offerings of goods and services in outlying shopping areas were psychologically prepared for the advent of shopping centers throughout the metropolitan area in the 1950s and after. Southgate began the trend in 1951 as a strip of stores with adjacent parking west of 27th Street in the Town of Greenfield; before long the area was annexed to the City, and the City of Greenfield was incorporated to its south. Bayshore, also small and simple, was built north of Silver Spring Drive on the east edge of the newly incorporated City of Glendale in 1953; Capitol Court followed in 1957 on Milwaukee's northwest side and Mayfair the next year in Wauwatosa's recently annexed west side.

Along with many smaller and less complex centers came three more very large roofed-in malls between 1961 and 1972 — Brookfield Square in Waukesha County but serving the Milwaukee metropolitan area; Northridge on 76th Street and Brown Deer Road in Milwaukee; and Southridge on the northeast corner of 76th Street and Grange Avenue in Greendale. The enclosing of the new shopping malls was ironically an emulation of the downtown's Plankinton Arcade on Wisconsin Avenue between Plankinton and 2nd Streets, constructed in 1916 and expanded in 1924 as a cluster of retail shops under one roof. The Arcade became the centerpiece of the Grand Avenue of 1982, often described as a suburban shopping mall, with parking, superimposed on the downtown.

The outward thrust of such shopping malls in the 1950s contributed further to the perception of a precipitous decline in the role of the City's central business district. This perception was reinforced by the almost total absence of major building construction even in the post-World War II period, the razing of many downtown buildings for surface or ramp parking and for expressway construction, and the sudden loss of the downtown movie palaces as entertainment magnets. Conversely the new shopping centers utilized their ample parking facilities by spawning many small, almost primitive, first-run movie houses and some high-rise office buildings.

But the real villain of the piece for the historic downtown was the postwar economic boom, the sharp increase in automobile ownership and child-bearing it facilitated, and the pent-up demand for new single-family homes after nearly two decades of slack residential construction. Subdivisions mushroomed not only in the relatively small open space left in Milwaukee and its suburbs, but more importantly on the adjacent farmland of the County's seven towns. The City's annexation drive, which had been institutionalized in 1922, had succeeded in adding 17.7 square miles, or 67 percent, to the city's land area in just nine years (1924-32), but it produced less than a tenth of a square mile between 1933 and 1945.

The depression and the war years had hardly been propitious years to launch annexations which would require large infrastructure investments. When the City resumed aggressive annexation postings in 1946, however, it found itself confronted with formidable competition. Seven of the ten existing suburbs also annexed town lands, two of them — Wauwatosa and West Allis — quite substantially. More significantly, eight new suburbs were incorporated between 1950 and 1957. By the latter date all of Milwaukee County's land area had been incorporated as a village or city, and the seven historic towns had ceased to exist. The decade of annexations and incorporations which ended in 1957 might be termed the suburbanization of Milwaukee County. Not only did the eighteen suburbs — half of them villages, half cities — then occupy 145 square miles or 60 percent of the County's land area; in addition the City of Milwaukee itself had created in the northwestern corner of the County, formerly the Town of Granville, a segment with most of the physical, social, and economic characteristics of these same suburban entities, and it later promoted the area as "Milwaukee's suburb in the city."

The annexations and the incorporations were inextricably intertwined. Milwaukee's renewed effort to extend its borders now had a sense of urgency behind it never before present. The city had always been relatively small by American standards, and this remained true even after its relatively rapid growth between 1924 and 1932. The changing role of the city's central business district was sensed if not totally perceived and understood, and anyone familiar with the evolution of other large American cities knew that a major alteration of the relation of central cities to their suburbs was occurring. What later came to be known as exurbanization, the process of escaping from the core city not to the contiguous suburbs but beyond them to still open and unincorporated land, the urban sprawl enormously facilitated by the automobile, was clearly in prospect for metropolitan Milwaukee. Sociologists and demographers have explored the many forces contributing to these suburban and exurban trends, and public officials and politicians of the central cities and the suburbs have provided their often self-serving interpretations.

The fact remains that the postwar exodus from the city was bound to alter the political map of the County and even of the adjacent counties. It is worth noting that long before the Second World War, indeed before the widespread ownership of automobiles, individuals had commuted to work, to shop, and to seek professional services in Milwaukee from beyond the contiguous suburbs. Steam trains and electric interurbans had long served the Waukesha County lakes district as well as many small communities in all the counties bordering Milwaukee. For example, the Village of Chenequa, incorporated as early as 1928, provided high quality basic municipal services for year-round and summer residents in the exclusive Beaver and Pine Lakes area north of Hartland, quite in contrast to most rural areas.

Much more immediately threatening to the City of Milwaukee after World War II was the impending incorporation of the semirural areas abutting Milwaukee County to the north and west. Menomonee Falls to the northwest had become a village in 1892, following the arrival of the railroad in 1890; but as late as 1930 it had only 2,469 residents, one-third fewer than the Town of Menomonee which surrounded it. Nearby tiny

Butler, a railroad junction, had incorporated in 1913, as had Germantown to the north in Washington County in 1927 and neighboring Lannon in 1930. But the Milwaukee County incorporation binge of the 1950s produced a secondary wave which led to the 1957 incorporation of the City of Mequon — a forty-eight-square-mile community extending along Milwaukee County's entire northern border with Ozaukee County. The major physical expansion of Menomonee Falls in 1958 into the rest of the Town of Menomonee and the establishment of four new Waukesha County municipalities between 1954 and 1964 in turn closed Milwaukee's western border. Brookfield became a city in 1954, Elm Grove a village in 1955, and New Berlin and Muskego to the south became cities in 1959 and 1964, respectively. Any ambition the City of Milwaukee may have had to escape the "iron ring" of Milwaukee County suburbs by escaping into the counties to the north and west was now blocked by Butler, Menomonee Falls, and Mequon.

The more critical development from Milwaukee's standpoint, nevertheless, was the closing off of any further expansion within its own county. This was effected in two ways: the more significant was the incorporation of eight new suburbs; and these new suburbs, including their own post-incorporation annexations, gobbled up 93.6 square miles of town lands, almost exactly half of that remaining when the competition began in 1950. Annexations in the 1950s by the City of Milwaukee and six older suburbs accounted for the rest of the total absorption into incorporated communities.

The City of Milwaukee was by far the biggest player in the annexation game, acquiring forty-six square miles, some of it only after a protracted court fight which ended in 1962 in Milwaukee's favor. The most important acquisitions were toward the northwest corner of the County, in the former Town of Granville, by which means it drove a wedge between the seven predominantly residential suburbs along the north shore and the upper Milwaukee River and the three older west side suburbs — West Milwaukee, West Allis, and Wauwatosa. In a decade of postwar battling over turf, a fight which left many lasting political scars, Milwaukee thus more than doubled its prewar land area.

The expansionist mayor who presided over almost all of the acquisitions during his twelve-year incumbency (1948-60), Socialist Frank P. Zeidler, was widely respected, even by some of his bitterest opponents, for having a coherent and well-thought-out philosophy behind his actions. As a keen student of urbanization in mid-century America, Zeidler conceived of the classical, traditional central city — in this case Milwaukee — as a remarkable institution that had served society well in industrialization, in acculturation of diverse population stocks, and in the provision of educational and cultural advantages. This vehicle of modern urban America was now threatened with strangulation as suburbs, professing a much more limited role in American society, had ringed the central city and would soon deprive it of the spatial resources it needed for providing adequate housing and jobs.

Though a continuing member of the nearly moribund Socialist Party, Zeidler was not ideological but pragmatic. Frugal in his public as well as his personal life almost to the point of parsimony, he believed that his own economic and social objectives for local government and the city beautiful would be better served by a larger central city than by a congeries of fragmented suburbs or by a transfer of power to the County government or to a metropolitan authority, either piecemeal or in one fell swoop. During his three four-year terms as mayor, therefore, he pursued the same annexationist policies as his Socialist predecessor in the 1920s, Dan Hoan, and added more land area to city jurisdiction than all previous mayors since the city's birth in 1846.

That two or more could play the annexation game quite successfully was demonstrated not by the minor additions in the 1950s to West Milwaukee and River Hills, but by the substantial ones to four other suburbs. Fox Point increased by a third to its present still modest 2.8 square mile size, and Cudahy added 2.8 square miles to its original 1.9, but the two big suburban annexationists were West Allis and Wauwatosa. The former grew to one and a half times its pre-1950 size, reaching 11.6 square miles and becoming for a time the state's sixth most populous city; since 1910 it has been the County's most populous suburb.

In 1952 Wauwatosa made an even more spectacular leap to thirteen square miles, three times its previous size. This was the single largest annexation in county and state history and altered substantially the character of the community. Already a mature suburb with a surprising range of internal institutions stemming from a history about as old as Milwaukee's, Wauwatosa now undertook to service a rapidly growing residential area to the west of the original "village" and to assimilate the open space of the large and sprawling County Institutions grounds (approximately 1.6 square miles) and many County parks and parkways. It also provided for a major addition to its tax base through industrial sites west of Highway 100 and for a retailing and office district at the intersection of that route and North Avenue. So large an annexation entailed commitments to so high a level of basic urban services, and especially of schools, as to generate heated public debate prior to the official incorporation of the new area into the City in 1954, and to taint the community's politics for some years.

The combined annexation efforts of Milwaukee, Wauwatosa, and West Allis in the 1950s obliterated the Town of Wauwatosa. The fate of the

Town of Granville was the same, but its death was more convulsive and prolonged. As late as 1950 its original thirty-six square miles were not seriously disrupted, having yielded up only a small southeast segment to Milwaukee and a northeast corner to River Hills. The remaining twenty-nine square miles, or 80.5 percent, crisscrossed by railroad routes, the Menomonee River, and some major highways, still maintained its historic farm and rural character, though dotted here and there with evidences of urban sprawl, residential, commercial, and industrial.

One long-settled but informal crossroads community in the northeast of the Town was known as Brown Deer, and some of its businessmen, fearing annexation by Milwaukee, incorporated this 1.8 square mile area as a village with 1,323 residents early in 1955. Their plans for expanding to twenty-two square miles were thwarted in the courts by Milwaukee the next year, and after prolonged litigation the state supreme court reduced Brown Deer to only 4.3 square miles in 1962. Residents who were thus deprived of their suburban status by court action formed an informal independent Granville, but neither they nor Brown Deer officials could thwart the City of Milwaukee in its northwesterly drive.

Contemporary observers of a truncated Village of Brown Deer questioned whether the municipality could survive in its original form as a small suburb of single-family homes. Most doubts were removed by rezoning for multi-family units and an industrial park in 1965, and later by the Northridge development to its west along the old Wauwatosa Avenue, which stimulated intense commercial activity on the Village segment of Brown Deer Road. The new housing mix broadened the community's income base, and by 1980 had attracted more blacks than any other Milwaukee suburb and nearly as many as the other six northern suburbs put together.

The Town of Milwaukee, which had originally included the Towns of Granville and Wauwatosa as well as the Village which preceded the City of Milwaukee, also succumbed to a combination of incorporation and annexation by 1955. The spasms of eight incorporations within the County in the 1950s was begun with Glendale in 1950. Its area was a north-south ribbon along the Milwaukee River and the Green Bay Road lying between Capitol Drive and River Hills. It was a mixture of residential and industrial use, and some of its occupants had long hoped for and contemplated incorporation. Milwaukee's earlier aggressive annexations northward led to three abortive incorporation moves in the area in the 1920s, and the City unsuccessfully fought against the 1950 effort as well. The City of Glendale began with only 2.9 square miles but including the most valuable industrial property at the south end along Port Washington Road. Within the next five years it had added 2.8 square miles, some of it from the Town of Granville, and had thus effectively destroyed the viability of the remain-

Erected in 1872, the Town of Milwaukee Town Hall has been preserved on a new site. It is the oldest of the two remaining seats of town government in the County; the Oak Creek structure has also been moved for museum purposes.

ing Town of Milwaukee by removing its tax base. Its initial population of 3,152 had reached 13,426 by 1970, when it leveled off.

Incorporation of the Village of Bayside in 1953 with only 467 persons in just under a square mile illustrates the dynamism of the incorporation wave. Bayside occupies the far northeast corner of the old Town of Milwaukee, and by the 1950s had faced a choice of independent incorporation or cooption by a neighbor. It was as solidly residential as Glendale was industrial, and its tax loss meant an end to the Town of Milwaukee. Similar in residential character to its neighbor Fox Point, Bayside felt the need to expand almost immediately to 2.4 square miles, including a tiny portion of Ozaukee County. Its original strict residential zoning was relaxed in 1969 but without altering its essentially affluent nature. Its population reached 4,724 by 1980. The only aberration from its exclusive residential character is the presence in its southeast corner of the Schlitz Audubon Center, on the Uihlein family's famed Nine Mile Farm.

New Suburbanization in the Southern Tier of Towns

Dominant in the 1950's scramble for political hegemony in the northern half of the County were the City of Milwaukee and the annexation process; although three new suburbs ultimately came into being — Glendale (1950), Bayside (1953), and Brown Deer (1955) — they accounted for but a small portion of the still unincorporated northern town lands as of 1950. It was just the opposite in the southern half of the County. Here the City of Milwaukee gained far less by annexation; and five new suburbs came into being, two of them to become the largest suburbs in the County, one of average size, and two smaller ones. Once again the major consequence was that before the end of the decade the four original southside towns had ceased to exist.

The two smallest new southside suburbs had had early traditions of clusters of settlers, and the wonder may be why they had not incorporated earlier. St. Francis became a city in 1951, adopting its name from a religious community within its border since 1849. St. Francis Seminary for the training of priests, especially for so German-speaking a diocese as Milwaukee, opened in 1856 on a ninety-acre site four miles from downtown Milwaukee, known locally as South Point and to the Potawatomi Indians as Nojoshing or "a tongue of land." The importance of this educational institution to the health of an essentially German diocese far exceeded its role as a developer of this lakeshore corner of the Town of Lake. Like Bay View to its north, the area suffered from poor land access to Milwaukee's downtown, even after the main line of the Chicago and North Western Railway passed through west of the seminary grounds. When Patrick Cudahy relocated his packing plant outside of the City of Milwaukee in 1892, he chose to move farther south into the southeast corner of the Town of Lake.

Between 1921 and 1930 the Milwaukee Electric Railway and Light Company constructed a pioneer electric generating plant on the lakefront just south of the seminary; its three smokestacks became the identifying landmark of the South Point of Milwaukee's bay. Large state utility property tax revenues generated by this power plant were shared with the local town government and became both an incentive to incorporate the adjacent area and an obstacle to its severance from the Town of Lake. Three incorporation efforts met political and judicial rebuffs, but the fourth succeeded in making St. Francis a city of 2.9 square miles in 1951. An adverse change in the state's shared tax program, the absence of significant growth potential, and a high proportion of non-taxable religious and park real estate caused the community to consider consolidation with Milwaukee; but in keeping with a powerful tradition among Milwaukee suburbs, St. Francis opted for continued independence. Population peaked at 10,489 in 1970 and had declined 4 percent by 1980.

Hales Corners traces its origins to an original land claim of young William Hale, who had arrived from New York in 1837. A community largely composed of German farmers developed at the point where the Janesville Road exited the County to the west. As postmaster, farmer, and innkeeper for passenger and farm wagon traffic to the southwest, Hale lent his name to a community that soon declined with the advent of other transportation routes. But the persistence of a rudimentary village — with inns, saloons, a mill, stores, craftsmen — in the County's predominantly agricultural southwest led to the acceptance of limited municipal responsibilities in 1924 as an unincorporated village. In turn this attracted city residents who wished to escape to more rural surroundings. There were 1,382 residents upon incorporation as a village in 1952. Originally only half a mile square, the village added two square miles in 1955, thus paving the way for planned residential growth on large lots and curving streets to match the unchecked spread of a crowded retail strip along Highway 100. Like St. Francis, Hales Corners could not maintain its 1970 population high of 7,771, dropping 8.5 percent by 1980.

The predictability of the incorporation of St. Francis and Hales Corners was absent with respect to Oak Creek, Franklin, and Greenfield, yet all were the product of the same post-World War II wave of suburbanization and municipal expansion which swept the County. All three may also be said to be the consequence of the resumption of aggressive annexation by the City of Milwaukee, and the case of the pathbreaker among them — Oak Creek — involves melodrama.

Milwaukee's 1951 consolidation with the remaining southern portion of the Town of Lake, west of the City of Cudahy and including an expanding General Mitchell Field, gave it a substantial if irregular border with the Town of Oak Creek west of the City of South Milwaukee. Concern for the political future of this still predominantly rural if not largely farm area ran into three harsh facts. The only remotely urban sections of the town were few, small, and scattered. Just off the lake and south of South Milwaukee lay unincorporated Carrollville. Served by the Chicago and North Western Railway, this industrial community had developed just before the turn of the century and had some characteristics of a company town, for one firm had first built eight worker homes and then another fifty-four, and a company-sponsored cooperative served as general store and housed the post office. Beginning with a whiskey distillery in 1893, the community's industrial plants generally made products which were unwelcome in organized villages and cities — glue and gelatin from tannery waste, chemical fertilizers, tar products, TNT, dyestuffs, aluminum smelting — or, like Allis-Chalmers, engaged in R and D. At one time individual local plants were said to employ 500 or 600 workers while 700 persons lived in the community. Residents were often immigrant workers obliged to accept unpalatable entry-level jobs and to live amidst noticeable air and water pollution.

The manifest advantages of isolation and freedom from municipal regulation were matched for the factory owners by the proximity of rail and water transport and access to an unlimited water supply. The raw frontier life style of Carrollville tolerated many rowdy saloons before Prohibition, and bootleg liquor during that era. Several of the earlier firms operating in Carrollville, notably the glue and gelatin producers, were owned by Milwaukee businessmen who apparently sought to conceal their

Carrollville connection; later owners were eastern or foreign firms such as Peter Cooper and du Pont.

Even earlier settlements had been made at Oak Creek village in the northeast corner which had become a part of the City of South Milwaukee in 1892, and in Oakwood, which was a depot on the Milwaukee Road and a post office in the Town's southwest area. As of the census of 1950 the Town of Oak Creek recorded but 4,807 residents, exceeding in population only the neighboring Town of Franklin among the County's seven towns, most of them already severely truncated, and these residents were widely scattered on 28.2 square miles.

A second deficiency for Oak Creek was the almost total lack of tax-producing real estate. Even the Carrollville industries were by this time wholly inadequate to finance much of a municipal undertaking. A partial remedy appeared in 1951, when the Wisconsin Electric Power Company began construction of a hundred-million-dollar steam-generating plant in the Town's far southeast corner. But this development could only partially offset the low tax potential under state law of the Town's classification of 80 percent of its area as farm land, rich farm land though it was.

The harshest fact of all was the stringent state rules regulating municipal incorporation. To form a city, a minimum of 1,000 residents was required, as well as a minimum population per square mile. The imminence of a City of Milwaukee annexation effort, a posting of 9.7 square miles under current annexation law, might have deterred a less determined group than the Town Board of Oak Creek, but the latter, taking advantage of a long-standing rural-farm-small-town bias in the legislature amounting to open hostility to the state's only large city, and reinforced by inadequate decennial reapportionments of assembly and senate seats, won legislative approval for an amendment to Chapter 60 of the statutes governing towns.

This change, henceforth referred to as the Oak Creek law, provided that towns might become fourth class cities provided they were adjacent to a city of the first class (only Milwaukee qualified), had over 5,000 residents and over $20,000,000 equalized valuation, and were petitioned by at least 100 citizens and taxpayers representing the owners of over half the town's real estate. On the face of it this special legislation might be construed as violating sections 23 and 31 of Article IV of the state constitution, but Governor Walter J. Kohler had agreed to sign it, and a court challenge to its constitutionality by the City of Milwaukee failed after four years of litigation.

The drama of Oak Creek's last-minute rescue from the big city's grasp was not only legislative and judicial. In order to file required documents to complete their petitioning for city status, the Town officials had to drive to Madison with City of Milwaukee representatives hard on their heels, in an episode usually reserved for Hollywood thrillers.

The precedent set by Oak Creek in incorporating an essentially farm and rural area, in the face of state municipal incorporation traditions dating from the 1890s, was extended to Franklin in 1956, thus converting to city status an area of 34.6 square miles whose population swelled from 3,886 in 1950 to 10,000 by 1960. The threat of annexation for Franklin came less from Milwaukee than from Greendale, which already occupied some former Franklin acreage. A quarter century later Oak Creek had 16,932 residents and Franklin 16,871, or just below the average for the County's eighteen suburbs, but both were growing rapidly. Incorporation undoubtedly conferred benefits on both Oak Creek and Franklin residents, even though their property tax bases lacked the traditional strength provided other suburbs by commercial and industrial developments. Oak Creek welcomed the move to Howell and Drexel Avenues in 1962 of the large and sophisticated research and production units of the A-C Spark Plug (now A-C Spark Plug and Delco Electronics) Division of General Motors, employing as high as 7,000 at one time; and farther north on Howell Avenue the south campus of Milwaukee Area Technical College was located.

Franklin's vast expanse has had its own recent forms of recognition — the relocated County House of Correction; Tuckaway Country Club, since

The first German "free church" in the state acquired land in Franklin in 1851 for both a cemetery and this meeting house, constructed from hand-hewn logs. It is a County landmark, known as Painesville Memorial Chapel.

66 *Olson*

1973 host to the Greater Milwaukee Open on the PGA tour; the Hales Corners Speedway; and for many years, until its removal in 1983 to Oshkosh, the Experimental Aircraft Association headquarters and museum, sponsor of a spectacular small plane fly-in every year since 1953. Its historical traditions are particularly interesting for an area that remained agricultural so long. On its southeast still stand the Painesville Chapel and graveyard, a reminder of the "free church" Germans of the 1850s, and the Oakwood school, a true pioneer of rural high school education in 1883. An urban cluster southwest from Whitnall golf course is still informally known as St. Martins. Here the ubiquitous Reverend Martin Kundig, Bishop Henni's administrator and missionary, founded both a church and a settlement (which he named for his own patron saint) for both Irish and German Catholics. Kundig, imbibing the current economic development mania, proposed to link the Root River by canal to St. Martins. He failed, but his settlement survived and now hosts Hales Corners' annual pig fair. With their still largely undeveloped open space both Oak Creek and Franklin contain large park and parkway components of the County park system, especially along the meandering Root River.

To complete the extinction of the County's town land and the suburbanization of the County, a two-mile-wide east-west portion of the Town

MILWAUKEE COUNTY CITIES AND VILLAGES

NAME	YEAR OF ORIGINAL INCORPORATION	CHANGE IN STATUS OR NAME	1980 CENSUS	PRESENT SIZE (SQ. MI.)
Milwaukee	1838 Village	City in 1846	636,212	95.73
Bay View	1879 Village	Consolidated with City of Milwaukee 1887	—	—
South Milwaukee	1892 Village	City in 1897	21,228	4.5
Wauwatosa	1892 Village	City in 1897	51,308	13.1
Whitefish Bay	1892 Village		14,930	2.4
Cudahy	1895 Village	City in 1906	19,547	4.74
North Milwaukee	1897 Village	City in 1918; Consolidated with City of Milwaukee 1929	—	—
Shorewood	1900 Village	Renamed in 1917; originally East Milwaukee	14,327	1.59
West Allis	1902 Village	City in 1906	63,982	11.402
West Milwaukee	1906 Village		3,535	1.121
Fox Point	1926 Village		7,649	2.8
River Hills	1930 Village		1,642	5.5
Greendale	1938 Village		16,928	5.56
Glendale	1950 City		13,882	6.6
St. Francis	1951 City		10,066	2.6
Hales Corners	1952 Village		7,110	3.1
Bayside	1953 Village		4,724	2.5
Brown Deer	1955 Village		12,921	4.5
Oak Creek	1955 City		16,932	28.4
Franklin	1956 City		16,871	35
Greenfield	1957 City		31,467	12

of Greenfield incorporated as a city of that name in 1957. All five of the surrounding communities were already urban and/or industrial, and one — Milwaukee — was hostile to Greenfield's incorporation, helping to block its first such effort in 1954. Its 12.6 square miles contained only 17,636

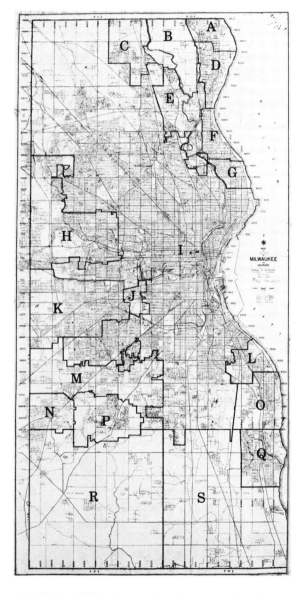

A- Bayside

B- River Hills

C- Brown Deer

D- Fox Point

E- Glendale

F- Whitefish Bay

G- Shorewood

H- Wauwatosa

I- Milwaukee

J- West Milwaukee

K- West Allis

L- St. Francis

M- Greenfield

N- Hales Corners

O- Cudahy

P- Greendale

Q- South Milwaukee

R- Franklin

S- Oak Creek

A 1959 City of Milwaukee engineering map, updated to 1962, which indicates the finalization of community boundaries within Milwaukee County.

residents in 1960, but growth was rapid in the next two decades. Freeway construction dealt harshly with the new city, as the airport, zoo, and Rock freeways bisected it in three directions, while a broad segment of the Root River Parkway had already removed from potential development much of the city's western reaches.

The impact of postwar urbanization and suburbanization, and even exurbanization, had not yet spent itself in metropolitan Milwaukee by 1957, but it had completed the County's political fragmentation. The City's boundaries were now fixed forever, short of a political convulsion which no one predicted or could foresee. Eighteen suburbs, an "iron ring" according to some city observers, held 60 percent of the County's land area and 28.5 percent of its population. They were strikingly diverse in age and maturity, in size and population, in social characteristics and economic function, and in political traditions. Two — West Allis and Wauwatosa — were by far the largest and displayed characteristics and tendencies very similar to Milwaukee's, due to their size, age, and complexity. There was no correlation between size and population among suburbs; in 1960 exactly half had 10,000 or fewer residents, and one (River Hills) as few as 1,257, while West Allis with 68,157 at the other end had more than all ten of the least populous.

Two decades later two pronounced demographic trends could be identified in the County for the period 1970 to 1980; the City of Milwaukee and ten suburbs were losing population (as little as 3.7 percent for Fox Point, as high as 19.8 percent for tiny West Milwaukee), as was the County as a whole, but the suburbs' share of County population was increasing at the expense of the City's and was now 34 percent of the County total. Between 1970 and 1980 the City had declined by 11.3 percent, while the suburban total dropped only 2.4 percent. Population flows were essentially outward, north, west, and south, from the historic old-city core to the suburbs, and in the suburban cases to the next outlying tier of suburbs. Milwaukee's losses were somewhat tempered by the large open spaces annexed on its perimeter in the 1950s and especially toward the northwest in the former Town of Granville. The countermovement of a residential revival accompanying the Downtown's renaissance during the 1960s and 1970s was not significantly reflected in the 1980 census. The centrifugal demographic tendency was underscored by population increases in all four neighboring counties, and especially by Waukesha County's 21 percent spurt; indeed, her neighbors' population increases almost exactly matched Milwaukee County's loss for the decade.

The Challenge of Fragmentation

The incorporation of eight suburbs in the County between 1950 and

1957 and the accompanying, or perhaps stimulating, expansionist annexations by the City of Milwaukee and some suburbs must be interpreted as popular responses by both public officials and residents to a wide range of economic, social, and political needs and opportunities. Similar popular responses were also represented by the population outflows. This is not to suggest that all County residents approved of the political actions which led to the extinction of the seven towns, nor even that the political fragmentation which resulted in Milwaukee County was inevitable. It is evident that there had long been a realization that economic, social, and technological trends — especially advances in transportation and communication — were rendering obsolete the traditional political forms and political thought inherited from farm and small-town nineteenth-century America. An urbanizing and industrializing society was obliged to adapt, or at least try to adapt, its political institutions to the new reality. In Milwaukee and Wisconsin this adaptation was slow, gradual, piecemeal, even reluctant, rather than sudden, dynamic, and revolutionary. On the whole it was an adaptation that used old forms to meet new challenges rather than fashioning new institutions. If Milwaukee's was different from the experiences of many other metropolitan areas in the United States, it was a matter of differences of detail rather than overall effect.

Before examining the public and private responses to dramatic changes in Milwaukee's governing structures after the Second World War, we might note that all of the newer as well as the older suburbs in the County moved systematically toward a nearly full range of municipal services. There were exceptions to this generalization. For example, River Hills, principally comprising a more affluent population on larger lots, did not develop the traditional inner city infrastructure of streets, sidewalks, street lights, and retail areas; and other suburbs as well and even the northwestern portion of the City of Milwaukee developed new residential areas that reflected the same urge to avoid the characteristics associated with old-fashioned city density. The larger, older, more industrialized suburbs more nearly resembled Milwaukee in appearance and in municipal services. Nevertheless during the forty years following the end of the war almost all of the County's municipalities accepted the same urban responsibilities — for police, fire, and civil defense protection; for public health, sanitation, sewer, and water services; for building inspection, zoning, and planning; and for schools, recreational, and library facilities.

In modest ways intergovernmental cooperation came into being — for example, by agreements to share protective services in an emergency. Suburban residents gained access to information sources beyond their own library capabilities, first by contract with the Milwaukee Public Library, later in 1982 through participation in the Milwaukee County Federated Library System authorized by state law; and through membership in the

Library Council of Metropolitan Milwaukee, they shared in the assimi-
lation of the holdings of the area's college, university, and special libraries
to those of the public libraries. Three suburbs, Whitefish Bay, Fox Point,
and Glendale, formed a joint water utility as the North Shore Water
Commission, operating since 1963, while others, such as Wauwatosa,
Brown Deer, Shorewood, and West Milwaukee, partly as a result of
successful legal action brought by Wauwatosa, gained wholesale access to
the water intake system of the City of Milwaukee while maintaining their
separate distribution facilities.

In almost all cases municipalities and their school districts had identical or nearly identical boundaries. In the northern and southern suburban
sections of the County, however, some non-urban (that is, common, high
school, or K-12) school districts persisted in crossing municipal boundaries. It is possible that the County's schools would have seen some major
redistricting as a result of the work of a County school committee appointed by the Milwaukee County Board of Supervisors through a mandate from the 1947 legislature. The committee's plan of reorganization
appeared, however, in mid-1950, just as the wave of municipal incorporations and annexations had begun to change the County's political map
so dramatically. It is clear in retrospect that the committee's proposal for
eight districts, however rational geographically and in equalizing resources, was too revolutionary to survive public hearings. One of the few
specific consequences of the County committee was the consolidation of the
West Milwaukee and West Allis urban districts in 1957. The major annexations by the cities of Milwaukee, Wauwatosa, and West Allis resulted
in school district consolidations influenced by and not unlike those proposed by the County committee, but the merging of suburban and school
district (town) schools — to the southeast, southwest and north shore —
and the proposed crossing of County boundaries into Racine and Waukesha County, never materialized as the committee recommended. The
school committee expired in 1965.

It may be concluded that the more than century-old public school
system in Wisconsin had such strong local roots and such good access to
state aids, both general and specific, that it could thus resist efforts at
rationalization in the name of equal student opportunities and equalization of district resources. Only later, in the 1970s and 1980s, in response
to two sets of lawsuits in the federal courts, the first against the Milwaukee
Public Schools in the name of minority students, the second by the Milwaukee Public Schools (joined by the NAACP) against suburban school
districts, were the questions of equal opportunities and resources raised
once again. Charges of racial segregation and discrimination thus complicated what had earlier been narrowly interpreted as a simple matter of
school system reorganization.

A separate but increasingly important tax-supported school system in metropolitan Milwaukee dealt with vocational education. Milwaukee area employers had taken the initiative for developing apprenticeships and continuing education programs early in the twentieth century, an obvious response to the city's large working class and immigrant population and to its growing dependence on manufacturing skills. A private local trades school was incorporated into the city school system as a technical high school, but it did not satisfy broader and more immediate industrial needs. As a consequence of a two-year international study of vocational education led by the state's renowned Legislative Reference Librarian Charles McCarthy, the 1911 legislature mandated that all cities of 5,000 or more maintain a continuation, trade, and evening school under a separate five-member board and with some state aid. The City of Milwaukee's, launched in 1912, grew rapidly and soundly, until it had expanded its curriculum and student body well beyond the model of 1911, including ultimately a two-year college transfer program as well as a large adult enrichment component.

In Milwaukee, as well as elsewhere in the state's urban areas, the need for vocational and continuing education ultimately transcended inner or central city boundaries and at the same time strained the city's financial capacity. The opportunity for the first major revison of the 1911 statute came in 1965 in the midst of widespread public interest in post-secondary education for the World War II baby boom crop. The result was the creation by the legislature of sixteen area vocational, technical, and adult education district boards covering the state, together with the promise of expanded state funding. Thus the state government, under the guise of a statewide reorganization, transferred from the jurisdiction of a City of Milwaukee citizens board the facilities and programs which had been built up locally over more than a half century. Under an area board which extended beyond county boundaries major new campuses were constructed in Oak Creek, West Allis, and Mequon, and instructional programs were fielded throughout the district. Local public school districts could and did continue, however, to offer additional adult education services deemed appropriate to each community.

State intervention to overcome political fragmentation had also appeared with regard to sewage. Milwaukee installed its earliest rudimentary sewers before it became a city in 1846, but its first efforts were piecemeal. Under a board of public works established in 1869 the City planned extensive sewer construction which had reached 165 miles by 1888. The state legislature authorized a city sewerage commission in 1913, and its more aggressive attention to waste and storm water gathering and to waste water treatment improved pollution abatement in the city's rivers and in Lake Michigan, especially upon the completion of an experimental activated sludge sewage disposal plant on Jones Island in 1925.

Meanwhile, the state legislature partially converted the City's facilities into a broader function by creating a Metropolitan Sewerage Commission in 1921. The latter body was empowered to construct sewers beyond the city limits and to draw upon the city's facilities for handling waste water. Subsequent state legislation also empowered a divison of the State Department of Natural Resources to exercise jurisdiction over local waste water and solid waste programs. The present Milwaukee Metropolitan Sewerage District, governed by a board of commissioners appointed from the municipalities represented in the district, now operates the Jones Island treatment plant and a new South Shore treatment plant, and is responsible for the court-ordered $1.75 billion deep tunnel projects intended to eliminate raw sewage discharges from the district facilities into the lake. The district now extends beyond the county into Ozaukee and Waukesha County municipalities.

The state's preemptive role in sewerage, exercised as early as 1921 by the formation of a metropolitan district, thus did not entirely solve the problem of fragmented local governmental units, especially after the suburbanization of the 1950s. Instead, the issues of extension of sewer facilities (both gathering and treatment) and of equitable charges, especially for capital expenditures, became acute in dividing the many affected constituencies in the 1980s without providing a seeming democratic and equitable means of resolution.

The exercise of state authority to reduce the effects of political fragmentation, as in the case of vocational education and sewers, clearly had severe limits. Alternatively one could seek an expanded role for county government, as more and more needs seemed to transcend municipal boundaries. Some functions almost from their inception were predominantly county oriented. This was true of airport facilities. The County acquired the Zimmerman farm in the northwest part of the Town of Wauwatosa in 1919 as an airport site, possibly the earliest effort of an American municipality to interject itself into commercial aviation. The site was inadequate — too small and wedged between a railroad and the Menomonee River — so it was abandoned in 1926 in favor of a private airfield in the Town of Lake acquired from Tom Hamilton, a wooden airplane propeller manufacturer formerly employed by Mathews Brothers as a furniture maker. The steady growth of commercial aviation, airmail, and army aviation brought physical expansion during the 1920 and 1930s to what was renamed General Mitchell Field in 1941.

In the wake of public enthusiasm following Lindbergh's flight, the City of Milwaukee had conceived of the advantages of a downtown airport and had opened a field on the lakefront north of the harbor mouth in 1926. Named for Lester Maitland, a local hero of a trans-Pacific flight, Maitland Field served for a time as the base for the Kohler Company amphibians crossing Lake Michigan, but the weather handicapped flights to and from the lake shore strip, and in 1956 the field was closed down in favor of a nike site. Meanwhile aircraft engine manufacturer Curtiss-Wright had opened one of its many small-craft franchised airports at Appleton and Silver Spring in the Town of Granville in 1929; this field also became County-owned in 1947 to serve general aviation, especially corporate and private flying, a portion of the aviation world no longer welcomed at Mitchell Field, and was renamed Lawrence J. Timmerman Field, honoring a former County Board chairman.

Urban sprawl after World War II accentuated the dominant role of the automobile in people's lives and dictated an interest in providing better access to the jobs, services, and amenities of the central city for the swelling population outflows. For the City of Milwaukee the provision of high speed freeways into downtown Milwaukee seemed essential to the maintenance of the traditional role of the downtown for the entire metropolitan area at the same time that it encouraged suburban and exurban living by making transportation access to the big city easier. The City began its formal expressway plans in 1952; but before it began construction, state legislation of 1953 transferred responsibility to a County Expressway Commission appointed by the governor. This quasi-independent commission was empowered to plan and construct a freeway system, which meant it could buy right-of-way, design, and award construction contracts, but it needed County Board approval of its projects and the appropriation of funds. The legislature later also obligated the commission to plan a mass transit system for the County.

Although the commission took over from the city in 1954, it did not open any part of the system for use until 1962. By that time the Federal Interstate Highway Act of 1956 was providing funds for those portions of the County expressways which could be incorporated into the I-state system. Initiation by suburban leaders of this transfer of expressway responsibility to a County body may have contributed to the popular hostility which later developed in Milwaukee regarding expressway plans. City neighborhood fabrics were torn apart; and significant older structures, like the historic Pompeii Church in the Italian Third Ward, were razed just as public awareness of historic preservation and ethnic values was growing. Even the new home for the Layton Art School on the lakefront fell victim to expressway plans. As a consequence of a growing public outcry against ambitious downtown expressway construction, some freeway routes in the County were scrapped, while others, such as the

Lake, Stadium, and Park freeways, were severely cut back even after major land acquisitions had been made.

The County and the Metropolitan Area: Solutions?

Gravitation toward the County of functions which transcended municipal boundaries became a greater likelihood as a metropolitan solution with the success of the merger between 1934 and 1937 of the City of Milwaukee parks, as well as of many suburban parks, into the County Park Commission jurisdiction. This move recognized that the open space available for future parks, especially of the larger and more complex sort represented by Whitnall Park, would be found not in the thoroughly urbanized sections of the County, but in the seven towns. Wider ownership of automobiles also made such park locations more accessible, and the City of Milwaukee, at least, could not understand why suburban and town residents should not share the cost of its excellent but expensive parks, including its Zoo in Washington Park.

Also persuasive was the reputation of the County Park Commission members as responsible, farsighted stewards for one of the nation's most respected park operations. When influential private citizens determined in the late 1940s to seek a major league baseball franchise, they turned naturally to the County Park Commission to construct and manage the stadium which was expected to attract a big league team. Later, under Commission auspices, the Zoo was transferred from Washington Park and expanded on a major west side site, and the Mitchell Park horticultural domes were developed, both to constitute major tourist attractions for the metropolitan area. A possible defect in such County as opposed to City responsibility for parks emerged in the 1970s with complaints that inner city — largely minority — areas were being neglected in the siting and development of parks and in the 1980s the County Board decided to cut back on park expenditures as the park system was viewed as overbuilt and too costly for property taxpayers to bear.

The possibility of added County responsibility was often moderated before 1960 by the realization that the structure of Milwaukee's county government was not equal to the assumption of new tasks. While a series of strong County Board chairmen and some remarkable and durable County administrators — in Parks, Highways, Civil Service, County Institutions, for example — allowed an antiquated nineteenth-century political and administrative structure to survive, it did not face up to the lack of an executive, of modern budgeting, and of financial and administrative controls. With the initiative from the County Board — which had most to lose — and through the authority of the state constitution, including the power of veto, a popularly elected county executive was authorized for Milwaukee County. County Board Chairman John L. Doyne served for the first sixteen years, beginning in 1960, and his successor William F. O'Donnell for the next ten years, thus providing surprising continuity for the new office.

Although Doyne clashed with the County Board chairman and with those department heads who had hitherto no strong administrator or executive to answer to, his open, generally disarming manner permitted him to impose upon the new office his own preconceptions. His most important weapons were the executive budget process and the rationalization of government units and functions so that County government would have the coherence and efficiency needed for its growing tasks. The general intent was to impose upon a County government which was constantly being asked to do more the same principles of accountability that had long prevailed in the City of Milwaukee.

The County's continuing accretion of such functions as services to veterans and the aging, responsibility for emergency government, and environmental protection could thus be readily assimilated. Considerably more complex was the County's absorption of the private mass transit system. Originally the electrified streetcar system had been linked to the local electric power company as a unit of the North American Company of New York, fashioned by Henry Villard into the nation's first electric public utility holding company. The Milwaukee Electric Railway and Light Company, or TMER & L, as it was popularly known, became a major economic and political force in the City and County during the forty years following its incorporation in 1896. By federal mandate the traction and power segments were separated in 1938, and both were spun off by North American as operating companies in 1947. The traction unit, now more bus than streetcar, became a separate privately held company in 1952.

Twenty years later it became evident that, like private transport companies all over the nation, it could not survive and provide adequate service under private ownership and operation. The Socialists had forced a City referendum on municipal ownership of the Electric Company in 1936 and had lost. Now, without question, it was the County that negotiated the purchase in 1972 of the rolling stock and other land and facilities of the bus company and that continued operation of the mass transit system. To many observers this logically followed from the County's role in expressways and air travel.

Mayor Henry Maier of Milwaukee, like his predecessors for half a century before 1960, lamented the City's declining resources for handling its many state-mandated and its voluntary responsibilities. Among the latter was the Public Museum. Established in the early 1880s, it had shared a handsome neoclassical building and a growing national reputation as a natural history museum with the city's Public Library. In 1962 the Museum began its move into a long-promised and costly new building better adapted to current exhibit and collection practices. The Museum's regional and state role and its national reputation now contrasted even more sharply with its narrow financial base under City governance as annual operating costs mounted in its new home. The City instituted an admission charge for non-residents, leading the County to negotiate a contract fee in lieu of such charges for surburban residents. After prolonged and sometimes acrimonious discussions, the County agreed in 1976 to buy the land and building of the Museum for $10 million — on a ten-year installment plan — and thereafter fund and administer it. The County, to blunt the fiscal impact of assuming full financial responsibility for the Museum, now charged everyone for admission.

The transfer of responsibility for a cultural asset of regional or metropolitan scope from City to County had a precedent in the merging of the private Layton Art Gallery, established in 1887, into the neighboring City-supported Milwaukee Art Institute under the name Milwaukee Art Center (now Museum) and their removal to the new War Memorial Building on the lakefront in 1957. The War Memorial Building was a County facility, and the County thus provided housing and some supplemental operating funds for the new non-profit art institution. While logic might suggest similar treatment for the City-financed Milwaukee Public Library's collections and services, in fact the parallel did not exist. The spread of suburban libraries in the County, their increasingly professional staffs, their growing collections and services, their linkage by contract and fees to the Milwaukee Public Library, and the launching in 1972 of a Milwaukee County Federated Library System with state funding obviated the need for such a step. The Milwaukee Public Library's Central (downtown) Library remains a critical resource in library services for metropolitan Milwaukee; but the Museum is a unique cultural institution.

The County's role in fostering and supporting other local cultural institutions and activities without accepting full responsibility as in the transfer of the Public Museum is varied. Almost from its founding in 1935 the Milwaukee County Historical Society benefited from County assistance, especially in the provision of space in the Courthouse and the assignment of County work program personnel. This assistance was converted to a contract budget for the Society's operations beginning in 1963 and the lease of the newly acquired Second Ward Savings Bank building as a historical center in 1965. The contract concept of support for the Art Museum in the Saarinen War Memorial Building on the lakefront was extended later to the Performing Arts Center and its major tenants, the Milwaukee Symphony and the Milwaukee Repertory Theater. The Symphony receives annual operating funds as well, the precedent for which stems from County support of local orchestras since the 1930s through the WPA and Music Under the Stars in the parks. The County also owns but assigns administration to the Milwaukee Art Museum for the decorative arts museum in Villa Terrace and the Charles Allis Art Museum.

The ad hoc treatment of county, metropolitan, or regional needs matched the local toleration of political fragmentation and urban sprawl and often represented a popular distaste for serious attention to planning and to guiding growth and change. Yet there always was a realization that the pace and magnitude as well as the character of changes in the metropolitan Milwaukee area differed radically from earlier periods. For one thing, a decade of depression followed by half a decade of wartime had bottled up economic and demographic forces which had accumulated unusual force before they were released. Consumer spending in Milwaukee for automobiles and homes had its own predictable consequences, as has been noted. Not surprisingly, the revival of the American economy after World War II was, at least for a quarter century, highly beneficial to Milwaukee's heavy industry economy and its factory-production labor force.

Less forseeable was the marked change that began in mid-century in the community's ethnic makeup. The First World War and restrictive federal legislation beginning in 1921 had brought to a halt the major immigration flow from Europe which had made Milwaukee so European from the 1840s on. The declining influence of European ethnicity on social, cultural, and political activities by mid-century was now matched, however, by growing numbers of three new minorities. Milwaukee's Black population, almost all of it resident in the city from its origins in the 1830s, had reached only 21,772 in 1950 (that was up from 8,821 in 1940), but catapulted to 62,458, 105,088, 123,689, and 146,940 for the next four censuses. The city's Spanish-speaking population — mostly Mexicans and Puerto Ricans, some of the former having arrived in the 1920s — had been negligible in 1950; by 1980 it was 26,111, or 4.1 percent of the city total. And Native Americans numbered 5,018 in 1980, up from 3,300 in 1970. The County's total minority population was only 6,544 higher than the City's in 1980, and half of this suburban total was Spanish-speaking.

Mayor Zeidler had perceived a potential problem in the changing ethnic mix of the city and before leaving office in 1960 had received a report from his study committee on Social Problems in the Inner Core Area of the City. For the first time residents of metropolitan Milwaukee could begin to see the implications of a major ethnic shift on the community's schools, housing, law enforcement, welfare caseload, employment patterns, and public and private social service agencies. But the problems and potential problems were still deemed to be essentially the City's and not even the whole City's. This view was reinforced by rioting in the inner city's Black area in the summer of 1967.

Open housing demonstrations and school desegregation suits, however, soon showed that municipal boundaries did not insulate a suburb from the social and cultural problems of the central city. The adoption of a state open housing law, and later suburban and City of Milwaukee open housing ordinances, while more than symbolic gestures, did not automatically open up the suburbs, or even all sections of the city, to Blacks, or even to large numbers of the Spanish-speaking or Native Americans whose economic status, if not their color, limited the probability of a move to a suburb. Ultimately, of course, a combination of public and private efforts, including intervention by the federal and state governments, broke down some geographical barriers for Blacks, as well as for some Spanish-speaking and Native Americans, but no metropolitan mechanism was developed which substantially altered the long-standing identity of the new minorities with the central city.

Studies But No Solutions

More malleable aspects of metropolitanism — the possible transcendence of political fragmentation and the reduction or elimination of some of the adverse effects of population outflows — were now considered in terms of structural changes within the County and in the contiguous urban areas of Ozaukee and Waukesha Counties in particular. The larger urban or metropolitan problems existing or developing in the suburbs beyond the City of Milwaukee were far from unique — indeed, despite important differences in state law, the stage of community development, and local traditions, there was a recognizable "urban crisis" almost everywhere in the United States.

Through the 1950s and 1960s local officeholders were conscious of the actual or impending consequences to their constituencies of the extremely fast rate of social change and the inadequacies of their political tools for coping with new needs. They became aware of the growing number of academic and government social scientists who called themselves urbanists — in history, geography, economics, sociology, anthropology, and political science — and who proposed to contribute to solving "urban" problems. By the early 1960s both major campuses of the University of Wisconsin, in Madison and Milwaukee, were developing new interdisciplinary or interdepartmental teaching and research units to confront such new public needs.

In the long run, however, metropolitan Milwaukee, like much of the nation, paid little heed to these academic approaches. The explanation for this seeming indifference to experience elsewhere and to scholarly or scientific analysis is to be found, at least in Milwaukee, in three influences: the problem was of recent origin and those who had helped create it were still in power; the adverse effects were unevenly distributed and those most severely impacted, even if in a regional majority, had insufficient power to effect the desired changes; and there was no consensus on the real problems, let alone on the proposed solutions.

The increase in suburban at the expense of central city political power and the multiplication of basic local governments in Milwaukee had occurred over a long period of time. The earliest era of suburban emergence had been at the turn of the century, and for nearly a half century thereafter the City's annexation thrust was at least as effective as the countervailing suburban incorporations and annexations. Only in the last stage — the decade of the 1950s — did the incorporation of new suburbs and the expansion of others foreclose any future expansion of the City's boundaries. If, as the City had long argued, there was an "iron ring" of suburbs, it was not until this last phase that the ring was closed. Beyond the birth and growth of suburbs within Milwaukee County, the City had now to confront the reality of suburbanization on its northern and western boundaries with Ozaukee and Waukesha Counties. Barring consolidation with one or more of the fourteen suburbs — three outside the County — with which it shared boundaries, a prospect no one dared predict, Milwaukee would never again be able to expand. If the obvious problems and inefficiencies of the multiplication of basic local government units — not alone of the County's nineteen municipalities but of its many single purpose instrumentalities for such things as public schools, vocational schools, and sewers — were to be dealt with, imaginative, not simple or common solutions were needed.

Since early in the twentieth century the Milwaukee area had not lacked quasi-public institutions of citizens and specialists offering advice on structural reforms. The City Club, representing the traditional and respectable genteel reformer of the Progressive Era, had studied, investigated, and advocated civic betterment since 1909. The Social Democrats, upon assuming the reins of City government under Mayor Emil Seidel in 1910, brought John R. Commons of the University of Wisconsin's Economics Department from Madison to direct a Bureau of Economy and Efficiency study of Milwaukee's social and governmental needs, modeled on Paul U. Kellogg's Pittsburgh Survey. The defeat of the Social Democrats in 1912 killed off the Commons Bureau, but at the urging of the City Club a private counterpart was formed by local businessmen in 1913. As the Citizens' Governmental Research Bureau, it has survived many changes of leadership and emphasis during more than seventy years, but always with an eye to efficient and economical conduct of local government as the contemporary general public defined what it wanted government to do. As one recent observer viewed the Bureau, it has represented the business viewpoint in government as the businessman himself increasingly withdrew from active participation in politics — and as he joined the suburban citizenry.

From time to time other citizens groups with narrower purposes and shorter lives entered the field of governmental scrutiny. More lastingly, upon the adoption of woman's suffrage in 1920, a local League of Women Voters, thoroughly non-political or non-partisan, came into being with a special interest in local government structure. Both the Downtown Association and the Milwaukee Association of Commerce emphasized the promotion of business, but not very distant was their concern with the politics of business.

At the end of the Second World War the Committee of 48 was formed by local businessmen, many now suburbanites, as the pressure point for the physical rebuilding of the metropolitan area and especially of the public facilities which had been neglected during a decade and a half of depression and war. What had formerly been — since the 1880s — an informal private power structure meeting irregularly in the Milwaukee Club or the Wisconsin Club or the Milwaukee Athletic Club, now had a sharper focus and a continuing institutional base. As the present Greater Milwaukee Committee, consisting of a broader base of 200 civic leaders, it has had some substantial success in shaping political decisions on such public facilities as a new zoo, a county stadium, the expressways, a sports arena, and a war memorial. Similar business-oriented organizations focusing on downtown renewal have been the short-lived Milwaukee Development Group and the present Milwaukee Redevelopment Corporation.

The persisting and respected interest of the City Club and the Citizens' Bureau in local governmental affairs, personified by Leo Tiefenthaler and Norman Gill in mid-century, nevertheless fell short of creating a consensus for the sort of political restructuring which some Milwaukeeans felt was needed. Indeed, if political restructuring was needed, some observers perceived a basic weakness in the absence of overtly partisan politics in Milwaukee's municipal elections, a Progressive Era reform the more readily embraced by some Milwaukeeans because it blunted the electoral power of the Social Democrats — now Socialists — at the time of its introduction in 1914. Thereafter only the Socialists had a coherent municipal platform, while the Democrats and Republicans, labeled as non-partisans, agreed chiefly on their opposition to the Socialists. And when the local Socialist Party decline set in very quickly following Mayor Daniel W. Hoan's defeat in 1940, the City at last was left without the Socialist Party as its traditional catalyst for political policy-making.

The successive events of the 1950s which redrafted the political map of Milwaukee County, however, led some Milwaukeeans to try for a step toward a solution, if not the solution itself, by invoking the assistance of a higher power, the state government. The result was the establishment, with a legislative mandate and the support of two successive Republican governors, of a Milwaukee Metropolitan Study Commission (MSC) in mid-1957. With an initial life of four years, bipartisan support, a broadly constituted citizen membership appointed by the governor, and a professional staff, the commission embarked on a highly visible effort to identify those problems and needs which crossed local government boundaries and to consider alternative solutions and remedies.

Not surprisingly in a community rarely given to rash and precipitate action, the commission was exclusively empowered to study and not to act. Even as a study body it had ample antecedents. The most significant in recent memory existed in the mid-1930s. Known as the Joint Committee on Consolidation, it consisted of fifteen City-appointed members and a like number from the County, reporting jointly to the Common Council and the County Board and adopting its agenda from a joint resolution of the state legislature. The citizen members were broadly representative and benefited from considerable research assistance for their reports. But their effectiveness was destroyed by a sharp city-suburban division which emerged during a referendum on consolidation, which carried, and a fight in the legislature for consolidation, which failed. And it became evident that even the consolidationists were divided between the total and the piecemeal advocates.

For the next two decades all studies on consolidation were on single subjects. Representative of these was the state-mandated County School committee, by 1957 winding down its decade of work with little formal action to report, for suburbanization of the County had in effect already reorganized the outlying school districts. The most proximate precedents actually led directly to the MSC: first, the Committee of 21 appointed by the County Board in September 1954 with equal representation from the County Board, the Common Council, and suburban governments. Stimulated by the transfer of responsibility for expressways and air pollution to the County, the Committee of 21 survived for three years in futility and frustration, failing even to be able to hire consultants because, according to some observers, it was dominated by public officials.

More promising was a second effort, a seven-member committee appointed by Governor Walter J. Kohler at the behest of the Greater Milwaukee Committee and headed by Robert E. Dineen of Northwestern Mutual Life Insurance Company. Limited by the governor's instructions to a very short life and only two subjects — sewer and water — and by its elitist social and business makeup, it nevertheless recommended in its December 1956 report not only a general broadening of the roles of the City's water utility and the Metropolitan Sewerage Commission but also a review of the distribution of the state's tax resources with municipalities and a citizen's study commission on all metropolitan problems in Milwaukee.

The MSC came into existence very quickly with the new governor's appointment of fifteen commissioners, only three of them from government. During its life of four years the Commission had three chairmen and seven replacement commissioners, as well as three research directors. Its broad mission was to study the principal services of the municipalities in the County, to determine the cooperative arrangements which were possible for some of these services, to recommend which services ought to be primarily local and which County-wide, and to report to the governor and legislature its findings, conclusions, and recommendations.

In its final report to Governor Gaylord Nelson, a close friend of the then chairman, Provost J. Martin Klotsche of the University of Wisconsin-Milwaukee, and to the legislature, on June 19, 1961, the MSC summarized the work of its staff and its committees, much of it already well-known from its previous four reports and over forty special studies. Few readers were surprised or disappointed that the Commission ordered no major governmental reform. Its original mandate had been very limited, and it had neither sensed nor created a consensus favoring a massive structural overhaul, thus reversing the suburbanizing fragmentation of the postwar era. It endorsed instead the retention by local governments of police, fire, library, planning and refuse and garbage collection services, although it recommended additional intergovernmental cooperation to improve police functions, the establishment of a county plan department to cope with land use and zoning across political boundaries, and the transfer of property assessment, always a sticky matter, to the County to insure greater uniformity. Refuse and garbage disposal, as opposed to its collection, should be unified.

The Commission's timid proposals and the obvious absence of public or political support for extending the Commission's life perhaps underscored the body's findings as to the causes of the present difficulties: rapid population growth, accompanying increases in automobile ownership and use, fragmentation of local political power, growing interdependence of discrete political units, an emerging fiscal crisis for local government, and public apathy. No local or state legislative initiatives subsequently emerged to carry out the modest changes called for by the Commission. And the Commission's failure may account for the total absence in the ensuing twenty-five years of any significant movement to study or to reform the county or the metropolitan area on a broad basis. The most recent effort to create a popular consensus for the area's future, a grass-roots movement calling itself Goals for Milwaukee 2000, revealed once again the absence of support for major structural change and a preference for dealing with finite, near-term needs.

The post-MSC quarter century in metropolitan Milwaukee has been marked instead by low-keyed and gradualist change. The County government has improved its capacity to serve as a modern municipality and has accepted responsibility for such additional obligations as the city's Public Museum and the private mass transport system. Through such devices as the War Memorial Center, Inc., contract services, and grants, the County Board has carved out a major role for itself in cultural affairs. But the County has shown no long range plan to enlarge its sphere of operations. The City has emphasized its search for more outside fiscal resources and has found allies on occasion among larger suburbs in the County and in larger cities out-state, particularly with the argument that older and larger cities historically have provided a disproportionate segment of the general needs of American society and that many urban services are legislatively mandated. The City has also aggressively counterattacked the economic development strategies of the nearby suburbs, in and out of the County, with its promotion of the open space in the old Town of Granville and its nurture of a downtown renaissance which would recreate and restore its earlier economic, social, and cultural primacy and rebuild its tax resource base.

Special-purpose government units dealing with sewerage, vocational education, and coordinated library services have strengthened their roles, not without some public grumbling, while most basic municipal services — public schools, fire and police protection, property assessment, land use and zoning, and public works — have remained parochial. Modest elements of intergovernmental cooperation, as in civil defense and water supply, exist, but their traditional supporters, such remnants of the Progressive Era reform impulse as the Citizens' Governmental Research Bureau, are as inclined to promote economy and efficiency in all local governmental units as to advocate major structural change among them.

There is no evidence of overt popular dissatisfaction with government fragmentation in Milwaukee County, nor of popular support for suburban consolidation with each other or with the City of Milwaukee, totally or by function. An incipient property tax revolt in those suburbs experiencing periodic jumps in their assessments or tax rates leads conventionally to demands for state tax relief, especially for public schools, rather than calls for economies of scale through consolidation of services or government units. The major private voice for metropolitan welfare, the Greater Milwaukee Committee, seems to have eschewed a political reform agenda in favor of the advocacy of community-wide economic and cultural projects and a rescue of the City's downtown.

It is always possible, of course, that forces outside of the County will intervene to affect or change existing political boundaries or structures. The state government has already done so regarding expressways, sewage collection and disposal, property assessments, and vocational schools, as well as on municipal incorporation. The historical record gives little reason to believe that the state legislature would move strongly counter to suburban views; hence state intervention is not likely to consolidate or centralize. It is also possible that the federal courts would order intercity school consolidation to desegregate public schools, as they already have regarding intergovernmental construction of storm and waste water sewers, but not likely.

If there is one new non-political element which supplies coherence to the metropolitan area in which the City and County of Milwaukee are the leading players, it is the Southeastern Wisconsin Regional Planning Commission. The body, one of nine in the state, was formed in September 1960, in accordance with general legislative authority from 1955. Its twenty-one members are designated for six-year terms by the governor, the secretary of the Department of Development, and the county boards, three each from the seven participating counties — Milwaukee, Ozaukee, Washington, Racine, Kenosha, Waukesha, and Walworth. Funding comes from the state and the participating counties; Milwaukee's share has dropped since 1961 from over two-thirds to less than half the local contributions, reflecting its population losses and the hinterland's growth.

SEWRPC has no authority to act. Its mandate limits it to conducting research, its most critical role; to plan for the physical, social, and economic development of the region and to adopt any such plans as its official recommendation for regional development; and to advise local governments on regional problems and to coordinate local unit plans. Despite its ostensibly non-political character the Commission has generated local conflict over the naming of commissioners, assessments for local units, and some planning recommendations, especially at the start.

SEWRPC has survived and gained respect during its quarter century of operation through skillful use of committees and subcommittees with additional citizen participation, extensive public hearings, the determination of its first chairman George Berteau, and the low profile and quality work of its long-time executive director Kurt W. Bauer and his able staff. Special concerns of staff studies and commission recommendations have been parks and open space, air quality, housing, land use, traffic circulation, public transit and railroads, population projections, retailing, and topographic mapping.

No regional planning agency, even one extending to six adjacent counties, can offset some of the handicaps that Milwaukee County municipalities have built in during their century and a half of political evolution. The laws of the Territory and State of Wisconsin reflected through most of the nineteenth century the outlook of a frontier people on the move, thinking more in terms of farms and small towns, not industry and large cities. Trade and commerce, transportation, and communication were to be revolutionized later in the nineteenth century and even more so in the twentieth, but the implications of social, economic, cultural, and technological change could not be readily discerned nor translated into more appropriate laws and institutions.

The growth and development of the City of Milwaukee for its first half century, often closely paralleling the history of other American cities from which it freely borrowed, was a marvelous achievement of the Victorian Age. Its leaders and its citizens foresaw for a long time no limit to its continued expansion and improvement. But from the 1890s on, political actions prompted by people with economic, social, and cultural views somewhat different from those of the the the citizens of the City of Milwaukee fashioned additional and separate political units from the former agricultural lands of the old seven towns within Milwaukee County; and state law gave these and any additional such villages or cities which were formed later roughly equal status with Milwaukee despite their obvious and major dissimilarities.

Throughout more than a half century, until the late 1950s, the new suburbs and the old central city vied with each other in converting farm land and a weak, archaic government form, the town, into nineteen municipalities encompassing all of the County's 240 square miles. No one had willed into being such widely disparate neighboring entities as the City of Milwaukee and the Village of West Milwaukee. Incremental steps, each seeming logical at the time, had produced what no one would have planned. Perhaps because these many political divisions of Milwaukee County were historical and evolutionary rather than planned, they work far better than contemporaries who are obsessed with intergovernmental conflict believe. It may also be that the intense urban-suburban rivalries of the 1950s, already three decades old, have receded so far into the past that appropriate accommodations have actually been made. What is reasonably clear is that there is at this writing no consensus for formal change. Change will undoubtedly come, as it has in the past, but we cannot now clearly predict what form it will take.

Bibliographical Essay

Most of the general references on Milwaukee County and its governmental units are applicable to this chapter.

Suburban histories have predominantly been prepared by devoted citizens for anniversary celebrations (or the nation's bicentennial in 1976) or as an adjunct to a guide to municipal services. They express the local loyalty which strengthens suburban separatism and display an affection for nearby people, places, and events so characteristic of local histories. Typical is *West Milwaukee Diamond Anniversary 1906-1981* (1981). The Federal Writers Project of Wisconsin produced *Shorewood* (1939) in the American Guide Series. Three suburban communities were covered by the Wisconsin Historical Records Survey: *Inventory of the City Archives of Wisconsin, Third Class, City of Wauwatosa, Inventory of the City Archives of Wisconsin, Third Class, Cudahy*, and *Inventory of the Local Government Archives of Wisconsin, Village Series, Greendale* (all 1942), each preceded by a short history.

Bay View has two complementary studies: Bernhard C. Korn, *The Story of Bay View* (1980), and John Gurda, *Bay View, Wis.* (1979). Ronald Wildermuth, "Greendale's Federal Years, 1938-1952" (M.A. thesis, University of Wisconsin-Milwaukee, 1968) represents scholarly interest in a New Deal experiment. Robert F. Morrow, *Carrollville in Retrospect* (c. 1981), illustrating the nature of communities which never incorporated, is based on interviews. The Milwaukee Department of City Development's promotional *Discover Milwaukee Catalog* (1986) tries to define the boundaries for the city's neighborhoods and characterizes the northwest corner of the former Town of Granville as a suburb in the city.

Insights into rural life in mid-nineteenth-century Milwaukee County may be found in Louis F. Frank, Margaret Wolff, and Harry H. Anderson, editors and translator, *German-American Pioneers in Wisconsin and Michigan: The Frank-Kerler Letters 1849-1864* (1971); Roger D. Simon, *The City Building Process: Housing and Services in New Milwaukee Neighborhoods 1880-1910* (1978); and Clay McShane, *Technology and Reform: Street Railways and the Growth of Milwaukee, 1887-1900* (1974) illuminate the city's spatial expansion, as does John R. Ottensman, *The Changing Spatial Structures of American Cities* (1975), using Milwaukee as a case study for technical analysis. Two business histories, Walter F. Peterson, *An Industrial Heritage: Allis-Chalmers Corporation* (1978), and Harold F. Williamson and Kenneth H. Myers II, *Designed for Digging: The First Seventy-five Years of Bucyrus-Erie Company* (1955), reveal a great deal about their relationship to two classical industrial suburbs, West Allis and South Milwaukee, while Msgr. Peter Leo Johnson's *Halcyon*

Days: Story of St. Francis Seminary Milwaukee 1856-1956 (1956) and *Stuffed Saddlebags: The Life of Martin Kundig, Priest 1805-1879* (1942) explain the religious origins of St. Francis and St. Martins.

"A Backward Glance — Historic Evolution of the Local Government Structure in Southeastern Wisconsin," by Eileen Hammer, appearing in the Southeastern Wisconsin Regional Planning Commission's *Technical Record* for March 1981, February 1982, and February 1984, together with Waukesha County Needs and Services Study, II, *Understanding Waukesha County, The Informal Survey Report* (1975), places Milwaukee County's suburbanization in the context of southeastern Wisconsin, while Jon C. Teaford, *City and Suburb: The Political Fragmentation of Metropolitan America, 1850-1970* (1979) provides a national perspective. Charles Davis Goff, in a 1952 doctoral dissertation in political science at Northwestern University, "The Politics of Governmental Integration in Metropolitan Milwaukee," provides a historical treatment from an integrationist viewpoint.

The reports of the Metropolitan Study Commission, 1957-61, are basic to the effort to move, however gradually, away from fragmentation. The best of them, by Charles E. Beveridge, *History of the Water Supply in the Milwaukee Area* (1958), reveals the role played by water supply in Milwaukee's annexation drives and in suburban frustration. David D. Gladfelter's short essay on "Water for Wauwatosa," in Richard T. Frost, editor, *Cases in State and Local Government* (1961), illuminates one important episode. A scholarly study of *The Milwaukee Metropolitan Study Commission* (1965) by Henry J. Schmandt and William H. Standing suggests why the Commission came to naught. The first effort at a major restructuring of local schools appears in *Your Schools: A Plan by the Milwaukee County School Committee for Reorganizing School Districts* (1950); it was overrun by the suburbanization splurge of the 1950s and the rapidly changing ethnic mix in Milwaukee, first described publicly in the Mayor's Study Committee on Social Problems in the Inner Core Area of the City, *Final Report to the Honorable Frank P. Zeidler, Mayor, City of Milwaukee* (1960). An early effort to see Milwaukee as "a case history of civil rights revolution" is Frank Aukofer's *City With A Chance* (1968). If Milwaukee's school desegregation case against the suburban school districts goes to trial in federal court, the trial record is likely to produce enormous documentation on the role of race in Milwaukee County and the metropolitan area.

A long and judicious essay on *Milwaukee: A Contemporary Urban Profile* (1971), by Henry J. Schmandt, John C. Goldbach, and Donald B. Vogel, while now seriously outdated, is the composite views of three political scientists with strong Milwaukee ties.

88   Olson

Bibliography

Aukofer, Frank A. *City With A Chance*. Milwaukee: Bruce Publishing Co., 1968.

Beveridge, Charles E. *History of the Water Supply in the Milwaukee Area*. Milwaukee: Metropolitan Study Commission, 1958.

Department of City Development. *Discover Milwaukee Catalog*. Milwaukee: Department of City Development, 1986.

Frank, Louis F., Margaret Wolff, and Harry H. Anderson, eds. *German-American Pioneers in Wisconsin and Michigan: The Frank-Kerler Letters 1849-1864*. Milwaukee: Milwaukee County Historical Society, 1971.

Gladfelter, David D. "Water for Wauwatosa," in *Cases in State and Local Government*, Richard T. Frost, ed. Englewood Cliffs, N.J.: Prentice-Hall, 1961.

Goff, Charles Davis. "The Politics of Governmental Integration in Metropolitan Milwaukee." Ph.D. dissertation, Northwestern University, 1952.

Gurda, John. *Bay View, Wis*. Milwaukee: Milwaukee Humanities Program, 1979.

Hammer, Eileen. "A Backward Glance — Historic Evolution of the Local Governmental Structure in Southeastern Wisconsin," (4:2-4) *Technical Record*. Milwaukee: Southeastern Wisconsin Regional Planning Commission, March 1981, February 1982, and February 1984.

Johnson, Peter Leo. *Halcyon Days: Story of St. Francis Seminary Milwaukee 1856-1956*. Milwaukee: Bruce Publishing Co., 1956.

——————. *Stuffed Saddlebags: The Life of Martin Kundig, Priest 1805-1879*. Milwaukee: Bruce Publishing Co., 1942.

Korn, Bernhard C. *The Story of Bay View*. Milwaukee: Milwaukee County Historical Society, 1980.

Mayor's Study Committee on Social Problems in the Inner Core Area of the City. *Final Report to the Honorable Frank P. Zeidler, Mayor, City of Milwaukee*. Milwaukee, 1960.

Morrow, Robert F. *Carrollville in Retrospect*. Oak Creek, WI.: Oak Creek Senior High Print Club, 1981.

McShane, Clay. *Technology and Reform: Street Railways and the Growth of Milwaukee, 1887-1900*. Madison: State Historical Society of Wisconsin, 1974.

Ottensmann, John R. *The Changing Spatial Structures of American Cities*. Lexington, Mass.: Lexington Books, 1975.

Peterson, Walter F. *An Industrial Heritage: Allis-Chalmers Corporation*. Milwaukee: Milwaukee County Historical Society, 1978.

Schmandt, Henry J., and William H. Standing. *The Milwaukee Metro-politan Study Commission.* Bloomington: Indiana University Press, 1965.

Schmandt, Henry J., John C. Goldbach, and Donald B. Vogel. *Milwaukee: A Contemporary Urban Profile.* New York: Praeger Publishers, 1971.

Shorewood. Federal Writers Project. Shorewood, WI.: Shorewood Village Board, 1939.

Simon, Roger D. *The City Building Process: Housing and Services in New Milwaukee Neighborhoods 1880-1910.* Philadelphia: American Philosophical Society, 1978.

Teaford, Jon C. *City and Suburb: The Political Fragmentation of Metropolitan America, 1850-1970.* Baltimore: Johns Hopkins University Press, 1979.

Understanding Waukesha County, The Informal Survey Report. Waukesha County Needs and Services Study, II. Waukesha, WI: United Community Services, 1975.

West Milwaukee Diamond Anniversary 1906-1981. West Milwaukee: Village of West Milwaukee, 1981.

Wildermuth, Ronald. "Greendale's Federal Years, 1938-1952." M.A. thesis, University of Wisconsin-Milwaukee, 1968.

Williamson, Harold F., and Kenneth H. Myers II. *Designed for Digging: The First Seventy-five Years of Bucyrus-Erie Company.* Evanston: Northwestern University Press, 1955.

Wisconsin Historical Records Survey. *Inventory of the City Archives of Wisconsin, Third Class, City of Wauwatosa and City of Cudahy; and Inventory of the Local Government Archives of Wisconsin, Village Series, Greendale.* Madison, 1942.

Your Schools: A Plan by the Milwaukee County School Committee for Reorganizing School Districts. Milwaukee: Milwaukee County School Committee, 1950.

The first Milwaukee County Courthouse, erected in 1836. Subsequent County office additions (right) were built in 1843 and 1846; all were razed in 1870.

Supervisors, Administrators, and the Executive: The Governing of Milwaukee County

by Donald B. Vogel _____

Introduction

For the purposes of the essay that follows the term *governance* refers to the operational activities involved in establishing public policy in those areas assigned to or permitted Milwaukee County by the state constitution and laws. Additionally, there is the legislative responsibility of oversight regarding the execution of public policy. *Administration* encompasses those support functions that either contribute to overall control and coordination or provide specialized support services for Milwaukee County's various legislative and executory functions.[1]

To answer the question of who controls how governmental decisions are made, attention must be directed to critical points of influence. Essentially, these influence points deal with who controls the acquisition and allocation of fiscal and personnel resources as well as information concerning these activities and operational concerns; i.e., information that permits the determination of how consistent operational activities are with legislative intent. Nothing significant can be decided or accomplished without these necessary resources. The individuals and units controlling these critical points of influence become key determiners of what the County does and how it achieves operational objectives. Basic change normally occurs as the result of a shift in control over the points of influence. Such change is reflective of both internal gains and losses as well as the ascendancy or decline of political forces outside the County governmental structure. Tracing these shifts in control over the critical points of influence provides a contextual framework for specific occurrences. This perspective seeks to provide greater understanding of the relative impact individual events have had on the way Milwaukee County government conducts its affairs.

An examination of governance and administration within Milwaukee County entails the discussion of changes in the points of critical influence. Most major change is not precipitous but rather the result of an accumulation of many developmental adjustments. Nevertheless, in the course of Milwaukee County's history there have been a number of milestones that permit the identification of distinct periods. While differing perspectives may give rise to disagreement regarding emphasis, it is hoped the most critical alterations within the governance and administration areas are given their due. Specifically, five trend periods are examined. Initially attention is directed to the start-up period from 1835 to the turn of the century. The second major development is the reform era from the 1900s to the 1920s, when a pervasive dissatisfaction with graft and corruption led to significant changes within governance and administration. Following this period of reform is one of governmental expansion and bureaucratic growth covering the years from the 1920s to the 1950s, which is in turn capped by a decade of administrative modernization and improvement from the 1950s to the 1960s. The last major trend, from the 1960s to the present, deals with the establishment of the County Executive and the effect of this office on preexisting relationships. In all cases primary attention is directed to changes in the critical points of influence and their impact on governance and administration.

Major Trends in Governance and Administration

Milwaukee County government is often misperceived as playing an exclusively supplemental role to other jurisdictional bases — cities, towns, and villages on the one hand and the state on the other. In terms of political bonding, the city, town, or village in which one lives or the state becomes the focal point. Rarely does anyone think of being from the County. Everyone is aware of the County's existence, but it simply does not engender the kind of loyalties and affiliations associated with the other bases. To many, Milwaukee County government is what's left over. The reality of state dominance over County affairs also contributes to its peripheral status. All local governments in Wisconsin, from special districts to cities, are creations of the state. Legislative home-rule, however, allows most other local entities to institute policy options regarding scope of services without recourse to the state for authorization to do so; this is not the case of Wisconsin county government.

From the outset, county government was established to facilitate the execution of territorial and then state policy. Specific state legislative action is required whenever additional county functions are deemed necessary or desirable. In essence, the county serves as an administrative agent for the state.[2] Without question it is not feasible to carry out state law from one administrative center; geography, if nothing else, makes it inconvenient. Its agency role notwithstanding, Milwaukee County increasingly occupies a central position on the local scene as a result of needs it is best suited to fill. Understandably, the County's split role of state agency and local government contributes to current ambiguities that surround the public's perception of its status. Such was not the case during the early years of Milwaukee County's operation when state-mandated activities dominated.

Getting Started. — In a sense the history of Milwaukee County begins in ninth-century England. The American county is a direct outgrowth of the English shire. ". . . [T]he affairs of each shire were managed by a semiannual court, composed of the representatives of each township and the individual landowners. . . ."[3] Administration of justice was the shire's primary activity, and to this end shire officials were established, including the earl, shire-reeve (sheriff), and bishop. Subsequently, administration of what was now called a county became dominated by the sheriff who served as the chief representative of the King. Not unexpectedly, the English settlers brought this well-established form of government with them to colonial America, where it enjoyed wide usage. The post-Revolutionary period witnessed continued popularity of the county, with the major change being a shift to local selection of officials.[4] Clearly, the creation of Milwaukee County follows a long heritage.

This heritage is apparent when noting the first officials designated for the County. The territorial governor of Michigan (Milwaukee County began its existence as an entity of the Michigan territory) appointed a chief judge and two associates, a county clerk, sheriff, and a judge of probate. In terms of compliance with the law, the administration of justice, and the keeping of vital records order was the concern. By substituting the territorial government for the King, the basic shire structure and functions are embodied in the 1835 Legislative Council actions creating Milwaukee County. This pattern was further reinforced with the establishment of the County Board three years later under the auspices of the newly created Wisconsin territorial government.

When Milwaukee County began operation, the specific form of county government generally followed one of the two distinctive variations. Support for one or the other usually depended on the county system an individual had lived under prior to his moving to the new territory, for much the same reason his forefathers had brought the county form of government to America in the first instance. The variation known as the Supervisor or "New York" form emphasized the town and other incorporated areas as the basic subdivision in the county, with local functions of government being carried out at this level. Under this approach the County Board was a confederation of these various local units with appropriate services coming from individual units rather than the county. The alternative approach, known variously as the "Southern" or "Pennsylvania" plan, concentrated the provision of local services at the county level and was overseen by a Board of Commissioners that represented the county as a whole.[5]

STEVENS T. MASON,

Secretary, and at present Acting Governor in and over the Territory of Michigan.

To all to whom these Presents may come, Greeting:

Know Ye, That, reposing special trust and confidence in the integrity and ability of Albert Fowler, I have nominated, and by and with the advice and consent of the Legislative Council of the said Territory have appointed him County Clerk in for the County of Milwaukee

AND DO HEREBY AUTHORIZE AND EMPOWER him to execute and fulfil the duties of that office according to law: **To have and to hold** *the said Office, with all the rights, privileges, and emoluments thereunto belonging, during the end of the next Session of the* **LEGISLATIVE COUNCIL** *of the said* **TERRITORY,** *unless the* **GOVERNOR** *of the said* **TERRITORY,** *for the time being, should think proper sooner to revoke and determine this* **COMMISSION.**

In Testimony Whereof, I have caused these **Letters** *to be made* **Patent,** *and the* **Great Seal** *of the said* **Territory** *to be hereunto affixed.*

Given under my Hand, at **Detroit,** *this twenty fifth day of August in the year of our Lord one thousand eight hundred and thirty five and of the* **Independence** *of the* **United States** *of America the Sixtieth*

BY THE GOVERNOR:

Stevens T. Mason,

Secretary of Michigan Territory, and at present Acting Governor.

The Acting Governor of the Michigan Territory appointed Albert Fowler the first County Clerk on August 17, 1835. The Wisconsin Territory was not established until 1836.

The choice of the Wisconsin Territorial legislature was the commissioner form, but almost from the start residents of the County agitated to replace it with the alternative plan and did so six years later. The Board of Commissioners was abolished and replaced with a Board of Supervisors.

The 1841 enabling legislation provided for the election of town super-visors, with the chairmen of the various town boards becoming members of the County Board as well. When the city of Milwaukee was incorporated in 1846, each town and each city ward was given County Board represen-tation.[6] By statehood in 1848 the basic format for the governance of Milwaukee County was established.

Because of the sparse population throughout the territory, much of the early legislation was anticipatory and the various specific governmental arrangements were left as generally applicable as possible. The issue of scale is important. It is difficult, given today's population densities, to visualize a much larger Milwaukee from a land area standpoint con-taining fewer than 3,000 persons. Demands on County government were miniscule, and then most activity centered around the administration of justice and hardly required intervention by the County Board, save for budgetary authorizations. Growth, however, was rapid and soon out-stripped other areas in the state. This led to increased pressure to alter the very casual and incidental role of the Board to one of increased activity. It also created a need to organize more effectively to deal with the increased pressure for governmental services at the County level. The initial re-sponse to the expanded activity was the designation of standing com-mittees in 1841. These initial subdivisions of the Board were committees on Assessment Rolls and Equalization, Claims and Accounts, Clerk, Courts, Printing, Condition of Public Buildings, Roads and Bridges, Trea-sury and Taxes, and Miscellaneous Matters and Expenses.[7]

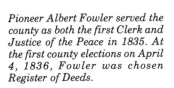

Pioneer Albert Fowler served the county as both the first Clerk and Justice of the Peace in 1835. At the first county elections on April 4, 1836, Fowler was chosen Register of Deeds.

Between the Clerk and the Board all appointments, records, and budgetary allocations were handled on an individual basis. Individual accounts were the responsibility of the various standing committees and then referred back to the whole board for pro forma approval. The internal audit responsibility was assigned to the Clerk. It was not until 1864 that legislation provided for the election of a county board chairman. The chairman's tenure was for the term in which he and the rest of the Board were elected. Once officially designated, the position of chair became the focal point for board leadership, particularly with regard to the assignment of standing committee membership.[8]

In addition to the committee structure just described, the County Board during this period utilized special committees to deal with every other specific matter that could not be clearly assigned to one of its standing committees. The necessity for such special arrangements reflects the fact that everything was run through the Board with the exception of the constitutional functions such as the courts, sheriff, district attorney, et cetera; even in these cases all budgetary supports required Board approval. An examination of the special committee designations between the years 1838 and 1879 reveals over 200 such entities. Their range of focus is truly comprehensive with nothing too small being beyond their scope. A typical array included special committees on County Paupers, County Records, Dispute of Supervisor, Examine Town Laws, Poor Laws, Pauper Accounts, Procure Lot, Reducing Tax Certificate Fees, Select Jurors, Unredeemed Lands, all for the year 1843.[9] By definition, such committees were single purpose and usually did not extend beyond the year they were created. The most extreme example of this pattern of work allocation on the Board was a special committee created in 1871. In that year a "Special Committee on Crazy Kate's Property" was designated to ". . .ascertain what property, if any, belongs to a person known as 'Crazy Kate' now confined in the Insane Department of the Poor House."[10]

This level of minutiae illustrates the small scale of operation present during this start-up period and helps to indicate the eventual need to deal with County affairs in a different manner. The early years of governance and administration in Milwaukee County were characterized by the highest degree of concentration and lack of differentiation for governance and administration it would ever again have, for understandable reasons of scale. The business of the County that the Board was designated to address simply was not sufficiently complicated or extensive to warrant anything else, at least during the first twenty years of its existence. Thereafter, a growing number of activities and increased complexity in those that already were underway exposed the weakness of this Board-centered method of operation.

It should be noted that the Board recognized this problem and, start-

ing in the late 1850s, began to respond to the difficulties resulting therefrom by instituting appointed commissions to deal with specific administrative and oversight functions. Following state legislative authorization, the first example of this approach was the forming of a
Commission for the House of Refuge in 1858. This was the first time a
non-Board group was given the task of setting up a County function.
Subject to Board approval, the Commissioners were assigned the role of
procuring a site, plans, and specifications for the erection of the House of
Correction.[11] The Board also recognized the need to retain administrators
for extended periods of time, for without such tenure the running of the
various enterprises then being set up would be difficult. Consequently,
Superintendents of the Poor House, Alms House, and Inspector of the
House of Correction were elected by the Board for fixed terms.[12]

Even when keeping the scale of growth in mind, the expansion of
needs unique to Milwaukee County became increasingly evident. To
impress the state legislature with the County's expanding needs, the
County Board instituted a Lobbying Committee in 1876. The Board resolution dealing with this concern established ". . . that the Chairman of this
Board together with the District Attorney be and are hereby appointed as a
Committee to go to Madison and wait on the Milwaukee Delegation to the
effect of securing the passage of the Laws recommended by the Board."[13]
The first formal recognition of Milwaukee County's unique status due to
its size and complexity came in legislation of 1885.[14] Because the Wisconsin Constitution specifically prohibited special treatment by the requirements of the "Uniformity Clause," the state legislature employed the
device of creating a separate category based on population.[15] The fact that
Milwaukee County was the only one in the state with a population of
100,000 or more allowed special treatment without violating the uniformity requirement. Although the category is now designated at 500,000,
the initial effort for special status has remained to the present day.

Another characteristic in the governance and administration areas
present during this time period was the lack of any extended tenure on the
Board of Supervisors. Only towards the end of the century did any member
of the County Board serve for more than six years and only one Supervisor
at that.[16] Since the Board served as the locus of administrative policy as
well as legislative activity, the absence of continuity resulted in an environment where little ongoing oversight could be applied. Lack of experience on the part of the Supervisors helped obscure any problems and also
contributed to the general directionless character of the various administrative enterprises the County was beginning to institute. Lastly, developments in American jurisprudence during the 1800s further established the status of the county within the governmental context. The
landmark pronouncement took place in an 1857 Ohio case, and it clearly

makes the distinctions that set the county apart from other municipal enterprises.

Counties are local subdivisions of a state, created by the sovereign will, without the particular solicitation, consent, or concurrent action of the people who inhabit them. . . .

A municipal corporation proper is created mainly for the interest, advantage, and convenience of the locality and its people; a county organization is created almost exclusively with a view to the policy of the state at large, for purposes of political organization and civil administration. . . .[17]

Until very recent times in Wisconsin, as well as elsewhere in the United States, the point of view enunciated in the above judicial decision has remained an accepted principle of law. Only with the establishment of the County Executive and the increasingly local nature of Milwaukee County's activities has this principle been challenged. For the start-up period no such doubts were entertained, and the general assumption of agency for the State continued into the other periods that followed directly thereafter.

Enough Is Enough. — By the end of the nineteenth century Milwaukee County government, though still extremely small, had instituted a number of activities that provided the foundation for future functional expansion. Although the state still controlled governance issues, it had shown a willingness to support the special needs of the County. As noted earlier, the most serious impediment to expansion was the lack of organizational continuity. Because all personnel were hired on the basis of personal preference of the appointing authority, their tenure usually lasted only to the next election. As a result, high turnover in elected positions within the County government led to constant breaks in administrative activity. While the scope of functions remained narrow and small scale, this was usually overcome; but it precluded any substantial expansion.

Additional factors also presented barriers to future effectiveness. Using political loyalty instead of adminstrative competence as the critical factor in making personnel selections further hindered effective management of County operations. Also of concern was the absence of meaningful fiscal control. Even though there was recognition for the need of a financial audit function, assigning this duty to the County Clerk ensured that it would be at best a peripheral undertaking, given the wide range of other responsibilities assigned to that office.

Construction of the west wing of the second courthouse began while the first building was occupied. Completed in 1870, the structure faced south and dominated the Courthouse Square. St. John's Cathedral is on the right.

Unfortunately, because earlier expansion in County functions was so gradual, it had not produced sufficient motivation to make change imperative. While growth was discernible and increased difficulties evident, there was no strong impetus to do things in a significantly different manner. At the same time there was strong support for keeping existing arrangements because of influence that had accrued to the Board in terms of political and monetary favors. Given the climate of the day, certain practices had evolved that placed those who controlled the critical points of influence in a position to gain personally. Until something occurred that made such arrangements unacceptable, it was evident that the required changes would not take place. Unbeknownst to the Board and its minions, however, the necessary agent for change was at hand.

Motivation for change in the way the governance and administration functions were carried out in Milwaukee County came as the result of the most widespread government scandals ever experienced at the local level in Wisconsin. For a generation that has experienced other transgressions in other governmental settings such an occurrence hardly seems noteworthy, regardless of its dimensions. At the time, however, the effect was nothing short of catastrophic for the established order of doing things. To get some sense of the Milwaukee political climate that prevailed in the early 1900s, a broader perspective is useful.

The previously mentioned issue of scale was equally applicable to the state and national levels as well. When compared to the breadth and scope of present governmental activity, the pre-twentieth century public enterprise was a comparatively simple affair. Critical influence points were, in general, legislatively controlled, and most administrative positions were either popularly elected or patronage appointed. This is reflective of the Jacksonian-based Spoils System. Essentially, such a system assumes that since most government work could be accomplished by a reasonably intelligent person without special skills, it is always better to have individuals whose political perspective is consistent with the dominant political elements as reflected by the electoral process. Patronage or direct election ensured the highest degree of political responsiveness from this point of view. In practice, however, such responsiveness often proved illusory. Not only did it encourage special favors and lead to graft and corruption, but it also failed to produce the technical skills and length of tenure required of an increasingly complicated array of governmental activities. While patronage appointments were feasible during its earlier stages, by the end of the nineteenth century problems stemming from the Spoils System were threatening to render the machinery of government to a great degree ineffectual.

Boodling, or the giving and receiving of political bribery, was the rule. An examination of the accepted order of things during this time period reveals political bribery either as an accepted cost of doing business in the public sector or as a "fringe benefit" of public employment or office. Although certainly not legal, it had become such a common practice that not to do it was noteworthy. Milwaukee was by no means immune from the general practices just described. At the turn of the century the local environment was characterized by a high degree of permissiveness regarding vice, gambling, and political corruption. In light of today's image of the Milwaukee scene it is often hard to visualize such a "loose" condition; nevertheless, the situation at that time had reached a point where the opportunity for reform was ripe. For those who sought to change the corrupt order of things, both the County and City presented ample opportunity.

The first efforts for reform initially met with failure in Milwaukee because the Grand Jury system under which such reform would have to take place was flawed. At that time jurors were selected by the local legislative bodies. Since there would be interest in protecting the prevailing system, not unexpectedly, individuals named to Grand Juries were usually sympathetic to maintaining the status quo. Before indictments would be forthcoming, the law governing Grand Jury selection would have to be changed. The required change was instituted in 1903, thus removing the major roadblock to legal action by preventing any political influence over the selection of jurors.[18] The opportunity was now present for a major drive to correct the widespread conditions previously described.

The specific instance of wrongdoing that opened the floodgates of change concerned the County's House of Correction, permitting the District Attorney's office the latitude to examine all areas of County and City operations to uncover wrongdoing. Of immediate concern here was the range of corruption the initial House of Correction investigation revealed regarding Milwaukee County governance and administration.

A chair factory was established at the House of Correction in 1878 to provide work for the inmates and produce revenue for the County.[19] It appears that the major beneficiaries, however, were neither the prisoners nor the taxpayers but the Inspector and his associates. Following extensive investigation, it was revealed that arrangements had been made between the Inspector and the supplier of lumber to defraud the County by overcharging and retaining the excess amounts thus produced. Additionally, the Inspector received payoffs for special treatment extended the company that had exclusive rights to sell the finished chairs the prisoners produced. When this was coupled with gross mismanagement of the accounts and the general operation of the House of Correction, the opportunity to bring action that would lead to conviction was extremely favorable.[20] A closer examination of the specifics involved here reveals just how favorable the House of Correction's scandal would prove in developing the kind of public indignation that would eventually lead to a general housecleaning.

Undoubtedly, no public organization whose operation comes under extraordinary scrutiny could escape criticism of at least some aspects of its stewardship. Even when criminal activity is not present, there will always be some segment of the community at large which feels things should have been done differently. In the case of Inspector Fred Heiden, Jr., the level of criminality was both extensive and blatant. Because a law in 1897 put the House of Correction in a unique position, Heiden was permitted a length of tenure that allowed him to develop a wide range of illegal practices.[21] Until that year the Inspector had been elected by the Board in the same manner as the other superintendents. Following the passage of the 1897 legislation, a Civil Service Commission was established whose purpose was to oversee the staffing of the House of Correction. As the incumbent, Heiden was appointed, following Board approval of the Commission action, to continue as Inspector; which he did for an additional six years until his resignation, under fire, in 1903.[22]

Many of the Inspector's activities were brought to light as the result of investigative reporting by the *Milwaukee Journal,* which began with the discovery of accounting discrepancies in the House of Correction's account. In an attempt to forestall further questioning the County Board appointed a special committee to examine the books, and this body quickly determined that the errors had resulted from a faulty accounting system rather than any misappropriation. The *Journal* continued to investigate, however, and was successful in uncovering many more instances of discrepancies between actual purchase prices for materials and listed figures, prompting the District Attorney's office, as well as the Board, to scrutinize the financial practices of the House of Correction.[23] As part of the general inept state of bookkeeping the *Journal* also revealed that Inspector Heiden's regular accounting staff member did not control the House's ledger system. Instead he had assigned two prisoners to keep the books. Ironically, one of these inmates had been convicted of embezzlement, a circumstance which certainly qualified him for the job at hand.[24]

Once the District Attorney's Office became involved, the investigation into criminal activity by the Inspector intensified. Under the leadership of future governor Francis E. McGovern, it was further disclosed that Heiden had failed to solicit bids for the contracts to sell the chairs manufactured at the House of Correction's factory. Instead, he negotiated an agreement with the Western Chair Company of Chicago that was patently to the disadvantage of the County. Heiden also received payoffs from Western for unauthorized extensions of payments to the County for chairs sold by the House of Correction to the company. It was later established that the Inspector had illegally paid in excess of $3,000 to A.D. Martin, former salesman for the House of Correction, for commissions on chairs never paid for.[25]

With the extended publicity given the House of Correction scandal and additional complaints regarding illegal practices by the County Board and City Council members, a Grand Jury was called for the December court term in 1903. This was the first Grand Jury to operate under the new law and promised to produce true bills where previous attempts had failed because of the old appointing procedure. The first indictments forthcoming were against Fred Heiden for embezzlement, but the Grand Jury was just beginning. Although its term expired in February of the following year, a total of sixty-nine true bills of indictment against twenty-four men were reported.[26] By the end of September 1905 and two additional Grand Juries later a total of 276 indictments against eighty-three public officials were returned.[27] It would be difficult to exaggerate the impact this had on how Milwaukee County government conducted its affairs. The cumulative effect of these numbers was devastating, and the specific nature of the illegal activities accentuated the shortcomings of a governance and administration system that had proved itself incapable of honest or effective operation.

Once the early indictments were prosecuted, additional illegal activities became known in the course of the Grand Jury proceedings, and this produced the need for the subsequent Grand Juries. Of particular note were the acts of members and former members of the County Board of Supervisors as well as other County officials such as the County Clerk and Register of Deeds. Generally, the impropriety involved the taking of bribes for favorable treatment in regard to contract letting and the appointment to positions in County government. Early examples from the

Fred Heiden, Jr., embattled Inspector of the House of Correction, resigned in 1903 after investigations revealed wrongdoings under his administration.

third Grand Jury (1904) are instructive. It was disclosed that Otis T. Hare, former County Clerk, had conspired with a printer to rig the bidding for the County printing contract by ensuring that the only other parties to bid for this contract were fictitious and then awarding an exorbitant contract price.[28]

Former Supervisor William J. Sutton was indicted for accepting a bribe to use his influence as chairman of the County Committee on Almshouse and Waterworks to obtain the appointment of a Mr. Hilger as steward and bookkeeper at the Almshouse. Supervisor A. C. Bade was charged with accepting a supply of coal for his home in return for using his influence as chairman of the Committee on Sheriff's and Coroner's Accounts to award the jail coal contract.[29] Even though the dollar amounts were never large, the extent of such practices was impressive. Virtually no construction project, supplies purchase, or repair contract was immune from boodling. The fourth Grand Jury involved more of the same, with indictments against former or current Supervisors for accepting bribes involving remodeling the Milwaukee County Hospital, roofing and heating contracts, and architectural planning contracts. Three indictments were reported for a general County Board conspiracy involving the sale of land to the Milwaukee Electric Railway and Lighting Company. Taken together, these Grand Juries produced thirty-eight indictments against twenty-one men, most of whom were or had been County Board Supervisors.[30]

The situation became so desperate for the County Board during this period that an effort was made to thwart the work of the Grand Jury by establishing a special investigating committee within the Board. The value of such a move was to protect Board members from having to testify before the Grand Jury, thus escaping prosecution. This attempt was unsuccessful because District Attorney McGovern obtained a court order blocking the Board's action and charging the Board with an attempt to undermine the Grand Jury system. With the court order in hand, McGovern was able to secure quick agreement by the County Board committee not to undertake its own investigation.[31]

Revelations about criminal activity occurring within Milwaukee County government paralleled similar disclosures for the City, thereby discrediting both the Republicans, who dominated County affairs, and the Democrats, who controlled the City. The political environment was ideal for a clean sweep, and the presence of the Social-Democratic party provided Milwaukee with real alternatives. Additionally, a number of civic improvement organizations were established during this period and helped to focus reform efforts. The most noteworthy instance of public protest against governmental graft and corruption had come early and served to provide the District Attorney's Office with the kind of strong public support that would reinforce its efforts. On September 29, 1903 three thousand people gathered at West Side Turn Hall and demanded the removal of criminals from public office.[32] In addition to the strong leadership of the clergy, such organizations as the Milwaukee Voters' League and the Municipal League of Milwaukee continued to keep the need for reform at the top of the local political agenda.

A significant factor in sustaining reform in Milwaukee was the success of the Socialists. Beginning in 1908 the party was able to enjoy significant electoral success by being characterized as the agent of reform both in the County and City. Although the major part of the Socialists' effort went into correcting practices within the City of Milwaukee, they also sought to extend major reforms to the County as well. From the beginning the party realized that success depended on the support of other groups who might not endorse socialistic principles but could support the Social-Democrats for other reasons, such as local reform. As a result, great pains were taken by the local Socialists, led by Victor Berger, to separate their efforts from those of the national party. By concentrating on the correction of local corruption and the introduction of modern and efficient managerial practices, Berger and his followers were able to enlist a broad spectrum of support and create the clear association between the Social-Democratic party and municipal reform.[33]

The election of 1910 demonstrated just how successful these tactics were. Not only did the party win the mayoralty, the three top administrative positions, and twenty-one out of twenty-five on the Common Council, but their success was equally impressive at the County level. All of the Milwaukee County constitutional offices were swept by the Socialists as well as ten out of sixteen on the Board. Two-thirds of the County's state legislative delegation and one of the Representative's seats to the U.S. Congress were also won by the party. This sweeping victory permitted a wide range of changes and a means to demonstrate that the Socialists meant what they said. An examination of the Party's campaign literature of 1912 reveals in copious detail specific governmental improvements instituted in County and City government.[34]

The success of the Socialists also facilitated the transfer to County government of administrative reforms implemented first in the larger City operation. This pattern would continue until as late as the 1950s, long after the party's influence had waned. Further, the injection of a third political party that was perceived as providing a real alternative gave a strong impetus for sustaining governmental reform in a way not usually found in other metropolitan areas in the United States. Although governmental misdeeds did not end, the Milwaukee environment became so changed as to convince later generations that honest and effective government was a feature that had always characterized this area. New

The Milwaukee County Board of Supervisors of 1911 in the board room of the second courthouse. Standing at left is Chairman James Sheehan.

reform groups such as the City Club and the Milwaukee Citizens' Bureau of Municipal Efficiency (later to become the current Citizens' Governmental Research Bureau) were created to counter the Social-Democratic center of reform. Nonpartisan elections also reflected the desire to blunt the influence of the Socialist party on local affairs. Both efforts indicate the substantial success the Socialists had in changing very unsatisfactory governmental operations in Milwaukee.

Direct outgrowths of the reform movement were two crucial changes in administrative practice that would have profound effect on governance and administration. These changes dealt with the central issues of fiscal management and personnel practices. Although the state had specifically required an internal audit function as early as 1849, it never had assigned this function to a separate office but had instead added it to the other functions of the County Clerk. In 1915 the legislature mandated the establishment of a County Auditor for Milwaukee.[35] Originally placed under the direction of the Clerk, the Auditor was charged with keeping the accounts of all the administrative operations within the County. This included not only the audit function but accounting and budgeting activities as well.

Since very little was previously done in these areas, the opportunity to develop a sweeping system of fiscal control was present; and the initial efforts sought to introduce appropriate cost accounting and modernize the bookkeeping practices. More importantly, the creation of the County Auditor began the process of concentrating fiscal information and the development of an independent control point that had the potential of substantially altering influence relationships within County government. In 1915, however, all this was only potential rather than actual. Nevertheless, the significance of this fiscal reform should not be understated. It provided for a meaningful oversight capability and assured the modernization of the County's fiscal affairs. As problems with the House of Correction had demonstrated, the need for an independent source of fiscal information was critical if the County Board was to be in a position to make sound decisions regarding the administration of its policies.

Equally important were developments that occurred two years later when the state legislature passed a comprehensive civil service law for Milwaukee County.[36] Prior to this action the only legislation regarding civil service was "lipservice" legislation that had been in response to efforts on the part of reformers for change.[37] The 1897 state law that established a Civil Service Commission in Milwaukee County was specifically restricted to the House of Correction (of all places).[38] Given the previous account of practices in the House of Correction, it is clear that the desired effect by the reformers did not take place. Not until after the scandals that followed this modest reform was a comprehensive personnel system instituted within the County.

Chief architect for the 1917 legislation was a state senator from the ninth district in Milwaukee, David V. Jennings; his interest in civil service was a great deal more than legislative. While an attorney, he did not have any special expertise in the personnel field, but that was to be rectified in the years to come. The crucial provisions in the state law established a Civil Service Commission under whose direction a Chief Examiner was to administer a personnel system based on merit and the application of appropriate job classification and compensation practices. In 1918, when the County Board appointed this Commission, which included some holdovers from the earlier House of Correction's body, its first act was to appoint David Jennings to the Chief Examiner position.[39]

Article IV, Section 12 of the Wisconsin Constitution provides that

"No member of the legislature shall, during the term for which he was elected, be appointed or elected to any civil office in the state, which shall have been created . . . during the term for which he was elected." This constitutional provision would appear to disqualify Mr. Jennings, and concern within the County was serious enough to request an advisory opinion from the District Attorney. While admitting that the question of the legality of his appointment was not "free from doubt," the opinion concluded that no constitutional violation had occurred. This determination was based on the faulty reasoning that the position of Chief Examiner was so minor that it was not intended to be included in the prohibition. The opinion stated in part:

> Upon examination of the law under which Mr. Jennings was appointed, it is found that all his work and duties are done under the direction and control of the Civil Service Commission; that he is not required to give any bond, nor take any oath of office, and that he is appointed by the Commission for such terms as it may desire. It would seem that the "Chief Examiner" merely becomes and is an assistant to the Commission in carrying out the objects and purposes of the law.[40]

Anyone with an understanding of how a civil service system works would know that the key position was Chief Examiner and not that of Commissioner. Given their lack of independent knowledge and the part-time nature of their role, the Commissioners were, from the start, little more than "rubber stamps" for the Chief Examiner. In the fifty years following, little took place to change this basic relationship. For the next thirty-two years Mr. Jennings would be without question the most influential person within County government when it came to personnel matters.

By October 1917 Jennings had established an office and drawn up the first standardized scale of wages and salaries of all positions over which the Board had control. This represented the beginning of a merit system for County personnel. It removed the direct involvement of the Board and established an operation that provided Milwaukee County with the capacity to effectively recruit, examine, and certify qualified employees. Just as importantly, it removed patronage as the primary criteria for appointment and protected individuals from dismissal for political reasons. The new merit system instituted by Civil Service did not initially bring about any radical change in the quality of employee because most incumbents were retained; but this would soon be altered as employees came in under the new arrangement and holdovers retired.

Once again it is essential to note the small scale involved here. In a 1915 publication, the Civil Service Committee of the City Club noted that

The 1922 Civil Service Commission. Chief Examiner David Jennings (lower center) while State Senator had initiated legislation creating the commission in 1917. He was subsequently appointed the first chief and held that key position for thirty-two years.

out of a total of 600 employees only forty were under civil service. The latter referred to the House of Correction personnel, who could hardly be viewed as superior to the remaining 560 patronage appointments. This committee's strongest argument was the tenure issue, pointing out the short length of service ensured administrative inefficiency.[41] With the small numbers involved, it did provide the County with the opportunity to do a proper job at the outset in establishing the basic tenets of an acceptable merit system without the pressure of having to deal with an overwhelming number of positions and classification levels.

Another important development during this second trend period was the establishment of Boards and Commissions with administrative powers. Characteristic of the reform era that swept the country was the conviction that the administration of governmental policy needed to be insulated from the negative aspects of political activity. Once policy was determined, the theory claimed, then it was essential there be no political interference in the administrative process. After all, the purpose of establishing a merit system was to acquire and retain those individuals who possessed the highest technical knowledge in how best to administer specific governmental functions. The strong conviction that there was a technical "best" way to accomplish such functions meant that politics simply must be prevented from meddling. Boards and commissions provided the buffer that was deemed essential if such political interference was to be prevented.

Also, the recurring concern for continuity could be alleviated by staggering terms and making the terms longer on these bodies. Reformers in Wisconsin were early and enthusiastic advocates for the concepts that supported Boards and Commissions. By 1910 most functional areas at the state and local level either had the enabling legislation in place or had created these insulating structures. At the local level, the establishment of police and fire commissions throughout the state signaled a strong desire to depoliticize these security functions. Within Milwaukee County a similar manifestation was evident. Preceding the establishment of the Civil Service Commission was the institution of Boards and Commissions dealing with parks and the various health and welfare enterprises carried out by the County. Such structures predated the scandals which provided a strong impetus for their proliferation. For example, Boards of Visitors for the House of Correction existed in the 1870s. They proved problematical. The County Board's *Proceedings* indicates that in 1879 the Board of Visitors of the House of Correction was ordered by the Supervisors to comply with the law that required them to file an annual report. It appears that the Visitors had failed to fulfill their obligations over a period of years and were now being ordered to ". . . proceed to said House of Correction and inspect the same and file their written report. . . ."[42]

The unfolding scandals in County government during the first decade of the twentieth century provided strong impetus for the formation of non-County Board entities to oversee the administration of both the Institutions and Parks. Supervision of the Hospital, Poor Farm, Alms House, and Water Works shifted from direct supervision of the Board of Supervisors to an appointed citizens board in 1905. The Asylum for the Chronic Insane came under a non-Board committee, and the Milwaukee Hospital for the Insane was to be governed henceforth by a seven-member board appointed by the Governor.[43] Generally, these oversight units had the power to ". . . let contracts; make purchases; audit all accounts; appoint the [various] . . . superintendents; appoint the county physicians who visited the indigent sick in their homes, and fix salaries for all employees in the above named institutions."[44] Following the enactment of state legislation, the County was allowed to form a Park Commission, which it did in 1907. Although its scope of responsibility differed, given the functional area it dealt with, this Commission also served to remove the Board of Supervisors from direct involvement.[45] In all cases, however, the County Board still had final oversight responsibility, primarily through control over the budget.

Governance and administration underwent substantial changes during this period. While the County operations were minor in scale, the inefficiencies that came from having the Supervisors handle all administrative and policy concerns were marginally tolerable. Ongoing County growth harbingered government expansion. The scandals accentuated the unsatisfactory nature of existing administration and hastened change. Although the potential to become involved in most aspects of County activity still remained, the Board of Supervisors was now removed from the direct role it had played during the County's early history.

The critical area of fiscal control still resided in part with the Board because of its budget power, but now other actors moved center stage. Originally all lists of accounts were maintained by the County Clerk acting in his capacity as agent to the County Board of Supervisors. Standing committees were assigned the primary role of auditing the accounts of the functional units within their purview. Following such audit functions the Board, as a whole, passed individual resolutions "to allow and list [sic] of accounts audited by standing committees." As a rule, such legislative action was strictly pro forma and amounted to placing chief fiscal control within each of the standing committees. With the creation of the County Auditor, however, the focal point of fiscal influence shifted. All financial information was now funneled through this position, not through the standing committees.

A similar shift in the control over personnel acquisition and allocation took place. Prior to the establishment of the comprehensive merit system the County Board either directly elected administrators or would act on the recommendations made by the various superintendents. Political appointment was the rule rather than the exception, and most patronage attached to the Board. After 1918 control over this critical point of influence was for the most part removed from the direct sphere of the Supervisors and allocated ostensibly to the Civil Service Commission. In reality, the administrative role of Chief Examiner became the focal point in this area.

The Era of the Administrator. — The period from the 1920s to the mid-1950s represents an unprecedented period of stability in the County. Although the range and scope of operational activities were greatly expanding during this time, the third period in the County's historical development was marked by a high degree of continuity of service for the top-ranking administrators charged with executing public policy. Further, the congruency between these officials and the County Board as well as the general public was at its highest level. The general assumptions were ones of confidence and trust and the belief that the County's business was being run in the most efficient and effective manner. This was in sharp contrast to the preceding era where overall dissatisfaction with County operations was the order of the day.

In large measure, the general assumptions of confidence and trust were due to the good fortune of having recruited a large number of highly qualified and dedicated administrators. In addition to the merit system that established a career service within the County, the economic conditions created a favorable situation where talented personnel were attracted to public service. It was also a time where a strong conviction

The County Board of Supervisors 1922. William E. McCarty (center) contributed to the stability of the board during his long tenure as chairman from 1914 until his death in 1932.

prevailed that technical expertise when applied appropriately and protected from political interference would produce governmental services at the highest possible level. Instead of reform groups pushing for wholesale changes and being highly critical of public service as had previously been the case, these groups served to bolster the legitimacy of administrative activity.

Stability also was increased within the Board of Supervisors due in part to the extension of the term of office from two to four years. Although this had occurred at the end of the preceding period, its effect was not felt until the twenties. The role of the Board Chair became dominant mainly by control over committee assignments. The crisis caused by the Depression also served to increase the visibility of the County Board, which had been completely overshadowed by the activities of the legislative bodies of the cities, towns, and villages.

Another noteworthy characteristic of County government during this time period was the dispersal of influence. Administration and governance no longer were centered in the Board. Instead, individual Supervisors interacting with key administrators and citizen members of appointed boards and commissions became the focal points of influence. While the County Board of Supervisors remained in "control" of the allocation of resources through the budget process, its ability to effect wholesale changes in the patterns of governmental activity through this process was severely limited. Since there was no centralized administrative point of accountability through the office of a chief executive, the various operational administrators working in concert with individual Supervisors were generally able to dictate the overall direction of their functional areas.

A similar pattern regarding the administrative functions of personnel and fiscal control also developed. As the result of control over much of the information that drove the decision-making processes in these areas, the positions of Chief Examiner and Auditor became key points of influence within the administrative area of County government. Long periods of tenure for the incumbents, David Jennings in personnel and Frank Bittner in fiscal, guaranteed their being at the center of the decision-making process in their respective areas. As their length of service increased, these individuals became critical "gatekeepers" through whom one went for the necessary resources to accomplish operational objectives. Although neither position ever possessed authority to direct the functional activities, the high degree of deference given these men by the top administrators ensured that a measure of informal influence would accrue to them.

Part of the support services included in County administration is the provision of legal support. This involves not only representing the County on legal matters but also drafting resolutions and ordinances as well as rendering opinions on matters relevant to County operation. An example of the latter activity is the previously mentioned question of David Jennings' appointment as Chief Examiner. All such service was the charge of the District Attorney's office; and while this would continue as such for this era as well, in 1927 a specific position in this office was created to fulfill the above duties exclusively.[46] The position of Corporation Counsel also was responsible for representing the County in Madison. As the position developed, it too followed the pattern of long tenure (it was included in the civil service system), and yet another area of administrative influence became a point of critical influence for the incumbent.

In all cases the key administrators developed a strong sensitivity to understanding the political realities that the environment of County government presented. To the extent that the concerns of key citizen members of the critical administrative boards and commissions as well as key Supervisors were responded to, then the substantial administrative policy decisions were usually left to the administrators' direction. The more complicated and technically intricate operations became, the more most legislators and commission members were likely to defer to the expertise of the department heads and key staff officials. In the absence of any evidence of wrongdoing, the inclination as well as ability to question administrative decisions was not usually present during the era of the administrator.

Lest the reader be misled, however, these days of administrative well-being were not without some noteworthy regressions to earlier troubles. Not surprisingly, the House of Correction again became the center of controversy. When last discussed, its Inspector had resigned in disgrace and the criminal activity disclosed had helped ignite an overwhelming protest against governmental improprieties. At the time of Fred Heiden's departure from the House of Correction in 1903 the County Board of Supervisors approved the action of the Milwaukee County Civil Service Board in appointing William H. Momsen the new Inspector. The pattern of long-tenured administrative officials got its start with the Momsen appointment; by the time he came under the 1918 merit system he had already served fifteen years.

It was not until 1934, however, that the House of Correction's management was seriously questioned and that it once more was the object of notoriety. The stewardship of Momsen, now a veteran of over thirty years' service, sparked the single most noteworthy instance of Board wrangling that took place during the third period of County development. Most significant was the marked contrast regarding the results when compared to the House of Correction's problems during the Heiden tenure. In part, this difference was due to the general trust in the administration of County affairs by the public that was totally absent during the period following the widespread local scandals. The other major distinction between the two situations was the high level of astuteness displayed by Momsen in establishing strong political support on the Board.[47]

Potentially, the issues raised in 1934 were most damaging. Prohibition had resulted in the incarceration of a number of House of Correction inmates for bootlegging. The resources available to these individuals allowed them to "improve" their situation through special treatment and visitations. Although there was never sufficient proof generated to implicate Momsen, there was ample evidence to remove some of his subordinates for inappropriate conduct regarding the provision of special privileges to influential prisoners. The *Milwaukee Journal* was vociferous in its denunciation of practices at the House of Correction, charging that illicit sex, drug trafficking, and unauthorized absences had taken place.[48]

Things came to a head when the *Journal* discovered that one of the staff at the House of Correction had maintained a diary documenting many of the newspaper's allegations. Additionally, other employees and prisoners had indicated to *Journal* reporters that they were prepared to testify that illegal activities had occurred on a large scale at the House of Correction. Crucial to proving these charges was the suspension or removal of William Momsen and his key staff to allow an impartial investigation to take place. The prisoners, in particular, had indicated that without such action they would not risk the reprisals they felt Momsen was certain to take against them.[49]

As a result of the pressure from the *Milwaukee Journal* and other concerned groups, the County Board Chairman, Eugene Warnimont, asked the Board to launch an official investigation; and subsequently the Institutions Committee held public hearings to establish whether the facts warranted filing charges against the House of Correction's staff with the Civil Service Commission.[50] Based on these hearings, the Commission recommended the suspension of seventeen House of Correction employees, including Inspector Momsen.[51] This led to a motion before the Board to approve the action of the Civil Service Commission on March 29, 1934. Based on eyewitness and newspaper accounts, the Board meeting that day was highly charged and emotional, for it clearly established publicly the strong antagonisms that existed within that body.

Essentially, two factions existed, one strongly supporting Momsen and opposing his suspension, the other equally committed to his removal. In large measure the Supervisors supporting Momsen were a most improbable association. Leading this group was Chairman Warnimont, who was joined by Willard P. Lyons, the Supervisor member of the Institutions Board and an acknowledged friend of Momsen, as was Warnimont. The remainder of the pro-Momsen faction was composed of the nine Socialist

members of the County Board. Although the party had previously abandoned any meaningful effort designed to promote its role in County
government, the Socialist representation on the Board had increased from
six to nine following the 1932 election due mainly to the economic conditions caused by the Depression.[52] Despite the non-partisan ballot, the
Social-Democrats ran as a bloc and usually voted in concert. In addition to
the friendship that Momsen had developed with them as a group, their
defense of him was motivated less by ideology than a desire to frustrate the
other faction on the Board headed by Lawrence Timmerman.[53]

To bolster its case, the *Journal* revealed that Momsen, Warnimont,
Lyons, Highway Commissioner William Cavanaugh (another long ten-
ured and respected administrator), and citizens Frank Klode (a local
furniture businessman who held contracts for the entire output of the
House of Correction's furniture products) and Julius Heil (then serving as
Chairman of the local National Recovery Act Compliance Board) were all
stockholders in the Water Edge Realty Company. The realty company's
sole undertaking was the ownership of what the *Milwaukee Journal*
identified as an ". . . exclusive summer resort near Eagle River, Wisconsin,
frequented by Milwaukee businessmen and politicians."[54] No attempt was
ever made by any of the aforementioned parties to deny their association;
on the contrary, all asserted the complete propriety of such an
undertaking.

It is testimony of the public's acceptance of this association that little
support for the *Journal's* outrage was generated. At the Board meeting
where the Momsen matter was voted on, a large and vocal audience led by
Klode and Heil strongly protested the action on the part of the Civil
Service Commission in suspending the Inspector. Their major argument
was that the Commission's action had been taken without permitting
Momsen to clear his name. A further telling point highlighting the essential difference between 1934 and 1903 was reported at the meeting by
Momsen's attorney. The House of Correction had been examined in February 1933 by Federal Inspector for the Bureau of Prisons J. H. Strief, and
a glowing report had resulted. Most noteworthy were the marks received
in the areas of administration and personnel where scores of 95 out of a
possible 100 were awarded. In short, it was much easier to overlook the
Journal's accusations in light of the fact that Momsen had been officially
recognized as running an efficient and effective operation.[55]

After heated exchanges between Supervisor Timmerman and Momsen supporters, the Board voted eleven to nine against the motion to
approve the Civil Service Commission's suspensions.[56] The Board's failure
to sustain the suspension caused the Commission to rescind its original
action and launch an investigation instead. Although some minor irregu-
larities were revealed, it became clear that the major transgressions would

The third and present courthouse on Ninth Street, completed in 1931, became the west side anchor for the civic center development along Kilbourn Avenue to City Hall, on the east side of the Milwaukee River. This 1943 view shows the safety building on the right.

Chairman Lawrence J. Timmerman presided at a 1937 County Board of Supervisors session; he served from 1936 until his death in 1959. The WPA art project mural, painted by Francis Scott Bradford, Jr. in the 1930s, depicts the growth and development of Milwaukee.

not be addressed as long as Momsen remained in charge of the House of Correction. A further setback came when a challenge to the Commission's authority over Momsen was sustained, the court ruling that since the Board appointed the Inspector, only it could suspend him. With the continued support of the eleven Supervisors on the Board, Momsen was easily able to prevail and continued to serve without further incident until his retirement in 1938.[57]

While the House of Correction imbroglio did not extend much beyond the middle of 1934, the relationships between administrators and Supervisors that it hinted at continued to prevail. Although joint partnerships and other business arrangments were not common, the general environment of close and cordial relationships was the rule rather than the exception. When this is added to the insulating effect the boards and commissions provided administrative officials, the unassailability of most operational activities was quite clear.

Within the administrative realm another action serves to indicate the support afforded appointed administrators. The Chief Examiner, as previously indicated, continued to accrue influence as the size and complexity of County operations increased; by the mid-1930s employment had reached approximately 4,500. Recognition of the real influence residing in the "support" role of Chief Examiner was evidenced by proposed state legislative action to institute greater control over this position. In 1935 Milwaukee Democratic Assemblyman George A. Weissleder introduced a bill that would eliminate the position of Chief Examiner (a merit system position) and replace it with the position of Secretary to the Commission, which would be exempt from Civil Service. In addition, Weissleder proposed that the Civil Service Commission be reduced from five to four members to include one member from each of the dominant political parties, such members to be certified by the party chairmen.[58] While most critics correctly argued that this legislation would politicize the personnel system, the fact that it also would have acted to establish the kind of control over the key administrative position totally absent under existing arrangements was generally overlooked. The bill created such vociferous opposition that no further attempts to alter the merit system were made during this period.

Although this thirty-year period witnessed the County's greatest employee growth, from less than 1,000 to over 5,000, the stability that was its most noteworthy characteristic permitted such growth to take place without any significant dysfunction. This was primarily due to attracting and retaining competent and trustworthy administrators as well as a strong supporting cast of highly qualified and committed County employees. Again, the economic conditions, coupled with the status public employment then engendered, ensured that the County's merit system would produce a personnel resource that was a strong asset. Turnover remained low during this period, and most employees sought to make a career within the County system. With a constantly expanding base of operations, the opportunities for advancements were most favorable, and this too contributed to creating the kind of organizational environment where productivity and morale could be sustained.

In the 1940 Legionnaires parade in Boston, a County Supervisors' sign extended an advance welcome for the 1941 convention that would be held in Milwaukee. The County, along with the city and state, appropriated money to win this major gathering to the city.

The stability that characterized the administration of County operations was extended to the administrative boards and commissions charged with overseeing these activities. Patterns of long tenure ensured that established relationships would support the control exercised by the appointed heads of the functional units within the County. Since relationships with the Board of Supervisors as a unified body were never at issue, the requirement for Board stability was of small concern. Nevertheless, the County Board of Supervisors, at least with regard to its Chairmen, maintained a similar pattern of continuity. In 1914 William McCarty became County Board Chairman and remained in this role until his death in December of 1932, when Eugene Warnimont took over to fill his unexpired term. At the next election in 1936 Lawrence J. Timmerman became Chairman and remained in the position until his death in 1959. In effect, for this third era of development, only two individuals occupied the Board's official leadership position.

Without considering the individual merits of McCarty or Timmerman such long tenure is not surprising, given the general stability within Milwaukee County government. Since the County Board no longer directly controlled the critical points of influence, concern over who controlled that body was muted. Individual Supervisors, because of their relationship to specific administrators or their specific Board responsibilities, became substantially more influential than the Board as a collective entity.

Administrative Improvement. — This fourth period from the early 1950s to 1960, though comparatively brief, is nevertheless significant in the historical development of Milwaukee County governance and administration. Most importantly, it serves as a staging period that provided the necessary impetus for the wholesale changes that were to come with the establishment of the County Executive. In a real sense those changes were made possible by the developments occurring in the decade of the fifties. In the same way that earlier reforms had permitted the extensive growth of County operations and employment, the fifties initiated another period of expansion that saw a doubling of the County's labor force by 1970 and a substantial expansion in County activities.

The earlier degree of congruity between administrative leadership and the general public noticeably waned in the fifties. The unqualified belief in technical expertise was beginning to be questioned, and many of the key individuals who had made the system work were nearing retirement or had ended their County service. While scandal would no longer serve as the impetus for change, a general belief that the governance and administrative functions of the County were basically flawed provided ample rationale for questioning the established order of doing things that had prevailed for such a long period of time.

Consistent with the governmental reform movements throughout the country, the Milwaukee experience had included the establishment and sustained influence of organized civic groups. Initially created to address widespread graft and corruption at the end of the nineteenth century, civic bodies had continued to provide an independent source of ideas about and critical examination of governmental operations within Milwaukee County. Most influential of such organizations were the City Club and the Citizens' Governmental Research Bureau (CGRB). Not uncharacteristically, the directors of these associations, Leo Tiefenthaler of the City Club and CGRB's Norman Gill, established strong reputations as resident "gadflies," and the long careers of both men enhanced their influence. While these individuals in their unceasing efforts to improve governmental activities never stopped making local officials uncomfortable, they were able to command a high degree of grudging respect for the usefulness of what they advocated.[59]

An early effort to institute changes in the way County government ran its operations was made by the City Club's Committee on County Affairs in May of 1939. The major thrust of its recommendations, echoed in subsequent efforts, finally culminated in the 1956 Public Administration Service Study, the most influential undertaking in this regard. Essentially the City Club argued that too many positions in County government were elective when the roles required administrative expertise and the need for a unifying and coordinative executive function. The report suggested the establishment of a county manager rather than an elected chief executive.[60]

Milwaukee County government had emerged during the preceding period of expansion as a disjointed confederation of operational departments, each functioning independently. The absence of a coherent body of interrelated activities became the major concern of all subsequent reform efforts. Since the civic groups need not concern themselves with political impediments, they advocated the institution of what they felt was the "ideal" construct rather than what would be feasible within the local environment. Consequently, the advocacy of a professionally trained and certified manager became the unquestioned position of such associations.

Additionally, attention was drawn to the absence of an effective fiscal control agency within the County. The ability to generate financial information independent of departmental influence was for the most part missing. Although the establishment of the Auditor's position and subsequent augmentation of this office had enhanced the Board's ability to exert control, it was severely limited by the scope of information generated as well as the consistent focus on the minutiae of items-of-expenditure. Clearly, the need for budget reform was overdue, and just as obviously a more comprehensive administrative function in this area would have to be established. To this end, most reform efforts sought to establish a staff capability that would be designed to provide not only budget development and monitoring services but would also serve an internal administrative oversight role. This latter function would focus on suggesting improved methods in the manner in which administrative departments accomplished their objectives.

Efforts to secure this staff capability culminated in the 1952 County Board resolution calling for the establishment of a budget and efficiency research unit.[61] Two more years were required to create enough pressure for additional action that reflected the increasing demands for governmental reform. The Finance Committee, to whom the 1952 resolution had been referred, determined that the creation of such a unit ought to be preceded by an administrative study of County operations to help the Board ascertain how best to utilize such a unit. To this end, a resolution was passed, calling for the preparation of specifications and the securing of proposals to make this study.[62]

There was strong local precedent for the kind of study proposed by the Finance Committee and advocated by the reform groups. In 1949 the City of Milwaukee had engaged the private consulting firm of Griffenhagen and Associates to evaluate administrative organization, policies, and procedures and make recommendations for improved coordination and simplification within Milwaukee's governmental operation. One of the major outgrowths of this study was the institution of a Department of Management and Budget within the city. This too provided substantial support for the advocates of a counterpart unit within County government. With Tiefenthaler and Gill as members, a special subcommittee was created by the Board to draft specifications for hiring a consultant for the County's administrative survey. Not surprisingly, the contract that resulted was in many instances a direct restatement of the City's agreement with Griffenhagen.[63]

Public Administration Service (PAS), a consulting firm of national stature, was awarded the study contract in January of 1955, and its final report was submitted to the County Board of Supervisors one year later.[64] Supplementing this document was a series of interim reports on specific functional areas within County government. These served to stimulate community interest, as the press coverage was extensive for each of the interim sets of findings and recommendations. With over three hundred specific recommendations as well as comprehensive proposals contained in close to one thousand pages, the prospect of effectively dealing with the PAS analysis proved daunting for the Finance Committee. Although the study was completed in January, it was decided to delay consideration and hold public hearings after the County Board elections in April.[65]

Following the elections, a Special Committee on Public Administration Service Reports was created, and it was still engaged in its deliberations in 1962.[66] As was the case with the City, action was taken by the Board in April of 1957 to create a Management and Budget Analysis Unit.[67] This new department was placed under the direction of the Finance Committee of the County Board and charged with carrying out three major functional assignments. First was the requirement to provide analysis and recommend changes regarding the administrative practices of the various operational units within the purview of the County Board. Secondly, the department was charged with augmenting the budget preparation and monitoring activities carried out by the various operating units and the Auditor's office. The third area of responsibility charged Management and

Budget Analysis with providing staff assistance to the operating departments in conducting studies and surveys as well as assisting in the
installation of new procedures and methods. This last area of responsibility also stipulated that budget and management analyses required by
Board Committees were to be included as a regular part of its assigned
duties.[68]

Of all the recommendations acted on by the Board pursuant to the
Public Administration Service study none had more long-term impact on
affecting control over critical points of influence than the establishment of
Management and Budget Analysis. Potentially, the new department had
authorization to generate information about virtually any aspect of any
operating unit. It represented the first substantial source of independent
information and analysis since the establishment of the Auditor's office.
Unlike the Auditor's role, which was primarily one of compilation and
reconciliation, Management and Budget Analysis would be seeking to
determine the appropriateness of administrative practices and budgetary
choices that had previously been exclusively the domain of department
heads and the boards and commissions that ostensibly guided them. The
first years of its operation would fulfill or surpass expectations. Without
the control base established by this department, shifts in governance that
subsequently occurred would have been, at the very least, delayed.

While most critical, the creation of Management and Budget Analysis
(which had been proposed prior to the study and strongly endorsed therein)
was only one of many recommendations acted on. Of particular interest
here were several changes instituted within the administration area. In an
attempt to consolidate purchasing activities previously conducted on a
decentralized basis the Board instituted the Department of Purchasing in
1958. Another action to increase control over crucial fiscal information
was taken this same year, when all accounting functions were placed in
the Auditor's office. To further increase the effectivenes of this shift,
electronic data-processing equipment was acquired to facilitate this activity. The next year elimination of the time-consuming and ineffective
practice of individually approving voucher payments by the Board was
effected; instead, this activity was delegated to the Auditor for monitoring.
In 1960 the Board also stopped taking bids and issuing orders for routine
purchases of supplies and commodities and shifted this function to the
Purchasing department.

There was literally no significant change in operations subsequently
made that could not find support in the Public Administration Service
study. It provided that most comprehensive compendium of analysis ever
undertaken for County government. The impact of the study was enhanced
because of its timing, coming as it did at a point in the County's development when the need was acute for substantial alterations in the manner in

which governmental operations were conducted. The study provided an independent and respected impetus for the kind of changes that otherwise would have been considerably more difficult to implement. Most noteworthy was the creation of an executive function independent of the Board and the operational departments. Clearly, the conditions for instituting this latest major shift in County government were immeasurably assisted by the study, and it would be difficult to understate its impact on the developments that occurred during the last developmental period discussed in this essay.

Who's In Charge? — The final period of historical development regarding governance and administration begins with the establishment of the County Executive in 1960 and continues to the present time. Without question, more significant changes were instituted within the governance and administration areas during this last period than in all previous eras. This in no way diminishes the importance of these earlier segments of the County government's development. In the absence of evolutionary changes occurring throughout the County's history, it is doubtful that the events recounted in this section would have taken place in the form they did. In short, the fifth period represents a culmination of the many historical developments that occurred in Milwaukee County government.

Raising the question of who controls usually takes place as a result of dissatisfaction with governmental outcomes. That the decision-making process in Milwaukee County government was questioned is a clear indication that there was sufficient concern with County affairs to support making fundamental changes. By the end of the 1950s it was clear to a number of the County Supervisors that the role of the Board in governance and administration was peripheral at best. With the possible exception of decisions dealing with capital projects the County Board was clearly in a spectator role, and what it was observing no longer seemed appropriate.

The long-term enhancement of other elements of County government, namely the operational unit administrators, had been further supported by an increased involvement of state and federal bureaucracies in the administration of County-based programs. The additional complexities created by the state and federal governments served to further complicate an already intricate administrative operation and render it increasingly impervious to legislative intervention at the county level. Additionally, long-term inertia within the County's Civil Service had led to a system that was paternalistic and seniority driven rather than merit based. The Board of Supervisors felt there was a loss of accountability.

The need for a separate executive function either in the form of a legislatively controlled manager or independent chief executive officer had long been advocated. Impetus from within the Board to create a

County Executive came in 1958, when Supervisor William F. O'Donnell introduced a resolution to study such a move.[69] Accountability was of critical importance. Previous experience with appointed Administrators suggested that an appointed manager would not manifest the necessary political responsiveness. When questioned regarding the genesis of his approach, Mr. Donnell traced the development of his ideas to a protracted series of discussions with long-time *Journal* reporter Avery Wittenberger.[70]

The O'Donnell initiative obviously had strong support on the Board, for in 1959, at the request of the County, state legislation creating the office of County Executive in Milwaukee was enacted.[71] In part, the Board was motivated by its perception that the reform provided an opportunity to alter power relationships within the Board. Board Chairman John L. Doyne had declared his interest in becoming a candidate for County Executive if and when the position became a reality; with the passage of the enabling legislation he entered the race. If Doyne were successful, his departure would provide an opportunity for other leadership on the Board.

The state legislature created the office of County Executive in 1959. John L. Doyne, former state legislator and County Board Chairman, was elected the first Executive in April 1960 and served until 1976.

Elected County Executive in April of 1960, John Doyne sought to establish the position as an independent source of administrative power and as an instrument of the Board to establish a greater degree of accountability to legislative prerogatives. Almost from the beginning, however, some elements within the Board had second thoughts concerning the degree of control that would actually return to that body. They realized that the Executive could effect greater control over existing administrative agencies, but such a move would probably not benefit the Board itself. Consequently, resistance to the institution of required changes intended to support the new position developed early on. When a Wisconsin Supreme Court ruling acted to restrict the original grant of powers to the County executive, the Board unsuccessfully sought to withdraw its support from an earlier position for a broad range of powers.[72]

This change of heart notwithstanding, the County Executive emerged considerably strengthened following voter approval of amendments to the state constitution granting veto and appointive powers that had previously been ruled unconstitutional. In the statewide elections of November 1962 voters approved amendments to the constitution specifically addressing the position of County Executive in Milwaukee. The amendments to Article IV, Section 23 and Article VI, Section 4 permit the aforementioned administrative powers.

Even before these actions had taken place, Mr. Doyne had taken several critical steps to establish his position as something considerably more than a mere ceremonial head of government. Sensitivity to the central concern regarding control over the critical points of influence was evident in his clear acknowledgement that his budget-making powers were vital. In an analysis dealing with the institution of the executive budget Doyne stated:

> Among the powers and responsibilities of the county Executive both major and minor, the broadest and most effective to date has appeared to be the power he exerts over the annual budget. The ceremonial power, the appointment power, and the general administrative power have been used...but none has had the over-all force in shaping policy and directing management — none has accomplished more in forging the beginnings of a dynamic and responsive organization out of a heterogeneous collection of unrelated departmental units — as the *budgetary power.* [73] [author's emphasis]

County Executive Doyne freely acknowledged that the successful transition from the previously employed legislative budget was the direct result of the creation of the Department of Management and Budget Analysis. Installation of a new accounting system and chart of accounts and the establishment of centralized purchasing, both occurring in 1959, were also credited as essential "building blocks" that provided a firm foundation for his efforts.[74]

Doyne was able to establish a strong working relationship with Richard Harter, the head of Management and Budget Analysis, after that unit was shifted from the County Board's jurisdiction to serve the Executive directly. Harter had previously served with the Milwaukee County Civil Service Commission and after failing to gain the position of Chief Examiner had sought another assignment.[75] Nationally recognized for his work in preparing and presenting the County budget by the Municipal Finance Officers Association in 1961, Harter, along with his staff, permitted the Executive to establish increased control over the operational units.

Seeking to further consolidate his ability to command the major staff services, Doyne proposed the creation of a Department of Administration in 1967.[76] His original proposal sought to include all administrative support functions, but strong opposition from the Chief Examiner and his supporters on the Board prevented the inclusion of Personnel. As a result, the final version of the Department of Administration did not include the Civil Service Commission but represented an important gain nevertheless. After considerable delay the Administration Department began operation in 1970 with Donald A. Schauer, an alumnus of Management and Budget Analysis, named as Director. Consisting of four units, it included a Division of Procurement, which took over all purchasing activities; the Division of Planning and Research, charged with capital planning and management analysis; the Division of Administrative Services, encompassing data processing, central reproduction, and mail; and, most importantly, the Division of Fiscal Affairs which was assigned the budget, accounting, and pre-audit functions. Management and Budget Analysis was eliminated as a separate entity, with its functions divided between the fiscal affairs and planning and research units. Gone too was the Auditor's office, and in its place was created a Department of Audit, whose role was narrowed to conducting post-audits. It reported directly to the County Board.[77]

The creation of the Department of Administration provided the County Executive with the ability to directly control the critical points of administrative influence. Not only had he been able to consolidate a wide range of activities, but with this consolidation came the opportunity to augment the resources originally allocated to the various staff activities involved. It should be noted that such gains took inordinately long to accomplish, most of the proposals for change having been developed during Doyne's first term in office. Board resistance, coupled with a growing concern for a loss of power on the part of departmental heads, served to

EXERCISE YOUR RIGHT TO BE HEARD!

Thursday, Nov. 7, 7 P.M.
COURTHOUSE ANNEX
Room 406
907 N. 10th St.
The Milwaukee County Board's Finance Committee
invites you to the

COUNTY BUDGET REVIEW

Special Public Hearing

Take advantage of this opportunity for you, as a Milwaukee County Resident to express your views and opinions on the proposed 1975 Milwaukee County Budget, as published in the October 7, Monday Journal and October 7, Sentinel. **There is still ample time to use many of your ideas and suggestions prior to final budget adoption in November.**

SOME OF THE MAJOR ITEMS TO BE CONSIDERED

Mass Transit—Freeways — Welfare — Mental Health — Sheriff's Dept. — Courts — Institutions — Parks — Metro Sewage — Airports — Art Center — General Hospital — D. A.'s Office

PARK FREE! Enter from 10th St. just west of Milwaukee County Courthouse

The official public hearing on the budget for the year 1975 will be held by the County Board of Supervisors, October 21, 1974, at 7:00 P.M., in the County Board room on the second floor of the Courthouse in the City of Milwaukee, Wisconsin.

delay his efforts. The major factor working in the County Executive's favor was his willingness to "stay the course" and his continued reelection; it proved very difficult to wait him out. Although the changes that eventually were made would have occurred sooner had there been more cooperation, the Executive was particularly sensitive to not wanting to do too much too fast. The Director of the Administration Department, Donald Schauer, recalled Doyne's constantly repeated caveat that the "time has to be right" before a major change was implemented.[78]

Emphasis should be given to the fact that while the Board sought to delay the Executive's initiatives, he was not without support among the Supervisors. Doyne was, after all, a former Board member and its formal leader for three years of his eight-year tenure. Even his much publicized feuding with his successor Eugene Grobschmidt did not extend to the personal level. In fact, without his strong Board ties and his understanding of Board prerogatives, it is doubtful if the progress that was made would have taken place. In an environment where few things are ever decided precipitously, the need for patience and perseverance was essential. Ultimately, had the Board of Supervisors chosen to do so, few if any of the changes needed to make the new position of County Executive meaningful would have been forthcoming.

In conjunction with his efforts to concentrate administrative control within his office, Doyne also sought to deal with problems created by the absence of any coherent interaction between the many departments within the County structure. It was extremely difficult to view County government as much more than a loose confederation of unrelated units. When the County Executive took office, there were thirty-six such units, far too many for meaningful control or supervision by an Executive. A further impediment to Executive influence was the authority possessed by the various boards and commissions to exercise control and supervision over the specific functional areas under their jurisdiction. Drawing in part from the Public Administration Study for support, Doyne had formulated an extensive reorganizaion plan by May of 1962. It envisioned restructuring all departments except the District Attorney and Superintendent of Schools into six comprehensive departments: courts, public safety, welfare, health and institutions, public works, and parks, recreation and culture. Under this plan, control exercised by the boards and commissions would be eliminated, and department heads would be appointed by the County Executive.[79]

Although, for the most part ultimately successful, these changes were not fully realized until the administration of his successor. The consolidation of staff operations within the Department of Administration not only served to enhance the Executive's control but also abetted his consolidation efforts in other areas as well. Understandably, the proposed reorganization of County operations faced a formidable set of obstacles. In addition to opposition from those elements in County government that would lose influence, the requirements involved in the passage of enabling state legislation ensured delay. Most importantly, however, under the Doyne administration the basic foundation for fundamental change was established. It would be up to the succeeding administration to continue the momentum begun during Doyne's tenure.

Not the least of the impediments to change was the appointment process of top administrators, whose reponsiveness to direction or new approaches requires some ability to sanction and cooperate. Since these administrative positions were either elective or under civil service, they could ignore the direction of the Executive with impunity. Certainly, the ability of the Executive to exert increased influence depended on this situation being altered. To this end, County Executive Doyne proposed removing top operational administrators from the merit system and changing the Sheriff's position from elective to appointive. While his desire for a Director of Public Safety to replace the Sheriff failed to elicit any substantial support, he was considerably more successful regarding other key administrative officials. Again, the climate for change was favorable, due not only to a growing dissatisfaction with the results of an unresponsive merit system but also to similar restructuring efforts underway at the state level.

The concept of cabinet government came late to Wisconsin because of its strong belief in separating administration of public policy from political interference. The experience at the national level as well as the existence of cabinets within other states and their local governments notwithstanding, a strong enough impetus for shifting to this construct within the executive function had not been present until this period. Under Doyne's leadership a strong effort was launched to bring about this change. In opposition were those elements within County government which stood to lose most from the institution of a system that would concentrate administrative power in the Executive's office. In the face of strong resistance from key administrators and their supporters on the County Board, over ten years passed before the Executive was successful in getting the system to budge. While he was not able to establish a cabinet system within the County, Doyne did realize a significant modification in the current state of affairs.

State legislation passed in 1973 provided that the Milwaukee County Executive appoint the administrative heads of the parks, institutions, civil service, and transportation. Thereafter such positions would no longer be within the merit system or classified service. With the exception of those operational heads elected to their positions, this represented virtually all the operating functions within the County. The price exacted for this landmark change was the agreement to permit those individuals currently occupying the affected positions to remain; i.e., be "grandfathered" in.[80] Consequently, the effect of the legislation was not immediately felt, and the ability to increase control and accountability over these administrators was not substantially increased until the incumbents vacated their jobs.

William F. O'Donnell, present County Executive, assumed the post in 1976 following twenty-eight years service as a County Supervisor. He was elected chairman of the County Board in 1975.

John Doyne and those who supported his efforts were able to provide a broad basis for altering the control over critical points of influence. While a high degree of frustration accompanied their efforts, a longer view of the changes begun during the 1960s and 1970s establishes the fact that opposition elements were serving to make such changes more complete rather than preventing their occurrence. Doyne had "set the table"; it would remain for his successor, William F. O'Donnell, to "serve the meal."

The 1958 resolution that O'Donnell had introduced envisioned a legislatively oriented executive position. The resolution refers to a "President of the County Board, Area Chairman of the Board, and/or County

Commissioner."[81] For O'Donnell, after twenty-eight years of Board service, it would be hard to imagine that this orientation would have been diminished when he became County Executive in 1976. It is certain that his original concerns for administrative accountability and responsiveness had not altered. Accountability, in particular, has remained a professed rationale for much of his effort as County Executive.[82]

As previously discussed, the vulnerability of the system to change was strong, and developments during O'Donnell's administration helped to further erode support for the old order. Instead of criminal practices being the chief factor in this regard, noteworthy instances of administrative insensitivity and mismanagement proved to be pivotal in strengthening the Executive's efforts.

Because of the inevitable displacements it caused, the construction of the County expressway system had generated dissatisfaction. As construction expanded, greater segments of the public began to question the appropriateness of the decisions being made by administrators involved in this activity. Often these objections would take the form of pressure by constituents on County Supervisors for action to affect the process. Support for what appeared to be unrestrained road construction became markedly less until few advocates beyond the Expressway Division and its Commission could be found. This was an obvious instance of a failure on the part of administrators to adjust to changing expectations; they failed to alter a position that no longer enjoyed its former support and hence provided a strong argument to institute changes that would ensure greater responsiveness.

Mismanagement became a crucial issue when deficiencies in the billing and collection activities in conjunction with health care services were publicly revealed to have resulted in the County losing large amounts of money. The November 19, 1976 *Milwaukee Journal* initiated an investigative series on the problems associated with these activities. With the lead article headlined, "County Fails to Collect Millions Due in Medicaid," the newspaper focused public attention on a problem that had been festering for years. Although criminal activity was never at issue, such detailed examination did disclose just how ineffective the management of this area was. Ultimately, it was a significant factor in leading to the resignation of the Institutions Director. An operational area that had long been insulated from public examination was now viewed as being far from the picture of administrative efficiency. This added further argument for increasing control over the County's operational activities. Since the primary reason for protecting agencies from political interference had been effectively undermined, a strong movement to increase accountability gained strength as a result.

Another major area of administrative activity that serves to illustrate the favorable environment for change is the personnel function. Prior to the creation of the County Executive all issues concerning compensation and new positions were under the exclusive control of the Civil Service Commission, which reported directly to the Joint Committee on Finance and the Judiciary, thus bypassing the budgetary review procedures. Since personnel resources made up such a substantial part of the operating budget, control over these matters was critical. For the 1963 budget this control was shifted from its previous locus with Civil Service and the Joint Committee to the Management and Budget Analysis Department, where it could be reviewed in the executive budget.[83] This shift was an early indication of an erosion of the influence centered in personnel.

The practices of the Civil Service staff under the direction of the Chief Examiner had long been a source of dissatisfaction. With the growth of governmental activities within the County structure, the demand for a process that would effectively deal with the various requirements involved in the recruitment, examination, and certification of potential employees was at a premium. Instead, complaints from the operating departments regarding delays in these areas were constant. Unless one had a personal relationship with key Civil Service staff, it was extremely difficult to achieve the kind of expeditious response necessary to allow expanded operations without inordinate delays.

Added to the general unhappiness regarding the execution of personnel functions are the issues surrounding the major changes that the whole personnel environment was undergoing. Collective bargaining in the public sector, after a long period of dormancy, was beginning to become the norm rather than the exception. The 1950s and 1960s witnessed rapid growth in public sector unions within Milwaukee area governments. Although labor relations is generally recognized as a key personnel function, the control over contract negotiation and administration was early on centered within the Corporation Counsel's office. Had Civil Service enjoyed its previous level of influence, it might have been anticipated that this new and critical area would remain its responsibility.

While developments in the labor relations field were an indicator of slippage in influence for Civil Service leadership, developments in the emerging area of affirmative action put the long-established practices of the Civil Service Commission at risk and made it highly susceptible to attack. Theoretically, a merit system is designed to produce the best qualified personnel for the various functional roles within the organization it serves. Within the County's Civil Service system, giving preferential treatment to certain groups such as women and minorities was not deemed acceptable to the extent that such treatment ran counter to the requirement of producing "best" candidates. The Civil Service Commission staff and the Commission it represented had never demonstrated interest in accommodating its practices to the strong societal support increasingly enjoyed by affirmative action. As a result, Civil Service failed to take the necessary steps to adjust to a situation that was increasingly putting the County at risk.

Not unexpectedly, in light of the foregoing, a class action suit, *Johnnie G. Jones, et al.* v. *Milwaukee County et al.*, alleging race and national origin discrimination in hiring, promotion, and transfer within the classified service, was brought against the County in 1974. Consistent with its general approach, Civil Service failed to alter its practices until the county found itself burdened with a Consent Order in 1980 that severely limited its choices. Instead of anticipating the effect affirmative action would have on its practices, Civil Service resisted until the least desirable arrangements were forced on the County. In addition to putting the County in a bad light, the episode again demonstrated just how outdated the Civil Service Commission was regarding personnel developments.

With the above examples of insensitivity and mismanagement aiding his position, the County Executive was now able to extend the advances sought by Doyne and himself. The most significant development in this

F. Thomas Ament, County Supervisor since 1968, was elected County Board Chairman in 1976 and continues in that post. Television cameras and a news table provided coverage of board actions.

regard was the passage of state legislation that permitted the County Executive to establish a bona fide cabinet system and further extend his ability to remove additional key administrative positions from the classified service.[84] Following this 1977 legislation, the shift in control over the administrative operations of the County was marked. In effect, after 1977 the County Executive operated in the same manner as the federal model. Unlike this model, however, the pattern of tenure thus far exhibited for the County Executive ensures that the level of control will extend, relatively, beyond that of the President. If there is rapid turnover in top administrative positions resulting from the election of new chief executives, then the impact of such a shift will be blunted because reliance on those within the classified service is not diminished. In the case of the County, however, it appears that a pattern of extended tenure of the Executive will continue for the foreseeable future.

Having effectively wrested control over the critical points of influence from elements in County government that had previously been pre-eminent, it remained for the Executive and the Board to complete the process by removing the insulating effect that various boards and commissions had provided. In this regard, the County Board was in a position to gain considerable influence as well. Heretofore, key boards and commissions such as the Welfare Board, Civil Service, Expressway, and Park Commissions had exercised both administrative and policy control over the operational units they headed. Although some degree of influence was afforded the Board and Executive through the appointment and budgetary functions, the fact remained that such influence would remain secondary to that of the boards and commissions.

Following the successes regarding appointment powers, the elimination of the Welfare Board in 1982 marked the end of an era that had prevailed since the 1920s.[85] The earlier demise of the Park Commission[86] and the substantial restructuring of the personnel function completed a series of changes that clearly places the locus of influence over administrative activities within the Executive's office and governance within the Board of Supervisors. In terms of losers and winners the operating departments as well as the boards and commissions were eclipsed by the Executive and Board. Not only do the various Board Committees replace the policy role of the boards and commissions, but the introduction of politically sensitive administrators ensures a greater degree of cooperation and consultation with the Board on administrative concerns as well.

To increase the effectiveness of these shifts in influence, steps have been taken on both the Board and within the Executive's office to provide adequate staff. Both have gained significantly over the last ten years in developing their capacity to generate independent sources of information and further their ability to exert control. The expectation is that enhance-

The sesquicentennial Milwaukee County Board of Supervisors.
Left to right: Row 1: Lawrence J. Kenny, Penny E. Podell, Susan L. Baldwin, F. Thomas
Ament, Bernadette T. Skibinski, John D. St. John, Betty L. Voss, Bernice K. Rose;
Row 2: Terrance L. Pitts, Robert L. Jackson, Jr., Anthony J. Czaja, Richard H. Bussler,
Dorothy K. Dean; Row 3: Harout O. Sanasarian, James Koconis, Daniel F. Casey, Daniel
Cupertino, Jr., Thomas Bailey, Richard D. Nyklewicz, Jr., Richard B. Kuzminski;
Row 4: Gerald D. Engel, Fred N. Tabak, Thomas W. Meaux, Paul F. Mathews, John J.
Valenti.

ment of administrative and governance functions directed or controlled by the Executive and Board will continue, and the significant shifts in the control over points of critical influence begun in the late 1950s will proceed apace.

Inevitably, disagreements will occur between the Board and Executive; to some extent this is due to the natural competition that exists between these two critical elements within County government.[87] There are, however, factors that will serve to temper such disagreements. A tradition of Executives with Board experience, if continued, will increase the Executive's sensitivity for legislative prerogatives. Secondly, with such a tradition in mind, it would not serve the interest of the Board's leadership elements to significantly erode the Executive's influence, lest they find the office seriously diminished when they accede to it. This is reenforced by the present practice of appointing Supervisors to unclassified administrative positions since enactment of the landmark legislation establishing the cabinet system in 1977.

There is every expectation that governance and administration in Milwaukee County will continue to evolve, with future developments drawing on the evolutionary shifts recounted herein. Throughout the foregoing essay attention has been focused on the milestone changes that resulted in gains and losses for the various elements that sought to control governance and administration. In all instances these changes have been preceded by a desire by those both internal and external to the governmental operation for a different way of doing things. While some changes were driven by evidence of criminality and others by mismanagement or administrative insensitivity, in all cases a dissatisfaction with the current state of affairs existed. For the entire history of County government, adjustment has been a constant characteristic, and it is not likely that future patterns will be different.

Endnotes

[1]From an organizational perspective all activities can be divided into two areas: operational and administrative. Operational activities are those functions for which the organization is created. In the case of governmental organizations the fundamental purpose is the establishment of policy to determine the distribution of societal values and the execution of such policy. Hence, legislative activity is an operational function which is the primary responsibility of the Board of Supervisors at the county level in Wisconsin. The other major category of operational activities is executory and is the responsibility of the functional departments such as Health and Human Services, Parks, Sheriff, Judiciary, District Attorney, Public Works, and Register of Deeds. Examples of such activities include social services, welfare, recreation, law enforcement, criminal justice, transportation, and the maintenance of marriage, birth, and death certificates.
Administrative functions are those activities that support the organization's efforts to accomplish its operational goals. These support functions deal mainly with dual concerns of control and coordination. This involves both the managerial hierarchy or command structure as well as a range of specialized units. The latter are concerned with the acquisition and management of fiscal and personnel resources, procurement of supplies and equipment, legal services, and data processing (which includes acquisition, storage, and analysis of data as well as the communication of information both inside and outside the organization). While these administrative functions are not the reason the government exists, it is certain that the operational activities could not be accomplished without them. In most cases where the government is small there is considerably less separation of function between operation and support activities. When the organization becomes large in terms of individuals and operational areas, then a high degree of specialization occurs. In fact, such growth usually cannot take place without differentiation of functions.
[2]"The Annals of Milwaukee County," an unpublished history by the Milwaukee County Employees' Association, 1923, contains an itemization of the Michigan Territory legislation that established the various functions to be administered at the county level. These provisions were carried forward with statehood.
[3]Russell W. Maddox and Robert F. Fuquay, *State and Local Government* (Princeton, N.J.: D. Van Nostrand Company, Inc., 1962) p. 493, quoting John A. Fairlie, *Local Government in Counties, Towns and Villages* (New York: The Century Co., 1906) p. 5.
[4]Ibid.
[5]James R. Donoghue, "Local Government in Wisconsin," *Wisconsin Blue Book*, 1979-1980, p. 125.
[6]"The Annals of Milwaukee County."
[7]*Proceedings*, 1841, Milwaukee County Board of Supervisors, p. 23.
[8]*Laws of Wisconsin*, 1864, Chapter 208.
[9]The information for these early years comes from copies made of the original handwritten records of the County Board *Proceedings* done as a W.P.A. project in 1937 (Project No. 7133-6476) which copied and indexed in typescript the *Proceedings* for the years 1838 to 1879 inclusive; this project also included a separate Consolidated Index for these same years.
[10]*Proceedings*, 1871, Milwaukee County Board of Supervisors, p. 243.
[11]This was authorized by state legislative action in *Session Laws*, 1855, Chapter 318, Section 1.
[12]*Proceedings*, 1877, p. 36.
[13]*Proceedings*, 1876, p. 52.
[14]*Laws of Wisconsin*, 1885, Chapter 53.
[15]*Wisconsin Constitution*, Article IV, Section 23.
[16]Only Fifteenth Ward Supervisor Herman Haasch qualifies; he served from 1892 to 1904 and was Board Chairman from 1900 to 1904.
[17]*Commissioners of Hamilton County* v. *Mighels*, 7 Ohio St. 109 (1857) quoted in Maddox and Fuquay, *State and Local Government* p. 496; the authors point out that the real distinction, from their point of view, between the county and other municipal corporations is one of degree only. The county is *primarily* a subdivision of the state, and the municipal corporation is *primarily* an instrumentality of local government.
[18]At the conclusion of this Grand Jury's two-month term on February 1, 1902 the panel failed to report indictments but indicated that there had been substantial evidence available demonstrating criminal activity. *Milwaukee Sentinel*, February 1, 1902; *Laws of Wisconsin*, 1903, Chapter 136.
[19]*Manual of Duties of All Elected and Appointed County Officials and Commissions*, WPA Project No. 4418 (Milwaukee, 1937) p. 102.

[20]For a more extensive examination of developments that focus specifically on the District Attorney's Office during this period of time see David George Ondercin, "The Early Years of Francis Edward McGovern, 1866-1910," unpublished Master's thesis (Milwaukee: University of Wisconsin-Milwaukee, 1967).

[21]*Laws of Wisconsin,* 1897, Chapter 342. The law, entitled: "The Board of County Civil Service Commission," was restricted to counties with over 100,000 population (of which Milwaukee was the only instance) and was to deal only with "persons . . . in any house of correction, work house or other similar institution. . . ." p. 771.

[22]*Proceedings,* 1903, Milwaukee County Board of Supervisors, p. 149.

[23]*Milwaukee Journal,* June 22; July 6 and 29, 1903.

[24]Ibid., September 23, 1903.

[25]Ibid., August 21, 1903; *Journal,* March 19, 1904, also reported the findings of a County Board hired special accountant that revealed that House of Corrections had operated the chair factory, which had been intended to defray expenses of the institution, at a loss of $182,719 during Heiden's eight-year tenure; Heiden had failed to report most of this loss.

[26]*Journal,* February 1, 1904.

[27]Ibid.; *Sentinel,* May 25, 1904, and October 1, 1905.

[28]*Journal,* March 16, 1904.

[29]Ibid.

[30]*Milwaukee Free Press,* July 1, 1905.

[31]*Proceedings,* 1905, Milwaukee County Board of Supervisors, p. 91.

[32]*Sentinel,* September 29, 1903.

[33]Frederick I. Olson, "The Milwaukee Socialists, 1897-1941," unpublished Ph.D. dissertation, Harvard University, 1952, pp. 131, 133, 145, 149, 163, and 168.

[34]*Milwaukee Municipal Campaign Book 1912* (Milwaukee: County Central Committee of the Social-Democratic Party, Milwaukee County, Wisconsin, 1912) pp. 142-50, deals specifically with improvements made within County government.

[35]*Laws of Wisconsin,* 1915, Chapter 37, Section 709.

[36]*Laws of Wisconsin,* 1917, Chapter 259.

[37]Olson, p. 136.

[38]*Laws of Wisconsin,* 1897, Chapter 342.

[39]*Proceedings,* 1917, Milwaukee County Board of Supervisors, p. 99.

[40]This opinion was written by Special Assistant District Attorney William L. Tibbs and appears in *Proceedings,* 1917, Milwaukee County Board of Supervisors, p. 136.

[41]*The Need of Civil Service in Milwaukee County,* a report by the Civil Service Committee, George A. Chamberlain, Chairman, City Club Bulletin, February 1915; a flavor of the employment situation the committee was attempting to rectify is given in the following excerpt from the Bulletin:

The placing of this conglomerate list of appointments in the hands of the board has been the outgrowth of a long series of uncoordinated laws, rather than the result of any logical plan. As a result, most incongruous situations are tolerated. For instance, the County Board appoints three employees at the county jail, while the sheriff appoints the other five. Again, the two elevator men at the courthouse are gravely elected by ballot for a term of two years by the 19 supervisors.

Tenure of office among the male employees of the janitorial service at the courthouse depends upon the political complexion of the Board. Everyone of these long standing, experienced employees was discharged on January 1, 1914, when their terms again expired. The scrub-women, who of course have no votes, were not discharged with the men. [p. 11]

[42]*Proceedings,* 1879, Milwaukee County Board of Supervisors, pp. 374-75.

[43]*Manual of Duties,* p. 107.

[44]Ibid.

[45]Ibid., p. 74.

[46]*Laws of Wisconsin,* 1927, Chapter 22, Section 1.

[47]Interview with George Lorenz, former Milwaukee County Board of Supervisors Committee Clerk, January 23, 1986. Mr. Lorenz began his service with the County as Committee Clerk in 1932 and remained in that capacity until his retirement in 1968; for much of his tenure he was the only professional staff serving the Board on a day-to-day basis.

[48]*Milwaukee Journal,* March 30, 1934, contains a review and editorial of the newspaper's perspective and understanding of the situation.

[49]Ibid.

[50]*Proceedings,* 1934 Milwaukee County Board of Supervisors, p. 906, contains the Warnimont request and Institutions Committee report is found at page 975.

[51]Ibid., p. 982.

[52]Olson, p. 486, cites the *Twelfth Election Report - 1933* of the Social-Democratic Party.

[53]Lorenz, interview.

[54]*Milwaukee Journal,* March 30, 1934.
[55]*Manual of Duties of All Elected and Appointed Officials and Commissions,* p. 104; the section on the House of Correction highlights this 1933 inspection in the treatment of its operations.
[56]*Proceedings,* 1934, Milwaukee County Board of Supervisors, p. 982.
[57]The *Proceedings* indicates that Momsen resigned effective May 31, 1938 after thirty-five years as Inspector; there is no indication in the *Journal* accounts of the resignation that Momsen left for any other reason than age. *Milwaukee Journal,* April 1, 1938 (in the account which featured the retirements of two other longtime House of Correction staff members no references were made to the 1934 efforts of the *Journal* to have Momsen removed).
[58]*Milwaukee Journal,* March 30, 1934.
[59]Although neither Tiefenthaler nor Gill was the original administrative head of his respective organization, each enjoyed a long tenure which greatly enhanced his influence within the community. Tiefenthaler in particular spanned four of the five developmental eras described herein. Although Gill did not assume the directorship until 1944, his previous experience with the City of Milwaukee provided him with a strong local knowledge. Gill remained with the Citizens' Governmental Research Bureau until 1984. Often one or the other or both would be called on to serve on official study boards and commissions examining various aspects of governmental operations within the Milwaukee area.
[60]"Reorganization of Milwaukee County Government," an unpublished report by the Committee on County Affairs, The City Club of Milwaukee, May 1939.
[61]*Proceedings,* 1952, Milwaukee County Board of Supervisors, pp. 1522-24.
[62]Ibid., 1954, p. 248.
[63]A comparison of the two contracts on file with the Citizens' Governmental Research Bureau indicates that the Purpose sections for both contracts are identical for paragraphs (b) and (c) and are essentially the same with obvious City and County organizational and functional differences accounted for.
[64]A brief review of the background and results of the study is provided in Robert E. Boos and Norman N. Gill, "Milwaukee County Plans To Get Its Money's Worth," *The County Officer,* 15 (October 1956): 230, 241-42. PAS was part of a consortium located on the University of Chicago Campus that represented the most comprehensive assemblage of associations devoted to State and local affairs. In addition to the highly respected PAS were Public Administration Clearing House, International City Managers' Association, Council of State Governments, American Municipal Association, Municipal Finance Officers Association, Federation of Tax Administrators, American Public Welfare Association, American Public Works Association, National Association of Housing and Redevelopment Officials, National Association of Assessing Officers, American Society of Planning Officials, Civil Service Assembly, and the National Municipal League; all the directors of whom served on the Public Administration Service governing board. PAS had previously done a personnel study for Milwaukee County in 1952.
[65]Boos and Gill, p. 242.
[66]Letter from County Executive John L. Doyne to Special Committee on Public Administration Service Reports regarding disposition of remaining (93) PAS recommendations not acted on; as per February 28, 1961 County resolution. (Letter dated May 17, 1962.)
[67]*Proceedings,* 1957, Milwaukee County Board of Supervisors, pp. 624-28.
[68]Ibid., p. 625-26.
[69]*Proceedings,* 1958, Milwaukee County Board of Supervisors, p. 947.
[70]Interview with William F. O'Donnell, Milwaukee County Executive, December 11, 1985; Mr. O'Donnell indicated that he and Wittenberger would often have lunch together and their discussions on the subject helped to shape his thinking with regard to the value of an elected position as opposed to an appointed one. Mr. Wittenberger, when interviewed, corroborated the discussions and indicated that while originally an advocate of the county manager plan he came to support O'Donnell's position largely on the grounds of greater accountability. Interview with Avery Wittenberger, reporter for the *Milwaukee Journal,* January 16, 1986. Mr. Wittenberger enjoyed a unique position in the County. Court House reporter from the mid-forties to the mid-seventies, he enjoyed a high level of respect from County personnel and was able to informally influence many key individuals because of the degree of trust he was able to establish over the long years of his assignment; the O'Donnell relationship was by no means an isolated example, based on the testimony of a wide range of Milwaukee County employees both elected and appointed.
[71]*Laws of Wisconsin,* 1959, Chapter 327.
[72]Henry J. Schmandt, John C. Goldbach, and Donald B. Vogel, *Milwaukee* (New York: Praeger Publishers, 1971) pp. 86-88.
[73]"The County Executive Budget in Milwaukee County," an unpublished paper by Herman John and John L. Doyne, June 8, 1962, pp. 2-3.

74Ibid., p. 22.
75Interview with Herman John, Deputy District Attorney, January 28, 1986; Mr. John was a member of the staff of the Department of Management and Budget Analysis under Richard Harter during the writing of the paper cited in the preceding note and was directly involved in the developments regarding the executive budget.
76"Recommendations for the Establishment of a Department of Administration," a report from John L. Doyne, County Executive, to the Finance Committee, Milwaukee County Board of Supervisors, February 16, 1967.
77Milwaukee County Government Report, 1971, pp. 10-11.
78Interview with Donald A. Schauer, former Director of Milwaukee County Department of Administration, February 4, 1986.
79"Reorganization Proposal for County Government," John L. Doyne, County Executive, May 8, 1962, Exhibit I.
80Laws of Wisconsin, 1973, Chapter 262.
81Proceedings, 1958, Milwaukee County Board of Supervisors, p. 878.
82Interview with William F. O'Donnell, Milwaukee County Executive, December 11, 1985.
83Herman John and John L. Doyne, p. 35.
84Laws of Wisconsin, 1977, Chapter 433; for a more extensive examination of this development see "S-484: Milwaukee County's Quest For Civil Service Reform," an unpublished undated paper by David R. Zepecki (Senate Bill 484 became Chapter 433).
85Ibid., 1981, Chapter 329. Although part of the 1981 Laws, Section 32 of Chapter 329 provides that: "This act takes effect on the first day of the 2nd month commencing after its publication," which in this case was May 6, 1982.
86Proceedings, 1981, Milwaukee County Board of Supervisors, p. 2233. Since the establishment of the Park Commission, unlike the Welfare Board, was permissive, state legislation abolishing it was unnecessary; consequently, such action was effected by the passage of County Ordinance found at the above page.
87For a detailed treatment of the issues associated with Executive-Board relationships see A. Clarke Hagensick, "Propositional Inventory of Executive-Legislative Conflict," Transactions of the Wisconsin Academy of Sciences, Arts and Letters, 56 (1967-1968): 81-92.

Bibliography

Public Documents

County of Milwaukee, Authorized Positions in Organizational Units, February 23, 1965.

Milwaukee County Board of Supervisors, Proceedings, 1841, 1855, 1864, 1871, 1876, 1877, 1879, 1888, 1903, 1905, 1917, 1934, 1952, 1955, 1981.

Milwaukee County Government Report, 1971, 1984, 1985.

Wisconsin, Constitution, Art. IV, Sec. 12 and 23.

Wisconsin, Laws of Wisconsin, (1897), Ch. 342.

Wisconsin, Laws of Wisconsin, (1903), Ch. 136.

Wisconsin, Laws of Wisconsin, (1915), Ch. 37.

Wisconsin, Laws of Wisconsin, (1917), Ch. 259.

Wisconsin, Laws of Wisconsin, (1927), Ch. 22.

Wisconsin, Laws of Wisconsin, (1959), Ch. 327.

Wisconsin, Laws of Wisconsin, (1973), Ch. 262.

Wisconsin, Laws of Wisconsin, (1977), Ch. 433.

Wisconsin, Laws of Wisconsin, (1981), Ch. 329.

Works Progress Administration, Manual of Duties of All Elected and Appointed County Officials and Commissions, Project No. 4418, 1937.

Books

Anderson, Harry H., and Frederick I. Olson, *Milwaukee: At the Gathering of the Waters*, Tulsa: Continental Heritage Press, Inc., 1981.

Austin, H. Russell, *The Milwaukee Story*, Milwaukee: The Journal Company, 1946.

Crane, Wilder, and A. Clarke Hagensick, *Wisconsin Government and Politics*, 3d ed. Milwaukee: Department of Governmental Affairs, 1981.

Maddox, Russell W., and Robert F. Fuguay, *State and Local Government*, Princeton, N.J.: D. Van Nostrand Company, Inc., 1962.

Schmandt, Henry J., and John C. Goldbach, and Donald B. Vogel, *Milwaukee*, New York: Praeger Publishers, 1971.

Torrence, Susan Walker, *Grass Roots Government*, New York: Robert B. Luce, Inc., 1974.

Articles and Periodicals

Boos, Robert E., and Norman N. Gill, "Milwaukee Plans to Get Its Money's Worth," *The County Officer*, 15 (October 1956):230, 241-42.

Cape, William H., "The Emerging Patterns of County Executives," University of Kansas Governmental Research Series No. 35, 1967.

Donoghue, James R., "Local Government in Wisconsin," *Wisconsin Blue Book*, 1979-1980.

Hagensick, Clarke A., "Propositional Inventory of Executive-Legislative Conflict," *Transactions of the Wisconsin Academy of Sciences, Arts and Letters*, 56 (1967-1968):81-92.

Larson, Lawrence M., "A Financial and Administrative History of Milwaukee," University of Wisconsin *Bulletin* No. 242, 1908.

Milwaukee Free Press, July 1, 1905.

Milwaukee Journal, June 22, July 6 and 29, 1903; September 23, 1903; February 1, 1904; March 16 and 19, 1904; March 30, 1934.

Milwaukee Sentinel, February 1, 1902; May 25, 1904; October 1, 1905.

Mowry, Duane, "The Reign of Graft in Milwaukee," *Arena*, 34 (December, 1905):589-90.

Treleven, J.E., "The Milwaukee Bureau of Economy and Efficiency," *Annals of the American Academy of Political Science*, 41 (May 1912):270-278.

Wehrwein, George S., "County Government in Wisconsin," *Wisconsin Blue Book*, 1933.

Younger, Richard D. "The Grand Jury That Made Milwaukee Quake," *Historical Messenger*, 11 (March 1955):7-9.

Unpublished Materials

Ames, Kathleen F., "A Socio-Political Profile of Candidates for Milwaukee Common Council and County Board in General Elections (1944-1964)," Master's thesis, University of Wisconsin-Milwaukee, 1965.

County Central Committee of the Social-Democratic Party, "Milwaukee Municipal Campaign Book 1912."

Goff, Charles Davis, "The Politics of Governmental Integration in Metropolitan Milwaukee," Ph.D. dissertation, Northwestern University, 1952.

"The Government of Milwaukee County," The Educational Foundation of the League of Women Voters of Milwaukee, 1955.

"The Government of Milwaukee County — A Concluding Report," Public Administration Service, January 12, 1956.

Institute of Governmental Affairs. The University of Wisconsin Extension Division, *Government in Action,* August 1964.

John, Herman, and John L. Doyne, "The County Executive Budget in Milwaukee County," typescript paper, June 8, 1962.

Letter from County Executive John L. Doyne to Special Committee on Public Administration Service Reports, May 17, 1962.

Milwaukee County Employees' Association, "The Annals of Milwaukee County," 1923.

"Milwaukee County Government," A Manual of Duties of Elected Officials prepared by the Staff of the Corporation Counsel of Milwaukee County, October 1954.

The Need of Civil Service in Milwaukee, report by the Civil Service Commission, City Club Bulletin, February 1915.

Olson, Frederick I., "The Milwaukee Socialists, 1897-1941," Ph.D. dissertation, Harvard University, 1952.

Ondercin, David George, "The Early Years of Francis Edward McGovern, 1866-1910," Master's thesis, University of Wisconsin-Milwaukee, 1967.

"Recommendations For the Establishment of a Department of Administration," a report from John L. Doyne, County Executive, to the Finance Committee, Milwaukee County Board of Supervisors, February 16, 1967.

"Reorganization Proposal for County Government," John L. Doyne, County Executive, May 8, 1962.

Interviews

Ament, F. Thomas, Chairman, Milwaukee County Board of Supervisors, December 27, 1985.

Dembinski, Doris C., Milwaukee County Board of Supervisors Committee Clerk, January 14, 1986.

John, Herman, Milwaukee County Deputy District Attorney, January 28, 1986.

Lorenz, George, former Milwaukee County Board of Supervisors Committee Clerk, January 23, 1986.

O'Donnell, William F., Milwaukee County Executive, December 11, 1985.

Schauer, Donald A., former Director of Milwaukee County Department of Administration, February 4, 1986.

Weber, Donald F., Assistant to the Milwaukee County Executive for Legislative and Fiscal Liaison, January 24, 1986.

Westbrook, Mackie G., Milwaukee County Board of Supervisors Director of Operations, January 28, 1986.

Wittenberger, Avery, former reporter for the *Milwaukee Journal,* January 16, 1986.

Courts and Criminal Justice: Law Enforcement in Milwaukee County

by Karel D. Bicha ─────────────────────────────

Introduction

Systems of law and jurisprudence have been primary characteristics of civilized society for nearly five thousand years. Formal procedures to discipline individuals who violate the rules of society and mechanisms to resolve disputes between members of society or between society itself and its members effectively define civilized life. Agencies designed to investigate violations of law and organizations charged with the ongoing responsibility for the enforcement of law originated later in time. And institutions such as the jail and the prison, created to neutralize the impact of criminal or deviant individuals on society, emerged even more recently. The latter institutions were, in effect, civilized alternatives to socially approved private vengeance or to such summary techniques as execution, mutilation, or banishment.

In a broad sense, all of these processes and institutions comprise judicial services. Thus, judicial services encompass more than the procedures administered by persons called judges in places called courts of law. They include all of the functions preliminary to judicial resolution — the investigation of wrongful acts, the preparation of evidence for judicial determination, and the elastic area of law enforcement itself. Judicial services also include the processes which succeed judicial action — the detention of individuals in penal institutions and such modern variants of penal procedure as probation, diversion, and parole. Essentially, judicial services consist of four distinct but interrelated elements — investigation, prosecution, judgment, and incarceration.

Each of these elements had undergone a complex evolution in the United States before the creation of Milwaukee County in 1835. In its legal posture, the County[1] has always been reflective of national trends rather than innovative. Like all American counties, moreover, judicial services in Milwaukee County centered in a court system. Without an effective system of courts, the investigative and prosecutorial work of the District Attorney, the law enforcement, court service and penal responsibilities of

the Sheriff, and the County prison known as the House of Correction would
have been superfluous.

A survey of the history of judicial services in the County must com-
mence with its central element, the court system. The preliminary work
which produced the contemporary judicial system in the County began in
April 1971. Governor Patrick J. Lucey, responding to numerous pressures
for judicial reorganization in Wisconsin, appointed a Citizens Study Committee on Judicial Organization to develop proposals for reform of the
state's judicial system. The committee, chaired by Milwaukee banker John
C. Geilfuss, consisted of forty members and omitted, by design, both judges
and members of the state legislature. By January 1973 the committee had
concluded its deliberations and shortly thereafter submitted a substantial
report. Among the numerous proposals contained in the report, three were
particularly crucial. The citizens committee recommended the establishment of a single trial court for each county in the state to exercise
jurisdiction over all matters currently divided between the circuit courts
and county courts. It recommended further that the state create a new
appeals court with jurisdiction intermediate between the proposed trial
courts and the Supreme Court. Finally, the committee suggested the
reduction of existing municipal courts to the status of "ordinance bu-
reaus." In addition, the committee proposed the periodic rotation of the
judges in the trial courts between the relevant areas of judicial responsibility — civil, criminal, juvenile, and family.[2]

In the form of amendments to the state constitution, the voters
approved the trial court and appeals court recommendations in April 1977.
Implementation proceeded expeditiously, and by the end of the 1970s each
county possessed a single judicial agency known as a Circuit Court. The
nomenclature derived from the original state constitution. Upon the
expiration of their terms, judges of the abolished county courts became
judges of new branches of the Circuit Court system.[3]

By the end of the 1970s, therefore, Milwaukee County possessed a
single court of record, the multibranch court of the Second Judicial Circuit.
The County had been part of the second circuit since 1848, and it had
comprised the entire circuit since 1882. Hence, in 1980 the County was in
the same judicial position as it had been in 1848. The judicial situation had
come full circle. Instead of one court and one judge, however, the new
system encompassed one court, thirty-three branches, thirty-seven judges,
and areas of responsibility never envisioned by the constitution makers in
1848.

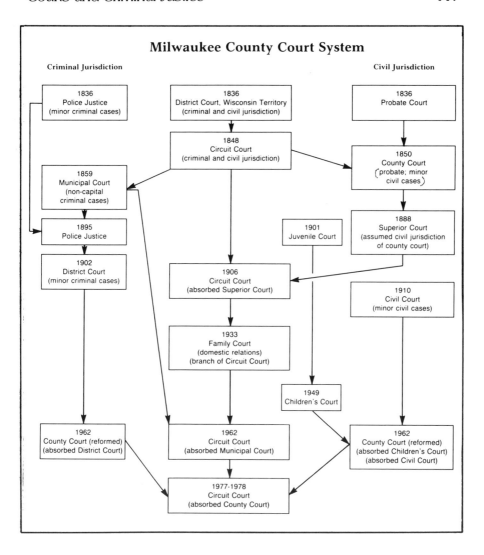

Milwaukee County Court System

Criminal Jurisdiction   Civil Jurisdiction

1836 Police Justice (minor criminal cases)	**1836** District Court, Wisconsin Territory (criminal and civil jurisdiction)	**1836** Probate Court

1848
Circuit Court
(criminal and civil jurisdiction)

1850
County Court
(probate; minor
civil cases)

1859
Municipal Court
(non-capital
criminal cases)

1895
Police Justice

1901
Juvenile Court

1888
Superior Court
(assumed civil jurisdiction
of county court)

1902
District Court
(minor criminal cases)

1906
Circuit Court
(absorbed Superior Court)

1910
Civil Court
(minor civil cases)

1933
Family Court
(domestic relations)
(branch of Circuit Court)

1949
Children's Court

1962
County Court (reformed)
(absorbed District Court)

1962
Circuit Court
(absorbed Municipal Court)

1962
County Court (reformed)
(absorbed Children's Court)
(absorbed Civil Court)

1977-1978
Circuit Court
(absorbed County Court)

The Court System, 1836-1977

In the 130-year interim between the creation of the second circuit and the absorption of all courts of record into that circuit there lay a long and tangled juridical history. In that interim the creation of courts and the reallocation of their responsibilities occurred with regularity, and peculiar areas of overlapping jurisdiction occasionally characterized their operation. While proposals for reform or reorganization were frequent enough, the court system grew increasingly complex and cumbersome. In 1931, for example, the *Milwaukee Sentinel* editorially commended Governor Philip La Follette for his veto of a bill providing an additional judge for the

County's Municipal Court, the court which then exercised the criminal jurisdiction in the County. Noting that the County already had the services of nineteen judges in six distinct courts, differentiated in responsibilities, caseloads, and compensation, the *Sentinel* argued that the County's residents would be better served by a single court with unlimited original jurisdiction and nineteen branches.[4] Nearly a half-century elapsed before the state legislature acted favorably upon this and related recommendations.

Between 1848 and the reform of 1977 judicial institutions proliferated in the County. Earlier, in Wisconsin's territorial period (1836-1848), a District Court, one of three in Wisconsin Territory, exercised authority in the County. The state constitution mandated the creation of a circuit court, police courts (justices of the peace), and a probate court. Subsequently the state legislature blessed the County with a County Court, a Municipal Court, a Superior Court, a District Court, a Civil Court, a Juvenile Court, and finally, as a part of the circuit, a Family Court. It also provided for the appointment of subordinate magistrates called court commissioners.[5] In the lexicon of American jurisprudence, all the County lacked was an appeals court, a chancery court, and a court of errors.

The first judicial agencies in the area of the County were products of Wisconsin's territorial experience. Initially, the County formed a part of the western circuit of Michigan Territory, and, after 1836, one of three district courts of Wisconsin Territory held occasional sessions in the County. In the Michigan phase the court operated from Green Bay or Prairie du Chien, and local petitioners of necessity journeyed to these settlements in their search for legal redress. Moreover, territorial courts were Federal institutions, constituent parts of the Federal district court system and the higher Federal tribunals, the circuit courts, and the Supreme Court. Their judicial personnel consisted of presidential appointees, most of whom were political operatives with claims on presidential favor who had exhausted their usefulness "back east."[6]

All accounts agree that the first session of the District Court of Wisconsin Territory held in the little village of Milwaukee was an unmitigated disaster. William C. Frazer, a Pennsylvanian appointed by Andrew Jackson to serve as judge, arrived in June 1837, to organize the court. He promptly secured quarters at an inn in the village, sought out a high-stakes poker game, and lost heavily. Proceeding to his court, he opened its first session by delivering an oration on the evils of gambling to the astonished petitioners and attorneys in attendance. After an unproductive session of two weeks' duration he departed for his home state. He turned up in Milwaukee a second time in October 1838, arriving by ship from Green Bay in an inebriated state and dying shortly after the vessel landed.[7]

The activities of the other territorial judicial officials in Milwaukee, the police judge and the probate judge, seemed mundane in contrast to Frazer's performance. For example, the first criminal case tried in the County by the justice of the peace, Daniel Wells, Jr., concluded with a verdict of guilty. Wells fined the defendant five dollars, retaining half of the sum as his fee. He remitted the remaining half to the County Treasurer.[8]

While Judge Frazer surely left a negative personal impression in Milwaukee, apparently he did pay due regard to legal proprieties in his conduct of the court. His successor, Andrew G. Miller, a Pennsylvanian appointed by Martin Van Buren, enjoyed both judicial success and public acclaim during a long tenure in the County. He was the last of the territorial judges, and when Wisconsin achieved statehood in 1848, Miller remained in Milwaukee and served until 1873 as judge of the United States District Court for Wisconsin. This court, which eventually exercised authority only in the eastern half of the state, merely continued the Federal jurisdiction begun in the territorial period.[9]

The District Court of Frazer and Miller concerned itself primarily with civil matters between 1837 and 1848. Essentially, the sources of litigation which required the attention of the tribunal were those associated with land claims and bankruptcy. The Pre-Emption Act of 1841,

Andrew G. Miller created a positive image for the early court system as territorial judge from 1839 until Wisconsin attained statehood in 1848. Miller then served as judge of the U.S. District Court for Wisconsin until 1873.

which generally validated the claims of settlers who "squatted" on the public domain prior to survey and administrative control by the Federal land offices, led to a plethora of disputes between rival claimants to parcels of land. Moreover, in the 1840s the nation witnessed its second experiment with a uniform national bankruptcy law for individuals. Most of the bankruptcy petitions adjudicated in Judge Miller's court resulted from the financial misadventures of settlers before their arrival in the territory. Between 1839 and 1848 Miller decided more than 8,000 cases in the land claims and bankruptcy categories alone.[10]

When Wisconsin achieved statehood in 1848, a dramatic change occurred in its judicial situation. The Federal jurisdiction exercised by Judge Miller's District Court paled in significance as the new state created its own judicial institutions and embraced the idea of an elected judiciary. Under the terms of its constitution the legislature of the new state established a Supreme Court, police courts, probate courts, and, most importantly, circuit courts. The police and probate courts were, in essence, extensions of those created in the territorial period, and the original Supreme Court consisted of the circuit judges sitting *en banc*. Hence the most important judicial by-product of statehood was the formation of a circuit court system. Milwaukee County became a part of the Second Judicial Circuit, one of five circuits created by the first state legislature. Originally the circuit encompassed a five-county area, but with the periodic establishment of new circuits to serve a rapidly growing population the legislature of 1881 decided that, effective in 1882, Milwaukee County alone was to comprise the second circuit.[11]

The Circuit Court in Milwaukee County assumed unlimited original jurisdiction over all civil and criminal matters, but the constitution also permitted the legislature, at its discretion, to allocate the authority of the Circuit Court to inferior courts or to fashion new judicial agencies with jurisdiction concurrent with the circuit. In practice, the legislature frequently employed both of these options, but the Circuit Court retained appellate jurisdiction over all subsequently created inferior courts. Within a decade after statehood the Circuit Court lost much of its authority and became primarily a court of civil procedure. It retained jurisdiction over major suits at law and equity, exclusive control over divorce proceedings, and ultimate responsibility for the issuance of the major writs, especially the writ of *habeas corpus*. But the Circuit Court exercised no control over probate or minor crime, for the legislature vested jurisdiction in these areas in a probate court and in justices of the peace.[12]

In spite of mushrooming population growth, the Circuit Court functioned until 1900 with the services of a single judge. The legislature authorized a second branch in that year and added third and fourth branches in 1903 and 1906. These latter branches, however, represented

Officials of the municipal and police courts in 1897. Standing, left to right: John W. Wollen, deputy clerk; Charles W. Lane, municipal court reporter; Charles Reichenbach, assistant clerk; Frank J. Grutza, deputy clerk; A. O. Wilmot, police court reporter; C. A. Groeling, assistant clerk. Seated, left to right: Thomas V. Dally, deputy clerk; Emil Wallber, municipal judge; Neele B. Neelen, police justice; Frank E. Woller, clerk.

the transference to the circuit of two judges of the disbanded Superior Court. Additional branches, all designated as civil divisions of the court, became operative in 1908, 1910, 1926 (2), 1934, and 1954. By 1954 ten judges presided over the affairs of the Circuit Court, all of them concerned with cases originating in the realm of civil procedure.[13]

Six men served as circuit judges between 1848 and 1900. Some were notable and some were nondescript. By origin and legal training, they included three New Yorkers, a Pennsylvanian, a Scotsman, and a Canadian. The first to sit on the circuit bench, Levi Hubbell of New York, endured and survived the only impeachment trial in the history of Wisconsin judiciary. Another, Scottish-born Arthur McArthur (later MacArthur), eventually secured a Federal judgeship but was perhaps most notable, historically, for the lineage he created — a son, Arthur and a grandson, Douglas. Yet another, the New Yorker Charles A. Hamilton, was the grandson of Alexander Hamilton. New Yorkers dominated the Circuit Court, and it was not surprising that all courts subsequently established in the County followed a decision of the Circuit Court in 1856 to adopt "New York rules" of pleading and procedure in civil actions.[14]

In addition, the 1849 session of the state legislature, after reconsidering the probate court structure which carried over from the territorial period, decided to assign probate responsibilities to a new institution, the County Court. This court, which functioned in Milwaukee County from 1850 to 1978, had a distinctly cyclical history. Expansion, contraction, and revision of its prerogatives occurred with frequency. Originally designed to provide a mechanism for the probating of wills and the disposition of estates and for managing the property of persons who died intestate, the County Court acquired, and lost, a number of ancillary functions in its history.

Aside from its probate duties, the original County Court functioned as an inferior civil court, adjudicating claims for debts and damages in amounts of less than five hundred dollars. It also operated as the court of appeal from decisions of the police courts. Unlike the judges of the Circuit Court, who served six-year terms and received salaries from the state, judges of the County Court held office for four years and subsisted upon fees for their services. Conflicts of interest arose from this situation, for judges of the County Court supplemented their incomes by practicing law in the Circuit Court. Since the Circuit Court was the court of appeals from decisions of the inferior courts in the County, a County Court judge might serve as attorney of record in a case in which he had rendered the original judgment which provoked the appeal.

Nevertheless, in the 1850s the legislature increased the legal domain of the County Court. In 1856 Wisconsin abolished the traditional rule that law and equity pleading occur in separate courts and, following New York rules, allowed equitable defenses in cases at law. This compelled the legislature to confer limited equity jurisdiction upon the County Court, and it later increased the maximum value of claims adjudicated by the court to five million dollars. From 1871 to 1888 the civil jurisdiction of the County and Circuit courts paralleled each other. But the legislature in 1887 summarily stripped the County Court of all civil functions and reduced it to its original status as a probate court. A newly established institution, the Superior Court of Milwaukee County, assumed its civil responsibilities.[15]

From 1888 to 1962 the judges of the County Court devoted their attention to probate matters. Nevertheless, the court remained an influential institution. It supervised the administration of wills, trusts, and estates, eventually collected the state inheritance tax, and managed the property of minors, orphans, and incompetent persons. The legislature also delegated social service functions to the court. It granted marriage licenses, administered adoption proceedings, and ruled on questions as diverse as the commitment of persons to mental hospitals and petitions to recall elected public officials. After 1905 it controlled the County's general assistance program, officially known as "outdoor relief" and eventually given the shorthand title of "welfare." By the 1930s an authority on the work of the court estimated that every piece of real property in the County passed through its jurisdiction at least once each generation.[16]

In 1888 the civil jurisdiction of the County Court devolved upon a new judicial agency, the Superior Court of Milwaukee County. This court existed briefly, but it was the first judicial institution in the County to be equipped with two judges and the requisite two branches. But the legislature abolished the first branch in 1903 and the second in 1906. The title "superior" misstated its importance, for the court possessed limited jurisdiction at law and none at equity. It functioned primarily as a conduit between the County Court, whose civil responsibilities it assumed, and the Circuit Court, which absorbed its caseload and its judges. Typically, three of the five judges who sat on the superior bench in the abbreviated history of the court were New York-born and trained.[17]

The abolition of the Superior Court proved untimely. By 1909 the burden of minor civil litigation forced the legislature to provide the County with another low-level tribunal, the Civil Court of Milwaukee County, a juridical agency unique in the legal history of Wisconsin. The Civil Court commenced its work in 1910 and existed, with a constantly expanding caseload, for fifty-two years. It functioned as the successor to the County and Superior Courts, but it also absorbed the civil powers of the vestigial justices of the peace.

The Civil Court operated as a catchall institution. The legislation creating the court required the division of the County into districts, with a chief judge to supervise the calendar and perform routine administrative tasks for other judges, eventually six in number, who serviced the districts. Hence the court became the largest employer of judicial personnel in the County until a similar proliferation of judges occurred in the Circuit Court. Organizationally, it was reminiscent of the justice of the peace system. Although the Civil Court operated as a court of record, ultimate authority over its activities resided in the Circuit Court, which filed the transcripts of its proceedings and promulgated its decisions.[18]

From 1910 until 1962 the Civil Court was the most utilized noncriminal court in the County. Its judges processed thousands of cases each year and received for their efforts comparatively substandard compensation. Most of the work of the court involved mundane or petty issues, and the procedures employed by its judges were decidedly informal. The

Circuit Judge Robert M. Curley presided as television cameras captured trial events in April, 1978. The State Supreme Court had approved the media coverage on an experimental basis that month.

court adjudicated paternity and illegitimacy suits, cases incident to minor torts, breaches of contract, eviction actions, garnishments, replevins, the collection of debts, petty libel and slander, and civil actions resulting from cases of assault and battery. In 1947 it assumed control of trust accounts established pursuant to illegitimacy proceedings. The court in 1957 disposed of 44,803 cases, more than 31,000 of them by dismissal. But the court also confirmed 12,326 default judgments and held 855 trials, only twenty-nine of which required the services of juries.[19]

Throughout the history of Milwaukee County the necessities of civil jurisprudence dominated the court system. Since all human communities contain deviant elements, however, the requirements of criminal justice became a matter of concern in the early days of the County. At first the concern was not serious, but the County's good fortune quickly came to an end. Criminal jurisdiction in the territorial period resided in the District Court, while in the first years after statehood the Circuit Court adjudicated the serious criminal cases. In both periods, however, resolution of minor criminal complaints often occurred in the so-called police courts, administered by part-time, non-professional officials know as justices of the peace. These minor magistrates, who became elected officials in the first years after statehood, subsisted largely on a system of fines and fees for service. Although the police court apparatus existed in Wisconsin until 1966, in Milwaukee County the criminal jurisdiction of the justice of the peace ended by 1910. In any event, the "jp's" normally served as village, town, or city officials rather than as county officers.[20]

The police court system quickly proved inadequate to serve the needs of a growing community. In 1859 the state legislature obligingly established the Municipal Court of Milwaukee County as a formal criminal court. This institution, which functioned until 1962, was the first of twenty such courts provided by the legislature for Wisconsin counties. The justices of the peace retained jurisdiction only over ordinance violations and a few misdemeanors, and the new Municipal Court assumed appellate authority over their decisions. Moreover, the jurisdiction of the Municipal Court was concurrent with that of the Circuit Court, with appeals from its decisions handled by the state Supreme Court. Hence the court enjoyed an independent existence in the County.

On the other hand, the legislature imposed some limitations on the authority of the Municipal Court. Jurisdiction over capital cases, cases in which defendants judged guilty faced sentences of life imprisonment or death, remained the prerogative of the Circuit Court and comprised the whole of that court's jurisdiction in the realm of criminal justice.

Among the courts which the legislature provided for the County, the Municipal Court had the most confused and injudicious beginning. The legislation establishing the institution became effective in March 1859, and in April of that year the County's voters elected a New Yorker, Erastus Foote, as judge. Foote immediately commenced the hearing of criminal cases and pronounced a number of guilty verdicts. Official "publication" of the Municipal Court Act occurred on June 29, 1859. Earlier in 1859, the Supreme Court, in deciding an unrelated question, decreed that laws affected with a "general public interest" became effective only on the date of publication. This decision cast doubt on the validity of Foote's decisions before the date of publication of the law, and it cast further doubt on the legality of the judge's election. Foote's adversaries, including a former law partner he had defeated for the judgeship and a number of attorneys for defendants he had sentenced before the publication of the law, quickly grasped the meaning of the decision and the opportunities it afforded them. If the court had no legal existence before June 29, 1859, its decisions were superfluous; and if the judge had been illegally elected, the possibility of ouster clearly existed. In fact, the Supreme Court invalidated Foote's election in March 1860 and ousted him from his position. While the high court validated his post-June 29 decisions, it also invalidated those rendered in the April-June 29 interim. A number of persons who had been judged guilty of crimes in that interim escaped the clutches of the law, and Foote gave way to a fellow New Yorker and ex-District Attorney, James A. Mallory, who served as municipal judge until 1890.

Aside from its inauspicious origins, the Municipal Court also utilized extraordinary procedures during much of its history. In spite of a caseload which grew more than proportionally with the population of the County,

James A. Mallory, twice elected District Attorney in the 1850s, served as Municipal Court Judge for nearly thirty years beginning in 1860.

the court operated for more than a century with the services of a single magistrate. That the institution performed its duties with such sparse resources resulted from a conscious policy. Its respective judges eschewed jury trials, preferring instead a summary brand of justice. The court disposed of criminal matters as inconsequential as ordinance violations and as serious as non-capital felonies. This obliged the respective judges to conduct the affairs of the court in a bifurcated manner. Judges reserved the morning hours for preliminary hearings and assemblyline resolution of ordinance violations and conducted a trial court with formal procedures in afternoon sessions. As criminal cases proliferated in the final years of the nineteenth century, the state legislature granted the municipal judge a modicum of relief. In 1895 it reestablished the office of police justice to adjudicate criminal cases and elevated the Municipal Court to the status of an appellate court for decisions of the police justice.[21]

The reconstituted office of police justice existed briefly. In 1899 the legislature authorized the creation of another subordinate criminal court, the District Court of Milwaukee County. This institution, which commenced the hearing of cases in 1902, represented an upgrading of the police justice, and the last police justice became the first judge of the

District Court. The District Court and its non-criminal companion, the Civil Court, comprised the lowest level of the County judiciary, the juridical agencies which ordinary citizens were most likely to encounter in their lives. This was particularly true of the District Court when the automobile became a pervasive element in community life. Since the District court assumed responsibility for the statutes and ordinances pertinent to the use of motor vehicles, a generation of errant Milwaukeeans came to know the institution as "traffic court." In fact, the District Court possessed considerably broader jurisdiction.

A weekly radio program broadcast directly from Judge George E. Page's traffic court in 1937 promoted safety. John Olson is seated at the microphone; clerk Charles Weiss is administering the oath to the arresting officer.

It was clearly the intent of the legislature to confer upon the District Court the authority to try all of the ordinance and misdemeanor cases in the County, including ordinances of the City of Milwaukee. Its prerogatives also extended to all violations of state statutes in which the appropriate penalties did not exceed fines of $1,000 or imprisonment for one year. Both the County and the City shared responsibility for the maintenance of the court and the salaries of its incumbent judges. The

District Court functioned as a subordinate branch of the Municipal Court, which heard appeals from its decisions and also returned or confirmed its decisions. Until 1950, when the legislature finally approved a second branch for the court, a single judge not only disposed of all of the traffic cases in the County but also adjudicated the actionable instances of theft, petty larceny, "bad checks," and the misdemeanors associated with alcoholic overindulgence.[22]

Alcohol-related misdemeanors, especially the categories of drunk and disorderly conduct and common drunkenness, added a special dreariness to the work of the court. However unintentionally, public policy occasionally afforded the judges a measure of relief. In June 1920, shortly after the effective date of national prohibition, Judge George Page of the District Court reported that the dry experiment had produced a more tolerable distribution of offenders brought before the court. He noted that arrests for drunkenness had not diminished, but the inebriates who once overwhelmed the resources of the court on Monday mornings, the result of overindulgence on weekends, had dwindled in number. Since the sale and distribution of alcoholic beverages now violated both Federal and state laws, committed drinkers pursued their avocation, and endured arrest, at any time in the week they managed to secure the appropriate potables.[23] (A Federal prohibition agent observed that Wisconsinites seemed oblivious to the prohibitory laws and that Milwaukee County led the state in non-compliance.)[24]

In the course of time the District Court acquired jurisdiction over matters other than ordinance violations and misdemeanors. Among its subsequent duties were the disposition of persons judged mentally incompetent and the supervision of sexual deviates. By the 1950s the two judges of the court struggled with a calendar which sometimes exceeded 250,000 cases a year. Most of its cases concluded summarily with pleas of guilty, and the court rarely presided over a jury trial. Not unsurprisingly, the District Court generated more revenue than all of the other judicial institutions in the County.[25]

Ancillary to the traditional areas of civil and criminal jurisprudence, the state legislature also equipped the County with two specialized courts, both of which operated at the juncture of law and social service. The first of these, the Juvenile Court (renamed the Children's Court in 1949), made its debut in 1901. It was an agency peculiar to Milwaukee County, and since its inception the judges who served this court have accentuated its role as a social service institution. Until 1949 judges elected to other courts fulfilled the duties of juvenile judge on a part-time basis. To be appointed to the juvenile bench was, in the estimation of some of its incumbents, a form of temporary judicial exile.

The Juvenile Court of Milwaukee County constituted one example of a nationwide movement to provide distinctive institutions for problem children and to segregate them from adults in both legal and penal environments. At a more profound level it was a reflection of a growing scientific interest in childhood as a developmental stage in the life cycle, an interest which emanated largely from the influence of such new fields as psychology and social work. To the reformers of the early twentieth century, characteristically depicted as "progressives," the cause of child welfare occupied a prominent part of their agenda for social change. Their efforts bore fruit in such innovations as the juvenile court, the reformatory, the detention home, the concept of probation, and the first tentative programs of financial aid to dependent children, originally known in Wisconsin as "mother's pensions."[26]

Surprisingly, the juvenile court movement began in Chicago. In 1899 the Illinois legislature authorized the creation of a special facility in the Circuit Court of Cook County to exercise jurisdiction over children under the age of sixteen. The Chicago experiment was the culmination of the efforts of leaders in the settlement house movement, especially Julia Lathrop of Hull House, who had ingratiated herself with both the state legislature and the bar association. But the Illinois law provided only that a designated judge conduct juvenile proceedings outside of a courtroom environment and supervise the work of an unpaid, volunteer probation officer. Unfortunately, Milwaukee County and many other urban counties adopted the same minimalist attitude during the formative years of the juvenile movement.[27]

Another source of the juvenile court idea emanated from Denver, especially in the person of that city's flamboyant "kids' judge," Benjamin Barr Lindsey. Lindsey's approach involved the manipulation of such existing laws as truancy statutes to gain jurisdiction over minors.[28] The Chicago and Denver practices both influenced Wisconsin legislators, and the lawmakers in the 1901 session sanctioned the creation of a juridical agency in Milwaukee County with supervisory authority over three categories of juveniles — the delinquent, the dependent, and the neglected. The categories quickly became sacrosanct and have existed unchanged since 1901.[29]

The Wisconsin statute, like its Illinois precursor, limited the jurisdiction of the new court to delinquent, dependent, and neglected children under the age of sixteen and carefully defined each of the pertinent categories. Dependent and neglected children consisted of those considered destitute, homeless, abandoned, publicly supported, deprived of parental care, reduced to beggary, domiciled in houses of ill repute or with vicious persons, or victims of parental depravity. In an ancillary category the legislation placed children under the age of eight found peddling, playing musical instruments on the streets, or offering public entertainment without a license. None of these categories, of course, involved wrongdoing. Yet the statute also defined all violators of state law or local ordinances as delinquent, regardless of the gravity of the alleged offenses.

A circa 1906 photograph of those who served the newly created Juvenile Court. Seated, left to right: Edward Van Vechten, assistant district attorney; Neele B. Neelen, Juvenile Court Judge; William F. Zuerner, chief probation officer. Standing, left to right: first two unidentified; Samuel Minturn, probation officer; Alfred O. Wilmot, court reporter; Louise Tillson, probation officer; Rev. Karl Eisfeldt, volunteer; Clara Smith and Marion Ogden, probation officers; Bruno Schlert, acting court clerk; and Clement Malek, probation officer.

In the early days of the Juvenile Court the County's judges ordinarily selected the judge of District Court to serve as juvenile judge, apparently reasoning that the kinds of offenses commonly committed by juveniles were those which fell within the authority of that court. After 1933, however, the circuit bench always provided the juvenile magistrate. Throughout the court's history, moreover, the trial of juvenile offenders for crimes which carried the possibility of incarceration was the province of the Circuit Court. The juvenile facility did not exist as a court of record and obviously possessed no authority to conduct criminal proceedings.

    Since the Juvenile Court functioned partly as a welfare agency, its sessions were customarily informal. They first occurred in a designated room in city hall rather than the courthouse, but after the construction of a detention center in 1909 that facility domiciled both the juvenile judge and his administrative subordinate, the probation officer. The latter official first served on a voluntary, uncompensated basis, but the County upgraded the position to professional status in 1906. In addition, the state legislature in 1913 enacted a "mother's pensions" law, and the operation of this financial assistance program became the responsibility of the juvenile judge. By the end of the 1920s the duties of the court had expanded to the point that the County found it necessary to create both a Juvenile Court Department and an ancillary agency, the office of Director of Pensions.[30]

Unfortunately, the effectiveness and the efficiency of the Juvenile Court were often in doubt. Dependent and neglected children far outnumbered the delinquent, but they seemed to slip through the interstices in the system. The first published report of the court, detailing its activities for the 1907-1908 fiscal year, revealed that the judge had contact with only 170 children in the dependent and neglected categories while administering some form of discipline to 726 delinquents. Even with the broad definition of delinquency permitted by law, it is difficult to believe that delinquents constituted such a significant proportion of problem children. Nevertheless, the most frequent juvenile crimes were burglary, larceny, assault, truancy, and, among girls, "immorality." Other minors found themselves before the court for such heinous offenses as "shooting firecrackers" or violations of the bathing or spitting ordinances. Most of the cases concluded with dismissal or probation, and only twenty-nine juveniles received sentences to the various semipenal institutions in the state.[31]

A decade later the situation remained unchanged, although the number of children who appeared before the court exceeded 2,000. The delinquents again outnumbered the dependent and neglected by a wide margin, and this pattern persisted in all subsequent reports. It appears that the court served the needs of few of the guiltless and unfortunate children in the County and that it concentrated its efforts on the alleged wrongdoers. Then, having brought the errant youths before the bar of justice, the judge offered probation to the guilty in most cases. While the Juvenile Court represented itself as a social service agency, it really dispensed a brand of justice reminiscent of the schoolmarm.[32]

For good reasons the procedures of the Juvenile Court underwent a lengthy evolution in the 1920s. Recommendations for a rationalization of its procedures emerged from the evaluative process, and after sustained pressure by the Wisconsin Conference on Social Work the state legislature in 1929 enacted Chapter 48 of the state's statutes, the "Children's Code." The code writers reaffirmed the three traditional areas of juvenile concern, repealed a few obsolete laws pertinent to minors, extended the court's authority over delinquent juveniles to the age of twenty-one, and, in a controversial section, granted jurisdiction to the court over adults who contributed to the dependency, neglect, or delinquency of children.[33]

Expansion of the legislative base of the court's authority was not the only objective of reformers of juvenile services in the 1920s. These reformers, principally social workers and interested members of social service organizations, also initiated a movement to provide the Juvenile Court with a full-time judge, a specialist in the legal affairs of youth who might fulfill his duties independently of the County judiciary. Critics of the court contended that the present procedure, the assignment of the judge to perform juvenile duties for two years, devoting only two days a week to the expanding responsibilities of the office, denigrated the importance of the position. It also violated the standards for juvenile institutions devised by the National Children's Bureau and the National Probation Association. Both of these organizations envisaged an aggressive role for juvenile courts, proposing to extend their authority to adoption procedures, paternity suits, disposition of the mentally incompetent, and even the disciplining of adults who failed to make support payments mandated in divorce decrees.[34]

In Milwaukee County, however, most of the proposed revisions in the court's powers and procedures stemmed from a study of juvenile agencies in 1925 sponsored by the State Board of Control and conducted by Francis H. Hiller, field secretary of the National Probation Association. The Children's Code of 1929 embodied some of the recommendations of the Hiller Report, but Hiller's argument in favor of an independent, full-time juvenile judge proved unavailing. Hiller's recommendation languished for nearly twenty-five years, but the County's experience with neglect and delinquency during World War II, the era of "eight-hour orphans" and "latch-key children," provoked the Board of Supervisors in 1948 to unearth the old report and reassess its content. The Board, finally convinced of the need for a full-time judge, found the idea acceptable to the county judiciary and prevailed upon assemblymen from the County to introduce appropriate legislation in the 1949 session of the state legislature. The bill cleared the legislature with little opposition, and the County soon possessed the authority to create a Children's Court, provide for the election of a judge, and appropriate the funds necessary to support the new agency.[35]

The replacement of the Juvenile Court by the Children's Court was the only important change in juvenile institutions to occur since 1901. Similarly, in the area of legislatively defined responsibility for juvenile welfare there was little progress for nearly fifty years after the enactment of the Children's Code in 1929. The 1977 session of the legislature, however, accomplished a fundamental revision of juvenile procedures and substantively amended the 1929 code. Implementation of the 1977 reforms required the Board of Supervisors to create a central office with supervisory authority over all children within the jurisdiction of the court, directed the Chief Judge of the County to formulate written policy governing intake procedures and the subsequent handling of juveniles, and obliged the Board of Social Services for the County to devise regulations for all of the nondisciplinary operations of the Children's Court.

These amendments to the Children's Code finally clarified the lines of authority in juvenile matters. They also represented a confirmation of the view that the primary function of the court was to assist the unfortunate rather than to discipline the errant. In addition, the legislation dictated the establishment of procedures for holding children in protective custody and clarified the rules for appeals from the decisions of the court, for adoption proceedings, and for the termination of parental rights. The court also acquired authority over the operation of foster homes and day care centers. In essence, with the implementation of the regulations enacted in 1977, the Children's Court became a social service agency in which its role as disciplinary agent assumed secondary importance.[36]

The most significant contribution to juridical processes to emerge from the County's experimentation with juvenile justice was a product of the old Juvenile Court. This court pioneered the technique of probation in Wisconsin, and probation quickly became the normative method for the disposition of adult offenders as well as juveniles. Probation, of course, is a simple concept. It involves the discretionary use of judicial authority on a case-by-case basis and allows judges to offer continued freedom on a supervised basis to guilty offenders as an alternative to confinement in penal institutions. The technique originated in the 1840s in Massachusetts, a state which for much of the nineteenth century led the nation in penal reform and experimentation.[37] Its use did not become widespread in the United States until the early twentieth century when "progressive" reformers embraced it as a one of many of their causes. But probation did afford judges a flexible and convenient mechanism to individualize the sentencing process and to alleviate the overcrowding of prisons. Only six probation programs existed in American states in 1900, while in the year 1915 thirty-three states either established probation systems or modified existing ones.[38]

Underlying the concept of probation was the belief that in criminal proceedings the judges should try offenders and not their offenses. Probation accentuated the uniqueness of the individual in the sentencing procedure. Max Raskin, who served on the circuit bench in Milwaukee County from 1963 to 1973, once explained that the effectiveness of a sentence involved "varying degrees of uncertainty concerning its ability to produce an improved behavior."[39] Since uncertainty characterized the process, liberal jurists like Raskin believed that, on balance, institutional confinement should normally be minimized. Probation neatly fulfilled this objective.

Judges of the Juvenile Court routinely probated the majority of juvenile offenders from the inception of the court. The probation department associated with the court grew from a single staff member in 1901 to an organization which, by the 1950s, employed four administrators and twenty-eight staff officers to supervise the 6,000 minors under its stewardship.[40] By the 1930s probation had also become the customary method of sentencing adults convicted in the Municipal Court.[41] It possessed great appeal as a technique, despite evidence which soon accumulated to cast doubt on its effectiveness.

Unfortunately, the use of probation for both juvenile and adult offenders proceeded from unproven and possibly unprovable assumptions about human behavior. The day-to-day administration of the probation system was the province of frequently undertrained and always overburdened officers. Violations of the terms of probation occurred routinely, and both the presentence and postsentence investigations of probated individuals seemed to be haphazard. Officials rarely observed probated persons in their home environments. In spite of these defects in the system, the technique retained its popularity for easily comprehended reasons. It was less expensive than imprisonment, and County government bore its costs, making it popular with legislators struggling to control state budgets. District Attorneys used the promise of probation to secure guilty pleas, often by reducing the charges, and thereby improved their conviction rates. Hence probation became ingrained in that peculiarly American phenomenon, the plea-bargain system. And judges learned quickly that probation afforded them more authority over guilty offenders than its alternative, the suspended sentence.[42]

The second of the special courts established in Milwaukee County and one whose operation frequently involved interaction with the Children's Court was the Family Court. This institution, technically known as the "family court division," was an integral part of the Circuit Court and never enjoyed an independent existence. Established in 1933 by the legislature as part of a revision of marriage and divorce legislation which became known as the "Family Code," the agency was, like the Civil, District, and Juvenile Courts, peculiar to Milwaukee County. The special provision for the County in the 1933 legislation specified only that one (or more) judges of the Circuit Court exercise jurisdiction over the processes of "domestic conciliation." While the essential concern of the Family Court was divorce litigation, its authority also extended to a variety of other marriage-related problems, investigations of the circumstances of problem families, reconciliation efforts, and child custody proceedings. Subsequent to the 1933 law the Family Court and the Juvenile Court, both of whose judges came from the circuit bench after that year, became known officially as "family court branches." In addition, the law mandated the creation of the office of Divorce Counsel, the predecessor of the contemporary Family Court Commissioners. It was the intention of the legislation that the Divorce Counsel represent the interests of the state in every divorce action, a role unenthusiastically fulfilled before 1933 by a representative of the District Attorney's office.[43]

Circuit Judge William R. Moser in the new seventh floor courthouse chambers which opened September, 1968 as part of a $1.5 million family court complex. From left: Bernice Schuckit, clerk; Stan Mocarski, court reporter; and David Hoffman, bailiff.

Fortunately, the Family Court appeared on the juridical scene at a propitious time. It was able to develop its procedures in the stable familial environment of the depressed 1930s. But the following decade constituted the first truly disastrous period for the institution of marriage in American history. An abnormally large number of marriages occurred in the early years of World War II, and the aftermath of the conflict witnessed a wholesale reconsideration of the wisdom of these alliances. For a number of years following the war divorce became a national pastime. The Family Court awarded 833 divorce judgments in 1940; in 1946 it awarded 1,969, an increase of 230%.[44] By the end of the 1940s the incidence of divorce declined, but within a decade the rate of marital dissolution began a dramatic rise which continued until the end of the 1970s.

Concern with the prevalence of divorce and the social dislocation which it produced prompted the state legislature in 1959 to revise the divorce provisions of the Family Code. The revision placed significant new burdens on the Family Court. After 1959 the law required that the pretrial segment of divorce proceedings be divided into two constituents, the summons and the complaint, separated in time by at least sixty days. Moreover, the new law provided for two sixty-day "cooling off" periods prior to the trial date and prescribed that a judicially controlled reconciliation effort occur in each case. Not only did divorce become more prevalent after 1959, it also became significantly more complicated.[45]

As a result of this added complexity, the legislature in 1965 authorized an auxiliary judge to serve both the Family and Children's courts. In 1966 the County redeveloped an entire floor in the courthouse into a "family court complex." The new facility housed courtrooms, hearing rooms for the Family Court Commissioners (the post-1960 title of the office of Divorce Counsel), and quarters for the domestic conciliation staff.[46] By the end of the 1970s the discord associated with contemporary marriage and family relationships in Milwaukee County absorbed the attention of nine judges, six commissioners, and a department of domestic conciliation. Since the human constituency served by these officials almost uniformly comprised persons undergoing abnormal stress, it was not surprising that the Family Court became a frequently criticized branch of the judiciary.[47]

Judges and courts, however, never constituted the entirety of the County's judicial services. The circuit court statute also provided for the appointment of officials known as court commissioners. In creating this

Municipal Judge Max W. Nohl (right) and jurors investigated a site involved in a sensational 1941 murder trial. Alice Dornblasser was convicted of bludgeoning her landlady, Carrie Seymer, to death during an argument over interior decorating.

judicial office, Wisconsin's legislators borrowed from a practice common to the Federal judiciary, but in Federal parlance the title pertinent to the office was "magistrate." Court commissioners functioned essentially as sub-judges, thereby relieving the jurists of preliminary, administrative, routine, and off-the-bench duties.

Court commissioners in Milwaukee County never existed as a singular body. Historically, they have been of three types — commissioners appointed by and attached to individual judges, permanent commissioners unattached to any judge, and commissioners of the Family Court. They have functioned predominantly, but not entirely, as adjuncts to the Circuit Court. Until recent years, most of the court commissioners were attorneys or retired judges selected by sitting judges of the Circuit Court and empowered to perform specific judicial functions for established fees. They served at the pleasure of the judges who appointed them. In 1959, for example, the legislature authorized each judge of the Circuit Court to appoint two commissioners and permit them to take depositions, administer oaths, certify acknowledgements, issue subpoenas, injunctions, and writs, fix bail, punish contempt, and create a record of proceedings. As an exclusive prerogative of the second circuit, its commissioners also possessed the power to foreclose mortgages and to execute the state mechanic's lien law. For a period circuit judges regularly used commissioners, but in recent years the practice has fallen into disuse.[48]

On the other hand, the County has also been served by two kinds of permanent commissioners. The first of these consisted of individuals who possessed the same prerogatives as judicially appointed commissioners but who worked for salaries. The second, and currently the most important constituent in the system, are the commissioners of the Family Court, the successors to the office of Divorce Counsel. Since 1960 the number of these functionaries has grown from one to eleven. These officials primarily make determinations regarding support and child custody in the pre-trial phase of divorce actions. Recently, however, the commissioners have acquired additional domestic relations responsibilities, especially in such sensitive areas as paternity questions and allegations of family abuse.[49]

Since the inception of a court system in Milwaukee County, moreover, another judicial office has been of fundamental importance. This is the office of Clerk of Court, known contemporaneously as the Clerk of Court and Director of Court Services. The original state constitution mandated the establishment of the clerk's office as an elective position, following a precedent which is virtually uniform in the United States. Functionally, the statutes which amplify the constitution, the ordinances of the County, and the rules of the Board of Judges determine the operations of the Clerk's office.

The duties of the Clerk of Court have changed little since statehood, but they have increased greatly in importance and complexity. As a judicial official, the role of the Clerk is administrative and clerical, and most of the obligations of the position have been historically constant. They include the maintenance of the court's records, judgment and order books, the preparation of the calendar and the docketing of cases, and the collection and disbursement of alimony payments, child support, and other funds held for the benefits of minors in cases of family dissolution. Appointment of some of the court's personnel, especially bailiffs, permanent court commissioners, and jurors, has also been a prerogative of the Clerk.[50]

The duties performed by the Clerk and his subordinates have been

Implementing a new policy to speed up Circuit Court cases, calendar clerk Edward J. Mitten (center) introduced a blackboard system in 1933. Mabel Bastian posted 71 mortgage foreclosures and 320 receivership cases to judges by number.

indispensable to the operation of the courts. In 1968, for example, the Clerk assembled 673 juries and apportioned the cases heard in that year among 101 judges, the majority of whom served the County's courts on a temporary or interim basis.[51] While the Clerk of the Circuit Court has been the most prominent court administrator since the organization of the

County, the lesser courts have had the services of similar officials. The Municipal and District courts shared an elected clerk, and the County Court employed a clerk known as the Register in Probate. Occasionally, clerks performed unusual supplementary duties. For a period in the 1920s and 1930s the Clerk of the Municipal and District courts served as neighborhood "peacemaker" in Milwaukee, a kind of ombudsman responsibility which required soothing the feelings of complainants in neighborhood disputes while the police simultaneously dealt with the offending persons.[52]

By the 1950s the judicial system in Milwaukee County had grown to formidable size and complexity. Citizens, public officials, and many attorneys routinely criticized the courts and their related institutions as unwieldy and inefficient. Excluding the justices of the peace, the state legislature since 1848 had established eight distinct courts for the County and terminated the existence of only one, the old Superior Court. Court reform became a serious public issue in the 1950s, and in 1959 the legislature finally responded by enacting a law which substantively revised the organization of the judicial system in the state and formed the basis for the "final" reform of 1977. The 1959 legislation represented the acceptance of the proposals of the state's Judicial Council, the advisory body on court administration in Wisconsin, which spent most of the decade reviewing the performance of the courts in the state.[53]

Implementation of the 1959 law commenced in January 1962. In Milwaukee County the impact of the legislation was of great consequence, for the law abolished all of the statutory courts created for the County since 1859, i.e., the Municipal, District, Civil, Children's, and Family courts. It also repealed all of the special acts which conferred powers on the County Court. To fill the resulting judicial void, the law established a dual system composed of the Circuit Court, with expanded authority, and a revitalized County Court. In effect, the two surviving institutions absorbed the jurisdiction and the judicial personnel of the abolished courts. The Circuit Court absorbed the Municipal Court, and the judges of that court filled two new criminal branches of the circuit. For the County Court, long accustomed to probate responsibilities and the provision of a few essentially non-judicial services, the 1959 law had more significant implications. That court acquired the jurisdiction and the judges of the six-branch Civil Court, the two branches and judges of the District Court, soon renamed "misdemeanor and traffic branches," and the Children's Court. In effect, the transference of juvenile responsibilities from the circuit to the county divided the jurisdiction of the so-called "family court branches," for the divorce and domestic relations prerogatives of the Family Court remained, as always, with the circuit.[54]

By January 1962, therefore, a simplified, dual-level court system existed in Milwaukee County. The duality was more apparent than real, for the two courts overlapped considerably in the civil realm and the judges of the "misdemeanor and traffic branches" of the County Court often performed "intake" services for the judges of the criminal branches of the Circuit Court. In addition, the legislation also permitted the Chief Justice of the Supreme Court to transfer judges on a temporary basis between circuit and county duties. The new system established by the 1959 law also contained a number of anomalies and quirks. Only circuit judges, for example, might preside in cases involving treason against the state of Wisconsin.[55] And the reorganized court system itself soon came under criticism. Dissatisfaction with the performance of the dual-level system led directly to the 1977 reform and the implementation of a single-level trial court apparatus for all of Wisconsin's counties.

In a fundamental sense the courts of Milwaukee County have been the peculiar province of the judges who administered them and supervised the performance of subordinate judicial officers, the commissioners, bailiffs, and reporters. Thus it is important to inquire into the origins of the County's elected judiciary. Obviously, all of the early judges were transplanted persons, men who migrated to Wisconsin for diverse reasons. The predominance of men born and trained in the law in the state of New York was the most obvious characteristic of the early judiciary. Unlike most of the upper middle west, Yorkers rather than Yankees shaped the juridical traditions of the County. Men of local birth who secured their legal training in Wisconsin did not supplant the migrants until the early years of the twentieth century.

Secondly, until 1920 the ethnic origins of the County's judges reveal that old-stock Americans of English or Scottish lineage clearly dominated the judicial offices. Since 1920 the ethnic backgrounds of the judges reflect greater diversity, although men with Anglo-Saxon surnames continued to represent a disproportionate influence among the growing body of jurists. Judges with Irish surnames, in relation to the Irish-American component of the County's population, have clearly overrepresented that group on the bench, but the German and Polish stock has been distinctly underrepresented. Jews and blacks have also been underrepresented, while individuals from smaller ethnic groups have only occasionally won election to the bench.[56] The ethnic composition of the judiciary, of course, reflects the composition of the law schools and the bar.

Origins and ethnic backgrounds aside, another characteristic has figured prominently in the process of judicial selection. In their prejudicial careers in the law, a clear majority of the individuals who won election to the bench had worked, often exclusively, on the public, prosecutorial side of the law rather than in private practices. This has been particularly true of the post-1945 period, the years in which judicial offices in the County proliferated. The future judges had labored either in the District Attorney's office or on the staff of the City Attorney of Milwaukee. In the 1940s and early 1950s the latter office acquired a reputation as the "cradle of judges."[57]

More importantly, since its creation Milwaukee County and its residents have been a microcosm of a larger society and its values. That society quickly developed a schizophrenic attitude toward the judiciary. Judges seem to evoke both fear and reverence, and Americans have constructed a judicial ethos which critics have depicted as the "cult of the robe." An aura of solemnity and remoteness surrounds American judicial institutions, but judges as individuals can be as injudicious and flawed as other persons. They exist on pedestals erected by society, and that society expects them to adhere to a code of personal and professional conduct more rigorous than that which governs any other professional group.[58]

How well the judges of Milwaukee County have measured up to this severe standard and how well they have collectively acquitted themselves professionally in comparison to the judges of other populous counties cannot be known. In any event, it was not until 1968 that the Supreme Court found it necessary to devise a "code of judicial conduct" for the judges of the statutory courts of the state. The code, technically Chapter 60 of the *Supreme Court Rules,* promulgated elaborate standards for appropriate judicial behavior.

In the courtroom, the code dictated that judges conduct proceedings with dignity, reserve, decorum, propriety, fairness, gravity, and courtesy to litigants, attorneys, and witnesses. At all costs, judges were to eschew flamboyant or attention-provoking tactics. To govern the general behavior of the jurists, the code proscribed "gross personal misconduct."[59] Ideally, it appears that the perfect judge would prudently blend the personalities of Gary Cooper and Mr. Chips. But Wisconsin judges have been elected officials since 1848; and despite passionate assertions to the contrary, the judicial office is an extension of political values and partisanship. Criticism of a political nature routinely surrounds the judiciary, and individual judges make political enemies.[60] What is the effect on the judiciary when one of its members falters, departs from the expected standards, and publicly displays his personal or professional frailty?

Fortunately, it appears that the citizens individualize the indiscretions of errant jurists and refrain from inappropriate generalizations about judicial misconduct. The "cult of the robe" survives unblemished. Since the organization of Milwaukee County in 1835, some 170 individuals, including five women, and excluding police justices and the early probate judges, have served in judicial offices. Most performed their duties without raising the eyebrows of the citizenry, and this may well have reflected community satisfaction with their efforts. The exceptions, of course, have been notable.

It is virtually axiomatic that an errant judge achieves instant notoriety. Instances of judicial misconduct have been few in the history of the County, and most of them resulted from personal rather than professional behavior. William C. Frazer, the territorial judge who conducted the first session of court in the village of Milwaukee, left an unfortunate legacy, but it was the result of indiscreet behavior rather than judicial ineptitude. Levi Hubbell, a New York native who served as the first judge of the Circuit Court (1848-1856) and as a member of the original Supreme Court, endured the only impeachment proceeding ever brought to trial against an incumbent judge in the history of the Wisconsin judiciary. The trial and subsequent acquittal of Hubbell in 1853 pitted all of the luminaries of the early Wisconsin bar in dramatic conflict, but Hubbell's deficiencies were essentially political in nature. Factional warfare in the Democratic party of Wisconsin, a party experiencing rapid disintegration in the decade preceding the Civil War, generated the eleven counts and seventy-two specifications of "high crimes and misdemeanors" preferred against the jurist. Apparently Hubbell was an unusually abrasive personage, but his difficulties stemmed from his allegiance to the wrong faction in his party. His prosecutors, or, as his supporters contended, his persecutors, were the Democrats of a rival faction. The quality of his jurisprudence was, if anything, a minor consideration in the impeachment proceedings.[61]

In the recent past, residents of Milwaukee County absorbed the unsavory details surrounding the death of Judge John A. Krueger. A judge of one of the "misdemeanor and traffic" branches of the County Court, Krueger committed suicide in his chambers on August 28, 1968. The investigation which followed the judge's demise produced some salacious revelations about his personal affairs and, more importantly, led eventually to the temporary suspension of the licenses of two prominent attorneys whose purported "harassment" of the judge possibly hastened his fateful decision.[62] However temporarily, the Krueger incident cast an ugly shadow over both bench and bar.

The most celebrated and protracted case of alleged judicial misconduct in the County centered on Judge Christ T. Seraphim of the Circuit Court and unfolded over a seventeen-month period in 1979 and 1980. A member of the judiciary since 1961, Seraphim's occasional courtroom theatrics and well-publicized off-the-bench remarks on criminal justice won him a loyal following in some quarters and provoked hearty disdain in others. The judge's difficulties began in earnest in February 1979, with the publication in the local press of the first of a long series of allegations of personal and professional misconduct. The allegations, involving indiscretions of a financial, judicial, and amorous nature, were unique in the history of the

Wisconsin judiciary. A movement to unseat the judge gathered momentum, but Seraphim responded by adamantly denying the growing list of charges against him. Ultimately, after investigation by the state's Judicial Council and a formal hearing before a three-judge panel drawn from the new Court of Appeals, the Supreme Court found the evidence against the judge sufficiently persuasive to pronounce a three-year suspension from official duties. Seraphim, clearly a man of unusual resilience, departed from office on July 7,1980, and returned, with aplomb, precisely three years later to resume his duties.[63]

The District Attorney

Fortunately, the judiciary of the County has been able to function with few blemishes on its character. But judicial services have never been solely the province of the judges and their subordinates. Other important institutions play a role in the judicial process before and after the determinations made by judges in chambers and courtrooms. One of the most fundamental of these judicially-related offices has been that of the District Attorney. Known in some states as county prosecutor or county attorney, the office has long existed in virtually all counties in the United States. It is also a peculiarly American office, owing little if anything to its English equivalent, the King's (or Queen's) Counsel. In Wisconsin, the District Attorney, like the Circuit Court and the Clerk of Courts, was an office established in conformity to the provisions of the original constitution. The essential duties of the District Attorney have changed little since statehood.

The District Attorney performs as the County's lawyer, as its representative in all legal actions to which the County is a party, as the legal advisor to all departments and officers of County government, and as attorney for the state in actions resulting from violations of state law which occur within the County. Since statehood the District Attorney's primary duties have been twofold — to investigate criminal acts and to prosecute the perpetrators of those acts. Hence the duties of the office relate primarily to criminal rather than to civil law. In addition, as an elected, salaried public official, the District Attorney has been forbidden to represent individual municipalities, common carriers, public utilities, or any private interests.

While the investigative power of the District Attorney has been virtually without limit since statehood, certain restraints have characterized the prosecutorial authority of the office. District Attorneys rarely participated in cases tried in the District Court or the police courts. In practice they appeared primarily in the Circuit Court or the Municipal

Court. Other responsibilities, however, have added important dimensions
to the office. The District Attorney served as legal advisor to the County
Board of Supervisors, as initiator of John Doe investigations, and as
attorney for the County in cases appealed to the Supreme Court. Until
1933, when the office of Divorce Counsel commenced operations, the
District Attorney also represented the interests of the state at every
divorce trial in the County.[64]

*District Attorney Francis E. McGovern (seated at right) gained recognition as a crusading
county prosecutor during the tumultuous years between 1905 and 1909. This led him to the
governor's mansion in 1910 for two terms.*

Since its inception the office of District Attorney has had a high public
profile. It has ordinarily attracted ambitious young attorneys who have
used it as a springboard to more prestigious office — judgeships, the
Congress, or the governorship. Thus, until recent years, there has been a
regular turnover of incumbents in the position. In the sixty years following
statehood, 1848-1908, twenty-three men held the office in the County,
none of them for more than six years. James A. Mallory, the second District
Attorney, subsequently became judge of the Municipal Court, while Francis McGovern, the last incumbent in this period, proceeded directly to the
governor's mansion.[65]

Although the District Attorney exercises both criminal and civil powers, the former has always been the dominant concern of the office. In the early years of the County the incidence of crime was not serious and occupants of the office found that the County placed little value on their services. Their compensation consisted of a small salary plus a supplemental stipend for each case which they prosecuted. Apparently the District Attorneys themselves determined the amount of their additional compensation. In 1855 James A. Mallory won a conviction in a homicide case and presented the County Treasurer with a voucher for $500. The County Board deliberated the matter at its next meeting and concluded that Mallory's fee was excessive. Learning that Mallory had already secured payment from the treasurer, the Board summarily reduced his salary by $400.[66] Within a generation circumstances apparently changed, and the Board secured for the District Attorneys salaries commensurate with the responsibilities of the office. In 1885 the Board authorized a salary of $1,300 and in 1887 dramatically raised it to $4,000 per year.[67]

The obligation of the District Attorneys before 1933 to participate in divorce cases also provoked occasional concern. This duty was unpleasant and probably irrelevant to the office, and after 1885 assistant district attorneys (ADA's) normally performed it. In 1929, for example, District Attorney George D. Bowman dismissed the assistant in charge of domestic relations and appointed in his stead a recent law school graduate, the daughter of a prominent Green Bay attorney. A number of ADA's resigned in protest, and various women's organizations in Milwaukee launched an attack on Bowman, alleging that he had demonstrated insensitivity to the domestic relations responsibility of his office. Bowman adamantly defended his decision and invited the new appointee to explain her credentials. In a formal press conference the young woman admitted that she did not possess "a lot of experience in life to fall back on" but that she regarded the opportunity to prepare briefs as "enthralling."[68]

More importantly, the responsibility of the District Attorney's office to investigate and prosecute criminal activity has increased disproportionately to the growth of population in the County. The crime problem, apparent even in the 1920s, became a major concern of the office in the years following World War II. Contending with the local contributors to the national crime wave required an ever-expanding staff. The first ADA appeared on the scene in 1885. By 1945 the number had grown to sixteen. It reached twenty in 1967 and fifty-five by 1975. Given the increasing burdens and marginal rewards of ADA positions, turnover became a serious problem, and during the crime-conscious 1970s resignations of ADA's often exceeded the availability of new appointees.[69]

By the 1970s the office of District Attorney had grown into a complex and cumbersome operation consisting of three "sections." A pre-charging

Present District Attorney E. Michael McCann, elected in 1965, during a 1980 news conference on a victim witness bill of rights. From left: Jo Beaudry, Victim Witness coordinator; County Supervisor Dorothy K. Dean; McCann; and then State Representative Barbara Ulichny.

section exercised authority over investigations, the processing of complaints, cases of non-support referred by the Family Court, and instances of consumer and welfare fraud. A post-charging section prepared evidence for felony and misdemeanor trials, advised witnesses, provided a liaison to the general citizenry, and handled sensitive crimes. An administrative section assembled and preserved the raw data of the criminal justice system. In 1974 the District Attorney and his assistants prosecuted a daily average of 355 cases before sixteen judges.[70]

The District Attorney's office in 1976 underwent an elaborate management study of the kind often employed by troubled private corporations. Investigators reached mixed conclusions about the operation of the office, but they did declare that it needed to be "incrementally improved." Among defects which the investigators identified were inefficiency, an "assembly line" approach to cases, inadequate case preparation, discontinuity in strategy, and breakdown in the process of document location. However tacitly, the conclusion of the management study contained the admission that the prevalence of crime had overwhelmed the resources of the office.

A number of pertinent recommendations resulted from the management study. Recognizing that the burdens of the office would continue to outstrip its resources, the authors of the final report suggested the minimization of complaint screening in routine cases and the retention of the complicated screening process only in cases of serious crime. Since traffic-related misdemeanors alone had increased by fifty percent between 1968 and 1975, this recommendation was a concession to the inevitable. The authors strongly advised the addition of staff, especially in the new and growing field of paralegal support personnel.[71]

Even before the final report of the management study engaged the attention of the District Attorney, the department itself had begun to modify its procedures. In the process the historic role of the District Attorney as trial lawyer for the County underwent substantive revision. Commencing in 1974, the office implemented a program known as "diversion," a program which represented a major departure from past policy. Diversion, in essence, was a technique which offered a second chance to first offenders and substituted the velvet glove of the social worker for the mailed fist of the law. Two boroughs of New York City, Brooklyn and Manhattan, had pioneered the diversion concept in the area of juvenile crime, but it was clearly the inundation of the District Attorney's office by criminal complaints which prompted the adoption of the policy for adult offenders in Milwaukee County.[72]

In essence, diversion was a form of probation which avoided the sentencing procedure. First-time offenders in certain categories of misdemeanors underwent evaluation by a unit of the Sheriff's department and, if approved, avoided court action in favor of supervision by social workers on the Sheriff's staff. If a defendant failed to abide by the subsequent terms of the diversionary agreement, policy required the remanding of the defendant's case to the District Attorney's office. Diversion reduced the demands on the District Attorney, the courts, and, potentially, the penal institutions of the state. The diversion program applied to two categories of eligible defendants — the "regular" and the "worthless check" offenders. It excluded all defendants whose alleged crimes involved the use of weapons. Most of the diverted individuals were those whose arrests stemmed from neighborhood disputes, alcohol abuse, minor theft, and property damage cases in which defendants promised restitution in lieu of the prospect of court action. The new program both expanded the discretionary authority of the District Attorney's office and reduced its workload.[73]

The Sheriff's Department

The diversion program utilized the services of the Sheriff's department, and the Sheriff was another official who performed judicial services for the County. Like the District Attorney and the judges of the respective courts in Milwaukee County, the Sheriff was an elected official who derived his legal prerogatives from the state constitution. Unlike the District Attorney, however, the origins of the sheriff lie buried in the history of medieval England. The office is one of the stablest, most self-perpetuating institutions in the English-speaking world. It probably originated in the tenth century, but the official title of sheriff, or *shirereeve*, first appeared a century later.

Originally, the sheriff was an appointee of the monarch, charged to perform the duties of *reeve* (representative) of the crown in an English county. The authority of the *shirereeve* emanated directly from the crown, but the judicial authority attached to the office proceeded indirectly from the king through the office of Ealdorman (earl), the only county official who outranked the sheriff. Among the prerogatives of the early English sheriffs was the power to command the county militia, to raise and lead the assembly of able-bodied men in the county called the *posse comitatus*, to organize and maintain order in the county courts, to collect the revenues from the courts and the royal lands, and to safeguard the prisoners of the crown by keeping a secure jail.[74] Thus the responsibilities of the early English sheriffs were fourfold — law enforcement, revenue collection, court service, and jail administration. Despite the passage of time and the incomplete transplantation of English institutions to America, three of these historic responsibilities have persisted and still characterize the sheriff's office in the contemporary United States.

While the sheriff's office in America retained much of its English character, the relative importance of its specific duties underwent periodic revision in consequence of peculiarly American conditions. The military duties virtually disappeared, court-related responsibilities grew in importance, the tax collection obligations continued in many counties to the end of the nineteenth century, and the law enforcement aspects of the office became dependent upon a number of circumstances, especially settlement patterns and the impact of urbanization.[75] Historically, American sheriffs exercised their law enforcement powers primarily in rural or sparsely settled counties. The role of the sheriff as jail-keeper remained unchanged.

Undoubtedly the most important change in the office in America, however, resulted from the democratizing influences of the early nineteenth century. American sheriffs became elected officials, normally limited by state laws to abbreviated tenures. Limited tenure imparted a distinct character to the office. Moreover, as many parts of the United States became urbanized in the latter years of the nineteenth century, the establishment of urban police departments and state law enforcement agencies diminished the peacekeeping functions of the sheriff's office and revitalized the sheriff's role as officer of the county courts. Throughout the

Sheriff William R. Knell (seated second from left) and the department staff in 1907.
Personnel wore business suits; uniforms were first issued after World War II to motorcycle
patrol officers.

nineteenth century, however, the sheriffs of most counties enjoyed important administrative and fiscal perquisites. They were, in effect, businessmen performing public duties with public funds for private gain. As law enforcement officers they were amateurs at best. Limited by law in most states to one or two terms in office, they found the circumstances under which they labored conducive to the pursuit of self-interest. They appointed the undersheriffs and deputies and possessed thereby substantial patronage power. The elaborate system of fees, travel allowances, and per diem payments made the office attractive and often lucrative to the incumbent. In each county the sheriff served the "process," the legal papers generated by the courts, and received in return stipulated fees and mileage payments. As keepers of the jail the sheriffs customarily employed wives or relatives as jailers and cooks and billed the county for meals served to prisoners and jurors, including many who apparently never existed. An astute individual could obviously profit handsomely from a term or two as sheriff.[76]

Early sheriffs of Milwaukee County apparently emulated national "standards" — or lack thereof. Benoni Finch, the first occupant of the position, held office for less than a year and exercised authority in an area which eventually encompassed eleven counties. He kept a jail in two buildings attached to the original courthouse, a frame dwelling acquired by the County from two of Milwaukee's founding fathers, Solomon Juneau and Morgan L. Martin. How well Finch and his successor territorial sheriffs performed their duties seems to be a mystery. Their tours of duty were characteristically brief.[77]

Once Wisconsin achieved statehood, the Sheriff became a biennially elected official. Between 1848 and 1910 thirty men served as Sheriff, only one of them for two terms. They came to the office from a variety of occupations, including the dry goods business, the liquor trade, and even the Milwaukee police department. In terms of performance they ran the gamut from dedicated to opportunistic and from competent to inept. Few of them possessed previous experience in law enforcement. Before the early twentieth century most incumbents conducted the affairs of the Department loosely, and, in some cases, scandalously. A sheriff in the 1870s approved a deputy's claim for per diem service which indicated 378 days of employment in a nine-month period.[78] In the 1880s the Department became embroiled in a serious scandal when evidence surfaced that incumbent sheriffs routinely dismissed their deputies during the summer court recess with full pay, secured supplemental appropriations from the County Board to expedite the collection of property taxes, and rehired the deputies as special tax collectors. Undoubtedly the grateful deputies surreptitiously refreshed the personal finances of their superiors as part of the process.[79]

The first woman Deputy Sheriff, Hattie J. Baranowski, appointed by Sheriff Patrick McManus on August 6, 1921. Her career spanned thirty-three years and fourteen sheriffs.

The ethical climate in the Department improved markedly after 1900. By 1918 all of the sworn personnel except the Sheriff and the Undersheriff worked under civil service rules, and sheriffs no longer possessed the prerogative of dispensing patronage. A sustained effort to professionalize the Sheriff's Department occurred in the 1920s. For the first time deputies acquired the accoutrements associated with law enforcement personnel — uniforms and a departmental patch. (The city of Milwaukee uniformed its police force in 1874.[80]) And in 1933 Sheriff Joseph Shinners, a hard-boiled former Milwaukee police captain, abolished the last vestige of the patronage system, the office of Undersheriff.[81]

Moreover, as the County became increasingly urbanized in the twentieth century, newly incorporated suburban communities established police departments, thereby eliminating much of the area in which the Sheriff's Department performed police services. This prompted the reassignment of deputies to court service or to the jail. Although the land area of the County had been entirely incorporated by the early 1950s, the Sheriff continued to provide police protection to a few municipalities. Franklin, the last municipality to rely on the department for such services, established its own police force in 1965, and one of the historic duties of the sheriff in Milwaukee County thereby became superfluous.[82]

Largely because of its curtailed role as a law enforcement agency, it appeared that in the early 1950s the Sheriff's Department was in line for retrenchment in manpower and responsibilities. In order to demonstrate the need for this contraction, the Civil Service Commission in 1954 undertook the first systematic analysis of the Department in the history of the County. In that year the office of Sheriff consisted of the Sheriff, an Inspector (added in 1951), 167 deputies and thirty-eight clerical and service personnel. The administrative survey conducted by the Civil Service Commission concluded with a recommendation to eliminate at least fifteen percent of the department's positions.[83]

The recommendations of the administrative survey proved to be ill-considered. Within a generation the manpower at the disposal of the Sheriff had increased threefold. In 1983 the Department employed 576 personnel, including technical, clerical, and service workers. At least three reasons explain this unanticipated growth. The proliferation of judges and court branches required a proportional increase in the need for deputies to serve process or to staff the courts as bailiffs. Secondly, the dramatic growth in motor vehicle violations, plus the growth in criminal activity, forced the Department to expand its supervision of the County roads and the new freeway system and, at the same time, to transform itself into a sophisticated police agency. Thirdly, the crime problem also resulted in a doubling of the daily jail population between 1955 and 1980. In 1955, for example, the Sheriff's office booked 8,056 prisoners into the jail and served 97,538 legal papers. The comparable figures for 1981 were 20,309 and 115,596.[84]

Moreover, in 1954 the Department consisted of six divisions — headquarters, investigation, patrol, process and courts, administration, and jail. All of these divisions remained twenty-five years later, but the department had acquired a number of new obligations. Participation in the "diversion" program required the employment of social workers. The Sheriff also operated a detective bureau and participated, along with other governmental agencies, in the collection of child support, the investigation of welfare fraud, the protection of witnesses, and the enforcement of drug legislation. In 1973 the Department assumed responsibility for the security of Mitchell Field and Milwaukee County Stadium. It operated a crime laboratory and the only professional explosives dismantling unit, or "bomb squad," in southeastern Wisconsin. And it operated a bakery and a kitchen, supplying baked goods to all the County institutions and meals to the prisoners in the jail and jurors in the courthouse.[85] Early sheriffs in the County could never have envisaged such a multifaceted institution.

While many of the duties acquired by the Sheriff's Department since the 1950s resulted from the increasing incidence of crime, one of these crime-related obligations has remained constant throughout time. Sheriffs have always "kept" the county jail. Milwaukee County has operated a number of jail facilities since its creation. The first, dating from 1835, was an adjunct to the first courthouse. Completion of a new courthouse in the early 1870s required the construction of a new facility. Ultimately, the new jail appeared at Broadway and East Wells, but its completion did not materialize until 1885 and its "grand opening" ceremony occurred in May 1887. The last facility, located in the Safety Building, received its first prisoners in 1930.[86]

As an institution, the jail has fulfilled a limited purpose. Although it has often been used to accommodate convicted misdemeanants serving short sentences, the basic purpose of the jail has been to quarantine individuals accused of criminal acts whose cases have not been adjudicated or those, already convicted and sentenced, who awaited transfer to longer-term penal institutions. Since the function of the jail has been temporary in nature, the comfort of individual prisoners has seemingly been of minor concern to its administrators.

Jail-keeping in the early years of the County was not ordinarily an onerous burden. For example, in mid-winter 1872 the Sheriff reported that the facility housed a single prisoner.[87] Apparently its population increased substantially by the 1880s, for in 1888 the jailer found it necessary to initiate a procedure which became a jail tradition, the annual fumigation.[88] Appropriate hygienic standards proved impossible to maintain, and in 1890 the state Board of Charities declared the facility to be "in a deplorable condition, filthy, swarming with vermin, without bathing facilities, with foul bedding, and with disgusting and disease-breeding privies right in the jail."[89]

Most prisoners in the jail, of course, have sojourned there only briefly. On the other hand, it was once a common practice among inebriates deliberately to arrange arrest in the winter months in order to guarantee shelter from the elements. The daily population of the jail grew considerably in the course of time. From a handful in the 1880s it increased to an average of 370 by the 1980s.[90] Overcrowding of the facility became a significant problem by the 1950s. In 1968, officials of the John Howard Association, an organization with an eminent reputation in the analysis of jail and prison conditions, prepared an elaborate and stinging report on the facility. According to the authors of the report, the County had no alternative but to construct a new jail.[91] County officials temporized and, rather than implement this costly proposal, acquired the old city jail to secure additional space and eventually transferred the work-release prisoners from the jail's "Huber dorm" to the House of Correction.[92] These policy changes alleviated, but hardly resolved, the overcrowding problem.

Completed in 1885, the massive stone County Jail was located at the intersection of present Broadway and Wells Streets.

House of Correction

In addition to the jail, Milwaukee County has long operated another penal institution, an institution designed for longer-term, sentenced inmates. Known originally as the House of Refuge, this facility, in effect a county prison, has been called the House of Correction since 1865. The two crucial words in the title of the institution, "refuge" and "correction," represent a blending of two distinct penological concepts. Houses of "refuge" originated in England and first appeared in the 1820s in the United States. Their purpose was to provide a home for delinquent, wayward, and impoverished children, and, as such, they offered an alternative to jails and almshouses. Houses of "correction," on the other hand, initially appeared in the Netherlands and have existed in America since 1665.[93] They were facilities for adult offenders to serve short or intermediate sentences. In the history of Milwaukee County's House of Correction the maximum sentences of its inmates have varied from one to five years, with the former period clearly the norm. Over the 120-year life of the institution, however, the average sentence has been less than one month.[94]

While the administration of the jail has been the province of the Sheriff since the founding of the County, the operation of the House of Correction has been directly under the control of the Board of Supervisors of the County. The state legislature first considered a bill to provide the County with a house of "refuge" in 1853 and authorized its creation two years later. Delays in site selection and construction and the intrusion of local politicians into the project prevented the facility from materializing before 1865.[95] Early in 1866 the original House of Correction complex, the first of three in the history of the County, received a complement of inmates from the jail, and by 1880 the normal inmate population approximated 200. The original institution operated in a restricted space on Windlake Avenue, the site of the contemporary South Side Stadium.[96]

Both the legislature and the Supervisors intended the House of Correction to be economically self-sufficient. Since, in the 1860s, there were no restrictions on the distribution of prison-made goods in the normal channels of commerce, the Supervisors decided in 1868 to establish a factory on the prison site.[97] The inmates were to occupy themselves with the manufacture of chairs, both straight-backed and rocking chairs. It was a decision of dubious wisdom, but from 1868 to 1940 the inmates turned out thousands of chairs for sale in private markets and later for use in public institutions. Chairmaking required skill, and after the introduction of power tools it also posed the threat of serious injury to the inmates. Long-term prisoners performed most efficiently in the factory, but they were the smallest component of the prison population. If the average sentence served by inmates was approximately one month, the modal sentence was five days. That five-day prisoners could acquire proficiency in many of the pertinent duties seems unlikely. These considerations and the realization that most of the inmates were not criminals but alcoholics cast doubt on the prudence of the Supervisors' fateful decision in 1868.

After thirteen years of operation, moreover, the House of Correction became embroiled in a serious scandal. In October 1879 the *Milwaukee Sentinel* shocked the community with an article entitled "The Milwaukee Hell," an article which provoked the state Board of Charities to initiate an investigation of the policies and administration of the House of Correction. The investigation soon focused on the performance of the Inspector of the Institution and his immediate predecessor, the officials appointed by the Supervisors to manage the affairs of the prison. As the investigation proceeded, the city's leading newspaper provided its readers with titillating revelations of the inner life of the institution. According to the *Sentinel,* "unusual and atrocious barbarities" routinely occurred at the House of Correction. In a particularly unjustifiable instance of administrative misbehavior, the paper reported that the previous Inspector had doused a "half-witted convict" with cold water and forced the unfortunate inmate to work outside for an entire day in frigid weather.[98]

The scandal contained some embarrassing complications, for the past Inspector accused of inhumane practices happened to be the current Chief of Police in Milwaukee. When the mayor refused to suspend him from office pending the outcome of the investigation, the *Sentinel* branded the mayor as "narrow minded" and "illiterate."[99] Moreover, the District Attorney, neglecting his duties as a public official, offered to serve as counsel for the former Inspector.[100] There was reason to believe that officials in high places, both City and County, had coalesced to protect their own. In December 1879 the Board of Charities and Reforms submitted a blistering report on the operation of the House of Correction to the Board of Supervisors. Consistent with their self-interest, the Supervisors deadlocked on acceptance of the report, effectively killing its reform proposals and its recommendation for disciplinary action against the past and present administrators.[101]

Chairs and scandal were not the only products of the House of Correction. In their "zebra" uniforms, adopted in the 1870s, some inmates also served on rock-splitting details, providing the County with the raw material for road construction.[103] Service in the so-called "geological department" was a commonplace phenomenon, especially for individuals incarcerated for vagrancy. Nevertheless, by the end of the nineteenth century, it was clear that the facility on Windlake Avenue was no longer adequate to fulfill its purposes. Daily populations often exceeded 400, and officials processed more than 2,500 inmates a year. Relocation of the institution became a matter of imminent concern.

The Board of Supervisors won legislative authority to relocate the

House of Correction in 1903, but serious planning did not begin for another four years. Political complications soon developed, and the decision-making process atrophied until 1913 when a committee of prominent citizens delivered a report on the existing House of Correction so devastating in its revelations that plans for a new facility quickly jelled.[103] Consequently, the Supervisors decided to remove the facility to a 400-acre site in the Town of Granville and to recreate it, at least in part, as a prison farm. This site, immediately north of contemporary McGovern Park, currently serves as quarters for a reserve unit of the United States Army. Completed in 1917, the second House of Correction offered a markedly improved penal environment. Farm-related labor gradually displaced chairmaking as the primary occupation of the inmates. The House of Correction existed on the Granville site until 1945, when, in the aftermath of World War II, the Army acquired the property and converted it for use as a disciplinary barracks.

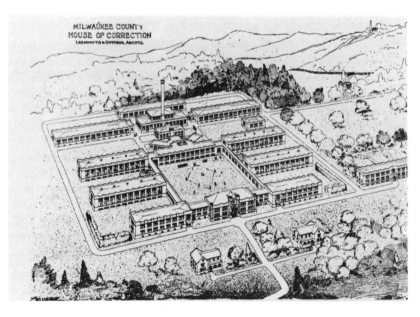

An architectural rendering, by the Milwaukee firm of Leenhouts & Guthrie, of the House of Correction facility completed in the Town of Granville in 1917.

Acquisition of the House of Correction by the Army forced the Supervisors to construct a third House of Correction. In 1946 they chose a 650-acre site in the Town of Franklin and authorized the erection of a dormitory, farm buildings, and an administrative complex. These facilities became fully operative in 1953, and subsequent additions to the original physical plant eventually put the County in possession of a modern, medium-security, self-sufficient prison farm. Inmates practiced diversified agricultural tasks, but the prison also housed a machine shop, a hospital, a chapel, a laundry, a tailor shop, a shoe-repair shop, and a barber shop.[104]

In its 120-year history the House of Correction's role as a prison has in reality been secondary in importance. Until the past decade the majority of its inmates have not been individuals convicted of felony or misdemeanor offenses. Instead, the typical inmate has been an alcoholic. Of 5,572 persons sentenced to the institution in 1951, for example, alcohol-related offenses accounted for fully eighty percent of the commitments.[105] Such infractions of the law as drunk and disorderly conduct, intoxicated use of motor vehicles, and the elastic category of "common drunkenness" generated the basic constituency of the House of Correction. It was not until the 1950s, however, that the institution engaged the services of counselors and social workers to deal with the root cause of the problem which plagued the majority of the inmates.[106]

Nevertheless, after World War II the inmate population began to display disturbing new characteristics. The House of Correction in 1948 processed 4,925 commitments. A profile of the inmates revealed that the "typical" prisoner was white, aged forty to forty-nine, and serving a modal sentence of five days. In fact, 120 of the 1948 prisoners had been sentenced to the institution at least fifty times.[107] Four years later the Superintendent complained that inmates used the facility "to get over one jag and in condition for the next one," a state of affairs which he described as "detrimental to the individual and a costly proposition to society."[108] By 1961, however, the normative inmate was an individual in the age group twenty to twenty-nine, alcohol-related offenses accounted for less than thirty percent of the commitments, and nearly a third of the inmates were black or Hispanic in racial origin.[109]

While alcohol abuse populated the House of Correction for most of its history, the inmates represented virtually every occupational and age category of the adult population. The largest number of prisoners came from the ranks of common laborers, restaurant workers, and the building trades, but the data indicate that no physician, dentist, university professor, or judge ever served time in the institution. Accountants, attorneys, architects, and teachers were not so fortunate. A significant change in the institutional population, however, occurred immediately after the state legislature decriminalized the offense known as "common drunkenness," effective in August 1974. Subsequent to that date the inmates came to represent a normal prison population, consisting of lesser felons, misdemeanants, and, after 1979, the work-release prisoners transferred from the jail.[110]

Conclusions

The problems which have confronted the judiciary and ancillary institutions in the County since World War II have been typical of American society as a whole. Easily the most compelling of these problems has been the extraordinary increase in serious crime. The days in which one or two branches of a criminal court sufficed to administer criminal justice in the County belong to a simpler, more innocent past. In 1975, for example, the District Attorney noted that 48,787 crimes had been reported in 1974 and that his office had prosecuted 35,573 persons in that year. Seventy percent of these criminal acts were ordinance and/or motor vehicle violations, but thirty percent, or more than 10,000 offenses, consisted of felonies or misdemeanors punishable by imprisonment. Most disconcerting of all was the revelation that crimes of violence exceeded 3,000 in number for the first time.[111]

Criminal activity on such a significant scale clearly taxed the resources of all judicially-related agencies and necessitated positive, innovative responses. Prosecutable cases inundated the District Attorney's office, and cases scheduled for trial clogged the court calendars. Witnesses and jurors often wandered aimlessly in the courthouse after futile searches for the location of appropriate proceedings. In order to mitigate this deteriorating situation, the District Attorney initiated in 1974 the "diversion" program for selected categories of first offense misdemeanants. But the most ambitious effort to ease the pressure on the justice system was an experimental program in the mid-1970s called Project Turnaround.

In the 1960s a central concern of American jurisprudence, especially at the rarified level of the Supreme Court of the United States, was the definition and expansion of the rights of accused persons. The 1970s witnessed a legal and juridical reaction to this liberalization phenomenon, and one of the byproducts of the reaction was an emphasis on the rights of victims and other innocent participants in the criminal justice process. It was to the needs of these individuals that the creators of Project Turnaround directed their attention. Underlying the project was the conviction that witnesses and jurors experienced "intolerable inconveniences" under the prevailing circumstances and that "victims of crime have been in turn victimized by the system."[112] The project originated in the District Attorney's office and operated with a grant from the Law Enforcement Assistance Administration (LEAA), an agency of the United States Department of Justice. It employed a staff which eventually exceeded fifty and functioned under the guidance of an executive committee composed of representatives of the judiciary, the Clerk of Courts, the District Attorney, the County Executive, and the Board of Supervisors.[113]

The objective of Project Turnaround was to provide needed assistance to the innocent participants in the criminal justice process — the victims, the witnesses, and the jurors. In developed form the project comprised six distinct but related "units," each administered by specialized personnel. The first, concerned with "citizen contact and support," apprised witnesses and victims in forthcoming hearings and trials of their responsibilities and oriented them to court procedures. A second unit, "citizen-victim complaint," addressed the needs of the victims of crime in such areas as the preparation of formal complaints and the operation of referral procedures in the office of District Attorney. The third, dealing with "witness emergency," undertook to protect witnesses and informants from outside intimidation. Fourthly, an experimental unit centered on the malleable concept of "advocacy." Its personnel attempted to identify problem areas in the justice system and to select test cases which might yield a determination of the precise rights of witnesses to crime. A fifth unit concerned itself with "sensitive crimes," the preparation of cases and the counseling of victims primarily in the aftermath of rape or child molestation. Finally, the sixth unit explored "information systems," the prospective computerization of selected components of the justice process. Technicians assigned to this unit undertook to devise programs to automate the court calendars, witness notification, the indexing of the status of cases in progress, and the issuance of subpoenas. They subsequently designed the capabilities to link the courts, the District Attorney's office, the Clerk of Courts, and the Sheriff's Department into a single system with a common data base.[114]

A number of the units of Project Turnaround continued to function after the expiration of official funding, but others, such as the "advocacy" unit, existed for only two years. An elaborate post-project analysis, conducted in 1979, gave the experiment a mixed review. The reviewers accorded the project high marks for cost effectiveness, but they also interviewed seven judges of the criminal branches of the Circuit Court and learned that six of them professed little if any awareness of the effort to expedite and humanize the criminal justice procedures. Two of the jurists recalled that the courts seemed to operate more efficiently during the existence of Project Turnaround. This was, at best, a tepid endorsement of the experiment.[115]

The long-term effect of Project Turnaround resulted largely from the achievements of the "information systems" unit. From this aspect of the program emerged the Justice Information System, or JUSTIS, the computerization and linkage of the relevant agencies responsible for the administration of criminal justice. In final form JUSTIS permitted the elimination of most manual procedures and automated the calendaring and docketing of cases, the issuance of warrants, subpoenas, summonses, capiases and commitments, jail booking, and the jail census. It also allowed the officials in the participating departments to track the progress of all criminal cases within the court system.[116]

Computerization produced efficiency and cost effectiveness, but it also generated some dehumanizing consequences. In the spring of 1985, for example, the public learned that nearly 900 individuals had received sentences to the House of Correction during the last quarter of 1984 for inability to pay fines resulting from local ordinance violations. These luckless individuals, predominantly unemployed, legally unrepresented members of minority groups, had received fines ranging from $100 to $300 for loitering, shoplifting, disorderly conduct, obstructing police officers, or carrying weapons other than firearms. Failure to make timely payment of the relevant fines activated the JUSTIS computer to issue the commitment orders, and the system possessed no capacity for reconsideration or individualization of the effects of the procedure.[117]

The majority of the indigent ordinance violators served sentences averaging twenty-eight days. Less than a month after the press divulged this information to the public, the Chief Judge of the County announced a change in policy which converted the outstanding commitments to bench warrants. This, in effect, allowed the indigent individuals an opportunity to explain their circumstances to a judge before commitment. Persons arrested when the courts were in recess, moreover, at least found themselves in the jail rather than the prison.[118] Apparently a measure of human discretion was still necessary to insure that JUSTIS rendered justice. Undoubtedly many people found this a comforting thought. It proved, at least, that the system still worked. Its continuity, of course, had never been in doubt.

Endnotes

[1]In this chapter the word County in upper case refers exclusively to Milwaukee County. All other uses of the word appear in lower case.
[2]Citizens Study Committee on Judicial Organization, *Report to Governor Patrick J. Lucey, January, 1973* (Madison: Citizens Study Committee, 1973), pp. 11-12, 26-28.
[3]*Wisconsin Blue Book, 1979-1980*, pp. 658-59.
[4]*Milwaukee Sentinel*, June 25, 1931. Hereafter cited as *Sentinel*.
[5]*Wisconsin Blue Book, 1979-1980*, p. 657.
[6]Citizens Study Committee, *Report*, pp. 65-66; Alice E. Smith, *James Duane Doty: Frontier Promoter* (Madison: State Historical Society of Wisconsin, 1954), pp. 48-95.
[7]Parker M. Reed, *The Bench and Bar of Wisconsin: History and Biography* (Milwaukee: Reed, 1882), pp. 22-23; Joshua Stark, "Origin and Development of the Judiciary System," in Howard Louis Conard (ed.), *History of Milwaukee County; From Its First Settlement to the Year 1895*, 3 vols. (Chicago: American Biographical Publishing Company, 1895) 1:193; Jerome A. Watrous (ed.), *Memoirs of Milwaukee County*, 2 vols. (Madison: Western Historical Association, 1909) 1:505-09.
[8]Reed, *Bench and Bar*, p. 24.
[9]Watrous, *Memoirs* 1:509-14.
[10]Reed, *Bench and Bar*, pp. 27-29.

[11]Watrous, *Memoirs* 1:514.

[12]Ibid., 515.

[13]"Capsule History of Milwaukee County Court System" (mimeographed; [rev. 1971]). Milwaukee County Law Library.

[14]John Berryman, *History of Bench and Bar of Wisconsin*, 2 vols. (Chicago: H.C. Cooper, 1898) 1:383-92; Watrous, *Memoirs* 1:515-20; Stark, "Origin and Development" 1:197-200.

[15]Watrous, *Memoirs* 1:520-26; Stark, "Origin and Development" 1:200-03.

[16]James Westfall, "The Courts of Milwaukee" (typescript [1936]), pp. 9-10. Legislative Reference Bureau, Milwaukee City Hall.

[17]Watrous, *Memoirs* 1:526-31.

[18]Wisconsin Statutes, *Laws of Wisconsin, 1909*, chap. 549. Hereafter cited as *Laws of Wisconsin*.

[19]*Sentinel*, January 3, 1958; "County of Milwaukee 1960 Budget Review," pp. 2090-93. (mimeographed). Milwaukee County Law Library.

[20]Stark, "Milwaukee County as a Judicial Circuit," in Conard, *History of Milwaukee County* 1:204; *Laws of Wisconsin, 1909*, chap. 544.

[21]Watrous, *Memoirs* 1:531-36.

[22]"County 1960 Budget Review," pp. 2032-33.

[23]*Sentinel*, June 27, 1920.

[24]Richard C. Crepeau, "Prohibition in Milwaukee" (Master's thesis, Marquette University, 1967), pp. 43-44.

[25]Westfall, "Courts of Milwaukee," p. 9.

[26]David J. Rothman, *Conscience and Convenience: The Asylum and its Alternatives in Progressive America* (Boston: Little, Brown & Co., 1980), pp. 43-44, 51-53, 66, 72-73.

[27]Martin Gilbertson, "A Study of the Social Action for a Full-time Judge of the Juvenile Court in Milwaukee County, Wisconsin" (Master's thesis, University of Wisconsin-Madison, 1949), pp. 13-16.

[28]Charles Larsen, *The Good Fight: The Life and Times of Ben B. Lindsey* (Chicago: Quadrangle, 1972), pp. 27-54.

[29]Gilbertson, "Full-time Judge," pp. 15-19.

[30]Children's Court, *Report, 1954: The Activities of the Court, Probation and Detention Home for 1954 in Addition to Historical Background and Statistics*, pp. 2-13; Robert U. Stolhand, "The Milwaukee County Juvenile Court as a Social Service Agency" (Master's essay, University of Chicago, 1942), p. 32.

[31]"Report of the Juvenile Court of Milwaukee County, Wisconsin, 1907-1908," pp. 7-29, 31, 38, 40-41. (mimeographed).

[32]"Report of the Total Number of Cases Disposed of in Juvenile Court, Milwaukee County, from January 1, 1917 to January 1, 1918" (mimeographed). Milwaukee County Law Library.

[33]Stolhand, "Juvenile Court," pp. 19-26.

[34]Gilbertson, "Full-time Judge," pp. 20-22.

[35]Ibid., pp. 24-27, 49-57.

[36]*Laws of Wisconsin, 1977*, chap. 48, secs. 48.06, 48.12, 48.18, 48.22, 48.44.

[37]Blake McKelvey, *American Prisons: A History of Good Intentions* (Montclair, N.J.: Patterson-Smith, 1977), p. 159.

[38]Rothman, *Conscience and Convenience*, p. 44.

[39]Max Raskin, untitled paper [1974], p. 6. Raskin Papers, Area Research Center, University of Wisconsin-Milwaukee.

[40]Children's Court, *Report, 1954*, p. 8.

[41]Westfall, "Courts of Milwaukee," p. 9.

[42]Rothman, *Conscience and Convenience*, pp. 83, 87, 90, 98-99, 103, 110-11.

[43]Family Court, "Annual Report, 1964" (mimeographed). Milwaukee County Law Library.

[44]"Milwaukee County Divorce Statistics" (typescript [1948]). Milwaukee County Law Library.

[45]Family Court, "Annual Report, 1964"; *Laws of Wisconsin, 1959*, chap. 252, sec. 252.016.

[46]Family Court, "Annual Report, 1966" (mimeographed). Milwaukee County Law Library.

[47]*Sentinel*, April 1, 2, 1985; August 15, 1985.

[48]*Laws of Wisconsin, 1959*, chap. 252, sec. 252.14.

[49]Family Court, "Annual Report, 1965" (mimeographed). Milwaukee County Law Library.

[50]Clerk of Circuit Court, "Annual Report, 1977" (mimeographed). Milwaukee County Law Library.

[51]Ibid., 1968.

[52]Westfall, "Courts of Milwaukee," p. 14.

[53]*Laws of Wisconsin, 1959*, chap. 252, sec. 252.031.

[54]*Wisconsin Blue Book, 1979-1980*, p. 658.

[55]*Laws of Wisconsin, 1959*, chap. 252, sec. 252.031.

[56]"Capsule History of Milwaukee County Court System." Author's conclusion from list of surnames.

[57]*Sentinel,* August 25, 1966.

[58]Fred Rodell, *Nine Men; A Political History of the Supreme Court from 1790 to 1955* (New York: Random House, 1955), pp. 3-32.

[59]*Wisconsin Supreme Court Rules, 1984,* pp. 193-200. Revision of the code occurred in 1974, 1977, 1978, and 1979.

[60]See, for example, the Appendix to Bruce Allen Murphy, *The Brandeis/Frankfurter Connection: The Secret Political Activities of Two Supreme Court Justices* (New York: Oxford University Press, 1982), pp. 345-63.

[61]John Bell Sanborn, "The Impeachment of Levi Hubbell," *Proceedings of the State Historical Society of Wisconsin* (1905): 194-213; Alfons J. Beitzinger, *Edward G. Ryan: Lion of the Law* (Madison: State Historical Society of Wisconsin, 1960), pp. 26-39. See also Raoul Berger, "The Impeachment of Judges and 'Good Behavior' Tenure," *Yale Law Review,* 79 (July 1979): 1475-1531.

[62]*Milwaukee Journal,* August 26-31, September 5, October 1, December 1, 2, 1968. Hereafter cited as *Journal.*

[63]The Seraphim case may be traced in both the *Sentinel* and the *Journal.* Pertinent issues are: *1979:* February 20,22, 23, 25, 28; March 1, 14; April 11, 22; May 2, 4; June 7; August 2, 14; November 11, 12, 13, 14, 16; December 1, 18, 21, 27; *1980:* January 2, 31; February 7, 24, 26, 27, 28, 29; March 6; May 9, 22; July 7; *1983:* July 7.

[64]Ovid B. Blix (comp.) "Duties of the District Attorney" (typescript [1932]). Milwaukee County Law Library.

[65]Watrous, *Memoirs* 1:535-38.

[66]*Sentinel,* January 8, 1855.

[67]Ibid., March 28, 1885; November 13, 1889.

[68]*Wisconsin News,* August 6, 1929.

[69]District Attorney, *Management Study Final Report, July, 1976,* chart following p. 20.

[70]District Attorney, "Annual Report, 1974," pp. 4-5 (mimeographed). Milwaukee County Law Library.

[71]*Management Study,* pp. 12-13.

[72]Raskin, untitled paper, pp. 27-30. Raskin Papers.

[73]District Attorney, "Annual Report, 1974," pp. 10-11.

[74]William A. Morris, *The Medieval English Sheriff to 1300* (Manchester, England: Manchester University Press, 1927), pp. 1, 3, 23-29, 55-56, 186-87.

[75]Cyrus Harreld Karreker, *The Seventeenth Century Sheriff; A Comparative Study of the Sheriff in England and the Chesapeake Colonies, 1607-1689* (Chapel Hill: University of North Carolina Press, 1930), pp. 7, 11, 14-28, 63-159.

[76]Ernest M. King, *Sheriff's Manual* (Washington: National Sheriff's Association, 1960), pp. 1-23.

[77]n.a., "Milwaukee County Sheriff's Office Revisited," *Wisconsin Sheriff and Deputy,* 21 (October-November 1969): 1-3.

[78]Ibid., 4.

[79]*Sentinel,* April 29, 1881.

[80]Eric Monkkonen, *Police in Urban America, 1860-1920* (New York: Cambridge University Press, 1981), p. 166.

[81]"Sheriff's Office Revisited," p. 9.

[82]Sheriff's Department, "Annual Report, 1965," p. 2 (mimeographed).

[83]"Administrative Survey of the Milwaukee County Sheriff's Department, 1954", p. 13 (mimeographed).

[84]Sheriff's Department, "Annual Report, 1955", p. 3 (mimeographed); *Annual Report, 1983,* pp. 11, 17.

[85]"Administrative Survey, 1954," p. 14; Sheriff's Department, *Annual Report, 1979,* pp. 6, 9, 12, 14, 16, 18.

[86]"Sheriff's Office Revisited," pp. 3-4; John Howard Association, "Survey Report, Milwaukee County Jail Complex, 1969," p. 1 (mimeographed); *Sentinel,* November 29, 1871; January 19, 1872; May 7, 1887.

[87]*Sentinel,* January 27, 1872.

[88]Ibid., June 3, 1888.

[89](Wisconsin) Board of Charities, *Jail Report, 1890,* pp. 10-11.

[90]Sheriff's Department, *Annual Report, 1983,* p. 11.

[91]John Howard Association, "Survey Report," p. 1.

[92]Prisoners governed by the work release provisions of the Huber Act of 1913 had been quartered in the jail since the 1930s. To alleviate overcrowding at the jail, in 1979 the Huber prisoners underwent transfer to the House of Correction, effectively concluding the responsibilities of the Sheriff's Department in the work-release program.

[93]David J. Rothman, *The Discovery of the Aslyum: Social Order and Disorder in the New Republic* (Boston: Little, Brown, & Co., 1971), pp. 209; 237-40, 293-94; McKelvey, *American Prisons*, pp. 2-3, 11, 69-70.

[94]Joseph B. Drewniak, "History of the House of Correction," pp. 1-2 (typescript [1954]). Milwaukee County Law Library. Drewniak was Superintendent from 1940 to 1954.

[95]*Sentinel*, November 24, 1853; September 9, December 15, 1858; February 4, 1865.

[96]Ibid., February 13, 1866; June 27, 1882; House of Correction, "Annual Report, 1966," p. 2. (mimeographed).

[97]House of Correction, *Twelfth Annual Report, 1878*, p. 4.

[98]*Sentinel*, October 29, 30, November 6, 1879. Quotations from issue of November 6.

[99]Ibid., October 30, 1879.

[100]Ibid., November 6, 1879.

[101]Ibid., December 3, 1879.

[102]Ibid., January 22, 1879.

[103]*Report of the Citizens Committee on Construction of a New House of Correction for Milwaukee County, Wisconsin* (Milwaukee: Schueppert-Zoeller Printing Co., 1913), p. 5.

[104]Drewniak, "History," pp. 1-2.

[105]Joseph B. Drewniak, "Background and Purpose of the Milwaukee County House of Correction," p. 2 (mimeographed [1952]). Milwaukee County Law Library.

[106]Drewniak, "History," p. 3.

[107]House of Correction, "Annual Report, 1948," pp. 12-27 (mimeographed).

[108]Drewniak, "Background and Purpose," p. 4.

[109]H. Samuel Hughes, "An Examination of 1681 Admissions to the Milwaukee County House of Correction, October 1, 1960 - February 28, 1961" (Master's thesis, University of Wisconsin-Milwaukee, 1961), pp. 21, 34, 76.

[110]All House of Correction reports previous to 1974 provided data on age, sex, occupation, religious affiliation, frequency of admission, and duration of sentence. These data and the modal five-day sentence indicate the predominance of alcohol-related reasons for sentencing.

[111]District Attorney, "Annual Report, 1974," appendices A and B-2.

[112]Ibid., p. 27.

[113]"Discretionary Grant Progress Report: Milwaukee County Project Turnaround, October 15, 1975" (mimeographed). Milwaukee County Law Library.

[114]"Project Turnaround — Summary of Program" (mimeographed [1976]). Milwaukee County Law Library.

[115]"Executive Summary, Final Report, Milwaukee County Project Turnaround, January 31, 1979" (mimeographed). Milwaukee County Law Library.

[116]"Justice Information System in Milwaukee County" (mimeographed [1976]). Milwaukee County Law Library.

[117]*Journal*, April 22, 28, 1985.

[118]Ibid., May 16, 30, 1985.

Bibliography

"Administrative Survey of the Milwaukee County Sheriff's Department, 1954" (mimeographed).

Beitzinger, Alfons J. *Edward G. Ryan: Lion of the Law.* Madison: State Historical Society of Wisconsin, 1960.

Berryman, John. *History of the Bench and Bar of Wisconsin.* 2 vols. Chicago: H. C. Cooper, 1898.

Blix, Ovid B. (comp.). "Duties of the District Attorney." (typescript [1932]). Milwaukee County Law Library.

"Capsule History of the Milwaukee County Court System." (mimeographed [rev. 1971]). Milwaukee County Law Library.

Children's Court of Milwaukee County. *Report, 1954: The Activities of the Court, Probation and Detention Home for 1954 in Addition to Historical Background and Statistics.*

Citizens Study Committee on Judicial Organization, *Report to Governor Patrick J. Lucey, January, 1973*. Madison: Citizens Study Committee, 1973.

Clerk of Circuit Court. "Annual Reports, 1968, 1969, 1977. (mimeographed). Milwaukee County Law Library.

Conard, Howard Louis. *History of Milwaukee County; From Its First Settlement to the Year 1895*. 3 vols. Chicago: American Biographical Publishing Company, 1895.

"County of Milwaukee 1960 Budget Review." (mimeographed). Milwaukee County Law Library.

Crepeau, Richard C. "Prohibition in Milwaukee." (Master's thesis, Marquette University, 1967).

"Discretionary Grant Progress Report: Milwaukee County Project Turnaround, October 15, 1975." (mimeographed). Milwaukee County Law Library.

District Attorney. "Annual Report, 1974." (mimeographed). Milwaukee County Law Library.

——————————. *Management Study, Final Report*, 1967.

Drewniak, Joseph B. "Background and Purpose of the Milwaukee County House of Correction." (mimeographed [1952]). Milwaukee County Law Library.

Family Court, "Annual Reports, 1964, 1965, 1966." (mimeographed). Milwaukee County Law Library.

Gilbertson, Martin. "A Study of the Social Action for a Fulltime Judge of the Juvenile Court in Milwaukee County, Wisconsin." (Master's thesis, University of Wisconsin-Madison, 1949).

House of Correction, *Twelfth Annual Report, 1878*. (professionally published *Reports* of this institution are extant from 1872 to 1896. Subsequent *Reports*, in mimeographed form, are sporadic in the public domain)

House of Correction, "Annual Reports, 1948, 1953, 1966." (mimeographed).

Hughes, H. Samuel. "An Examination of 1681 Admissions to the Milwaukee County House of Correction, October 1, 1960 - February 28, 1961." (Master's thesis, University of Wisconsin-Milwaukee, 1961).

John Howard Association. "Survey Report, Milwaukee County Jail Complex, 1969." (mimeographed). Milwaukee County Law Library.

"Justice Information System in Milwaukee County." (mimeographed [1976]). Milwaukee County Law Library.

"Milwaukee County Divorce Statistics. (typescript [1948]). Milwaukee County Law Library.

"Milwaukee County Sheriff's Office Revisited." *Wisconsin Sheriff and Deputy* (October-November, 1969):1-9.

"Project Turnaround-Summary of Program." (mimeographed [1976]). Milwaukee County Law Library.

Raskin, Max. Papers. 11 Boxes. Area Research Center, University of Wisconsin-Milwaukee.

Reed, Parker M. *The Bench and Bar of Milwaukee: History and Biography.* Milwaukee: Reed, 1882.

"Report of the Juvenile Court of Milwaukee County, Wisconsin, 1907-1908." (mimeographed).

Report of the Total Number of Cases Disposed of in Juvenile Court, Milwaukee County, from January 1, 1917 to January 1, 1918." (mimeographed). Milwaukee County Law Library.

Sanborn, John Bell. "The Impeachment of Levi Hubbell." *Proceedings of the State Historical Society of Wisconsin* (1905):194-213.

Sheriff's Department. "Annual Reports, 1955, 1965." (mimeographed). Reports appeared sporadically after 1933.

Sheriff's Department. *Annual Reports, 1979, 1983.*

Smith, Alice E. *James Duane Doty: Frontier Promoter.* Madison: State Historical Society of Wisconsin, 1954.

Stolhand, Robert U. "The Milwaukee County Juvenile Court as a Social Service Agency." (master's essay, University of Chicago, 1942).

Watrous, Jerome (ed.). *Memoirs of Milwaukee County.* 2 vols. Madison: Western Historical Association, 1909.

Westfall, James B. "The Courts of Milwaukee." (typescript [1936]). Legislative Reference Bureau, Milwaukee City Hall.

Wisconsin Blue Book, 1979-1980.

(Wisconsin) Board of Charities, *Jail Report, 1890.*

Wisconsin Statutes. *Laws of Wisconsin, 1909, 1959, 1977.* Chaps. 48, 252, 253, 549.

Wisconsin Supreme Court Rules, 1984. 193-200.

Health, Hospitals, and Welfare: Human Services in Milwaukee County

by Steven M. Avella _____

From its inception as a distinct socio-political entity in 1835, Milwaukee County has recognized its responsibility to provide for the poor and sick of the community. As is the case with other County services and institutions, assistance to the poor and needy has undergone a process of evolution in concept and practice over the past 150 years. Beginning with a program of ad hoc "outdoor" relief, social welfare services have expanded and multiplied into a giant complex of institutions and programs that constitute the single largest function of County government. Under the administration of the County Board of Supervisors and its Department of Health and Human Services (DHHS), an appointed director oversees an "empire" of social welfare operations. Changes in these services have come about as the result of a complex interaction of public need, technological and conceptual advances, and the exigencies of County politics. It is my purpose to provide a summary overview of the evolution of social welfare services for the needy of Milwaukee County.

Assistance to the Poor: Conceptual Considerations

The belief that society and its institutions have a responsibility for the poor and disadvantaged is the universal mark of a civilized society. American concepts of assistance to the poor derive most directly from the heritage of the English Poor Laws of the sixteenth and seventeenth centuries. These statutes firmly established the principle that local units of government were to be responsible for the care of the poor and that funds for their relief were to be raised by general levy. While the Poor Laws did insist that the able-bodied should work and that families bore an important responsibility to care for their own, nonetheless, the community recognized its role in caring for those who could not care for themselves.[1]

These concepts of poor relief were replicated in North America (as were many other English laws and institutions) especially in New England, where care of the poor was an accepted function of colonial townships. Established citizens who fell on hard times received aid from their neighbors in their own homes or were taken in until they could gain their independence. Only the itinerant poor were "warned away" from taking advantage of this colonial largesse. It is important to note that colonial Americans did not struggle unduly with the causes of poverty and destitution. Although they looked askance at idleness and immorality, frequent causes of indigence, they seemed to accept, at face value, the biblical injunction of Christ, "The poor you will have with you always" (John 12:8). In their estimation, poor people were simply part of the Divine Plan for the world. Moreover, living in close proximity with one another, they could readily observe that one could be reduced to poverty by accidents, death, or other misfortunes that afflicted the righteous and unrighteous equally.

As America became a nation in the late eighteenth century, the ideological mainspring of national expansion and self-expression was a strong emphasis on liberal individualism.[2] The drive to "make one's way," coupled with the abundant opportunity waiting for the taking, produced an important shift in the manner in which Americans considered the presence of the poor and needy among them. The limitless possibilities of the young nation meant that anyone who truly wanted to "make it" could do so. The converse of this enterprising self-confidence was the belief that persons who could not make their own way must somehow be personally weak or flawed: "loafers" or "malingerers." The best way to help such people, it was maintained, was to compel them to work in order that they might regain the independence and self-respect necessary for the citizenry of a virtuous republic. It was seldom asked whether persons were poor due to personal folly and indolence or for reasons beyond their control. The environmental considerations which had qualified colonial conceptions of poverty figured less prominently, if at all. Only as a last resort was public charity to be bestowed; and if it was, it was to be so designed as to repel any but the most needy.

It was in this socio-intellectual matrix that Milwaukee County's system of poor relief was begun. The subsequent history of nineteenth-century social welfare efforts in Milwaukee County generally reflected this attitude of disdain for the poor and the recurring suspicion that County funds expended in their behalf were misspent. One County supervisor summed up the attitude when, in protesting the system of outdoor relief, he declared, "Instead of being benefited, the poor become lazy and indolent, lose all self-respect, and finally, are utterly regardless of their own welfare." He earnestly wished that "the county would get rid of any army of hangers-on who are now bleeding this county to death."[3]

Laying the Foundations: The Territorial Era

Milwaukee County, like all counties, is a subunit of the state government. As such, the services provided by the County are dependent on the state for concept and legal sanction. Health and social services were (and still are) derivative from the specific statutes of the state code, which not only mandate local responsibility for the relief of the poor but also permit taxation for that purpose.

In its first territorial phase (1835), Milwaukee County's care for the poor was attended by two appointed Superintendents of the Poor, Solomon Juneau and Benoni Finch.[4] The job of these County poor officials was to receive applications from those in need and provide for their needs on an ad hoc basis, with reimbursement coming from County funds for their out-of-pocket expenses. This system, known as outdoor relief, provided the applicant with food, firewood, and occasionally lodging. While cash was rarely given, the County sometimes provided funds to transport widows and orphans to out-of-state family members who could support them. Finch and Juneau held the positions briefly, and new Superintendents were appointed annually by the County Board. Together with the "official" efforts of these designated officers, poor relief was also given by a number of private citizens, who then submitted their requests for reimbursement to the County Board.[5]

Wisconsin's formal organization as a territory in 1836 brought into existence the first poor laws specifically relating to the future state. Despite the fact that these enactments clearly defined the county (as opposed to the townships) as the chief channel of poor relief, what emerged was a confused and overlapping "mixed" system of county and township efforts on behalf of the needy. Milwaukee County continued its system of outdoor relief and annually appointed new Superintendents of the Poor, but so also did the City of Milwaukee look to the needs of its growing ranks of indigents by the erection of a poor house in the First Ward. What ensued was confusion over such issues as eligibility for poor relief (length of residence in the county/city to receive public assistance), who cared for the transient poor, and finally what were the precise boundaries of city and county relief efforts. This lack of clarity was aggravated as Milwaukee began to emerge as a major trade depot on the Great Lakes.[6] The attendant rise in population accelerated demands for assistance to the poor and sick and taxed the social welfare system to its limits. Dissatisfaction with the system and the amount of money being spent spilled out in an 1843 petition of the Board of Supervisors to the territorial legislature:

> The present laws for the relief of the poor in this Territory and especially in those counties which have adopted the County and Town system of government are so very defective that they are almost useless.

The County Board urged a serious reworking of the laws so that

> The whole control of this matter be placed under the authorities of the county exclusively to be regulated similar as in those

counties in the State of New York where all the poor are declared a County charge.[7]

The reference to New York not only was a plea to emulate the county-based plan of poor relief that existed in that state but also had other significant implications for the evolution of Milwaukee County's social welfare services.

Important developments in New York's care of the needy and sick provided a model for many other states of the Union. Having first tried the outdoor relief system, New Yorkers grew weary of the rising expenses and the dubious social results. In 1821 the report of a committee chaired by state Attorney General J.V.N. Yates was submitted to the New York legislature claiming that outdoor relief was not only too costly but scandalously ineffective in curing "pauperism." As a cost-saving and humanitarian alternative, Yates suggested the creation of county-based institutions that would provide succor for the "deserving poor" but would be less than enticing for those who could support and care for themselves if they really wanted to. Moreover, these proposed institutions were designed to be partially self-supporting by means of farming or light industry, thus defraying some of the costs of operation and lifting a portion of the burden from the backs of the taxpayers. The Yates Report won widespread acclaim throughout the nation and made an institutional response to poverty both palatable and politically expedient for hundreds of counties.[8] Alternately known as the Almshouse, Poor House, or County Farm, this "indoor relief" method of poor support soon found advocates in Milwaukee County.

Laying the Foundations: Statehood

Less than a year after Wisconsin's admission to the Union in 1848, laws were enacted dealing with poor relief. Section 49 of the Wisconsin Public Statutes assigned responsibility for the poor to the municipalities, but a further provision permitted county boards of supervisors, with the approval of two-thirds votes of their members, to assume the responsibility themselves.[9] Thus counties could abolish the distinction between town and county poor, a vexatious problem of the past. After some debate, Milwaukee accepted the county system, mainly at the insistence of City supervisors who feared that the whole brunt of poor relief might fall on City revenues.

It was the continually growing City of Milwaukee that brought the problems of poor relief to the attention of the County Board. Natural problems of destitution were seriously aggravated in 1848-1850, when a deadly cholera epidemic added even more names to the poor rolls. With no County hospital in existence, the Board was compelled to utilize the services of the Roman Catholic Sisters of Charity, who had opened St. John's Infirmary at the city's north point in 1848.[10] By 1852 Milwaukee County's population was well over 30,000, and rising costs for poor relief compelled the supervisors to look seriously at the indoor relief option. A committee of the Board reported on September 29, 1852 that "the system of Outdoor Relief ... is attended with great expense and ought to be entirely prohibited."[11] As alternatives, the supervisors suggested two possibilities: either purchase and improve the existing almshouse in the City of Milwaukee (which was being given rent-free to the County), or impose a poor tax (discretionary authority for this had already been granted by the state legislature) and use the collected revenue "for the purpose of purchasing or hiring a suitable farm and dwelling ... to which the poor in such county may be removed."[12]

Although the supervisors rejected the abolition of outdoor relief (the suggestion was to be made many more times in the history of the County), they did accept the need for a poorhouse. The Milwaukee site was rejected as far too decrepit, and the Board charged a committee under Supervisor William A. Prentiss with the task of selecting an appropriate location for the institution. Even though several offers were made, Prentiss and his committee looked no further than the membership of the County Board when Supervisor Hendrik Gregg offered his 160-acre farm in Wauwatosa as a potential site. Located near rail lines and the Watertown Plank Road,

The County Institutions depicted in a 19th-century oil painting. The scene includes the poor farm (center) and County Hospital (right). The structure at left is believed to be the newly completed insane asylum, occupied in March 1880, a month after the hospital burned.

the property contained the requisite large farm house, barns, livestock, as well as crops in the field that could be worked by future inhabitants. For the sum of $6,000 the Board approved the purchase (Gregg appropriately did not vote).[13] Subsequent purchases of adjacent farm land expanded the holdings to nearly 1,200 acres and permanently settled most functions of Milwaukee County's social welfare services in the Wauwatosa location.

The County Poor Farm or Almshouse began operations in November 1852 with twenty-four people comfortably housed in the remodeled Gregg farm house. Some of the County poor remained at the city location until it was finally closed and sold in 1859. From its beginnings the Almshouse posed problems and challenges to County administrators. Designed as an economy move, the Almshouse was more costly than the advocates of indoor relief had imagined.[14] Moreover, conditions soon developed inside the house that attracted the attention of reformers, the press, and certain politicians who made the institution a political football.

Like many almshouses, the Milwaukee site became a catchall for society's misfits and rejects. These included not only men and women down on their luck (mostly the foreign, elderly poor) but the sick poor and children of county prisoners or paupers. The insane as well were often consigned to the Almshouse by legal authorities eager to clear them off the streets. As one might imagine, this medley of characters created problems of order and cleanliness, while periodically raising the hackles of reformers who perceived the conditions of the poor house as both inhumane and socially counterproductive.

Complaints about the conditions in the Almshouse did not take long to surface. Physicians, reformers, and at times the inmates themselves decried this or that aspect of the institution. In response, the County Board mandated regular inspections of the Almhouse, and a standing committee of the Board of Supervisors was established to oversee conditions. Investigations occurred with great regularity throughout the nineteenth century and helped bring about significant changes that subdivided the services rendered to the poor. It soon became evident that the "catch-all" Almshouse was not the best answer to the host of problems besetting the indigent of Milwaukee County.

The Sick Poor

Contagiously ill paupers who appeared at the County Almshouse alarmed administrators and prompted the adoption of several plans of action. The need to separate these cases from the others led the supervisors to renew their contract with the Sisters of Charity. The Sisters had performed heroically in the cholera outbreak of the late 1840s and until the construction of the County hospital in 1860 provided the only hospital services in Wisconsin.[15] Further, the Board urged the designation of a separate wing of the Almshouse as an infirmary for the sick poor, thus segregating them from the rest of the inmates. Finally the supervisors contracted the services of a number of Milwaukee area physicians, who attended to the needs of the sick poor in the Almshouse as well as to those who were receiving outdoor relief in their homes.[16] The County was divided into four medical districts (the fourth being the area that included the Almshouse and later the County hospital), and the physicians were assigned to attend to the needs of the sick poor of that area for an agreed-upon flat rate. Later the number of medical districts would be expanded.

The numbers of the sick poor descending on the Almshouse continually increased. The rising costs as well as the urging of local physicians prodded the supervisors to erect a separate thirty-one bed County hospital in 1860. Although its location in "far-off" Wauwatosa would engender some unhappiness, the construction of the hospital opened up an important phase of social welfare work in Milwaukee County.

The nature of this early hospital is not easy to determine, but no doubt it was regarded as were most hospitals of the day as a refuge for charity cases only.[17] Most nineteenth-century Americans received needed medical care in their homes and generally avoided hospitals not only because they bore the stigma of charity wards but also because of their chaotic ward arrangement and the general lack of differentiation in the placement of patients. A particularly offensive feature of these indigent-oriented institutions was the so-called "lying-in" or maternity wards. Because most "respectable" childbirths took place in homes attended by midwives, those who were forced to bear their children in hospitals were often unwed mothers who had come to "hide their shame." An inspector from the State Board of Charities and Reform spoke of this ward in the Milwaukee County Hospital in a report to her superiors:

> From May 1 to August 2, there have been ten women in the lying-in wards of the Milwaukee County Hospital. In the majority of instances they have been victims of men who promise marriage, only to betray and desert them when ruined, leaving both the betrayed woman and her offspring a burden upon our public charities.[18]

In addition to the "image" troubles of the hospital, hygienic problems also made it less than an enticing health care option. Before the advent of asepsis and antisepsis, hospitals were not noted for the high degree of cleanliness and germ-free conditions that are supposed to characterize them today. Surgery was rarely performed in these places, and doctors themselves were among their most vocal critics. The Milwaukee County Hospital shared many of the problems of the hospitals of the day. In periodic visits public officials generally commented that the hospital was "clean enough," yet flaws in its ventilation and sewerage systems created serious difficulties.[19] In the days when disease was thought to be caused by foul miasmas or vapors, this was a major blunder (one outraged supervisor referred to the hospital's construction as "a piece of arrant botchery").[20] Even additions to the building in 1868, designed to remedy recurrent complaints of overcrowding, did not ameliorate the problems of proper sanitation and care. About the only positive contribution of this early County hospital was to effect the needed separation of the sick poor from the rest of the Almshouse population.

The administration of the hospital was the responsibility of one of the three appointed Superintendents of the Poor. Generally a patronage appointment, the Superintendent of the Hospital often knew little or nothing of the world of medicine or health care (even in the primitive forms in which they existed in the mid-nineteenth century). Not until 1876 was the administration of the hospital put into the hands of a trained physician, Dr. Fisk H. Day. Day's contributions to the development of professional and humane treatment of the sick and insane are well worth noting.[21]

Fisk H. Day, a man of diverse talents and interests, had come to Wauwatosa from New York in 1854. He accepted an appointment as a Milwaukee County physician and made regular visitations of the Alms-

Dr. Fisk H. Day, Wauwatosa physician since 1854, became superintendent of the County Hospital in 1876. Dr. Day advocated humane treatment of the sick and insane and promoted many reforms. He is pictured in his home study amid scientific and geological items which reflect avocational interests.

house, farm, and later the hospital. Regular association with the County institutions made him a credible critic of certain practices and involved him in wrangles with the County Board. Much of Day's criticism was trained on County treatment of the insane, but he also kept up a drumfire of negative comment on the poor construction of the County hospital and the mismanagement of the County Board in accepting such a flawed edifice. Day's carping did not win him many friends on the Board but did eventually bring about many needed reforms in the County institutions.[22]

The metamorphosis of the County Hospital into the center of healing, antiseptic health care, and medical research we know today began tragically in 1880, when a disastrous fire killed two patients and completely destroyed the buildings. Although the loss of life and property was lamented, the destruction of the buildings came at a fortuitous time. Already underway among physicians were reforming and professionalizing impulses that would totally revolutionize health care, bringing about a whole new role for the hospital in the process.[23] Chief among these reforms was the so-called "Public Health Movement." Begun in England in the 1840s, this movement rejected the prevailing wisdom that sickness and disease were part of the plan of God for the world. Instead, public health proponents asserted that illness was caused by environmental factors, with filth, raw sewage, noxious odors, spoiled food, and bad water among the chief culprits.[24] These findings were reinforced in the 1870s, when Doctors Louis Pasteur and Robert Koch discovered that germs and bacteria were the causes of disease. The United States experienced the creation of numerous boards of public health as well as massive citizen drives to clean and sanitize public facilities and purify public water supplies. Milwaukee established its own Board of Health in 1867, and active programs of swamp drainage, milk and water purification, and city sanitation were put into action.[25]

The study and practice of medicine changed dramatically in the wake of these new discoveries. Newly formed medical associations enforced rigorous standards for the attainment of professional status. Care of the sick was to be undertaken in clean, orderly, and antiseptic conditions, and hospitals were to be built to accommodate these needs as well as provide facilities for the increasing amount of surgery done. Moreover, hospitals were to function as bases of clinical experience for doctors in training, as medical education was integrated into the very nature and purpose of hospital administration.

Milwaukee County Hospital moved along with the pace of medical developments. The appointment of Fisk H. Day as hospital superintendent brought, for the first time, a trained professional to the helm, the first of many doctors who would serve as permanent staff members of the institution. Techniques of modern surgery were first demonstrated in the

Dr. Anna Gregory Connell, first Superintendent of Nurses at the Milwaukee County Hospital, 1888-1889. The hospital assumed the role of training and certifying nurses after Dr. Connell and her physician husband, the hospital administrator, established the program.

Eight young women from the first class of nurses at the County Hospital. In the back, from left: Nellie Wells, May Ballenbach, Mary Baker, Denia Austin, Jennie Starr, Rilla Darling, Nellie Lehan, and Emily Fliegge in front.

County Hospital by the internationally renowned Dr. Nicholas Senn, a father of modern medicine in the Milwaukee area. Care of patients was also significantly upgraded in 1887, when hospital superintendent Dr. M.E. Connell and his wife, Dr. Anna Gregory Connell, established a class for the "instruction and training of nurses for service." The following year, the County Board allowed for the establishment of a school of nursing that awarded a diploma or certificate after two years of training. The first class, consisting of thirteen students, moved to the County grounds in 1888 and began studies. In 1889 Milwaukee County Hospital assumed full responsibility for the training and certification of qualified nurses. The quality of nurses training improved with every year under the direction of a succession of strong-willed and competent matrons.[26] The existence of the school and the visible improvements in the care and treatment of patients caused County Hospital to shed some of its reputation as a haven of last resort (although paying patients were not permitted until the 1960s). By 1900 County Hospital was a genuine center of health and healing, with an active surgical department and a growing corps of doctors who contributed their services to the hospital staff.

Child Care

The presence of children in the Almshouse also presented a difficult challenge to County administrators. Since the children were often consigned to this institution because their parents were reduced to poverty or incarcerated, sometimes if they were orphaned, concern for their safety was a major issue. Some of the children were "bound out," that is, apprenticed to local businesses or craftsmen until they reached the age of majority. Still others were adopted by families who wanted them. For those who stayed on at the Almshouse, the County Board effected some small degree of separation with the building of a school house in 1858 "for the purpose of educating the children and keeping them separated from the influence and often corrupt examples of the older inmates." These children could be taught, the Board maintained, to be "useful and respectable citizens ... instead of candidates for our jails and prisons."[27] The school was a step in the direction of completely separating the children from the baneful effects of the Almshouse. Yet even this measure could not adequately cope with the increasing numbers of indigent minors coming to the Almshouse who were orphaned by periodic epidemics that swept the Great Lakes region or tragedies such as the sinking of the *Lady Elgin* in 1860.

County care of poor children was a special object of public concern in the 1870s with the formation of the State Board of Charities and Reform. This state-appointed agency was created to oversee and report on the administration of state-sponsored penal and mental institutions. Similar to boards in other states, this body also collected copious amounts of information on conditions in various County institutions, and its written reports contain solid and revealing information about these facilities.[28] The membership of these boards appeared to be representatives of the Christian-oriented reforming groups that were so popular during the nineteenth century. Strongly imbued with religious zeal to right the wrongs that these institutions often perpetrated, these reformers placed at the very top of their priorities inquiries as to the care and treatment of children in public institutions.[29]

Mary E. B. Lynde strove to improve conditions for the poor and hospitalized insane as a member of the State Board of Charities and Reform and as a community leader.

In 1871 State Charities Board member Mary E.B. Lynde (a native of Milwaukee) conducted the first state inspection of the County institutions. While the thrust of her report was favorable, she upbraided County administrators for the condition of the children whom she found to be "ragged and neglected." Conditions did improve on subsequent inspections, but Mrs. Lynde took the occasion to report that

> I am fully convinced that a poor house is a most unsuitable place in which to rear children and take the liberty to recommend the foundation of a Children's Home where they can be removed from the associations and influences of adult pauperism.[30]

Lynde and other reformers pressed the child welfare issue forcefully with the state legislature and secured passage of a law in 1875 forbidding the placement of children over the age of five and under the age of sixteen in county or city poor houses. With the poor house option gone, child care in Milwaukee County entered a period of uncertainty. At about the same time a national debate raged among child care experts regarding the merits of institutional versus home child care.[31] The unresolved status of the issue resulted in only piecemeal efforts for the remainder of the century in Milwaukee County. Initially, indigent youngsters were dispatched to various state and private industrial schools, which boarded and educated them until they reached majority. City orphanages, mostly operated by Catholic groups, also accepted a number of the waifs. Yet for those children who needed only temporary care, until their parents were released from jail or the Almshouse, the industrial school or orphanage alternatives were not acceptable. In 1882 the County established a temporary children's home on the County grounds to deal with these temporary cases, while at the same time maintaining efforts to "place-out" as many of the children as were eligible to adoptive homes or work environments. As the century drew to a close, the home care advocates of the child care debate gained the upper hand and proceeded to press for a change in the methods of dealing with dependent children. Milwaukee County was slow to respond to the pressure, choosing instead to fret over the influence of adult paupers on the impressionable youth. In 1893 the County Board mandated that no outdoor relief be given to persons accompanied by

Youngsters enjoyed outdoor activities at the Home for Dependent Children in the 1920s. The facility began operation in 1898.

children over the age of three. "It has," they insisted, "a tendency to create a habit with the child to be supported by public alms."[32] Yet as in the case of other County institutions, the mere crush of numbers forced more substantive action on behalf of the children. Immigration, acute financial distress, and the effects of another disastrous cholera outbreak in the 1890s brought scores of dependent youngsters to the overcrowded and dangerous situtation in the "temporary" children's home. Moreover, a percentage of these youths were delinquents, consigned to the home rather than jail because of their youth. With conditions reaching a critical point, the County Board provided for the erection of a Home for Dependent Children, which opened its doors in 1898. True to the wishes of the home-care advocates, the new facility was designed to be a temporary holding place, until children could be returned to their parents or "placed-out" in adoptive homes or jobs. Yet despite the best efforts, a number of the children were compelled to become permanent residents when they were removed from the custody of their parents. To accommodate these long-term cases, school instruction and recreational programs were provided. Later, additions were made to the structure to accommodate infants and provide hospital care.

With the establishment of the Juvenile Court in 1901, and the creation of a youth detention center at Eleventh and W. Galena in Milwaukee, the separation of delinquent from dependency cases was effected. Until the late 1970s, the County Children's Home, funded by State and County dollars, constituted the bulwark of County efforts in the area of shelter for dependent children. Because of a change in State philosophy regarding the care of non-delinquent children in county-operated facilities, State funding for the Children's Home was gradually withdrawn during the decade of the '70s. The County began contracting with private vendors to provide child care services in smaller, scattered sites. By 1982, all such care was purchased from a variety of vendors and the Children's Home was closed.

Outdoor Relief and Administrative Developments

Despite the increased role of indoor or institutional relief, Milwaukee County never abandoned its system of outdoor relief. Its continued survival was assured by the fact that ward supervisors had a direct role in determining who would be eligible for the commissary-style assistance that County poor officers would provide. This ability to dispense relief to needy constituents was a helpful perquisite of incumbency, especially at election time. Moreover, outdoor relief simply worked too well and provided for the needs of those whose indigent status was not as severe as the inhabitants of the County institutions. As one might expect, however, outdoor relief was more tolerated than accepted by County officials, and the program and its administrators came under special scrutiny of the Board of Supervisors and its special standing committee (alternatively known as the Committee on Paupers, the Committee on the Poor Farm, and the Committee on the County Institutions). One of the first of the major investigations of outdoor relief came in 1858, when supervisors expressed dismay at the amount of money that was utilized not to assist the poor but "to support a throng of idlers under the name of officers, almost as great as the whole number of paupers maintained at the expense of the county."[33] In response to this "abuse" the committee issued a welter of proposals designed to tighten up operations and expenses of the relief system.

In 1858 the three state-mandated Superintendents of the Poor were to take over a phase of County social welfare efforts, one being responsible for the Almshouse, another for the farm, and a third for the outdoor relief. In addition, strict accounting was to be made of all money received and expended. The superintendent charged with outdoor relief was to establish an office in the city of Milwaukee, where he was to coordinate and direct efforts.[34] In subsequent additions to the welfare regulations, County supervisors maintained an important hand. Applicants for outdoor relief had to first submit an affidavit to their local supervisor, which in turn had to be witnessed by two taxpayers. Upon successful completion, this form was presented to the Superintendent of the Poor, who registered the persons on the poor rolls and gave them a weekly ration consisting of twelve pounds of flour, three pounds of meat, one-half cord of wood, and one-half bar of soap.[35] The petitioners could thus be supplied until a complaint was received that they were not entitled to such aid. The minutes of the Board of Supervisors are filled with such complaints.[36]

The commissary-style relief system necessitated the purchase of car-loads of food and supplies and involved any number of contracts with meat companies, wood suppliers, and dry-goods firms — all of whom angled to receive lucrative County business. The presence of these huge quantities of supplies often invited theft and fraud on the part of both provider and the needy. Indeed, one of the first complaints leveled at a Superintendent of the Poor came in 1854, when he was condemned for "fattening swine from the provisions furnished by the County for his own use and benefit."[37] More illustrative was the case of Superintendent Byron L. Abert. In 1872 Abert became the object of a special County investigation relative to complaints that he had grossly mismanaged the Poor Department and the County Hospital. A stinging report charged that Abert had "provided County Supplies [sic] to persons in possession of comfortable homesteads and bank accounts, and he had admitted persons to the Poor Farm and Hospital without authority in many cases." In addition, forty-two cords of wood, destined for the needy, had disappeared from County wood lots, to which

Abert appeared "Very indifferent." Perhaps worst of all, "Mr. Abert has assumed undue authority in dealing out supplies and taking persons into the Poor House without instructions from the Supervisors."[38] Abert strongly protested these accusations and, in retaliation, brazenly had one County Board member arrested. The other supervisors promptly bailed their colleague out and summarily removed Abert from office.[39] Yet the indomitable superintendent was not to be beaten. Mounting a series of court challenges to his removal and benefiting by a change in the membership of the Board of Supervisors, Abert was eventually reinstated and exonerated of the charges. Abert's case was typical of other investigations described in the minutes of the County Board. Accusations of mismanagement, theft, and fraud were often given a more lurid appeal by claims of drunkenness and immorality against the offending party. Indeed, Abert's successor was eventually removed because of accusations that he had seduced a ward of the Almshouse.[40]

The recurrent battles between supervisors and poor relief officials revealed larger tensions between alternate visions of proper administration. Older administrative models, largely derivative from the spoils system, held a high place for the so-called "citizen-politician," who, it was believed, was inherently competent to deal with all kinds of public problems and issues. Newer concepts, which gained increased popularity as the century unfolded, insisted that skilled administrators needed to be experts in their fields and should be removed from the rough and tumble of political concerns in the performance of their duty. Milwaukee County's approach to the administration of poor relief eventually moved in the latter direction. Under the lash of calls for reform, as well as the burden of their own increased duties, supervisors were compelled to abandon their direct role in the dispensing of outdoor relief. Moreover, the 1858 decision to apportion duties to the three Superintendents of the Poor led to the practice of picking qualified experts to direct and administer the growing number of institutions. By the end of the century, the administrative framework of the system had evolved into a series of virtually independent institutions, run by their own Board-selected administrators and respective boards of trustees. The title "Superintendent of the Poor" remained only with the official who had responsibility for the outdoor relief "department." This administrative diversity was to last until 1915, when unification was imposed by state law.

Treatment of the Insane

Of all the problems confronting County social welfare efforts, none were more vexatious than those relating to the mentally ill and insane.

Nineteenth-century knowledge of the causes and types of mental illness was even more primitive than the medical knowledge of the day. Because of this ignorance, the mentally ill were often poorly treated, sometimes with unspeakable cruelty.[41] Locked in city jails or, even worse, in bedlam-like lunatic asylums, the mentally disturbed were "treated" with chains, painful restraints, and shocking water treatments that were supposed to calm them down. Reforms in the treatment of the mentally ill came primarily through the efforts of Dorothea Dix, who lobbied untiringly for over forty years against the cruelties visited on the insane. Dix urged the creation of clean, well-regulated "asylums," where she hoped persons could learn to regain the balance and order they had lost in the unstable conditions of society.[42] While her expectations of effecting cures for these unfortunates ran high, more realistic reformers soon realized that some of the insane were far beyond any reasonable hope. Yet even in these so-called "hopeless cases," calls for humane and comfortable custodial treatment were loud and insistent.

The 275-bed County Insane Asylum opened in 1880, the first of two 19th-century facilities built for the care and treatment of the insane.

Before the County institutions were built, insane persons in Milwaukee County were often kept in the jailhouse, with violent cases shuttled off to one of the few insane asylums in the nation. The case of the "crazy man," Patrick McGowan, is illustrative. McGowan had been hauled into jail in the late 1840s so violently insane that his presence threatened the safety of the guards and the other prisoners. As a result, County officials put up the money to have him admitted to an insane asylum in Brattleboro, Vermont, where he remained on a County subsidy until he died.[43]

After the establishment of the Almshouse in 1852, the insane-poor found their way to its doorsteps and immediately posed serious problems of care and maintenance. Varying in the nature and extent of their respective disorders, the more violent inmates were soon confined to a special section of the Almshouse which was designated as the insane wing. This was the nucleus of County institutions for the mentally ill.

If criticisms of the officials and conditions of the Poor Department were legion, the controversy stirred up by County efforts in behalf of the mentally ill was even more strident. As in the institutions, the problems of overcrowding was present. The larger Milwaukee County grew, the more the poor and insane taxed the resources of the community and the institutions. One County supervisor complained in 1868 that

...the city of Milwaukee is the terminus of most of the railroads of the state, and of the steamboat lines from parts of the whole chain of lakes, and many insane persons are brought here, and left in the streets of the city, they are picked up by our police and being unable to give any clear account of themselves, humanity and public safety compel the Superintendents of the Poor to send them to the Insane Department of the County Poor Farm.[44]

Despite the supervisor's complaint, Milwaukee County was not alone in coping with the problems of the mentally ill. The state had also become an active partner in this problem with the opening of a state mental asylum at Madison in 1860 and another at Winnebago in 1873. Milwaukee County regularly sent its most acute cases to the new facilities; but when overcrowding occurred at the state institutions, disagreements developed between state and County officials over how many Milwaukee was entitled to send.[45]

The insane who remained in Milwaukee had only the slapdash, ad hoc efforts of the insane wing of the Almshouse. Even though additions had been made to the old Gregg farmhouse, they were ill-planned and soon hopelessly overcrowded. Pitiful descriptions of scantily clad human beings confined in cold, ill-ventilated cells, and initially not even segregated by sex were reported regularly to the Board of Supervisors by Dr. Fisk H. Day.[46] Day's complaints, which grew more shrill as needed reforms moved slowly or not at all, were soon reinforced by the State Board of Charities and Reforms, as well as local women's benevolent societies. In 1873 the State Board once again commissioned the indefatigable Mary E. B. Lynde to inspect conditions in the Milwaukee County institutions. Her report reaffirmed the stinging indictments made by Dr. Day.[47] Complaints of spoiled food, bad ventilation, and poor management elicited a defensive reaction from the supervisors, who maintained that conditions were basically good if only slightly overcrowded. Instead, the Board members turned their fire on Dr. Day, who, they insisted, "makes it his special hobby to exhibit all the defects of the Poor House and Hospital to the unfriendly gaze of every fault finder who may happen to come along." Angered Board members maintained that if Day had difficulties with the administration of County poor relief, it would be "infinitely more charitable...and in far better taste to have quietly informed some members of the Board of Supervisors."[48] In a blast at Mrs. Lynde, the supervisors decried a tendency toward "extravagance" in County institutions, fostered by "the periodical visits of well-meaning but visionary *Soi-dist-ant* [sic] reformers who imagine they are accomplishing a vast amount of good..."[49]

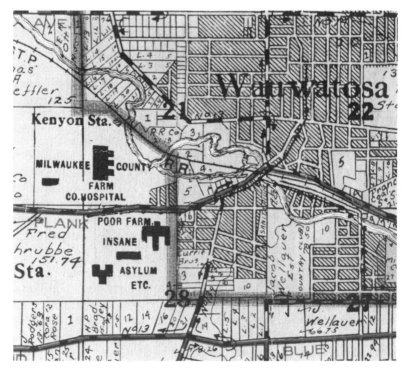

A 1916 map depicts the County Institutions grounds located near the City of Wauwatosa and six miles from downtown Milwaukee. Initially a 160-acre farm purchased from County Supervisor Hendrik Gregg in 1852, the complex expanded through the years to encompass nearly 1,200 acres.

Fire protection at the Institutions was another county concern. The fire station and horse-drawn ladder truck were part of the equipment available in 1910. The insane asylum is in the background.

This exchange did not end the controversy. In 1874 Mrs. Lynde enlisted the support of the Milwaukee Ladies Bible and Benevolent Society (of which she was a member), who launched their own independent investigation of the county's treatment of the insane. They, too, found conditions deplorable and singled out the harsh treatment meted out to the mentally ill by the director and matron of the Almshouse insane wing, one Mr. and Mrs. Boogk. Calls for their removal came amidst allegations of patient mistreatment and charges that the administrators were frequently intoxicated. While the Boogks were able to fend off the outcry, the point had been made; treatment of the insane demanded serious reformation.[50]

Once again, the State Board of Charities and Reform took the lead. Their lobbying efforts secured special legislation in 1878 which allowed for a program of county-state cooperation on behalf of the insane. Under the law, the state and the county were permitted to share financing and supervision of a new insane asylum. Milwaukee County quickly submitted plans for a new facility in 1878, and in 1880 the Milwaukee County Insane

Asylum opened its doors.[51] The 275-bed structure was quickly filled not only by Almshouse clients but also by those chronically insane persons whom the state returned to Milwaukee when there appeared little hope for their cure. So many came that by 1887 the County Asylum was awash with the mentally ill, and once again the State Board called for the creation of an additional facility to segregate the chronically insane from those who held some promise of a cure. In 1889 this building became a reality. The so-called "curable insane" remained in the older facility, which was re-named the Milwaukee County Hospital for the Acute Insane, and were subjected to a regimen of rest, quiet, and rehabilitation, including work on the County farm. The newer building, known as the Asylum for the Chronically Insane, provided custodial care for cases of incurable insanity, severe retardation, and senility, as well as serving as a receiving insti-tution for the retarded at the Northern and Southern Colonies. Physical additions and changes in treatment came slowly to these two County institutions, reflecting the relatively slow metamorphosis of theory and practice in the field of mental health.

The Groundwork Laid

By the turn of the century the main configurations of the Milwaukee County system of social welfare had emerged. A mixed system of indoor institutional and outdoor relief provided for the needs of thousands of Milwaukee County needy. Handicapped by funding problems, a funda-mentally negative attitude toward the poor, and the inevitable problems that a patronage-oriented system of administration brings, these insti-tutions made slow and painstaking progress. The percentage of Mil-waukee County expenditures given to poor relief was relatively small, and there was an ingrained resistance towards capital improvements on ex-isting facilities until there were absolutely no other options. With the onset of the reform movement known as Progressivism and the leadership of William L. Coffey, significant changes were to be made in both the structure and conduct of the County institutions and relief programs.

The Coffey Era: Consolidation and Expansion

The latter half of the nineteenth century had witnessed significant progress in the care and treatment of the needy of Milwaukee County. As the twentieth century dawned, new challenges were to redirect and inten-sify County social welfare efforts.

By the 1890s Milwaukee had begun her transformation from a com-mercial marketplace into a major industrial center. The city's burgeoning factories were like magnets for thousands of southern and eastern

European immigrants who descended on the upper midwest at the turn of the century.[52] By 1900, Milwaukee County's population had swollen to over 300,000 from the 138,500 it had been twenty years earlier.[53] Many of these newcomers found with their new life a measure of prosperity and a standard of living that they had only dreamed of in their homelands. Others were not so fortunate. Proportional numbers of the needy among the newcomers combined with "native" cases to overload the public institutions. To provide for them all, city and county agencies of assistance had to be expanded and rationalized.

Like the rest of America, Milwaukee County was facing the throes of modernization, a process of industrialization and urbanization that had accelerated since the end of the Civil War. The often unsettling dimensions of this process elicited a spectrum of reactions, but none so significant and enduring as the multifaceted national reform movement known as Progressivism.[54] This movement, especially prominent in Wisconsin, was to have significant implications for the administration of social welfare programs.

On one level, Progressivism challenged the predominant laissez-faire individualism of the previous century — an ideology that consistently cast the poor in a negative light. Progressive reformers such as Jane Addams challenged prevailing notions regarding the etiology of indigence by factoring in environmental and social considerations as major links in the "chain of poverty."[55] As these ideas were diffused, they created the inevitable ferment that led, particularly in Wisconsin, to a serious questioning of the basis on which the poor laws of 1838 to 1848 had been written. A brief written in the early twentieth century indicates this changing mood:

> ...the conception of the causes of poverty has changed from the idea that it is due entirely to a character defect, to a realization of the fact that it is often attributable to conditions over which the individual has no control.[56]

These altered perceptions of the causes of poverty came together with still another facet of Progressivism, namely, the so-called "search for order." Progressive reformers led the way in adapting the lessons of scientific management to a broad array of human affairs. In the realm of public relief to the poor they believed that they could decisively alter and rearrange "a distended society" by insisting on careful planning, rationality, and efficiency in social welfare activities.[57] The heralds of this new gospel of order were to be trained professionals who brought purposeful planning and efficient management techniques to Milwaukee County's social welfare efforts.

Administrative reforms led the way early in the new century. Throughout the nineteenth century, every aspect of the administration of

County social welfare had come under the direct supervision of a committee of the County Board. This system created a confused maze of superintendents and boards of trustees with intersecting lines of authority, duplicated services, and general administrative chaos. In 1905 a bill was enacted by the state legislature that began consolidating these varying lines of authority. A five-person board, selected by the County Board and the governor, assumed partial control of the Almshouse, Outdoor Relief, and the County Hospital. The mental asylums and the children's home remained under separate boards of trustees.[58] In 1913 the consolidation process lurched forward once again when County Supervisors secured legislation to permit formation of a centralized Board of Administration. Composed of a mixture of state and local appointees, this citizen-politician body reflected the abiding faith of the Progressives in regulatory boards that functioned as middle management organizations. Armed with a broad grant of authority to consolidate and administer the work of social welfare in Milwaukee County, the new Board of Administration took up its duties on October 1, 1915.[59] Among the members of the five-person panel was a thirty-six-year-old dentist, William L. Coffey, who became the Board's full-time secretary. From 1915 until his retirement in 1952 at the age of seventy-three Coffey dominated the social welfare establishment of Milwaukee County. The extent of his influence was such that this period can aptly be characterized as "the Coffey Era."

Born in Milwaukee in 1879, William L. Coffey attended parochial schools and Marquette College (for which he retained an enduring interest and affection). After graduation he pursued studies in dentistry at the College of Physicians and Surgeons (the predecessor of the Marquette School of Medicine) and graduated in 1901. His dental practice was cut short in 1904, when he assumed responsibility for a small trucking firm owned by his father. In this endeavor he apparently demonstrated the kind of managerial skills that were to serve him well in his County welfare work. He was recruited for the Board of Administration in 1915 by close friends on the Board of Supervisors and soon made the secretary's post the administrative hub of that body. From the outset, Coffey insisted that planning, coordination, and professionalization ought to characterize the social welfare efforts of the County.[60] Although neither a trained physician nor a social worker, Coffey nonetheless pressed for a greater degree of specialization of services that would bring Milwaukee County into a new era.

Coffey's hand was immeasurably strengthened in 1918, when a state civil service law went into effect mandating testing for specific positions in County government. As the demands for professional physicians and social workers increased, institutions of higher learning began to offer programs to supply the need. In 1918 Marquette University formally established its

William L. Coffey, director of
the County Institutions for
over thirty years, reshaped the
county's social welfare establishment through admin-
istrative consolidation and
expanded services to the
needy. A retirement picture
was taken of Coffey and his
wife in front of the County
Hospital in 1952.

own medical school. This institution soon moved into an informal, but close, relationship with County General Hospital (as it was now called), giving that institution the benefits of some of the latest and best of medical advances. Professional social work also received an important boost with the opening of a school of social work at the University of Wisconsin in 1920. This growing pool of trained social welfare professionals was augmented late in the 1940s by the establishment of an extension program at Milwaukee. Graduates from both programs provided a steady stream of employees and administrators for County welfare posts.[61]

The Board of Administration also reflected changing perceptions of the poor and mentally ill by renaming institutions that housed them. Illustrative of this was the case of the County Almshouse. This first of County institutions had finally received new quarters in 1890, with additions being made in 1907 and 1932. Its resident population, which usually hovered around five hundred, was generally the elderly poor and some mentally ill who were not totally disabled or bedridden. In 1917 the Board of Administration suggested that the name "Almshouse" (with its negative implications) be dropped in favor of the more euphonious (and technically correct) Milwaukee County Infirmary. This change was approved, and that title was retained until the institution was closed in 1978. So, too, other institutions reflected changes in their purpose or public image by different nomenclature. The Milwaukee County Home for Dependent Children became simply the Milwaukee County Home for Children; the Milwaukee County Hospital for the Acute Insane became the Milwaukee County Hospital for the Mentally Diseased; the Milwaukee County Asylum for the Chronic Insane became known as the Milwaukee County Asylum for Mental Diseases.[62] Later the two mental facilities came to be known simply as North and South Divisions.

The Board of Administration secured important changes in social welfare operations for Milwaukee County, but it was only to be a transitory body. The experiences of the Board had demonstrated that stronger and more coordinated executive management was necessary. To this end,

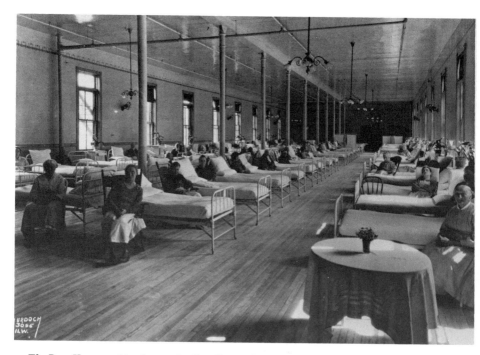

The Poor House or Almshouse, the first County facility established in 1852, became known as the Milwaukee County Infirmary in 1917. This is a typical interior view of the infirmary in the 1920s.

legislation was secured in 1921 creating a new body called the Board of Trustees for the County Institutions and Programs. The new law also contained a provision creating a civil-service rank managerial position that would function as an executive arm for the new body.[63] Quite naturally, the Board of Supervisors selected the hard-working Coffey as its interim manager and, after he had successfully completed the civil service examination, appointed him permanently to the post in 1922. The new arrangement made Coffey accountable to both the Board of Trustees and the County Board but gave him even fuller authority over the various superintendents and employees of the County institutions. Coffey further augmented the power of his position in the 1930s, when the Board of Trustees was renamed the Board of Public Welfare. A hard-driving, almost workaholic man, Coffey lived on the County grounds (as did other administrators) with his wife and ten children, immersing himself in all the details of the various institutions. Well connected with powerful allies on the County Board such as Eugene Warnimont, Willard "Mike" Lyons, Walter Celichowski, and Lawrence Timmerman, not to mention influential friends on the state and federal level, Coffey consistently expanded and consolidated the social welfare enterprise of Milwaukee County and his power over it.[64] Besides his natural managerial talents, Coffey brought a stability to the work. His long-term service, coupled with those of most of the superintendents with whom he worked so closely, assured continuity and a steady line of development.

Not only was the County refitting its administrative structures, but the entire environment of the institutions grounds was changing as well. From the 160-acre Gregg farm the County had expanded its holdings by subsequent purchases of adjacent properties. New facilities erected on these lands brought increased demands for utilities and services. Water disputes with the city erupted in the late nineteenth century, resulting in the construction of a separate pumping station and waterworks on the County grounds in 1896. Centralized services grew as well to handle the volume of patients and workers on the grounds. Plans for a central laundry and butcher shop were proposed in 1917, and later additions included a central bakery, garage, and power plant to replace the individual furnaces of the respective institutions.[65] The presence of patients, administrators, and workers (some of whom also lived in housing provided by the County) gave the grounds the aspect of a small city, attractively landscaped by a growing corps of groundsmen assisted by selected patients. A substantial brick administrative center was erected in the early 1920s as well as warehouses for commissary supplies.

The County farm was one of the more profitable institutions on the Institutions grounds. Farm acreage had increased so significantly that by 1919 farm superintendent Charles Evert boasted that barns, grain fields,

The Milwaukee County School of Agriculture and Domestic Economy operated between 1912 and 1928 in five buildings erected on 208 acres at the Institutions grounds. The school offered training in farming and home economics. These pictures illustrate classes in sewing and beekeeping.

pasturage, and stock flourished on land that was originally considered exhausted. Prize livestock, horses, swine, and cattle were cared for by County inmates and hired labor.[66] The County farm was also later connected to an interesting experiment inaugurated by the state in 1911. In that year a law was enacted permitting counties to establish schools of agriculture and "domestic economy" (housekeeping) for high-school-age youth. Milwaukee County established such a school in 1912 and erected a series of attractive buildings on the institution grounds that accommodated budding agriculturalists from all over the state. In 1923 the school was united with the County farm and in its brief existence managed to produce prize-winning agricultural exhibits at the state fair (a long tradition in County farming) together with a faithful alumni. Despite its apparent success, the school was far too costly for the relatively few students who entered. In 1928 the County Board closed its doors, and the agricultural program was absorbed by the state university system.[67] The farm itself continued in operation, providing work for able-bodied residents as well as supplying a portion of the needs of the County institutions and the Outdoor Relief Department. A destructive fire ravaged several of the farm buildings in the 1950s, and the County Board discontinued the livestock enterprise.[68] By 1964, virtually the entire farming program was phased out (although tomatoes were still raised in the County greenhouses until 1970), and the entire County farm was turned into an open field.[69]

The regimen of outdoor work was seen as an important form of therapy for a number of patients served by the County institutions. Nowhere did the need for fresh air and a healthful environment figure more prominently than in the care of the mentally ill and tubercular.

Progressive America looked more closely at the etiology of mental illness than previous generations. Not until the 1950s and 1960s would the County move away from the concept of asylum or custodial care for the mentally ill, but the dawn of preventive and aftercare therapies were emerging by the 1920s.[70] In 1919 Milwaukee County opened an outpatient facility known as the Dispensary (more below) on the third floor of the Saxe Building on Fifth and Grand (now Wisconsin) Avenue. As part of this new phase of patient care, a mental hygiene clinic was begun, which by 1924 was enlarged to accommodate additional psychiatric staff. In that same year, responding to both community needs and developments in the field, a Child Guidance Clinic was inaugurated. These agencies eventually came together in 1926 to form the Milwaukee Mental Hygiene Clinic, changed in 1939 to the Milwaukee County Guidance Clinic. Expansion of service and personnel caused the clinic to move out of the Dispensary building in 1937. Despite these innovations and the growing use of these clinics by social workers, the courts, and the children's home, the backbone of mental health care still remained the services provided at the North and South Division mental facilities.[71]

Of all the concerns of the Public Health Movement that were to affect Milwaukee County the care of the consumptive or tubercular was the most dramatic and ultimately successful.[72] Tuberculosis was one of the chief killers of children and young adults in human history. In 1884 the Medical Society of Milwaukee County drew attention to the increasingly serious problem of the disease in the area. By one count in 1911, over 2,000 persons were afflicted with the illness (in various stages), and nearly 500 had died of its effects.[73] Aided by city funds, Milwaukee physicians mobilized to combat the disease and soon effected a separation of TB patients from others in the hospital wards of the city. In 1904 public awareness of the disease was heightened when the exhibit of the National Tuberculosis Prevention Movement was brought to Milwaukee. National interest in this problem spurred local support in 1907 for the construction of one of the first professional treatment centers for TB in the area, the Blue Mound Sanatorium for Incipient Tuberculosis. County effort characteristically

Fresh air was an important part of treatment for tuberculosis. Young patients were housed at the Blue Mound Preventorium, a department of Muirdale Sanatorium, the large medical complex built in 1913 to combat the deadly disease.

lagged behind these private and city endeavors. Pressure from local physicians eventually brought about the designation of special wards for the tubercular at County General and the mental asylums. In 1911 County efforts took a step forward when the fifty-bed Greenfield Sanatorium, originally sponsored by the City of Milwaukee, was secured. A small "Social Workers Sanatorium" was also purchased. Encouraged by the Greenfield purchase, the city and private groups that operated the Blue Mound facility offered to sell the whole operation to the County. County officials rejected the offer, choosing instead to build a new sanatorium adjacent to the existing County institutions. Legislation and funds were secured in 1913 for a facility innovative in design and concept for the treatment of tuberculosis. Muirdale, as it was to be known (named for Wisconsin naturalist John Muir), comprised a series of multistoried cottages which kept adult patients together and maintained a rigorous schedule of fresh air, bed rest, and close supervision. Separate wings were later added for the tubercular insane. Muirdale was unique both in its insistence on the therapeutic value of cold, dry air, as well as the cottage-like arrangements that kept patients together.[74] In 1921 the County purchased the Blue Mound Sanatorium and rechristened it the Blue Mound Preventorium to deal with TB cases in the young. With these new facilities the County made it possible for hundreds of its residents to find some relief from the so-called "White Plague." But since indigency was the prime criterion for admission to the sanatorium, not everyone who had the dread illness could apply for treatment — even on the graduated scale of payments allowed for some patients. This fact, coupled with the advent of more effective treatment, i.e., chemotherapy and drugs, caused the facility gradually to decline in the numbers of patients it served in the 1940s. However, when war-time draft-board physicals revealed that the disease was from from eradicated, Wisconsin tackled the problem with a program of free treatment and prevention in 1945. This reinvigorated the use of the Muirdale facilities. In 1947 treatment and prevention programs were joined. Medical advances had begun to root out TB so effectively that by 1969 Muirdale was closed and TB treatment made a department of County General. In 1978 the Muirdale buildings became the home of the County Nursing Home (formerly the County Infirmary).[75]

Care of the children underwent significant changes in the early twentieth century as well. Stimulated by the conclusions of a major White House conference in 1908, child care professionals endorsed the findings of social welfare experts and urged that the family unit be preserved as the best possible environment in which to care for children. Institutionalization, the mainstay of child welfare efforts of the nineteenth century, remained as a last resort and a temporary arrangement at that. In 1911, acting under recommendations of the Board of Trustees of the Home for Dependent Children, Milwaukee County permitted the setting aside of

$5,000 from the County poor fund to be distributed to mothers of dependent children.[76] This proposal antedated by one year a program adopted by the state and became the forerunner of one of the most durable of later federal welfare programs, aid to dependent children. A unique aspect of this policy was its administration by County probate judges rather than appointed County officers. The interrelationship of the courts to the social welfare system is a long and complex matter, having grown from the regular court referrals of patients and inmates to the County institutions (particularly the mental health facilities). With the establishment of the Children's Court in 1901, the judiciary moved into the field of child welfare. Later old age pensions and benefits to the blind were added to the panoply of programs administered by the County judiciary. As such, it was a cause of much frustration to subsequent Boards of Supervisors and a perennial stumbling block to the centralizing ambitions of William L. Coffey.

County General had long ago surpassed the Almshouse/Infirmary as the most vital of County institutions. Important changes in the medical profession, and in medical technology had brought about the metamorphosis of this institution from a cramped and ill-ventilated charity ward to a professional health care facility. Increasing demands for the services of the hospital elicited the special concern of Institutions Manager Coffey (one of his daughters later referred to County General as "his baby") and led to major programs of administrative reorganization and physcial expansion.[77]

In 1920 the Board of Administration appointed Dr. Harry Sergeant as hospital administrator. A graduate of the Marquette Medical School, Sergeant had done his internship at County General and used his knowledge of the institution to assist Coffey in his work. The new administrator eventually secured the part-time services of Doctors Joseph M. King as chief of surgery, and Francis D. Murphy as chief of medicine. Both men served as volunteers until their positions were given official "part-time" status in the 1930s. The Coffey, King, Murphy, and Sergeant quartet constituted a working alliance that pressed constantly for an improved County General. Moreover, the appointments of King and Murphy, who also had positions on the staff of the Marquette Medical School, established even more firmly the unofficial links between that institution and County General.[78] Scores of young interns received their first hands-on experience of medicine from men like Sergeant, King, and Murphy.

Two other major concerns, outpatient care and the location of County medical services, coalesced in the 1920s to provide still another chapter in the development of professional health care in Milwaukee County. One of the long-standing disputes on the County Board and among the citizenry was the location of the County hospital in "far-off" Wauwatosa. Complaints that ambulance service was too slow and bumpy for emergency patients and that medical services were not easily accessible to city residents prompted the establishment of a number of privately run dispensaries or outpatient clinics. Operated by the good will and volunteer services of local physicians, these small operations attempted to respond to the needs of the urban sick and acutely ill.

The maturation of the preventive medicine and outpatient care concepts in the twentieth century brought about a sentiment to modify certain aspects of health care in Milwaukee County. When a report to the Board of Supervisors in 1916 related that inspectors of the Wisconsin Medical Association were dissatisfied with the status of outpatient care at County General, the Board recommended the establishment of a County-run Dispensary that would (in typical Progressive fashion) "promote social efficiency by preventing many things which the community is now called on to alleviate or cure."[79] Funding for the proposed facility was to be met by County resources together with substantial contributions from the Matthew Keenan Endowment Fund, which had been established in 1898. In 1919 enabling legislation was secured, and the County opened a temporary Dispensary in rented quarters on the third floor of the Saxe Building on Fifth and Grand Avenue. The seven County physicians made

The various County Institutions contributed to a public display, which described their functions and activities, for the 1926 state fair.

this facility their headquarters, spending time there as well as continuing their appointed rounds to those on outdoor relief. By 1923 the Dispensary had expanded its services with the establishment of night clinics for the treatment of venereal diseases (banned from County General for a time), as well as diabetes, prenatal, obstetrical, and child welfare clinics.[80]

The progress and popularity of the Dispensary resurrected long-standing concerns for an emergency facility. As in the movement for an urban dispensary, the City of Milwaukee took the lead. In 1892 it had established the Johnston Emergency Hospital on the corner of Third and Michigan, a small twenty-four-bed unit that rendered yeoman service until it was so overcrowded that it could no longer function effectively. Late in 1925 the city offered to sell the Johnston Hospital and turn over the funds to the County for the establishment of a new Dispensary-Emergency Clinic. This plan won the support of William L. Coffey, who promoted it as part of a larger master plan devised by himself and the superintendents of the institutions to extend and upgrade medical services. Coffey's careful planning had included a proposal that the new facility be located on a tract of County-owned property at 24th and Wisconsin Avenue, land known as the Schandein site. Ironically, at the same time, Coffey's beloved Marquette University was eyeing the same land as a potential site for a teaching hospital for its growing medical school. Intense rivalry ensued and Coffey ultimately prevailed, not only securing the Schandein site, but preserving County General as a teaching hospital for Marquette interns. The new Dispensary-Emergency Hospital opened in 1930, aided by physicians who donated their services and providing twenty-four-hour care for the urban sick and those whose illnesses did not require hospitalization. Moreover, the Dispensary-Emergency Hospital functioned as one of the many "intake" operations of the County system, separating those cases that required long-term hospitalization from those who only required outpatient care.[81]

County General itself, having undergone crucial conceptual and technological changes, still suffered from overcrowding. The original buildings erected in 1880 had been expanded in piecemeal fashion and accommodated about 350 patients. As early as 1916 calls had been issued to expand the hospital. In 1930 this became a reality when a $1.8 million, 650 bed hospital opened its doors on the County grounds.[82] The old hospital continued in existence for several more years as the so-called Unit II, until it was closed in 1934. However, by 1936 the new County General was bursting at the seams with patients, and Coffey secured federal assistance from the Works Progress Administration (WPA) to refurbish and renovate the old building. Finally complete in 1943, the renewed facilities were able to serve 400 new patients. Just as the new County General was opening its doors in 1930, the nation and the County were plunged into a major depression that would quite literally tax the health and social welfare services of both to their limits.[83]

Depression, War, and the End of the Coffey Era

The first thirty years of the twentieth century had witnessed tremendous advances in County welfare services. Significant progress in methods of treatment and medical technology were capped by an ambitious expansion of the physical plant. In all, it seemed a ringing endorsement of the consolidationist policies of William L. Coffey and the Board of Trustees.

Virtually the only division that remained outside this cavalcade of development was the Department of Outdoor Relief (DOR), headed by William Spindler. Spindler had been on the job since the turn of the century (he still signed himself "Superintendent of the Poor"), and his resignation in 1928 brought his assistant Willard "Pop" Notbohm to the post. Notbohm enjoyed the slow-paced complacency of the DOR for a little more than a year when an economic cataclysm of gigantic proportions hit the nation and the County — the Great Depression. The stock market crash of late October 1929 sent shock waves through the national economy that were soon felt in Milwaukee County. By late 1929 hundreds of businesses either closed or so curtailed their operations that thousands of Milwaukeeans were thrown out of work and compelled to seek public assistance. The DOR, which had tendered assistance to 383 families in August 1929, saw the numbers of applications skyrocket to over 2,500 by December. This was only the beginning. By December 1930, 10,593 cases were reported to the DOR, and $857,050.40 was spent on their behalf, more than the total amount distributed in the preceding seven years. The year 1932 saw expenditures three times that of 1931, and by 1935, the peak load of 40,176 cases was reached. By that year over half the budget of Milwaukee County ($14.3 million) was channeled into various kinds of outdoor relief.[84]

Notbohm, with a skeleton staff and little experience in dealing with disasters of this type, was soon overwhelmed by the work, and Coffey threw himself full time into the planning and execution of programs to feed and shelter the swelling number of the dependent.[85] Although the County had seriously debated the granting of food vouchers to outdoor relief recipients, the exigencies of the Depression caused these plans to be shelved as the commissary food program was dramatically expanded.[86] Twelve regional aid centers were established at key locations in the County, and dietician Ada B. Lothe devised nutritious and filling menus for the aid recipients who would collect them weekly. Children's coaster wagons and gunny sacks hauled home the rations of flour, rolled oats, fresh vegetables, and meat. Cheap-grade coal as well as vouchers for rent and utilities was also provided. Although complaints surfaced about particular aspects of the relief effort, by and large it was a success.[87] Indeed, Milwaukee was one of the few localities that did not have to establish a special emergency agency to handle the overwhelming tasks that hard times imposed.

Notbohm resigned his directorship in 1932 and was replaced by Benjamin Glassberg. Coffey had recruited Glassberg from Milwaukee's Federated Jewish Charities. A trained professional and a crack administrator, Glassberg expanded and refined the operations of the DOR, allowing Coffey to divert his attentions to the needs of the other institutions which were also besieged during the Depression, as well as to federal and state relief projects that sought his advice.[88] Glassberg remained at his post until 1943 and brought the DOR (which changed its name to the Department of Public Assistance in 1939) to a high level of national prominence by his own published work in professional journals as well as his consultations with officials of the federal government.[89]

In 1932, however, days of acclaim were far distant for Glassberg and his harried staff. The strains on County resources became painfully evident at the same time President Herbert Hoover was exhorting localities to take up the main burden of relief. One Hoover administration initiative did have some limited effect in Milwaukee County, namely, loans from the Reconstruction Finance Corporation (RFC). With these funds Milwaukee County was able to establish a work program in 1932 that supplied various units of County government with workers from the relief rolls. These workers received prevailing rates of wages "on paper" but were restricted to limited hours.[90] When Hoover's successor, Franklin D. Roosevelt, took office in 1933, he commenced a broad-based program of relief, recovery, and reform known as the New Deal that brought the federal government into full partnership with the states and localities in the work of social welfare. This represented a historic turning point in the expansion and development of social welfare services for Milwaukee County.

In late 1933 the Federal Emergency Relief Administration (FERA) established a branch of the Civil Works Administration (CWA) in Wisconsin. Joined with minimal aid from the nearly exhausted coffers of the state government, the CWA provided short-term employment to thousands of Wisconsin residents through the bitter winter of 1933-34. Road construction and improvement, playground construction, sewer pipe expansion, and airport construction were among the jobs CWA workers performed. Upon FERA's expiration in April 1934, the Wisconsin Emergency Relief Administration (WERA) was put into effect. Carrying on the projects of the CWA, over 17,000 men and women were employed in public service jobs throughout 1934. In 1935 the rolls were reduced to 8,000.[91] Despite these efforts, however, relief rolls continued to climb in Milwaukee County. In the spring of 1935 Roosevelt established the Works

Progress Administration (WPA), perhaps the best remembered of the myriad New Deal agencies. Similar in concept to the CWA, the WPA appeared at a crucial juncture in County social welfare efforts because by 1936 relief funds were totally exhausted.[92] The County WPA office was opened in November 1935, and armies of Milwaukee jobless found employment working on the city "infrastructure" (roads, bridges,and parks), as well as rendering important clerical and white collar work to County offices and agencies.

The WPA was designed only as a temporary measure to relieve those worst afflicted by the Depression. Although it left some enduring traces of its presence, a much more substantial legacy of the New Deal in Milwaukee County came with the enactment of the Social Security Act of 1935.

Assistance to the aged had been part of the Milwaukee County social welfare agenda since 1930. In that year the County Board utilized the discretionary power given it by the state legislature in 1925 to permit the distribution of funds to the elderly poor.[93] With the adoption of the Social Security Act of 1935, the Wisconsin program was adapted to fit the federal requirements. The two main provisions of the law, Title I, relating to old age assistance, and Title II, providing for unemployment insurance, permanently expanded and developed the role of the federal government in issues of social welfare. Subsequent amendments to the law further broadened the scope of the programs funded and administered by Washington. Local power over Social Security benefits, like child welfare cases and aid to the blind, was the province of county probate judges.[94]

This administrative divergence called to mind earlier scenarios of overlapping and confused responsibilities for relief operations. After Glassberg's departure in 1943 and the short tenures of William Greenya and Stanley White over the Department of Public Assistance, important developments continued in the area of public relief. The first phase of these changes came when the County abandoned the commissary-style relief program in favor of cash payments. Long arguments had raged over this proposal since Supervisor R. Metcalfe first suggested it in 1933. Proponents argued that it was administratively more simple as well as less demeaning for relief recipients to receive cash instead of victuals. Opponents, including Glassberg and Coffey, charged that it would be more costly and that the opportunity for fraud would be multiplied. Moreover, the commissary system had worked well enough during the Depression. Despite the controversy, the County Board approved the measure in 1945, and it went into effect January 1, 1946.[95]

Unification of the various public welfare services had been urged since 1938. In October 1947, the County Board created a separate Department of Public Welfare to handle old age assistance, aid for dependent children, aid for the blind, and the placing of dependent children in new homes. General supervision of these programs remained under County judges, but in 1948 a professional social worker from Gary, Indiana, Joseph E. Baldwin, was recruited to serve as the executive director of this County relief effort. General assistance to families remained under the aegis of Coffey and the Board of Public Welfare.[96]

In 1949 a report entitled the "Milwaukee County Survey of Social Welfare" criticized this administrative structure, calling for an end to the oversight of the judges and urging a unification of all relief services. Public pressure built for administrative reorganization which eventually took place in 1950, when Coffey succeeded in uniting the relief systems in one large department under the leadership of Baldwin and the supervision of the Board of Public Welfare. Baldwin set up his offices on the sixth floor of the County Courthouse and carefully organized the new agency into a welter of divisions to process, approve, and deliver legitimate claims for public assistance. As amendments to the Social Security Act were made and the federal role in social welfare expanded, the Department of Public Welfare (DPW) assumed added responsibilities for interfacing local, state, and federal aid programs. By 1964, having outgrown its courthouse quarters, the DPW moved the entire operation to the vacant Schuster's Department Store on Twelfth and Vliet Streets.[97]

Not only had the Depression vastly expanded the role of the DOR, but it also had placed strains on other County institutions. Adding to the burden the indigent placed on the existing facilities, the onset of war in 1941 created serious shortages of building materials and brought a virtual halt to all non-defense construction activity. Moreover, the Milwaukee Socialist influence in local politics continued to exercise a conservative hesitation about building unless the funds were already set aside for a project. This "pay as you go" mentality partially explained the traditional reluctance of County supervisors to expand County institutions even if they were seriously overcrowded.[98] As a result of all these factors, the natural, planned growth that would normally have taken place was stymied. County General hospital became the first target of dissatisfaction with the crowded and belt-tightened conditions. In late 1945 a group of interns staged a work slowdown to protest the lack of supervision they were receiving at the hospital as well as the quality of care and supplies provided to the patients. Specific objects of the complaints included hospital administrators Dr. Harry Sergeant and Dr. Joseph King as bitter and highly publicized hearings took place before the Board of Public Welfare throughout 1946.[99]

As the hearings unfolded, however, it became obvious that the criticisms of County General were only a pretext for attacks on William L. Coffey and the administrative "clique" that ran the County institutions.

Coffey indignantly protested the attacks on his stewardship and demanded an investigation of all the County institutions to clear his name. Although the Board of Public Welfare did not accede to Coffey's request, it ultimately exonerated him and his associates of any accusations of mismanagement; yet the level and extent of the public hostility, especially manifested in the pages of the *Milwaukee Journal*, shook him deeply.[100]

Whatever his private feelings about the events of 1946, Coffey continued to labor diligently to expand and improve County facilities. With the end of the war, press attention on the increasingly crowded facilities of the County institutions created public pressure for necessary expansion. A study of needs and costs conducted by Coffey was presented to a 1949 luncheon meeting of the County Board and drew stunned gasps as the Director revealed that $10 million would be needed to provide 300 new beds at County General, an equal amount for the hospital for the acute insane, 500 beds for the asylum for the chronically insane, 200 for the chronically ill, and 75 for Muirdale.[101] Postwar inflation stalled these ambitious plans, with only a substantial addition to one of the mental facilities being accomplished.

Coffey reached the mandatory retirement age of seventy in 1949, but special arrangements kept him on board for an additional three years. Finally in 1952, he stepped down to be replaced by thirty-four-year-old John Rankin.[102] Coffey's tenure of over thirty years was characterized by a consistent stress on administrative consolidation and the expansion of services to the needy. Because of his long tenure and that of his closest associates, he was able to build firmly on the nineteenth-century foundations of social welfare in Milwaukee County, as well as pioneering a few new directions himself. With the era of John Rankin, the period of long-tenured administrators appeared to be over. Social welfare activity was moving into a new and activist phase that would transform it as significantly as Coffey had the nineteenth-century heritage.

A New Era: Mental Health and the Medical Center

When William L. Coffey stepped down in 1952, it was the end of one age and the beginning of another. Coffey's thirty years plus had witnessed steady progress in the concept and delivery of social welfare services, while his longevity had assured the necessary stability to plan and execute a long-range vision. The next thirty years (1952-1982) would both continue and discontinue the broad patterns established in the Coffey years. On the one hand, the example of a long-tenured institutions chief began and ended with Coffey. Between 1952 and 1982 there were to be five directors: John Rankin (1952-1959), Orville Guenther (1960-1969), Edwin Mundy

(1969-1977), Symuel Smith (1977-1981), and James Wahner (1981-   ). Each of these directors would feel the heavy winds of political opposition and find himself besieged by a combination of political and professional pressures that might have toppled even the indomitable Coffey. Yet it was the combination of these forces that ironically continued the program of expansion and consolidation that Coffey had so single-mindedly pursued during his years in office. This process accelerated with such sweeping dynamism that it engulfed not only the County institutions but also brought about a joining of public and private health care services in a cooperative endeavor of significant historical importance. Moreover, as intercooperation was to change the face of Milwaukee County health care, important impulses were afoot in the field of mental health that would effect major changes in this crucial area. In short, two issues loom largest over the complex history of this last era, the metamorphosis of mental health services (the "Landis Revolution") and the development of the Milwaukee County Regional Medical Center.

Thirty-four-year-old John Rankin assumed office in May 1952 and moved on a number of fronts to complete the final phases of the Coffey agenda in addition to developing his own. Coffey's hopes to build on and improve the crowded County General found easier acceptance after he departed from office. A flush of prosperity swept the nation, and Milwaukee County government abandoned its traditional fiscal conservatism, pouring money into any number of projects that transformed the face of the metropolitan area. New public facilities included a stadium, a zoo, an arena, and the beginnings of a modern expressway system.[103] Plans for a new County hospital were part of this rush in improvement. Ground was broken for a new facility which would include 600 new beds, laboratories, and expanded facilities for every department. Moreover, emergency and outpatient clinics were to be transferred to the new site (a decision that engendered much controversy). The hospital was completed in late 1957 and opened its doors in 1958.[104] The decision to remove the Dispensary-Emergency Hospital to the new location was part of a larger plan that was destined to significantly reorganize the social welfare operation of Milwaukee County.

Commissioned by the Board of Supervisors in 1955, the Chicago-based Public Administration Service had undertaken a major study of all aspects of county governance. Their report, issued in 1956, suggested a number of changes for the social welfare departments and provided a blueprint for the shape of things to come.[105] Most significantly, the report called for the retention of the position of Director of the Institutions but suggested a degree of decentralization with the appointment of four separate department heads to oversee specialized areas of the work of social welfare. To be appointed were a medical director, a mental health director, a public welfare director, and a services director.[106] The position of Deputy Director was later added to oversee the purely fiscal aspects of the operation.

Institutions Director Rankin moved to implement this report with approval from the County Board. Joseph Baldwin was reconfirmed as public welfare head; Dr. Harold Cook, former head of the now dismantled Dispensary-Emergency Hospital, was eventually chosen as medical director.[107] But the most significant appointment was that of Dr. Charles Landis to head the mental health directorate of the newly reorganized social services.[18] Virtually single-handedly, Landis was to effect a major reorientation of the mental health services rendered by Milwaukee County, wrenching them from their dependence on outdated and ineffective custodial methods and redirecting them to modes of active treatment and outpatient care. The "Landis Revolution" emptied the mental institutions and helped to restore all but the most serious cases to some effective degree of engagement with the community.[19]

Mental health director Dr. Charles W. Landis in front of the nearly completed new day hospital in 1969. Landis reshaped the County's approach to mental health services.

Landis, a native of Indiana, assumed his post in May 1958. At the time of his appointment, the population of the North and South Division mental facilities was nearly 3,800. Projected estimates of the rates of admission warned that the numbers in these two institutions would exceed 10,000 patients unless something were done.[110] Landis approached the problem on two fronts: by the refinement of diagnostic techniques and by the development of more effective methods of treatment for those already in the institutions. A new diagnostic clinic designed to rigidly screen those who seemed candidates for institutionalization from those who could better profit from alternative forms of therapy had already opened in 1958 at the newly built County General.[111] Working with newly elected County Executive John Doyne and sympathetic state legislators, Landis worked to reduce the number of admissions by securing important changes in the mental commitment laws of the state of Wisconsin. By making it all the more difficult to consign a troublesome parent or relative to a mental institution, he hoped to discourage this as a form of punishment and encourage the use of outpatient care.[112] By the application of rapidly advancing medical technology, (i.e., drugs and outpatient therapies), further progress could be made. For those already in the County institutions, the same application of antidepressant drugs and therapy had so helped to thin out the populations of North and South Division that by 1968 Landis had succeeded in cutting the population in half. However, cutting the numbers was only half the game. Aided by provisions of the newly enacted Medicare legislation, Landis also simultaneously moved to bring about a whole new format for mental health care that significantly departed from the asylum concept.

Working closely with federal officials, who had taken a lively interest in mental health issues, Landis devised a plan for a centralized mental health center that would incorporate his vision of active therapy (as opposed to custodial care) and more refined specialization for different constituencies. Initially, federal officials resisted, recommending instead the construction of five new mental health centers in the Milwaukee area. Both Landis and his supporters in County government thought that this was excessive.[113] Instead, generous federal funding was utilized to bring about the construction of an attractive A-frame hospital for outpatient care of the mentally ill. Functionally named the "Day Hospital," this facility opened in July 1969 and stood as a testimony to Landis' abiding belief in this form of therapy.[114] To attend to the need for mental health services outside the institution grounds area, Landis developed the "catchment area" system. This interesting variation on the old county-physician practice established six regions of the Milwaukee County area, each with a population of 150,000-200,000. At an easily accessible site within that region a mental health center that would bring services and important diagnostic information to patients in the area would be established. Local professionals were encouraged to participate in the program, and the hope was expressed that catchment area services would one day include more than mental health treatment.[115] Landis' program also called for the building of a special facility to deal with mental illness in youth and adolescents. The fact that young people needed separation from the adult mentally ill was a lesson long known by mental health experts but only imperfectly acted upon. Landis first proposed the idea in 1966 and recommended at the time that the center for youth be in refurbished buildings in the old children's home. Later he pressed for the construction of an entirely new facility, a proposal that met defeat temporarily in 1969.[116] Landis left County service in that year, thoroughly exhausted with the travail of politics,[117] but his plans were later implemented and in 1973 the proposed center was opened. Ten years after his departure, the capstone of the "Landis Revolution" came with the opening of a new mental hospital, displacing the nearly century-old North and South Division facilities.[118]

Landis' death in early 1986 received far less press coverage than his prodigious accomplishments merited.[119] He had decisively altered the pattern of mental health care in Milwaukee County and broken the pattern of custodial care, substituting it with a flexible and professional program in the vanguard of contemporary developments in the field. The modern Mental Health Center on the County grounds is truly Landis' legacy.

Concurrent with the activities of Dr. Landis, major changes that would significantly alter the county institutions were sweeping the health care world. These issues were to coalesce in the 1960s to bring about the formation of the Milwaukee County Regional Medical Center, a cooperative endeavor of public and private health care interests on behalf of better service to the people of southeastern Wisconsin.[120]

The lesson of the Second World War served as a catalyst in expanding the role and influence of the federal government in health care. When draft-board examinations revealed that the state of American health was not good, government leaders determined to upgrade the quality and quantity of medical care. What emerged was a program of government-sponsored medical research and the encouragement of centralized medical service delivery systems that would bring the fruits of that research to bear as soon as possible. The vision was of regional health care centers that would unite research, teaching, and specialized medical services in one common endeavor. To these ends the government in the late forties established the National Institute of Health (NIH), which provided millions of dollars in research funds to physicians and scientists. Moreover, the Hill-Burton Act of 1946 made available generous federal aid for the construction of hospitals that served the poor. The findings of the Hoover Governmental Reorganization Committee of 1949 also promoted the concept of regionalized/centralized medical care.[121]

Milwaukee's attention to these activities of the federal government came about primarily through the efforts of the Greater Milwaukee Committee (GMC), a group of influential business and community leaders. Founded in the 1930s as a spin-off of the public-service-oriented Rotary Club, the GMC was formally incorporated in 1948 and became the spearhead of a number of major community projects in the Milwaukee metropolitan area. Their leadership was especially decisive because the fiscal conservatism of the socialist elements in county and city governments resisted anything but "pay-as-you-go" public projects. In 1948 the GMC succeeded in having a deficit financing referendum placed on the ballot and brought to an end an era of fiscal conservatism when voters approved the measure. This released the floodgates of public and private capital enabling the construction of any number of public facilities (i.e., the stadium, arena, zoo) that literally transformed the face of Milwaukee County. The GMC's interest in the establishment of a regional medical center was only a part of this larger program of metropolitan renewal to make Milwaukee a better place to live and work in. As such, the GMC was to be the guiding force in the formation of the Milwaukee Regional Medical Center, providing the necessary public support and the organizational knowledge to guide the proposal through its various phases.[122]

The GMC's quiet leadership in the health care question was significantly advanced with the establishment of the post of County Executive in 1959 (a position GMC influence had helped bring into existence). The selection of Supervisor John L. Doyne as the first incumbent in this position brought to the helm a leader who had greater than average interest and concern in health care issues. Doyne, a nephew of Supervisor Willard "Mike" Lyons, had long known of the social welfare scene in Milwaukee. Uncle "Mike," then head of the Board of Public Welfare, had one day taken the young Doyne to the newly built County General (c. 1930) and predicted that one day a huge medical center would be on those very grounds.[123] Doyne's interest in social welfare issues was evident from the time he first was selected to succeed his uncle on the County Board in the early '50s.[124] The Doyne-GMC combination was to mastermind the delicate and difficult process that culminated in the establishment of the Regional Medical Center in 1969. Moreover, the interest of Doyne assured the County Institutions a central role in the development of that plan. County medical care and services were to be expanded and consolidated in a way William L. Coffey never dreamed.

As the broad outlines of a regional medical center were being advanced, important developments were transpiring at the Marquette University School of Medicine (MUSM), providing an important link in the local chain of events leading to a regional medical center. Formally chartered in 1918, the Marquette Medical School had consistently worked to expand and develop its programs and upgrade the quality of its faculty and curriculum.[125] However, by the 1950s the school was experiencing major financial problems that raised serious questions with an accreditation team of the Association of the American Medical Colleges. In 1952 MUSM was placed on "confidential probation" and urged to deal with its deteriorating fiscal condition. Marquette officials moved quickly to shore up the status of the faltering medical school, and Dean John S. Hirschboeck entered into serious negotiations with the trustees of the Kurtis R. Froedtert estate to solicit funding.[126] Froedtert, a malt millionaire and a devout Lutheran, had died in 1951, leaving a substantial estate for the building of a teaching hospital to be named for himself. The negotiations were lengthy and complex and ultimately did not bear fruit. Not only was the Froedtert fortune tied up in local development projects (and would be for many years) but the Lutheran Men of America in Wisconsin filed suit against the Froedtert trustees to protest cooperation with a medical school operated by Jesuit priests of the Roman Catholic church. These obstacles combined to keep the status of the medical school questionable until the late 1960s. Good byproducts of the negotiations, however, were the findings of two commissioned studies, the McLean Report (1953), and the Willard Report (1959), which not only urged regional medical care but also encouraged the use of the Milwaukee County grounds as the nucleus of this endeavor.[127]

Public support in behalf of regional medical care open to all the citizens of Milwaukee was building. Already County General was feeling the impact of the generous NIH grants given to MUSM researchers, providing important medical breakthroughs in kidney and heart care. However, these services could only be given to the indigent and emergency patients.[128] In 1963, the GMC formed the Hospital Area Planning Committee, which further elaborated plans for the centralization of medical care and devoted itself to the task of preserving the faltering MUSM.[129] With the cooperation of Doyne a vision developed of a coordinated health care center located on the County Institution grounds, with the medical school and a host of other independent health care facilities in close proximity or attached by bonds of affiliation.

Major stimulus came once again from the federal government when Titles 18 and 19 were added to the Social Security Act in 1964. *Medicare,* a program of health care to the elderly, and *Medicaid,* health care to the poor, brought about seismic changes in the field of social welfare. With the aid of government funds the poor could now elect their own place of treatment rather than being restricted to public hospitals and institutions.[130] In another development Congress enacted the Regional Health Care Act in 1965. This law formalized what the government had indirectly urged since the end of World War II. Under its terms funds were appropriated to advance the establishment of regional health care centers. Congressmen Clement Zablocki and Henry Reuss quickly moved to secure the grant of research funds that this legislation made available.[131]

On October 6, 1965, on the very day President Lyndon Johnson signed the regional health care bill into law, County Executive John Doyne convoked a meeting of a Medical Center Steering Committee, a public and private sector body composed of fifteen members, whose task it was to generate public interest and support in a regional medical center.[132] The members of this board soon delegated the job of studying the possibilities and goals to be achieved to a special subcommittee of the GMC headed by Joseph Heil, Sr. The so-called Heil Committee met throughout 1966 and in January 1967 issued a landmark report entitled "Greater Milwaukee's Need for a Comprehensive Medical Center." This document, known as the Heil Report, brought together the diverse streams of federal and local concerns about regional health care and spelled out, with a clarity unique in such documents, the precise steps necessary to bring about a central health care center.[133] The Heil Report was both the *Magna Charta* and the blueprint for an idea whose time had come.

Among the findings of the report, the committee pointed out that Milwaukee was one of three major metropolitan regions of the country that did not provide a major comprehensive medical center. Moreover, the report, citing statistics on the physician manpower needs for metropolitan Milwaukee, found that a shortage existed and threatened to grow worse if adequate provisions were not made soon. In relation to this, the Heil Committee acknowledged that the Marquette University School of Medicine needed new sources of funding and suggested the possibility of a merger between the school and the University of Wisconsin. Finally, it pointed out that the Medical School, together with the Milwaukee County Institutions, Children's Hospital, the Milwaukee Psychiatric Hospital, and the Milwaukee Veteran's Hospital, formed a solid nucleus that could and should be developed into a comprehensive medical center.[134]

The Heil Report's enthusiastic reception by Doyne and the GMC accelerated the growing momentum for the regional medical center. On April 21, 1967, Doyne appointed another Medical Center Steering Committee to implement the recommendations of the Heil Report and develop the organization and administrative infrastructure of the proposed center. This action-oriented group consisted of thirty-four persons, with GMC member Delwin Jacobus as president. Doyne moved to secure the support of the Board of Public Welfare for the Heil Report and, upon their approval, worked with them to effect the statutory changes needed to open the County Institutions to the kind of public/private cooperation envisioned in the regional medical center concept. These changes, drafted by County General Medical Director John Petersen, permitted the Board of Public Welfare to admit paying patients to the County Institutions, to allow County lands to be leased to private enterprise, and to permit doctors serving at the County Institutions to charge for their services. These proposals were enacted by the state legislature in late July 1967 and signed into law by Governor Warren Knowles.[135] The County Board subsequently approved $49 million in improvements to the County Institutions.

The status of Marquette University School of Medicine was, throughout all this, highly problematic. The problem of securing adequate funding still remained, and suggestions that the University of Wisconsin-Milwaukee might open its own medical school further muddied the situation. While planning for the medical center went on, coordinated efforts to secure funds proceeded as well. GMC leader Edmund Fitzgerald exercised decisive leadership in pressing for the retention of MUSM as a key component of the medical center, while seeking to transform it into a nonsectarian organization, thus enhancing its eligibility for public funds.[136] On September 30, 1967, Marquette University ended legal ties with the medical school, and in February 1969 over $1 million in state aid was secured. After having fended off a court challenge to the aid, the school moved to a new status, changing its name in 1970 to the Medical College of Wisconsin.[137]

Plans continued apace to structure the new medical center. On February 3, 1968, a subcommittee of the Medical Center Steering Committee approved an organizational structure for the medical center that would be truly regional. A detailed and complex framework that permitted cooperative arrangements between public and private agencies was established. After further consultations the County Board of Supervisors approved the structure of the medical center on July 16, 1968. Articles of incorporation were drawn up and by-laws established providing for the representation of the public and private members of the new operation. The Medical Center Council of Southeastern Wisconsin and the initial board of directors of the Southeastern Wisconsin Medical Foundation, the umbrella organization that would coordinate the various components to the regional medical center, held their first meeting January 15, 1969.[138] On November 20, 1969, the regional medical center, the dream of "Mike" Lyons, John Doyne, and the GMC, was officially called into existence.

Fund-raising and the development of a master plan were on the top of the agenda for the Medical Center Council. On October 25, 1971, after lengthy consultations and studies with professional firms, the "Master Plan for the Development of the Southeastern Wisconsin Medical Center" was developed. Moreover, leases were negotiated with the Curative Workshop in Milwaukee, the Eye Institute, the Milwaukee Blood Center, and the Froedtert Memorial Lutheran Hospital. In 1975 the Eye Institute opened its doors, and in 1976 Curative Rehabilitation Workshop relocated on the County grounds. In that same year ground was broken for the Medical College of Wisconsin, which opened in 1978. In 1979 the new mental hospital took its place in the Regional Medical Center, and in 1980 the long-awaited Froedtert Memorial Lutheran Hospital commenced operating clinical programs transferred from the Milwaukee County Medical Complex. County General was renamed the Milwaukee County Medical Complex, and Froedtert began to divide areas of medical expertise, with Froedtert assuming care of acute cases. The Southeastern Wisconsin Blood Center established a donor station on the grounds in 1983. The Ronald McDonald House opened in 1984,[139] and on April 15, 1986 ground was broken for the new Milwaukee Children's Hospital. Slowly, the Heil Committee's recommendations came to life on the County grounds.

The naming of the center "Milwaukee County Regional Medical Center" came about in 1977, as the result of jurisdictional disputes between the County and the private members of the enterprise. Today, the regional medical center is a massive operation, employing thousands of persons and providing a plethora of services for virtually every conceivable health care need of the residents of Milwaukee County.[140]

The developments in mental health and the establishment of the regional medical center occupy the central place in developments of the last thirty years. Major shifts as well in the availability and delivery of various programs of public assistance also have figured prominently during this era. Joseph Baldwin's tenure as head of the Department of Public Welfare ended with his death in April 1970. The implementation of the social welfare programs of Lyndon Johnson's Great Society had fallen on the shoulders of local officials like Baldwin, and his successor, Arthur Silverman, continued his efforts. Delivery of the federally funded aid to families with dependent children, as well as coordinating Medicaid payments, challenged and at times frustrated the talents of Milwaukee County's social welfare operatives. Public controversies concerning welfare continued to rage as they always had throughout Milwaukee County's history. In 1979 the Department of Public Welfare was renamed the Department of Social Services (DSS), a broader and more conceptually pleasing title for a department that was a regular object of public scrutiny. Silverman retired in 1980 and was replaced by William Carr. In 1984 Thomas L. Brophy assumed the leadership of DSS.[141]

Milwaukee County's decision to establish the post of County Executive in 1959 had administrative implications for the social welfare departments. Centralized authority increased demands for accountability from high level County appointees. The various Directors of the Institutions felt the heightened level of public and political expectation, and thus the tenure of these directors was considerably shortened. Moreover, the lines of accountability between the Director of the Institutions (since 1984 the Department of Health and Human Services-DHHS) and the County Executive were strengthened when County Executive William F. O'Donnell succeeded in establishing a cabinet-style government in 1978. The Director's civil service status was removed and he became a political appointee, serving at the pleasure of the County Executive and the approval of the County Board.[142] DHHS Director Symuel Smith was the first to work under these new arrangements. He was succeeded in 1981 by James Wahner.

In 1974 the state legislature established monitoring agencies in each county to oversee the distribution of funds to developmentally disabled, mentally ill, alcoholic or drug abuse programs. The Board of Public Welfare assumed responsibility for the oversight of these combined community service responsibilities. However, the role of the BPW had become increasingly problematic. Until 1960 it had the primary responsibility for policy over the County institutions and programs. With the advent of a County Executive system in 1960 the BPW began to recede in importance. The jurisdictional snarls created by the addition of combined community service responsibilities brought this home. The BPW came to be viewed as an inefficient additional layer of bureaucracy. In 1981 County Executive William F. O'Donnell moved to abolish the Board and to transfer its policy-making responsibilities to the standing committees of the County Board, its administrative functions to the appointed director of the DHHS, and to reconstitute a Combined Community Service Board to carry out the statutory requirements of the state. This was accomplished in 1982.[143]

The winds of social change brought about additional modifications of social welfare services. The combined effects of the sexual revolution and the women's movement of the sixties and seventies removed barriers to the public discussion of hitherto unmentionable sexual problems such as rape and child molestation. At the urging of women's groups in the Milwaukee area, a sexual assault counseling unit was established under the auspices of the District Attorney's office in 1974. Extensive one-on-one counseling for the victims of rape not only facilitated the healing process but also strengthened the "prosecutorial clout" of the District Attorney.[144] In 1975 a Citizen Complaint/Battered Women Program was also established. Although intended to respond to a variety of citizen grievances, ninety percent of its complaints involved male/female battery or related issues. Advocates for Battered Women, a citizen action group founded in 1979, is also on the premises of the District Attorney's offices, providing volunteer assistance for the intake of cases as well as support and advocacy after a case has been charged.[145]

County concerns for cases of child abuse were long in the province of the Children's Home. In 1961 a special Child Abuse and Neglect Unit was established with federal money in Milwaukee County. The level of federal, and later state, funding for this program has steadily increased over the years. In 1982, the DHHS Administration chose to become a Consolidated Aids County. Under this system, federal and state aids earmarked for specialized county social service needs were consolidated and the allocation of these funds was incorporated into the County's annual budget development process.[146]

The election of Ronald Reagan as president in 1980 signaled a growing conservative mood in the nation that was destined to have an impact on social welfare programs at every level. Reagan's 1981 budget mandated significant cutbacks in spending for social programs that were quickly felt on the local level. The new national mood renewed outcries against welfare cheating and reviewed suggestions of "workfare" and restrictions on "welfare shopping." Yet, paradoxically, the cutbacks focused attention on those who had fallen through the so-called "safety net," especially the homeless poor. Since the end of walk-in services at the County infirmary in the '50s, there were no real provisions for the indeterminate numbers of "street people" that needed shelter, especially during the winter. Although County Executive O'Donnell opened the door of the abandoned emergency hospital on 24th and Wisconsin during the bitter winter of 1983-84, County efforts on behalf of the homeless consist mainly of subsidies to the privately owned Guest House on N. Thirteenth Street in Milwaukee.[147]

It is apparent from this brief study that Milwaukee County's commitment to its poor and needy is a steady and durable one. No doubt the structures of administration and the delivery of services will continue to change and adapt to meet new needs. Moreover, as County welfare services absorb a larger and larger share of the County tax levy, it appears that serious fiscal questions will pose challenges to administrators and County officials in meeting those needs. Those who have been left with the task of carrying on this 150-year tradition will need the right proportions of compassionate idealism and hard-headed fiscal realism to ensure the continuity of these services to the poor and needy, as well as to all other Milwaukee County citizens.

Endnotes

*I wish to thank the following people for their assistance: Jeff Aikin, Chuck Cooney, Walter I. Trattner, Margaret and Catherine Coffey, Nancy Abboud, Ralph Erdtman, Michael Bauer, David Verhasselt, and Gloria Szymanowski.

[1]Much of the information on early American social welfare can be found in Walter I. Trattner, *From Poor Law to Welfare State: A History of Social Welfare in America*, 3rd ed. (New York: The Free Press, 1984) pp. 1-28; and David J. Rothman, *The Discovery of the Asylum: Social Order and Disorder in the New Republic* (Boston: Little Brown and Co., 1971) pp. 2-55; see also Walter Trattner, *Social Welfare or Social Control* (Knoxville: University of Tennessee Press, 1983).
[2]For an incisive description of this spirit, see Daniel J. Boorstin, *The Americans: The National Experience* (New York: Vintage Books, 1965).

[3]Minutes of the Meetings of the Milwaukee County Board of Supervisors (hereafter MCBS), 1859, p. 163.

[4]Jerome Watrous, *Memoirs of Milwaukee County*, 2 vols. (Madison: Western Historical Association, 1902) 1:110; see also MCBS, 1838, p. 10.

[5]An example is in MCBS, 1838, p. 10 and 1852, p. 8.

[6]For a thorough but dated treatment of Milwaukee history see Bayrd Still, *Milwaukee: The History of a City* (Madison: State Historical Society, 1948) pp. 168-99.

[7]MCBS, 1843, p. 69.

[8]Rothman pp. 157-63, 166-67.

[9]"Development of Public Assistance Programs in Wisconsin and their Administration, 1848-1948" (State Department of Public Welfare, Madison, 1948) p. 23; see also Susan M. Drew, "The Milwaukee County Institutions and Departments" (unpublished paper, Milwaukee County Historical Society).

[10]Peter Leo Johnson, *The Daughters of Charity in Milwaukee, 1846-1946* (Milwaukee: Daughters of Charity, 1946) pp. 29-52; Peter Leo Johnson, "When Cholera Came," *Historical Messenger*, 8 (December 1952):11-13.

[11]MCBS, 1852, p. 91.

[12]MCBS, 1852, p. 92.

[13]MCBS, 1852, pp. 103-04.

[14]In the days before systematic bookkeeping and budgeting it is difficult to understand the nature of the expenditures for County social welfare services. A history of County government done by the Works Progress Administration reveals that in 1851, the entire County tax levy was only $4,898.60. This was before the purchase of the Gregg farm. In 1854, six months care for the poor cost the County $1,500. Prices had indeed gone up; by 1856, $18,893 was spent; in 1857, $27,249.96; and in 1858, $23,901.89. Cf. MCBS, 1859, p. 83.

[15]MCBS, 1859, pp. 251-52.

[16]MCBS, 1859, p. 5.

[17]For the best treatment of the evolution of the modern hospital, see Morris J. Vogel, *The Invention of the Modern Hospital: Boston, 1870-1930* (Chicago: University of Chicago Press, 1980); see also Paul Starr, *The Social Transformation of American Medicine: The Rise of a Sovereign Profession and the Making of a Vast Industry* (New York: Basic Books, 1982) pp. 145-79; and Judith Walzer Leavitt and Ronald L. Numbers (eds.), *Sickness and Health in America.* 2nd ed., rev. (Madison: University of Wisconsin Press, 1985).

[18]*First Annual Report*, 1871, State Board of Charities and Reforms, p. 14.

[19]*Third Annual Report*, 1873, State Board of Charities and Reforms, pp. 257-58; MCBS, 1870, p. 117.

[20]MCBS, 1873, p. 145.

[21]"Dedication of the Historical Marker on the Fisk Holbrook Day Residence" (dedicatory booklet), Wauwatosa Landmark Commission, Landmark No. 4, November 8, 1979.

[22]Two examples of Day's reporting are in MCBS, 1870, pp. 116-17 and 1872, pp. 258-60.

[23]Starr pp. 145-79.

[24]Trattner pp. 135-54.

[25]George A. Dundon, "Health Chronology of Milwaukee" *Historical Messenger*, 12 (June 1956):10-12.

[26]"A Short History of the Milwaukee County General Hospital School of Nursing: 1883-1963" (memorial pamphlet), Milwaukee County School of Nursing.

[27]MCBS, 1858, p. 127.

[28]These reports can be found at the State Historical Society in Madison, Wisconsin: Bernett O. Idegaard and George M. Keith, "A History of the State Board of Control of Wisconsin and the State Institutions 1848-1939," State Board of Control (1940).

[29]Good insights into the minds of these reformers can be found in Ronald G. Walters, *American Reformers, 1815-1860* (New York: Hill and Wang, 1978) pp. 193-211; see also Trattner pp. 77-102, for the period after the Civil War.

[30]*First Annual Report*, State Board of Charities and Reform, 1871, p. 14.

[31]For additional information regarding child welfare in the late 19th century consult, Leroy Ashby, *Saving the Waifs: Reformers and Dependent Children, 1890-1917* (Philadelphia: Temple University Press, 1984); see also "Conclusions and Recommendations of the State Board of Control Based on the 'Survey and Investigation into the Question of Aid to Mothers With Dependent Children' as Authorized by Section 11, Chapter 659, Laws, 1913," State Board of Control, 1913.

[32]WPA History, "County Government," p. 13.

[33]MCBS, 1858, pp. 120-21.

[34]MCBS, 1858, pp. 120-24. These recommendations had originally been made a year earlier. See MCBS, 1857, pp. 104-06.

[35]*Third Annual Report*, State Board of Charities and Reform, 1873, p. 147.

[36]MCBS, passim.

[37]Quoted in first draft of WPA History, p. 11, Milwaukee County Historical Society.

[38]MCBS, 1872, p. 278.

[39]Susan Drew, "The Milwaukee County Institutions and Departments," p. 14.

[40]MCBS, 1877, pp. 61-63.

[41]Gerald Grob, "Mental Illness, Indigency, and Welfare: The Mental Hospital in Nineteenth Century America," in Tamara K. Harevan, ed., Anonymous Americans (Englewood Cliffs: Prentice Hall, 1971); see also Trattner pp. 182-198, for later developments.

[42]Rothman pp. 109-54.

[43]MCBS, 1845, pp. 7-8, 26.

[44]MCBS, 1868, p. 24.

[45]MCBS, 1869, pp. 24-25.

[46]MCBS, 1872, pp. 258-60; see also Milwaukee Sentinel, November 15, 1865.

[47]Third Annual Report, State Board of Charities and Reforms, 1873; see also Milwaukee Sentinel, August 6, 1874.

[48]MCBS, 1873, p. 147.

[49]Ibid.

[50]The accusations against the Boogks were the object of special hearings before the Board of Supervisors. Cf. MCBS, 1874, pp. 205-23. The newspapers also picked up the accusations; see Milwaukee Daily Sentinel, August 14, 1874.

[51]MCBS, 1878, pp. 261-65, 408-11; Eighth Annual Report, State Board of Charities and Reforms, 1878, p. 198.

[52]Still pp. 257-78, 321-55.

[53]Sarah C. Ettenheim, How Milwaukee Voted: 1843-1968 (Milwaukee: Institute of Governmental Affairs, 1970) p. 12.

[54]There is abundant literature on Progressivism. Good general studies include: John D. Buenker, Urban Liberalism and Progressive Reform (New York: Norton, 1978); Samuel P. Hays, The Response to Industrialization (Chicago: University of Chicago Press, 1957); William L. O'Neil, The Progressive Years: America Comes of Age (New York: Dodd Mead, 1975).

[55]Jane Addams, Twenty Years at Hull House (New York: The Macmillan Company, 1910). See also Roy B. Lubove, The Progressives and the Slums (Pittsburg: University of Pittsburgh Press, 1963); Roy B. Lubove, The Professional Altruist (New York: Atheneum, 1971); Allen F. Davis, Spearheads for Reform (New York: Oxford University Press, 1967).

[56]"Conclusions and Recommendations of the State Board of Control Based on the 'Survey and Investigation into the Question of Aid to Mothers with Dependent Children' as Authorized by Section 11, Chapter 659, Laws, 1913" 1913 (State Board of Control), p. 17.

[57]For a discussion of these impulses see Robert H. Wiebe, The Search for Order: 1877-1920 (New York: Hill and Wang, 1967). See also Lubove, The Professional Altruist.

[58]"County Institutions" in Manual of Duties of All Elected and Appointed County Officials and Commissions (hereafter Manual), Works Progress Administration Project No. 4418, p. 107.

[59]Ibid., pp. 107-08. The minutes of these Board meetings are located in the offices of the Health and Human Services Department of Milwaukee County.

[60]"Head of Institutions Winds Up Long Job," Milwaukee Journal, June 15, 1952. Joint Resolution No. 835, May 2, 1957, Wisconsin State Senate. "Death Takes W.L. Coffey," Milwaukee Journal, February 22, 1957. Interview with Margaret and Catherine Coffey. MCBS, 1921, p. 661.

[61]Benjamin Lane, "The Development and History of the Milwaukee School of Social Work" (unpublished Master's thesis, U.W.-Milwaukee, 1949).

[62]MCBS, 1917, p. 189.

[63]Manual, pp. 107-08.

[64]Margaret and Catherine Coffey to writer.

[65]Biennial Report, Milwaukee County Institutions, 1925-26. p. 5. Minutes of the Board of Administration, passim.

[66]Marlon D. Dykas, "The Breadless of Milwaukee County at the Turn of the Century" (unpublished Master's thesis, U.W.-Milwaukee, 1974) pp. 55-56.

[67]"History of the Establishment of the Agricultural School" (no pagination). File "Agricultural School" DHHS, Milwaukee.

[68]Interview with Mr. Richard Scheller; "County to End Operations in Cattle, Swine," Milwaukee Journal, October 28, 1954; "County Holstein Herd is Sold for $43,787," Milwaukee Journal, May 26, 1955.

[69]Interview with Mr. Robert Wissing.

[70]Rothman pp. 293-323.

[71]Biennial Report, Milwaukee County Institutions, 1923-1924, pp. 10-11 and 1925-26, p. 7.

Jean Mosely, "A Study of the Adult Referrals to the Milwaukee County Guidance Clinic in 1949" (unpublished Master's thesis, U.W.-Milwaukee, 1950) pp. 6-11.
[72]Trattner pp. 142-47.
[73]MCBS, 1911, p. 171. See also Harold Holand, "Twenty-Two Against the Plague," *Wisconsin Magazine of History* 42 (Autumn 1958):29-34.
[74]Joan Seaman Murphy, "History of Muirdale Sanatorium," *Wisconsin Occupational Therapy Bulletin* 9 (1937) (no pagination). Muirdale patients wrote and published a journal called *The Town Crier*. Two interesting articles relative to the origins and conditions at the TB facility include Harry Walworth, "A Narrative History of Muirdale Sanatorium," *The Town Crier* 26 (July 1955):6-11, and "A Review," *The Town Crier* 9 (September 1938):4-5.
[75]Richard Scheller to the writer. A chronological summary sheet was compiled by a Miss Clare Czarnecki enumerating developments at Muirdale from 1932-1950. This can be found in the DHHS offices. See also *Annual Report* (1969), Milwaukee County Institutions and Departments, pp. 125-26.
[76]"The Children's Law and the Mother's Pension Law in Wisconsin," Wisconsin State Board of Control, 1921; see also Eugene Warren Gauns, "Wisconsin Mother's Aid Legislation Prior to 1935" (unpublished Master's thesis, U.W.-Milwaukee, 1951) pp. 30-42.
[77]Margaret and Catherine Coffey to writer.
[78]"Dr. Harry Sergeant Hears 900 Good-Byes," *Milwaukee Journal*, December 22, 1956; Edward A. Bachuber, M.D., "Dr. Joseph M. King: Man and Surgeon," *Wisconsin Medical Journal* 72 (November 1973):212-14; Margaret and Kate Coffey to writer.
[79]MCBS, 1916, p. 119.
[80]*Biennial Report*, Milwaukee County Institutions, 1923-1924, pp. 10-11.
[81]"Schandein Site Fades as Home for Structure" (unidentified clipping). "Milwaukee County Hospital Dispensary-Emergency Unit," *Manual*, pp. 124-25; MCBS, 1925, pp. 597-99; 1926, pp. 90-91, 414-15.
[82]"Milwaukee County Hospital," *Manual*, p. 123.
[83]"Hospital Filled to Capacity," *Milwaukee Journal*, August 28, 1936; "New Hospital Nearly Ready," *Milwaukee Journal*, September 5, 1943.
[84]"Outdoor Relief Department," *Manual*, pp. 98-99.
[85]Margaret and Kate Coffey to writer. Interview with Mr. Stanley White.
[86]These debates went on even after the Depression began. For an example of them see MCBS, 1932, pp. 885-88; 1939, pp. 177-79.
[87]Stanley White to writer.
[88]"Coffey Offered Post as Federal Aid Boss," *Milwaukee Journal*, January 25, 1934. "Heil Demands Coffey Accept," *Milwaukee Journal*, September 23, 1939.
[89]WPA History, pp. 15-16.
[90]"Development of Public Assistance Programs in Wisconsin and Their Administration, 1848-1948," (State Department of Public Welfare, Madison, 1948), p. 25.
[91]*Manual*, p. 99.
[92]"Development of Public Assistance...," p. 26.
[93]Ibid., p. 29.
[94]"Relief Set-Up Criticized as Burden for Judges," *Milwaukee Journal*, January 30, 1950.
[95]Interview with Arthur Silverman; Stanley White to writer; "End 'Coaster Wagon' Relief Board Urges," *Milwaukee Sentinel*, March 22, 1945. "Urge Stopping Relief in Kind," *Milwaukee Journal*, March 23, 1945; "Proposes Shift to Cash Relief," *Milwaukee Journal*, April 11, 1945; "Relief Plan Adopted," *Milwaukee Journal*, May 9, 1945.
[96]"Unify Welfare Work Experts Urge County," *Milwaukee Journal*, January 4, 1938; "Begin Unified Welfare Work," *Milwaukee Journal*, December 1, 1947; "Welfare Post to J.E. Baldwin," *Milwaukee Journal*, May 6, 1948.
[97]"Relief Set-Up Criticized as a Burden for Judges," *Milwaukee Journal*, January 30, 1950; "Veteran County Welfare Aide, Amy Allen Will Retire June 1," *Milwaukee Journal*, May 5, 1950; "Welfare Services Centralized to Cut Costs and Red Tape," *Milwaukee Journal*, May 7, 1950; "One Welfare Department," *Milwaukee Journal*, July 14, 1950; Stanley White to writer.
[98]"More County Institutions," *Milwaukee Journal*, February 25, 1946; "Need Modern Facilities at County Institutions," *Milwaukee Journal*, October 13, 1947; "Helpless, Needy and Ill Jam County Buildings," *Milwaukee Journal*, October 12, 1947.
[99]"Restive Aides Air Criticisms of Institutions," *Milwaukee Journal* (all citations hereafter are from the *Journal*), December 13, 1945; "This Astounding Hospital Inquiry," December 15, 1945; "Public Probe Aim of C.I.O.," December 16, 1945; "New Welfare Setup Is Aim," December 20, 1945; "Urge Hospital Probe Speed," December 30, 1945; "County Setup at Fault, Claim," December 28, 1945; "Board Limits Its Inquiry to the Hospital," December 29, 1945; "Interns Draw Fire in Probe," December 29, 1945; "Revise County Setup Is Plan," May 3, 1946; "Asks Reforms at Institutions," September 17, 1946; "Urges School Hospital Link," January 23, 1947; "Get Together Hospital and MU Are Told," June 14, 1948.

[100]Margaret and Kate Coffey to writer.

[101]"Building Cost Stuns County," *Milwaukee Journal*, February 1, 1949.

[102]J. W. Rankin Picked to Fill Coffey's Post," *Milwaukee Journal*, March 17, 1952; "Hard Worker, That's Rankin," *Milwaukee Journal*, March 18, 1952; "Praises Setup for Institutions," *Milwaukee Journal*, March 23, 1952; Rankin resigned in 1961 and was replaced by Orville Guenther.

[103]Interview with William F. O'Donnell.

[104]"County General Hospital Plans 578 Bed Addition," *Milwaukee Journal*, October 30, 1952; "Two Large Structures Being Built for County," *Milwaukee Journal*, August 14, 1955; Elizabeth S. Kletzsch, "The Institute Story: Milwaukee County Institutions and Departments," Milwaukee County (1954), pp. 5-6.

[105]"The Administration of Medical and Welfare Services in the Government of Milwaukee County," Public Administration Service (1956).

[106]"County Health and Welfare Unit is Urged," *Milwaukee Journal*, January 26, 1956.

[107]Memo to J. W. Rankin, March 31, 1959, DHHS files.

[108]"Dr. Landis Named Mental Health Chief," *Milwaukee Journal*, May 4, 1958.

[109]"Big Gains Have Been Made in Fighting Mental Illness," *Milwaukee Journal*, July 9, 1969; "Mental Health Day Center to Open Doors," ibid.

[110]Interview with John L. Doyne.

[111]"Milwaukee County Mental Health Center North Division" (Milwaukee County, 1961), Introduction (no pagination).

[112]Interview with Edwin Mundy. Mr. Mundy was the Institutions Chief from 1968 to 1977.

[113]John L. Doyne to writer; "Centralizing of Mental Services Hit," *Milwaukee Journal*, October 17, 1968.

[114]"Mental Health Day Center..."

[115]"Mental Health Ink," February 1970, Milwaukee County Association for Mental Health.

[116]"County May Scrap Child Care Center," *Milwaukee Journal*, May 2, 1969; "Child Care Center Plan Dies," October 3, 1969.

[117]Edwin Mundy to writer; John L. Doyne to writer.

[118]*Milwaukee County Government Report* (1985), p. 50.

[119]"Landis, County Leader in Mental Health, Dies," *Milwaukee Journal*, January 14, 1986.

[120]The best single account of the complex process leading to the formation of the Milwaukee Regional Medical Center is Louis J. Pascek's, "Milwaukee Regional Medical Center: Growth and Development" (unpublished Ph.D. dissertation, U.W.-Milwaukee, 1982).

[121]Pascek pp. 14-33.

[192]Ibid. pp. 40-52.

[123]Doyne to writer.

[124]For an example of this interest see, "Board Snubs Medic Boss Post Plan," *Milwaukee Sentinel*, September 18, 1956; Doyne to writer.

[125]Gerald W. Mullins, "Politics and Higher Education in the State of Wisconsin: The Case of the Marquette Medical School" (unpublished Ph.D. dissertation, Marquette University, 1971) pp. 59-70; see also Walter Zeit, "Marquette University School of Medicine: The First Fifty Years," *Wisconsin Medical Journal* 62 (July 1963):295-302.

[126]John Hirschboeck, M.D., "Milwaukee's Medical Center" (unpublished paper, Archives of the Medical Society of Wisconsin) pp. 7-11; see also Mullins p. 88.

[127]Pascek pp. 73-76, 80-82.

[128]Interview with Dr. John Petersen.

[129]Pascek pp. 105-20.

[130]Trattner pp. 304-05.

[131]Doyne to writer.

[132]Pascek pp. 131-35.

[133]Ibid. pp. 135-36, 138-40, and 164-71.

[134]Mullins pp. 93-118.

[135]Peterson to writer.

[136]Pascek pp. 200-13.

[137]"Dear Diary," Medical College of Wisconsin (1982), pp. 1-4.

[138]Pascek pp. 213-27.

[139]*Milwaukee County Government Report* (1985), pp. 48-49.

[140]Pascek pp. 248-252.

[141]Silverman to writer.

[142]O'Donnell to writer; *Milwaukee County Government Report* (1985), pp. 28-29.

[143]O'Donnell to writer; *Milwaukee County Government Report* (1985), p. 55; "Welfare Board A Center of Power and Controversy," *Milwaukee Journal*, July 24, 1980; "County Panel Back Welfare Board Plan," *Milwaukee Sentinel*, December 15, 1981; "Welfare Board's Days Numbered?" *Milwaukee Journal*, March 28, 1982.

[144]*Milwaukee County Government Report (1985)*, p. 43.
[145]*Ibid.*
[146]*Jeff Aikin to writer.*
[147]*Ibid.*

Bibliography

Primary Sources

Files of the Department of Health and Human Services.
Institution Reports, Milwaukee County Historical Society.

Books

Addams, Jane. *Twenty Years at Hull House*. New York: The Macmillan Company, 1910.

Ashby, Leroy. *Saving the Waifs: Reformers and Dependent Children, 1890-1917*. Philadelphia: Temple University Press, 1984.

Bremner, Robert H. *American Philanthropy*. Chicago: University of Chicago Press, 1960.

Bruno, Frank J. *Trends in Social Work, 1874-1956*. New York, 1957.

Buenker, John D. *Urban Liberalism and Progressive Reform*. New York: Norton, 1978.

Davis, Allen F. *Spearheads for Reform*. New York: Oxford University Press, 1967.

Ettenheim, Sarah C. *How Milwaukee Voted: 1843-1968*. Milwaukee: Institute of Governmental Affairs, 1970.

Harevan, Tamara K., ed. *Anonymous Americans*. Englewood Cliffs: Prentice Hall, 1977.

Hollis, Ernest V., and Alice L. Taylor, *Social Work Education in the United States*. New York: Columbia University Press, 1952.

Hays, Samuel P. *The Response to Industrialization*. Chicago: University of Chicago Press, 1957.

Johnson, Peter Leo. *The Daughters of Charity in Milwaukee: 1846-1946*. Milwaukee: Daughters of Charity, 1946.

Leavitt, Judith Walzer, and Ronald L. Numbers, eds. *Sickness and Health in America*. 2nd ed., rev. Madison: University of Wisconsin Press, 1985.

Leiby, James. *A History of Social Welfare and Social Work in the United States*. New York: Columbia University Press, 1978.

Lubove, Roy B. *The Professional Alturist*. New York: Atheneum, 1971.

Lubove, Roy B. *The Progressive and the Slums*. Pittsburgh: University of Pittsburgh Press, 1953.

Numbers, Ronald L., and Judith Leavitt. *Wisconsin Medicine: Historical Perspectives*. Madison: University of Wisconsin Press, 1981.

O'Neil, William L. *The Progressive Years: America Comes of Age*. New York: Dodd and Mead, 1975.

Robison, Dale W. *Wisconsin and the Mentally Ill: A History of the "Wisconsin Plan" of State and County Care, 1860-1915*. New York: Arno Press, 1980.

Rothman, David J. *Conscience and Convenience: The Asylum and Its Alternatives in Progressive America*. Boston: Little, Brown and Co., 1980.

Rothman, David J. *The Discovery of the Asylum: Social Order and Disorder in the New Republic*. Boston: Little, Brown and Co., 1971.

Rothman, David J., and Stanton Wheeler, eds. *Social History and Social Policy*. New York: Academic Press, 1981.

Starr, Paul. *The Social Transformation of American Medicine: The Rise of a Sovereign Profession and the Making of a Vast Industry*. New York: Basic Books, 1982.

Still, Bayrd. *Milwaukee, The History of a City*. Madison: State Historical Society, 1948.

Trattner, Walter I. *From Poor Law to Welfare State: A History of Social Welfare*. 3rd ed. New York: The Free Press, 1984.

Trattner, Walter I. *Social Welfare or Social Control: Some Historical Reflections on Regulating the Poor*. Knoxville: University of Tennessee Press, 1983.

Vogel, Morris J. *The Invention of the Modern Hospital: Boston, 1870-1930*. Chicago: University of Chicago Press, 1980.

Walters, Ronald G. *American Reformers, 1815-1860*. New York: Hill and Wang, 1978.

Watrous, Jerome. *Memoirs of Milwaukee County*. 2 vols. Madison: Western Historical Association, 1902.

Wiebe, Robert H. *The Search for Order: 1877-1920*. New York: Hill and Wang, 1967.

Government Documents

Wisconsin. State Board of Control (1940). "A History of the State Board of Control of Wisconsin and the State Institutions 1848-1939," by Bernett O. Idegaard and George M. Keith.

Wisconsin. State Board of Control (1921). "The Children's Law and the Mother's Pension Law in Wisconsin."

Wisconsin. State Board of Control (1913). "Conclusions and Recommendations of the State Board of Control Based on the 'Survey and Investigation into the Question of Aid to Mothers with Dependent Children'
as Authorized by Section 11, Chapter 659 Laws, 1913."
Madison, Wisconsin. State Department of Public Welfare (1948). "Development of Public Assistance Programs in Wisconsin and Their Administration, 1848-1948."

Pamphlets

"Dedication of the Historical Marker on the Fisk Holbrook Day
Residence."
"A Short History of the Milwaukee County General Hospital School of
Nursing: 1883-1963."

Unpublished Papers

Drew, Susan M. "The Milwaukee County Institutions and Departments."
Dundon, George A. "Health Chronology of Milwaukee."
Hirschboeck, M.D., John. "Milwaukee's Medical Center." Medical Society
of Wisconsin.
"History of Milwaukee County Institutions." Works Progress
Administration.

Articles

Bachuber, M.D., Edward A. "Dr. Joseph M. King: Man and Surgeon."
Wisconsin Medical Journal 72, November, 1973.
Holand, Harold. "Twenty-Two Against the Plague." *Wisconsin Magazine
of History* 42, Autumn, 1958.
Johnson, Peter Leo. "When Cholera Came." *Historical Messenger* 8 De-
cember, 1952.
Murphy, Joan Seaman. "History of Muirdale Sanatorium." *Wisconsin
Occupational Therapy Bulletin* IX, 1937. "A Review." *The Town Crier* 9,
September, 1938.
Walworth, Harry. "A Narrative History of Muirdale Sanatorium." *The
Town Crier* 26, July, 1955.
Zeit, Walter. "Marquette University School of Medicine: The First Fifty
Years." *Wisconsin Medical Journal* 62, July, 1963.

Unpublished Theses and Dissertations

Colbert, Roy Jefferson. "Social Work in Milwaukee County." Ph.D., University of Wisconsin, Madison, 1931.

Dykas, Marlon D. "The Breadless of Milwaukee County at the Turn of the Century." M.A., University of Wisconsin, Milwaukee, 1974.

Fenner, Martin A. "Administrative Factors Involved in Granting Public Assistance in Milwaukee County." M.S., University of Wisconsin, Milwaukee, 1960.

Fink, Ronald. "A Study of Relative Responsibility in the Old Age Assistance Division: Milwaukee County Department of Public Welfare." M.S., University of Wisconsin, Milwaukee, 1954.

Gauns, Eugene Warren. "Wisconsin Mother's Aid Legislation Prior to 1935." M.S., University of Wisconsin, Milwaukee, 1951.

Lane, Benjamin. "The Development and History of the Milwaukee School of Social Work." M.A., University of Wisconsin, Milwaukee, 1949.

Mosely, Jean. "A Study of the Adult Referrals to the Milwaukee County Guidance Clinic in 1949." M.S.W., University of Wisconsin, Milwaukee, 1950.

Mullins, Gerald W. "Politics and Higher Education in the State of Wisconsin: The Case of the Marquette Medical School." Ph.D., Marquette University, 1971.

Pascek, Louis J. "Milwaukee Regional Medical Center: Growth and Development." Ph.D., University of Wisconsin, Milwaukee, 1982.

Stefanik, Richard L. "Public Health in Milwaukee From Sanitation to Bacteriology." M.A., University of Wisconsin, Milwaukee, 1967.

Zillman, Carl J. "The History, Development and Present Status of the Care of Dependent Children in Milwaukee County." M.A., Marquette University, 1943.

Interviews

Coffey, Margaret and Catherine, daughters of William Coffey, February 25, 1986.

Doyne, John, first Milwaukee County Executive, April 22, 1986.

Mundy, Edwin, former Director of Milwaukee Institutions, April 8, 1986.

Petersen, Dr. John, Director of Medical Services, April 2, 1986.

Scheller, Richard, Deputy Director for Operations, Department of Health & Human Services, August 5-6, 1985.

Silverman, Arthur, Department of Public Welfare, January 28, 1986.

White, Stanley, January 15, 1986.

CHRONOLOGY OF KEY DEVELOPMENTS
IN
MILWAUKEE COUNTY HEALTH AND HUMAN SERVICES

1835-Appointment of Solomon Juneau and Benoni Finch as Superintendents of the Poor of Milwaukee County

1852-Purchase of Gregg Farm in Wauwatosa as site of County Poor House/Farm

1858-Children's Wing of Poor House established; Outdoor Relief Office opened in Milwaukee

1860-Erection of first County Hospital

1868-Addition to County Hospital

1870-Establishment of the State Board of Charities and Reform

1878-Milwaukee County Insane Asylum built

1880-New County Hospital built

1887-School of Nursing established

1889-Milwaukee County Hospital for the Acute Insane built

1890-New Almshouse built

1989-Children's Home established

1911-County Board appropriates money for dependent mothers

1912-School of Agriculture and Domestic Economy opened

1915-Muirdale Sanatorium opened; Board of Administration established for County Institutions

1917-Name changes effected in County Institutions

1918-Marquette Medical School chartered

1919-Dispensary opened; Mental Hygiene Clinic established

1921-Blue Mound Preventorium purchased

1922-William Coffey appointed County Institutions Manager

1924-Child Guidance Clinic established

1930-New County General Hospital built; Dispensary-Emergency Hospital opens

1939-Board of Public Welfare created; Department of Outdoor Relief renamed Department of Public Assistance

1946-Abolition of commissary style relief, cash relief payments inaugurated

1947-Department of Public Welfare created unifying old age, aid to dependent children, aid for the blind and placing out services

1948-Joseph Baldwin selected to head Department of Public Welfare

1950-Public Assistance added to Department of Public Welfare and entire Department is placed under the Board of Public Welfare

1952-Resignation of William Coffey; appointment of John Rankin as Institutions Manager; Marquette School of Medicine placed on confidential probation; McLean Report

1956-Public Administration Service Report; additions to County General
1958-Appointment of Dr. Charles Landis as Director of Mental Health; Dispensary-Emergency Hospital closed
1959-Willard Report; Orville Guenther appointed Institutions Director
1960-County Executive Position created; John L. Doyne elected
1963-Hospital Area Planning Committee formed by Greater Milwaukee Committee
1964-Medicare and Medicaid Legislation enacted; amendments to Social Security Act, Titles 18 and 19; County farms cease operation
1965-Regional Health Care Act; County Executive Doyne established Medical Center Steering Committee
1967-Heil Report issued; Marquette University School of Medicine cuts ties with Marquette University
1968-Changes effected in state law regarding acceptance of paying patients at County Hospital; laws permitting use of County Grounds for private concern enacted; Medical Center Organization devised
1969-Regional Medical Center comes into existence; Day Hospital opens; Edwin Mundy appointed Institutions Director; Muirdale closes; catchment areas devised
1971-Master Plan for Development of Regional Medical Center approved
1973-Child and Adolescent Treatment Center opened
1975-Eye Institute opens at Milwaukee County Medical Center
1976-Curative Rehabilitation Workshop opens facilities on County grounds
1977-Symuel Smith appointed Institutions Chief
1978-Medical College of Wisconsin opens; Institutions Director becomes cabinet post
1979-New Mental Hospital built; Department of Public Welfare renamed Department of Social Services
1980-Froedtert Hospital opens
1981-James Wahner appointed Institutions Director
1982-Board of Public Welfare ends
1984-Department of Health and Human Services formed
1986-Ground broken for new Children's Hospital on County grounds

Recreation, Entertainment, and Open Space: Park Traditions in Milwaukee County

by Harry H. Anderson ⸺

Introduction

Park lands of one type or another have been a feature of the Milwaukee community since the first settlements were developed here in 1835. The town plats laid out by Solomon Juneau, Byron Kilbourn, George Walker, and their associates contained provision for "public squares" in all three of the communities that formed the early city. Reflecting the traditions of New England and many eastern towns, these areas were included, in part, to offer pioneer residents the opportunity to enjoy open green space, relaxation, and fresh air while also serving as sites for public gatherings of a political nature.

To these modest beginnings were added, in the decades which followed, numerous private parks or "gardens" — many located outside of the limits of the central residential area. Here, more sophisticated opportunities for recreation and entertainment were offered to a rapidly growing population, many of whom were used to and had enjoyed this type of facility in their European homelands. Towards the close of the nineteenth century the City of Milwaukee responded to the needs of a large urban population that required improved transportation, utilities, health, and other public services. A municipally supported system of parks, featuring units designed in the classical tradition of European and eastern United States cities, was one of the results of this development.

Initially, Milwaukee's city park system emphasized facilities that were carefully and artistically designed, and largely artificial in their utilization of natural landscape features. Then, during the first decade of the twentieth century, park enthusiasts of more imaginative and broader vision promoted the creation of a countywide system. Anticipating the need for population expansion into the rural areas, they placed a strong emphasis on sound planning and the utilization of natural topography for both park lands and major routes of travel. Under the leadership of Charles B. Whitnall and others, the County's park system received widespread public and political approval. It eventually absorbed the financially strapped City parks in the midst of the depression years of the 1930s, continued both its physical expansion and program development during the postwar decades, and has become nationally recognized as one of the foremost urban park systems in the United States.

In more recent years this reputation has continued, but basic changes have also occurred in the system's method of operation. Rising real estate costs have all but terminated its physical expansion. Limitations on the ability of the County tax base to finance traditional programs have produced fundamental changes in funding support and administration, and the modernization of both the executive and legislative branches in Milwaukee County government has terminated the existence of the historic, nonelected citizen Park Commission as the policy-making body for park operations.

The century and a half of park tradition in Milwaukee County resulted in a product that passed through many stages and has been dramatically influenced by a variety of forces and factors. It exists today as an important feature of the community's personality and, in all aspects of its programs, provides recreation, enjoyment, and the opportunity to relate to the pleasures of nature for millions of park users annually. This growth and development is a tribute to the concern for the quality of life in Milwaukee County displayed over the past 150 years by both officials of local government and citizens of the community.

Milwaukee's Private Parks

Frontier Milwaukee, the three small settlements which grew out of the immigration of 1835, had little real need for park facilities during its first years of existence. Surrounded by combinations of stands of heavy timber and rolling prairie and drained by a network of rivers and streams, nature provided abundant opportunities for those pioneers who had the time to seek the pleasures of outdoor recreation or leisure. Yet, the early town plats surveyed and filed by Juneau, Kilbourn, and Walker bore evidence of their awareness for the need to include "public squares" in their townsite plans. More often than not, however, the designation of these open spaces reflected economic or political objectives as much as they did a concern for public health and recreation.

The early plats of Juneautown and Kilbourntown had land set aside for the location of a courthouse; and when Juneau and the east side interests proved victors in the struggle for the county seat, the half-block south of the white frame County courthouse became known as Courthouse Square or Park. This initial relationship between County government and public parks, in somewhat expanded form, survives today as Cathedral Park. Present-day Walker and Clarke Squares on the south side and Carl

Zeidler Park, west of the river in the heart of the downtown business section, are other reminders of this era of pioneer park planning.

The legal dedication of these tracts for public purposes by Milwaukee's founding fathers assured their continued protection when the process of urban development in the late nineteenth century made their use for commercial real estate purposes more attractive. Scattered throughout other parts of the city, and particularly on the lower east side, are additional tiny parcels of open land, oddly shaped through the process of street development. These were acquired by the City shortly after it was chartered in 1846, largely because they were too small or poorly located for residential or commercial use. Like the public squares, these accidents of urban development have assured that islands of open, green space would remain as a legacy of the pioneer era of Milwaukee's settlement. These spaces, often neglected or cared for only sporadically as the revenues of local ward government permitted, eventually came under the jurisdiction of the City's Park Board after that body began its work in the 1890s. Prior to that step, however, they also served to illustrate Milwaukee's glaring shortcomings in the area of public park service when compared to other American cities. Their presence was a challenge to the city fathers during the last quarter of the nineteenth century to provide something more substantial for a rapidly expanding urban population.

In the absence of effective municipal park efforts throughout much of the nineteenth century, it remained for the private sector to meet most of the community's needs for recreation, entertainment, and relaxation in an outdoor environment. Milwaukee's private parks played a major role in influencing the development of a strong park tradition in the community. By their location and the types of activities offered to patrons, they introduced many of the basic characteristics that were to highlight both the City and County systems when they became operative in later years.

Although the private gardens or parks of nineteenth-century Milwaukee were largely the product of the influx of European immigrants beginning in the 1840s, these types of facilities also existed during the earlier Yankee era. When the first lighthouse was located on the lake bluff at the head of present East Wisconsin Avenue, Eli Bates, the peg-legged lighthouse keeper, developed an informal outdoor recreational setting adjacent to the structure overlooking Lake Michigan. Better known, and more systematically laid out, was Lemmuel Week's Swiss Garden, near South Second and Mineral Streets in Walker's Point, where this Yankee physician from Vermont fenced in a large grove of plum trees and offered outdoor refreshment and entertainment to local residents.

The European tradition of the neighborhood "bier gartens," brought to Milwaukee by pre-Civil War German immigration, emphasized the opportunities for social contact and entertainment in an outdoor setting. Several of the earliest and most popular of these featured the planting and cultivation of flowers and bushes among the natural growth of trees at attractive locations. Ludwig's Gardens, on the east bank of the Milwaukee River near Pleasant Street, contained a large and valuable nursery to compliment the natural attractiveness of the river and a picturesque ravine which ran through the site. West of the river, on the high bluffs near Highland Boulevard and North Ninth Street, Francis Lachner terraced the grounds running downhill to Eighth Street and opened his property to the public. He provided his patrons with open air concerts by Christian Bach and his orchestra and an unobstructed view across the sparsely settled east side to Lake Michigan.

Natural landscape and topographical features were influential in site selection and entertainment activities at other Milwaukee private parks. Along the Milwaukee River present-day Hubbard Park in Shorewood was popularly known as Lueddemann's-on-the-River and later Mineral Springs Park and emphasized both water-borne access and water-related forms of recreation. On the south side the banker Alexander Mitchell developed a private park grounds (Mitchell's Grove) on the bluffs overlooking the Menomonee Valley for use by personal friends and his fellow Scots. The Lake Michigan shoreline proved equally attractive. Lueddemann's-on-the-Lake and later the Pabst Whitefish Bay Resort were established along the lake bluffs. Quentin's Park near Walnut and North Eighth Streets contained one of the highest of the numerous Indian mounds in the area. This became a feature attraction, particularly after the property was acquired by the Joseph Schlitz Brewing Company in 1879 and a large sightseeing tower erected upon the mound.

Other private park developments, particularly after the Civil War, took advantage of locations on main routes of travel and of the availability of large and relatively inexpensive acreage to attract a clientele. "Schuetzen Park" on upper Third Street and the road to Port Washington began as a firing range for local gun enthusiasts but soon acquired a reputation as an attractive spot for family or group picnics. Still farther north, far outside the then city limits, was Lindwurm Park on the Green Bay Road. On the south side there was Conrad's Grove (later National Park) on the western end of National Avenue and Greenfield Park on Greenfield Avenue, both of which had become spacious and popular beer gardens and picnic sites by the 1880s.

The original attraction for many of these facilities was a combination of the native beauty of the site, well cooked food, and ample supplies of Milwaukee beer. With the passage of time, however, the opportunities for recreation and pleasure were expanded. A wide variety of musical entertainment was introduced early. As its name implies, Schuetzen Park emphasized target practice and competitive shooting matches. Bowling, both indoor and outdoor, was featured at a number of park facilities. Cold Spring Park, near 35th and Vliet Streets, featured a race track where trotting races of national significance were often held. Another full-size race track was located on the so-called Stevens Farm in southern Wauwatosa township. The river parks, in addition to featuring rowboats, canoeing, and swimming activities, also developed water slides. With the advancement of carnival technology, ferris wheels became attractions at the Pabst Whitefish Bay Resort and also at Wonderland on the Milwaukee River, the former Pleasant Valley Park. This location became a modest replica of Coney Island because of the variety of its attractions. Most, if not all, of these activities were summer related, but some of the private parks featured cold weather sports as well. The early Bielfeld Gardens, near Ogden and Astor Streets on the lower east side, was a favorite for ice skaters during Milwaukee's long and cold winters.

One of the best documented of the nineteenth-century private parks is the famous Milwaukee Garden, located from 1855 until the early 1880s on an entire city block at Fourteenth and State Streets. A full-page engraving in the 1876 *Illustrated Atlas of Milwaukee County* visually details the

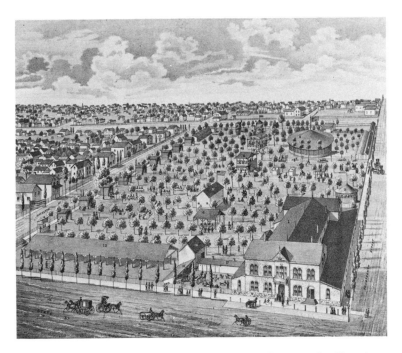

The Milwaukee Garden on State Street was an outstanding example of the private parks which provided outdoor pleasure to Milwaukeeans during the nineteenth century.

many activities featured at this and other similar facilities. Operated for most of its existence by Pius Dreher, a Wurtemberger who came to Milwaukee in 1855, the Milwaukee Garden when opened was situated some distance beyond the city's residential area. It was surrounded by a high board fence and contained numerous shade trees scattered about the grounds, along with gravel walkways, picnic tables, benches, numerous summer houses for private gatherings, and a decorative fountain.

Stands sold tobacco and ice cream, and there were half a dozen bars scattered throughout the park. A roofed eating area or restaurant served a variety of prepared foods for those who did not bring their own picnic lunches. "Kalter Aufschnitt" and snail dinners were house specialities. Recreational opportunities were provided by a bowling alley and shooting gallery, while the carousel and a "menagerie" (circular and rectangular cages) featured a variety of captive birds and animals. There was both an outdoor bandstand and a large circular summer dance hall. Theater performances were presented in an enclosed building in the center of the grounds, and in the southeast corner was a large brick concert hall, suitable for both summer and winter use. On weekends the gardens featured a carnival atmosphere, with cane racks, doll stands, wheels of fortune, and other games of chance.

When packed to capacity, the grounds were capable of holding almost 10,000 people. With its wide variety of activities, it was popular with all ages and was typical of the numerous centers of "gemuetlichkeit" which characterized the operation of private parks in nineteenth-century Milwaukee.

As evidenced by the facilities located on the Milwaukee Garden grounds, the performing arts were a prominent feature in the attractions offered by the private parks and beer gardens. Musical entertainment by orchestras and brass bands was a common feature of most facilities. The City's prominent musical organizations traditionally performed outdoors during the summer months. Bach's orchestra was a feature at Lachner's Gardens prior to the Civil War, various German societies presented folk festivals at Schuetzen Park, and the Milwaukee Musical Society gave occasional midsummer night concerts at Lueddemann's-on-the-Lake, although their favorite site for outdoor performances was at Schlitz Park. Here they appeared regularly as part of the summer programs which also included weekly operas. The first offerings were light Gilbert and Sullivan pieces, and later Italian and German operas made their appearance. In many respects Schlitz Park was the forerunner of the popular musical presentations that were later offered in the municipal park programs.

It is not surprising that Schlitz was but one of several major breweries identified with the private park tradition in old Milwaukee. This characteristic began with the Melms Brewery on the south side, where a public garden was operated near where present South Sixth Street ran down the hillside into the Menomonee Valley. The Best Brewery (later Pabst) purchased the Schuetzen Park in 1872, and it became a very popular attraction with the addition of a Katzenjammer castle, a scenic miniature railway, and an underground river complete with boat rides on the eight-acre site. One of the most enjoyable west side brewery parks was the Miller Gardens, a beautiful ten-acre setting on the high bluffs adjacent to the brewery at what was then the terminus of State Street overlooking the Menomonee Valley. In 1880 Blatz acquired what previously had been called Pleasant Valley Park, and the site was renamed the Blatz Pavilion or Park. It was frequently reached by river, in boats that could be rented near the North Avenue bridge.

The carnival atmosphere at Pabst Park highlighted good food and drink, games of chance, and roller coaster rides for visitors of all ages.

In addition to their role in providing outdoor recreation for the Milwaukee resident and his family, these private parks also served community organizations, churches, and schools in a similar manner. Many ethnic groups had their favorite locations for summer picnics, the Scots at Alexander Mitchell's private grove on the south side overlooking the Menomonee Valley, the Scandinavian element at National Park, and the numerous German organizations at the brewery-related sites. School children from the central city took the streetcars for annual outings at Lueddemann's-on-the-Lake. The Milwaukee Garden was the rallying point for many labor organizations and the scene of an immense May Day rally in 1886, prior to the labor troubles of that year. Even into the first decade of the twentieth century, the Labor Day parades would regularly tramp from downtown to Pabst Park on upper Third Street for the traditional speeches followed by an afternoon of social activities. Schlitz Park was a frequent scene of political rallies, with Presidents Grover Cleveland, William McKinley, and Theodore Roosevelt making appearances there, along with presidential aspirant William Jennings Bryan and numerous state and local candidates. Sports were also a part of the attractions offered in the private parks. Professional boxing and wrestling matches were held at Schlitz Park; and Turner festivals, both regional and national competitions, took place at the Milwaukee Gardens and other north side locations large enough to accommodate these meets.

The significance of the privately owned gardens and groves in the park world of Milwaukee began to decline sharply shortly after the turn of the century, and they had all but disappeared from the local scene by the close of the First World War. The reasons for this were several: the growth of the public park systems, both city and county; the demand for other uses of the park land, particularly for urban residential development and industrial expansion; and the greater mobility made possible by the automobile. Travel for recreational purposes became easier, more economical, and no longer the novelty that a horse-drawn or boat trip to Conrad's Grove or the Whitefish Bay Resort once was. Certainly, the final nail in the coffin was passage of the Eighteenth Amendment, which ended the availability of the amber fluid which had contributed so significantly to the social atmosphere of the beer garden era.

Important characteristics of the numerous private parks and gardens in the Milwaukee area did, however, become firmly engrained in the overall philosophy for the operation of their successors, the municipally supported public parks. Some, if not all, of these features would probably have been absorbed into the public systems through the experiences of other American cities. Yet, Milwaukee certainly benefited from the "gemuetlichkeit" emphasis generated by the enthusiasm of its European-born population for the gardens, groves, and private parks.

One definite long-range contribution of the private park era was to make available land, frequently within what had become by the beginning of the twentieth century the more developed residential areas of the city. A surprisingly large number of park sites in the modern Milwaukee public system were originally, all or in part, the location of the nineteenth-century private parks. The southern portion of Juneau Park had attracted the earliest Yankee settlers in the 1830s with its picturesque view of the

Wonderland, known today as Hubbard Park and as Pleasant Valley Park a century ago, featured stage performances by German-language theater groups and ample refreshments for viewers.

lake and refreshments provided by lighthouse keeper Eli Bates; Lueddemann's-on-the-Lake was one of the first tracts purchased by the City in 1890 to make up Lake Park; the Schuetzen/Pabst Park site, somewhat reduced, is today's Clinton Rose Park; Pleasant Valley Park on the west bank of the Milwaukee River was once Blatz Park, and the historic Quentin/Schlitz Park site now bears the name of Carver Park; a portion of today's Jackson Park was popularly called "Reynold's Grove" by south siders in the nineteenth century, and what they knew as Mitchell's Grove now comprises part of Mitchell Park; and the attractive old Lindwurm Park on Green Bay Road is the southwestern section of Lincoln Park. Other park areas within the County but not part of the County system also share this private park heritage. Hubbard Park, operated by Village of Shorewood, was once Lueddemann's-on-the-River, made famous in the poetry of Ella Wheeler Wilcox and still later known as Mineral Springs and Wonderland, while the popular Stevens farm and race track grounds of the 1870s today comprises much of State Fair Park in West Allis. The era of private parks in Milwaukee is now a distant memory, even for its oldest residents. But many of its contributions were significant and lasting. Partly because of their influence it became the responsibility of local government, first the City and later the County, to incorporate the best of their features into a municipally operated system.

The City Park System

As evidenced by the presence of public squares on the first town plats filed after the settlement of Milwaukee, there was some awareness on the part of early government officials of the need for park areas in the community. It was not until 1889, however, that obstacles in the path of a citywide park system were removed and such a program was established. The reasons for this lengthy delay were many. Prior to the Civil War, pioneer Milwaukee had more pressing needs for tax dollars, such as the subsidization of railroad construction linking Milwaukee with the interior of Wisconsin. The existence of the few ward parks, or public squares and triangles, offered an excuse that the City was already meeting its obligation in this direction. The growing number of private beer gardens and amusement parks and their popular acceptance also tended to dull whatever support there was for municipal involvement in this area of civic responsibility.

By the late 1850s there is evidence that some Milwaukeeans had begun to recognize a need for City efforts in this direction. That year Alderman Horace Chase offered to sell twenty acres of his farm on the south side to the City for park purposes. The proposal attracted some public and newspaper support, but the increased financial difficulties produced by the 1857 depression ended any serious consideration of such a step. Three years later, Alderman John Rosebeck introduced a resolution before the Common Council which would have allowed the several wards in the City to develop new parks or expand existing ones, with the costs to be borne by citywide taxation rather than on a ward basis. Amendments changing the funding to ward support only emasculated the basic objective of the proposal.

The treatment accorded the Rosebeck proposal highlighted a major obstacle to the creation of a City park system which was to plague proponents for the next three decades. The squares, triangles, and parks, where they even existed, were operated on a ward basis, and the individual aldermen and their constituents were opposed to any change in the system which would take away this control or, still worse, force them to pay taxes for park lands located either in other areas of the City or in their own wards when no sentiment for such amenities of life existed.

The system of ward-controlled parks was an uneven one. Some wards had no parks at all; others, such as the older Seventh Ward on the lower east side and the Fourth Ward west of the river had park areas that for the time period, were well developed. Newer sections of the City, populated by poor members of the working class, lacked park facilities. Here the local alderman, influenced by the attitudes of his constituents, viewed park acquisition and ongoing maintenance as an unwanted and unnecessary addition to the ward tax levy. Even the more affluent Seventh Ward bordering the lake shore, which boasted of the most successful of Milwaukee's early parks (the southern part of present Juneau Park), regarded the expansion of that facility by condemnation process in the 1870s as very expensive and unnecessarily burdensome to some residents.

As a possible alternative, efforts were made in the mid-1870s to obtain authority for joint funding for park development by two or more wards acting together. Opponents quickly raised arguments against such a plan because of possible difficulties in site selection and the unwanted addition of another layer of government in the form of the independent commission that was to oversee the arrangement. The depth of this ward-oriented mentality in City government was also illustrated by a dispute between City officials and ward aldermen over repairs made to Courthouse Square in 1875. When the Board of Public Works made necessary improvements to this small park area and paid the costs from the City's general revenues, the Common Council vigorously objected. The alderman regarded this procedure as a usurpation of rights and responsibilities that had heretofore belonged to the Seventh Ward (and, by implication, to other ward organizations in Milwaukee).

The strength of this ward tradition and the power of the aldermen proved a major stumbling block to the establishment of a citywide park system, governed by an independent citizen commission. Scattered proposals for enabling legislation on parks reaching the state legislature in Madison in the early 1880s failed to receive adequate support from the Milwaukee delegation whenever the measures even suggested a threat to ward control.

With the passage of time, however, these attitudes softened largely because the growing size and population of the city and the increased complexity of urban government produced demands for municipal services on an effective citywide basis. There was an expanded need for paved streets, water and sewer services, adequate police and fire protection, and the creation of an effective public health program. Park development became acceptable as the responsibilities of public officials for the welfare of the citizenry they served broadened. In its own right, and as an extension of the emphasis on health concerns, the establishment of a public park system became a plank in the platforms of progressive mayoral candidates by the mid-1880s. Influential citizenry also generated effective public support, stressing comparisons between Milwaukee's almost total lack of park services and the accomplishments of other American cities. Nearby Chicago was always held up as an example; but when smaller Wisconsin cities such as Sheboygan and Chippewa Falls made notable strides with park development by the late 1880s, the comparisons had an even greater effect. Milwaukeeans, it was now argued, should no longer have to rely on only the private amusement parks, Forest Home Cemetery, or the grounds of the Soldiers Home for their outdoor enjoyment.

Other arguments provided additional strength for the movement. In addition to basic municipal services — sewer, water, health, fire, and police — the City was enriching the quality of life for Milwaukeeans through public support of a library and museum. Parks would help make Milwaukee an even more attractive place to live for individuals and also stimulate business development. They would also reflect the maturing of the City, which had been, a little more than a half century earlier, only a fur trading post in the Wisconsin wilderness.

Leadership for the creation of a City park system came from a number of sources. Emil Wallber stressed the need for municipal parks in his victorious mayoral campaign in 1886. Assemblyman Michael Dunn unsuccessfully introduced a bill in Madison creating a park system in 1887, but only two years later did his renewed efforts secure the necessary enabling legislation. Others who strongly supported the movement included Theobold Otjen, local attorney and later a Congressman from Milwaukee, and businessmen Louis Auer and Moses H. Brand. And, of course, there was Christian Wahl, whose efforts then and later earned for him the reputation as father of Milwaukee's park system. Wahl, a native of Bavaria, came to Milwaukee with his parents in 1846 and grew up on the family farm in the old Town of Lake. After a very successful business career in Chicago, where he also served on both the city council and board of education, he retired and returned to Milwaukee in 1886.

A basic question facing Wahl and his associates was what type of a park system was best for Milwaukee. Suggestions that the city duplicate the New York effort with one large selectively located "Central Park" ran into the latent sectional objections left over from the years of ward control. The cost of acquiring land for a centrally situated site was also regarded as excessive, and spokesmen for the south side, cut off from the most likely sites by the Menomonee Valley, said emphatically that they would refuse to support the enabling legislation if park lands were not provided in all areas of the city.

Christian Wahl drew upon his observations of the park system in Chicago and argued for the selection of a broad program that included park development for all three major areas of Milwaukee, the east, west, and south sides. Assemblyman Michael Dunn guided the necessary enabling legislation through Madison, compromising where necessary but retaining what was regarded as the essential features of the new project. The borrowing authority for support of the program was reduced from $600,000 to an initial $100,000 to meet objections from fiscal conservatives in the city. An independent commission or Park Board of five members, to be appointed by the mayor and confirmed by the common council, was retained, however. The board was given basic responsibility to establish and maintain a system of parks (a more challenging and far-reaching task than the administration of a single central park would have been) and also to plan and develop a boulevard network for the city.

The Park Board appointments, made by Mayor Thomas H. Brown in May 1889, reflected several factors which had influenced the shaping of the bill in the legislature. Two supporters of the park movement were given key positions, Christian Wahl being chosen as president of the Board and Louis F. Auer its secretary. Their colleagues were John Bentley, a building contractor, Calvin E. Lewis, a commission merchant active in the Chamber of Commerce, and Charles Manegold, Jr., an elevator and flour merchant. Bentley and Manegold were residents of the south side, thereby assuring that section of the City that its interests would be protected in the selection of park sites. Three of the five members, including Wahl, were retired businessmen. This was a circumstance of considerable importance since the Board was to serve without compensation and would, initially at least, have no staff assistance. Its members would be required to spend a great deal of time dealing with park business.

When the new Board assembled in June 1889, its first major task was to work with the City Attorney's office to draft the necessary ordinance for issuing $100,000 in bonds to finance land purchases. Numerous offers of real estate were received, but the Board was forced to be specially selective because of both price and location. A major flaw in the enabling legislation became apparent when the Board realized it was prohibited from acquiring land outside the then City limits, where both desirable sites and reasonable prices were more readily available.

By October 1890, however, the Board had agreed upon five locations for their first land purchase. Two were situated between Lake Michigan and the Milwaukee River, and the other three south of the Menomonee River. These sites later became (with subsequent additions) Lake Park and Riverside Park on the north and Mitchell, Kosciuszko, and Humboldt Parks on the south side.

The inability of the Park Board to acquire land in the northwest part of the City with its rapidly growing population, plus the discovery of severe administrative limitations of the original park act, caused the City to go back to Madison in 1891 for additional legislation to broaden the Board's authority. Once the Park Board had acquired acreage for park purposes, it had found that there was no authority (or funds) to plan for, and facilitate, its use after acquisition. It was also discovered that the numerous administrative duties involved in land purchases and related matters took too much time even for retired businessmen, and some staff support was required.

Lily ponds in Humboldt Park were a part of the formal planning and design utilized in the City of Milwaukee parks.

New legislation enacted in Madison early in 1891 remedied these difficulties. The Board was empowered to purchase lands anywhere in Milwaukee County, with two new bond issues, $150,000 in 1891 and $90,000 in 1892, also being authorized. A one-half mill addition to the City tax levy was authorized for park development as was the employment of a full-time secretary at an annual salary of $1,500. Charles K. Lush, a local newspaper man, was hired for this position. With this new authority, the Board purchased sites for two new parks on the northwest side outside the then City limits — present-day Washington and Sherman Parks. Thus, during their first two years of operation the Park Board had acquired nearly 400 acres of land for a system structured to serve all sections of the City and to allow for further growth as well. Through judicious selection of park sites they also had provided the foundation for boulevard development in the City. Newberry Boulevard would subsequently link Lake and Riverside Parks, and Sherman Boulevard would connect Washington and Sherman Parks. In doing so, however, the Board had gone over $800,000 in debt, the bond issues apparently financing only the down payments for the seven new parks. No additional land would be purchased for sixteen years, until the original purchases were completed. Then the sites for Lincoln, Gordon, and Jackson Parks were acquired in 1907.

Limited finances for acquisition and development were not the only major problem the Park Board faced in its first years of operation. Although the Common Council had accepted the concept of an independent appointed Park Board in the passage of the 1889 enabling act, it rather naively saw the latter as being only an advisory group once it had been selected. Instead, under Wahl's leadership the Board took the initiative and, subsequently, sought clear-cut authority to make land purchases, hire staff and set salaries, and carry on program development independent of the Common Council. Fiercely protective of the responsibility for the spending of tax money, the aldermen attempted to rectify this situation. Before the 1891 legislation enlarging the scope of the Board's operation would be endorsed by the Common Council, a compromise between these two sharply divergent views had to be worked out. It was finally agreed that the City Comptroller's office (and thus, indirectly, the elected officials) would inspect and approve Park Board accounts. The Board was also required to submit to the Common Council an annual report which included itemized details of expenditures.

Control over and responsibility for the expenditure of tax dollars were issues that were to reappear in various forms in the years ahead for both the City Park Board and the County Park Commission. This may help explain why the City's park system was never adequately financed, and the issue was certainly a factor in the eventual demise of the County Park Commission in the early 1980s. It may also have been the reason why some lands used for park purposes in the City prior to the advent of the Park Board were not turned over to control of that body for a number of years. The historic Juneau Park and three newer facilities which evolved out of the City's development of a public water system — Kilbourn, Flushing Tunnel, and Water Works Parks — remained under the care of the Department of Public Works, as did a number of small squares and triangles scattered throughout the City. Most of these were shifted to the jurisdiction of the Park Board in February 1911 except for the Water Works sites, which remained under the Public Works Department until the City system was transferred to Milwaukee County in 1936.

The most notable step taken by the Park Board in its early years was to retain the services of nationally known Frederick Law Olmsted and his associates for the design and development of the new park sites. The Olmsted firm of New York eventually provided the basic landscaping for three of the new parks, Lake, Riverside, and Washington. Of the three, Lake Park has retained the greatest conformity to the Olmsted design, which emphasized the utilization of existing topographical features to provide a distinctive character to the park. Curiously, in submitting his preliminary proposals, Olmsted was critical of the sites selected by the Board because they were located considerable distances from the center of the City. This attitude not only tended to ignore the realities of Milwaukee land prices but sharply conflicted with the views of Charles B. Whitnall and his followers, whose vision of the importance of park land in rural areas to meet the needs of future urban growth was the cornerstone of the County park system's development.

The involvement of the Olmsted firm in the development of Lake Park

By the turn of the century, Lake Park had become a popular place for the afternoon drives in horse-drawn carriages.

indirectly reveals the active leadership provided by the Park Board. Christian Wahl kept up a steady correspondence with Olmsted's office regarding details of the design, while continuing negotiations with outside parties for the purchase of additional park lands and even becoming involved in directing tree planting and gardening.

Efforts by the Board to expand the boulevard network around the City linking the various park sites made little immediate progress beyond the development of Newberry Boulevard. Part of the problem was financial, but later difficulties resulted from the multiple jurisdictions involving other municipalities outside the City for some of the proposed routes. The potential for developing the lakefront between Lake and Juneau Parks also attracted the Board's attention. Legislation giving the City a 300-foot strip of submerged lands between the two parks was secured in the 1890s, but little was done towards its development until well into the next century.

Financial difficulties were a constant hindrance to the physical expansion of the City park system after the momentum of the first few years. As already noted, no new acquisitions were made for more than a decade and a half and thereafter only sporadically. A renewed interest in urban planning and beautification emerged in 1907, when a Metropolitan Plan Commission was created by the City. Its purpose, aside from the vigorous promotion of a Civic Center for Milwaukee, was to encourage overall urban planning of which park development would be a part.

One perhaps unanticipated result of the creation of the Metropolitan Plan Commission was to bring together, on a formal basis, a number of individuals destined to make their mark in park development in the Milwaukee area for the next decade. By 1907 the influential pioneers of the Christian Wahl era were gone, and it was now time for a new generation to focus park development in greater Milwaukee on broader objectives. Among the members originally appointed to the Metropolitan Plan Commission were Charles B. Whitnall, a local florist and political activist in the ranks of the rapidly developing Social Democratic Party, Alfred C. Clas, an architect with a special interest in community projects, and William Lindsay, head of a large local farm implement firm. All three were also to be appointed to the newly formed Milwaukee County Park Commission, created almost simultaneously with the establishment of the Metropolitan Plan Commission.

Creation of the County Park Commission

Formal creation of the Milwaukee County Park Commission was accomplished by action of the Wisconsin legislature in the spring of 1907, in response to the efforts of a group of concerned Milwaukee area park supporters. The official record is strangely silent on the role of Milwaukee County government in this development. The absence of any committee reports or special resolution in the *Proceedings of the County Board of Supervisors* supports a belief that much of the stimulus came from private sources. But certainly, influential members of the County Board must have been consulted, individually and informally on the matter, since appointive authority rested with the Board chairman and the enabling legislation contemplated use of the County's taxing power and other official forms of association.

Years later, Charles B. Whitnall, generally recognized as the father of the County's park system and a member of the Commission for forty years, recounted the circumstances under which he and others gave birth to the institution. During the first decade of the twentieth century a group of civic-minded men and women met regularly at a south side Milwaukee high school for lectures by faculty from the University in Madison. Prior to the lectures, they informally discussed problems in City and County government, including, on one occasion, the tendency of classical park planners to level the natural topography in order to later create artificial park grounds.

Whitnall was a determined advocate of the retention of natural features of the landscape for park purposes and felt equally as strong about the need to prepare for the orderly growth of urban centers of population by zoned planning. This objective included the early designation of desirable sites for park purposes, the dedication of sufficient land along principal routes of travel to allow for highway beautification and the development of parkways following the routes of existing rivers and streams in outlying areas.

Whitnall's discussion class agreed to try to put these concepts into practice through the creation of a County Park Commission that had authority to influence planning, highway development, and park acquisition in the rural areas outside the City of Milwaukee. Another member of Whitnall's group was Charles E. Estabrook, a Milwaukee attorney. Estabrook, a power in Civil War veterans circles, had gone from the Wisconsin legislature to the office of state treasurer in 1886. More importantly, he was at this time again a member of the state legislature, serving his second consecutive term as assemblyman for Milwaukee's thirteenth district.

On the scene in Madison, Estabrook guided the necessary enabling legislation through both houses of the legislature, the bill emerging as Chapter 250, Laws of 1907, to take effect on July 1 of that year. It provided that counties of over 150,000 population (Milwaukee was the only one to qualify) could create a seven-member Park Commission to be appointed by the Chairman of the County Board for seven-year terms, the appointments staggered so that one would expire each year. In addition to routine provisions concerning organization and officers, the measure went on to assign the new body responsibility for making a thorough study of the County to identify lands suitable for public use and to lay out a plan for open areas, roads, and boulevards as part of "a comprehensive plan for a county park system." Reports on this planning effort were to be submitted to the Board of Supervisors within two years, and, subject to the approval of the County Board, the Commission could acquire the necessary land to develop and maintain the proposed system of parks and parkways. Finally, the County Board was authorized to appropriate funds to implement the work of the Commission.

On August 20, 1907 Charles T. Fisher, chairman of the Board of Supervisors, made the necessary appointments to the Commission as called for by the law. These included William Lindsay, head of a farm implement company, appointed for the seven-year term; Alfred C. Clas, an architect (six years); Patrick Cudahy, president of the meat packing firm (five years); Emerson D. Hoyt, first Mayor of the City of Wauwatosa, (four years); Alvin P. Kletsch, influential Milwaukee hotel owner (three years); James Currie, a partner in a wholesale and retail florist business (two years); and Charles B. Whitnall, a landscape gardener by profession, for the remaining one-year term.

The choices were excellent. These first Commissioners were influential and respected members of the Milwaukee community who, either through their business activities or personal interests, were well qualified to serve. Hoyt was the only suburbanite, although Cudahy's substantial business interests in the rural community which bore his name could also be so classified. Whitnall was the sole member of the increasingly influential Socialist movement in Milwaukee County and was later able to count on strong support for Park Commission programs from elected Socialist party functionaries. There was a strong personal link within the Commission with similar municipal bodies in Milwaukee. Clas was a member of the City Park Board, and Currie would join him in a few years. Three of the County Commissioners, Lindsay, Clas, and Whitnall, were also members of the Metropolitan Plan Commission, appointed by the Mayor of Milwaukee about the same time the County body was established. This not only assured cooperation and a community of interest among the three groups but also provided broader contacts and influence beyond the make-up of the County Park Commission. The joint appointments of Lindsay, Clas, and Whitnall to new planning agencies appointed by the two major governmental bodies in the County certainly did nothing but enhance their reputations and influence in this area of civic progress.

At its first meeting of the County Park Commission on September 9, 1907, William Lindsay was elected president and Alfred Clas designated as secretary. Later, an official request was submitted to the County Board to include an appropriation for use of the Commission in the 1908 County budget. The amount eventually provided was $1,000 for general expenses. Clas served as secretary of the Commission for only a short time. By March 1908 Charles E. Estabrook had been retained as the salaried part-time secretary. Estabrook, although never appointed a member of the seven-man Commission, played a leading role in its activities for more than a decade until his death in early 1919. At that point Whitnall was selected as his replacement, serving as both secretary (which by that time had developed into an important administrative role) and an appointed member of that Commission. It required an opinion from the District Attorney's office to convince some members of the County Board that such a dual arrangement was legal, and after Whitnall's tenure of some seven years, Jerome Dretzka served in a similar dual capacity well into the 1950s. Upon Dretzka's retirement, however, he urged that the Park Commission secretary, as an active management position, be discontinued and administrative responsibilities shifted to professional staff.

The original enabling legislation creating the Commission reflected its goals and objectives as envisioned by Whitnall, Estabrook, Hoyt, and their associates. The identification and acquisition of desirable park land were major tasks, but only within the much broader framework of planning for the systematic development of the County outside the City of Milwaukee. An adequate highway network, with sufficient width for projected expansion of automobile travel and with rules governing setbacks for buildings along main roads, was seen as particularly essential to the relationship of residential sections with the outlying parks. A system of parkways, following the routes of major waterways in the County, would also provide connecting links between primary park areas. Eventually, the preservation and utilization of the Lake Michigan shore line for park purposes and the development of Countywide zoning ordinances would also become important duties of the Commission.

A review of the record of the Commission's actions during its early years suggests that the members, at times more concerned with rural planning concepts and land acquisitions, gave little real thought to public uses of the park system until public and political pressure stimulated efforts in this direction. Very early, the Commission found it necessary to go back to the state legislature to broaden its authority. In 1909 additional legislation placed the parkway and boulevard development on a more solid footing, provided for the use of the condemnation process to acquire lands, and substantially increased the appropriations from the County Board for Commission use. Additional legislative needs in 1913 sent Charles E. Estabrook into the political arena once again. Successfully campaigning for the Assembly after a four-year absence, Estabrook shepherded new bills through Madison, ironing out difficulties in the reappointment process for the Commission members, and authorizing the County Board to annually levy a one-tenth mill tax for use by the Commission in a greatly expanded program of land acquisition.

The first major project funded for the Commission was an appropriation of $4,000 in 1909 to carry out the comprehensive park and road study of Milwaukee County. In addition, the County Board annually made available $1,000 for expenses, including a part-time salary for secretary Estabrook. The appropriation was increased to $1,500 by 1912. After Estabrook's successful efforts to secure additional authority from the 1913 legislature for land acquisition, press reports based upon courthhouse gossip described him as receiving "a large salary" for his services. Indignant, Estabrook requested the opportunity to appear before the County Board, acting as a committee of the whole, to set the record straight about his modest monthly stipend of $125. The issue then died quickly.

The inclusion of a mill tax for parks in the annual County budget did substantially increase the ability of the Commission to embark on its land acquisition program. A separate fund containing $56,126 was set up for this purpose in 1914, and the 1915 budget provided an additional $57,425. Prior to the availability of these funds on a regular basis, the Commission had been required to secure special appropriations from the County Board, through either general funds or bond issues. Their first park purchases, Bluff Park located just north of the Soldiers Home and the initial sections of Jacobus Park in Wauwatosa and Grant Park in South Milwaukee, were acquired in this manner in 1910.

During the first dozen years or so of its existence the Commission had to work out methods of operation to accomplish its designated objectives and to meet new responsibilities which were assigned to it or which grew out of the expansion of its basic mission. Although the County body had the experience of the City Park Board to learn from, there were significant differences between the two park agencies. These were either mandated by law or developed from the philosophies of the members of the two bodies. It was frequently necessary for the County Park Commission to pioneer unexplored territory. The zeal and breadth of vision exhibited by Whitnall, Estabrook, and their early associates for emphasis on planning the development of the rural areas outside the City, the presence of a more varied topography in the outlying sections of the County, and the quantity of relatively inexpensive lands suitable for park use made the County Commission's task very different from the experience of the City Park Board during the first two decades of its existence.

It was necessary for the Commission to establish an effective and mutually satisfactory working relationship with the elected officials, particularly on the vital process of funding with tax dollars appropriated by the County Board the acquisition of lands for parks and parkways. In carrying out their organizational objectives, the Commission needed to show that it occupied an essential and productive place in County government, one that would also be useful to the other local governments in the County which ranged from first-class cities to the sprawling townships. And, finally, they had to accept and implement the additional responsibilities, large and small, assigned to them in a variety of ways as extensions of their primary concerns for development of parks and a Countywide network of highways and parkways.

An effective working relationship between the Park Commission and the County Board of Supervisors evolved within the decade or so which followed the creation of the Commission in 1907 but not without some problems and difficulties. In part, this was due to a substantial and far-reaching change in the make-up of the County Board in 1908, when its membership was reduced from a very large and unwieldy body of forty-nine members to a more streamlined group of sixteen Supervisors. It took the Board several years to fully adapt to this new arrangement and also to become responsive to new demands for both authority and funding being generated by the zealous leadership of Whitnall and Estabrook on the Park Commission. At the heart of the relationship between the two groups, however, was the question of money. As already noted, the Commission owed its existence in large measure to forces outside of County government. Its early success in obtaining legislative endorsement in Madison may have caused its members to underestimate the fundamental responsibility of the County Board for the shaping and financing of a County budget which included the funds for the Park Commission.

The newness of the Commission, the stature and reputation of its membership, the political influence of Estabrook, Hoyt, and Whitnall (the latter through his prominent place in the Social Democratic Party which became a force in City and County government after 1910), and the natural sympathy of many of the Supervisors for what the Commission was trying to accomplish made the first few years smooth enough, if also somewhat uncertain. The Commission's modest annual operating budget was rather routinely approved in this early period, while the more substantial financial arrangments for the purchase of park lands in 1910 in Wauwatosa and South Milwaukee involving over ninety acres and payment obligations of nearly $60,000 also were endorsed by the Board rather routinely. However, when the Commission took an option on a second parcel of some fifty-five acres for the South Milwaukee project requiring the commitment of an additional $22,000, the Board was not so quick to give its assent. Following some delay caused by the proposal being referred back to committee for study and an opinion from the District Attorney, the second South Milwaukee purchase (for present Grant Park) was approved by a resolution in which the Supervisors bluntly pointed out that no further land purchases were to be made without prior expressed authority from the County Board.

Passage of the 1913 park law, containing provision for a substantial mill tax for land purchases, disturbed some members of the County Board to the extent that a resolution was introduced in November 1914 to abolish the Park Commission along with several other public boards. Earlier that year, evidence of the Board's growing suspicions of the Commission and its land acquisition program was contained in action approving another acquisition for Grant Park which stated that the Commission must "pledge itself in writing" that the purchase would be funded by the park mill levy and be carried out through condemnation proceedings. A committee report on the abolition proposal was adopted by an overwhelming vote of the Board, the only opposition coming from Whitnall's Socialist colleague, Supervisor Frederic Heath. In reality, the problem was not so much the Park Commission alone but the combination of at least eight boards and commissions (most of them operating the County social service institutions) who were responsible for more than $800,000 in the County tax levy over which the Board had little operational authority. Although the District Attorney was instructed to draft legislation for introduction in Madison abolishing the various commissions, no action affecting the park body was forthcoming. Two years later, in 1916, park supporters in the state legislature (presumably with the assent of the Commission) proposed to amend the Milwaukee County park law by striking the requirement that purchase of land should be carried out "with the approval and consent of the County Board." The Board of Supervisors voted 16-3 to oppose the bill since it would have removed "a safeguard against excessive and improvident expenditures of public money." The three votes in opposition, and therefore in favor of giving financial independence to the Park Commission, came from Socialist supervisors, thus again suggesting Whitnall's hand in the Madison measure.

The final effort in the formative period of the Park Commission's existence to curtail the body's role occurred in 1919, when Supervisor Thaddeus Czerwinski proposed that a measure be sent to Madison "to abolish the County Park Commission." A committee report endorsing the proposal was rejected by the full Board by more than a two-to-one majority, as Supervisors from all political spectrums voiced support for the Commission's continuous existence and, by implication, its value to County government.

The message, however, had apparently been made clear to the Park Commission: the elected officials were going to maintain ultimate control over the purse strings of County government, including the operations of the park system. At the same time, however, there were other indications that the Commission was becoming not only accepted but recognized as a useful public body for expanding County services outside of parks and highways.

One other problem that plagued the relationship between the Park Commission and the County's elected officials in these early years was the matter of regularized Commission appointments. After the initial composition of the Commission was made by County Board Chairman Charles T. Fisher in 1907, the filling of vacancies due to the expiration of terms each year was not handled very effectively. Whitnall, whose one-year term expired in 1908, and James Currie, whose two-year appointment ended in 1909, were not officially reappointed to the Commission until Chairman James Sheehan acted to do so in March 1910. This sporadic attention apparently continued, for when the park law was amended in 1913 through Estabrook's efforts, one of the changes specifically allowed the remaining members of the Commission to fill vacancies if the County Board chairman failed to do so within ninety days. The result was that the Commission notified the Board in November 1913 that it had made the following appointments (actually reappointments) for terms commencing as noted: Alvin P. Kletzsch (1910), Emerson D. Hoyt (1911), Patrick Cudahy (1912), and Alfred C. Clas (1913). When questions were raised about this procedure, a County Board committee reported that in the opinion of the District Attorney the appointments were perfectly legal.

The following year, the County Board chairman again failed to act when Commission President William Lindsay's term expired, and he was selected to serve again by action of his colleagues on the Commission. By 1915, however, the lesson had been learned; and when Whitnall's second term was up, his reappointment was made by Chairman William E. McCarty, who did the same for the terms expiring in the next several years. When Commissioner Clas found it necessary to resign in 1917 and again when Patrick Cudahy died in 1919, McCarty made new appointments to fill the unexpired terms, with Fred Vogel, Jr. replacing Clas and William R. McGovern succeeding Cudahy. Both replacements were of high caliber. While Vogel only served until 1921, McGovern became a fixture on the Commission until his death forty-five years later and contributed immeasurably to the success of park development during that period.

Very early in its history, perhaps because of his close political association with Whitnall, Supervisor Frederic Heath was responsible for a number of steps which broadened the role of the Park Commission through new ways of service to County government and the community. In 1911 Heath successfully introduced an ordinance giving the Commission entire control of County forestry services after a double row of elm trees had been cut back improperly on the drive leading to the County Hospital. His other proposals also included that the Commission be directed to survey the County grounds in Wauwatosa, that its members serve on a special committee charged with beautifying the streams in the County which were then little better than open sewers, and that the Commission submit plans for the planting of trees along all designated County highways to beautify these routes.

Heath was also responsible for the first naming of a County park when he proposed in 1915 that one of the tracts in Wauwatosa be named Sholes Park after Christopher Latham Sholes, the Milwaukee newspaper editor who is generally credited with inventing the first practical typewriter. Deeply interested in Milwaukee history, Heath had also obtained County Board action in 1913 directing that one of the parks be specially designated as a historic park and that surviving landmarks such as log cabins, wind mills, and other similar structures be secured for location on this site. There is no indication that this farsighted project was ever implemented as he envisioned, however.

Other evidences of a growing involvement by the County Board in the development of the park system included the granting of broad authority to the Park Commission in 1917 to purchase lands in specifically named sections of the County, provided, of course, that funds were already available in the Commission's accounts and that these purchases would not require additional appropriations from the Board. In 1919 there were several proposals from individual County Board members which indicated that they felt the Commission was too much concerned with land acquisition and was not progressing quickly enough with the development of public services to satisfy the Supervisors' voting constituents. In a resolution introduced in April 1919 Eugene Warnimont pointed up the absence of bathing facilities in County parks, most notably the recently acquired lands on the upper Milwaukee River (Estabrook Park) and in the South Milwaukee park tract (Grant Park). The Park Commission was requested to erect bathing pavilions at these locations and at others that had river or lake frontage. Warnimont (whose district included the Grant Park site) also presented a second resolution aimed at stimulating the Commission's developments of the South Milwaukee tract, noting that it was almost impossible for citizens (meaning his constituents) to use the park lands due to inadequate roads in and around the park and the lack of benches and other conveniences.

Supervisor Charles Jacobus, long a supporter of the Park Commission's program, called attention to other needs within the system at the same meeting of the County Board. Noting that the Commission had not done much to improve park lands purchased almost ten years earlier, Jacobus said there was a special need for athletic and recreational facilities. Informal conversations with the Commissioners had indicated they were willing to proceed with the development of such a program if the County Board approved. Jacobus urged his colleagues to go on record supporting a broad recreational program through the creation of facilities for baseball, tennis, golf, and such other athletic activities. There was a particular need, he pointed out, for a golf course to be designed and developed at the South Milwaukee Park. (The apparent magnitude of this need and of Jacobus's influence on the Board is evidenced by the fact that his proposal was introduced, referred to committee, endorsed, and favorably voted on by the Supervisors all in one day!).

Perhaps the most significant indication that the Park Commission had, after ten or twelve years of existence, become a vital part of Milwaukee County government emerges from its role in the creation of the first County airport. On May 5, 1919, at a regular meeting of the County Board, Chairman William T. McCarty called the attention of his colleagues to the expanding network of air travel in the United States and said that it was to the interest and future benefit of Milwaukee County to develop the necessary landing field and facilities for air service to the community. At this time McCarty was also chairman of a citizen's committee working to bring regular air service to Milwaukee. McCarty proposed that the County, through the Park Commission, be empowered to develop an airport and to expend public funds to accomplish this end, and he had a resolution prepared directing that the legislature in Madison be asked to amend the park laws accordingly. This proposal was endorsed by the County Board.

Two days earlier the Park Commission had met to discuss McCarty's plan to involve the Commission in the airport business. It was agreed that the most suitable site was the so-called "Zimmerman Farm" in Wauwatosa, recently purchased for park development. A question was raised whether the Commission could legally use the land for what was clearly a non-park purpose. The Commissioners, and also McCarty, agreed it was necessary to have a ruling on this vital point. The District Attorney's office advised that it would be illegal to use park land for airport purposes involving private aircraft operations and that a change in the park law was necessary. The Commission assured McCarty they had no objection to such a change, and by its June 25 meeting the County Board chairman had secured passage of the necessary legislation by both houses in Madison and had the promise of the Governor's signature on the bill.

The Commission was then given the task of sufficiently developing the Zimmerman tract to accommodate various types of aircraft, including some large planes then being constructed in Milwaukee by the aviation pioneer Alfred Lawson. Park Commission funds already appropriated were to be used for this purpose, with McCarty having assured the Commission that the County Board would provide reimbursement for the development costs. Most of this work was completed by the fall of 1919, with Whitnall arranging for, and supervising much of, the grading and construction. The Commissioners, for their part, wrestled with such weighty matters as the preparation of rules and regulations for the use of the airfield and compensation for crop loss suffered by the farmer renting the Zimmerman property.

Airport management would remain the responsibility of the Park Commission until 1929. By 1925 aviation needs had advanced beyond the capacity of the original landing field at the Zimmerman site, and the Commission played a major role in selecting and purchasing Hamilton Field, present site of Mitchell International Airport, for use and subsequent expansion as the County airport. Although the objective was totally unrelated to its basic park function, the Commission was for several reasons a logical choice to play this important role in establishing airport facilities for the County. It was a governmental agency already in existence, made up of individuals who were respected in the community and experienced in undertaking new tasks for County government. It had control over two very necessary assets: land for the field and funds already appropriated for development costs. It appeared easier at the time to Board Chairman McCarty to have the laws governing the operation of the Park

Commission amended in Madison to allow for the development of an airport than to seek the creation of a totally new administrative entity. The effort was, on the whole, very successful. It provided a precedent for the Park Commission to perform a similar nonpark service resulting in an important benefit to the County after the Second World War, when it took over management of the Veterans Housing Program.

Expanding County Parks in the 1920s

By 1920 the County's park system had been in operation for more than a dozen years. During that time the Park Commission as a body had maintained a remarkable continuity of membership. By trial and error it had established an effective working relationship with the County's elected officials. It had also gained acceptance of the philosophy of its founders concerning the need for planned development of the rural areas. A rudimentary administrative procedure had been put into operation, although this was soon to be severely tested by the County Board's mandate for broad expansion of recreation activities. And it had displayed substantial progress in the physical acquisition of park lands for future development in locations well distributed throughout all parts of the County.

The initial flurry of purchases in 1910 of what would later be named Bluff Park overlooking the Menomonee Valley, Sholes Park in Wauwatosa, and the sprawling Grant Park site near South Milwaukee was followed by other key acquisitions later in the decade. Starting in 1916, substantial portions of Estabrook Park bordering the upper Milwaukee River were obtained, along with the Blatz Farm property (Kletzsch Park) farther north along the river two years later. In 1919 portions of what later became Currie Park, situated on both banks of the Menomonee River, were purchased and almost immediately developed for airport use. Control of the so-called Kneeland tract (later *old* Red Arrow Park), originally acquired by the County as a site for a new courthouse, was turned over to the Commission in 1916. With additions to the earlier park sites also being made during these years, in sheer acreage alone, the expansion of the system was both steady and substantial. A glance at a County map showing these sites quickly reveals the operations of two fundamental characteristics of Commission policy: the wide geographic dispersion of the park land and the selection of sites along the County's waterways.

During the decade of the 1920s the program of land acquisition was even more ambitious. Careful now to work closely with the County Board and responsive to the Supervisors' requests for cooperation in projects such as airport development, the Commission was able to fund the purchase of a remarkable amount of acreage during these ten years. Gaps in the geographic pattern were filled with the acquisition in the southwest for Greenfield Park (278 acres) in 1921 and with the purchase of a huge tract of farm land (over 600 acres) near Hales Corners for Whitnall Park beginning in 1929. On the north side the County Board turned over to the Commission property south of the House of Correction site in 1926, which is now known as McGovern Park, and two years later purchases were begun for Brown Deer Park. Smaller acquisitions also helped fill in the system. Nearly thirty-five acres along the lake shore south of the City of Milwaukee were purchased in 1929 and called Bay View Park. Hoyt Park bordering the Menomonee River was acquired in 1926. Several years earlier Saveland Park, in the old Town of Lake, had been donated to the

Private funding made possible the early musical performances in Milwaukee's municipal parks. Later, both the City and County governments supported concerts and other entertainment.

County by the descendants of John Saveland. Another site received by gift was Cudahy Park along the lake shore in the City of Cudahy. These park acquisitions, along with the land required for the development of the Root River and Menomonee River parkway systems during the 1920s and purchases expanding older parks, added more than 900 acres to the system, tripling its size between 1920 and 1930. The wisdom and foresight of this expansion became apparent during the depression era of the 1930s. Money for substantial land acquisition was then non-existent. Instead, great quantities of funding became available as part of government relief programs, and the vast undeveloped acres of the park system received attention that would never have been possible otherwise.

As the park system grew in size, so did the demands of both the politicians who were paying the bills and the general public for program and recreational development. In response to the urgings of the County Board, the Commission directed Whitnall to create and expand facilities within the parks as quickly as possible. With so much attention being paid to land acquisition, funding for development was sometimes a problem, and Whitnall resorted to a variety of stopgap measures. Lumber from a dismantled barn on the Blatz Farm was trucked to Grant Park for use in construction of temporary bathing facilities; and when this proved too slow, Whitnall borrowed a half-dozen voting booths from the Milwaukee Election Commission to serve as dressing rooms for bathers. The temporary nature of this arrangement was highlighted when the booths had to be returned for use by the City in a special election on the soldiers' bonus referendum in September 1919. Baseball diamonds and tennis courts were laid out, but only grounds and posts were provided for tennis enthusiasts. The players had to supply their own nets.

The creation of golfing facilities in Grant Park received the greatest attention. A nine-hole course was laid out initially, but the popularity of the sport soon caused it to be expanded to eighteen. Here again the Commission combined economy with ingenuity by purchasing used pipe from a wrecking company in Chicago for the sprinkler system. Layout of the course and its subsequent operation required a more experienced hand, however, and local golf enthusiasts recommended to the Commission that George Hansen, then in charge of a golf course in Racine, be retained. He went on the Commission's payroll in June 1919 and remained for more than thirty years, playing an immeasurable role in the development and operation of the park system during that time. When he died in 1950, Hansen held the position of Superintendent of Parks. As golf manager, his starting salary was $150 per month, plus the privilege of selling golf equipment, candy and cigars, providing lessons, and repairing clubs. Later, it became customary for the Commission to vote Hansen a bonus each January, based upon revenues received from golfing fees. The Fowle farm house on the grounds (the present Grant Park Clubhouse) was also made available to him as a residence.

This type of informal and individualistic arrangment was typical of the personnel policies of the Commission during the years of haphazard program expansion. At one point, the salary of the caretaker at Grant Park was calculated not only on his work performance but also on an allowance to keep cows and chickens and grow vegetables at the residence supplied for him by the Commission. Whitnall, as secretary, had responsibility for

Grant Park was the first facility in the County park system to feature an 18-hole golf course. This view, from the early 1920s, was taken near the clubhouse.

hiring the caretakers, laborers, watchmen, and tradesmen used in the parks, and his efforts suffered from lack of any overall direction or policy. In 1922 the caretaker at Estabrook Park was dismissed because the sheriff reported he had fired a gun at a woman in the park. On July 24, 1925 a tragedy pointed up the need for improved personnel policies for the Commission. Five employees were struck by lightning while working in a storm at the Grant Park nursery. One was killed instantly and others severely burned. Questions about insurance, benefit payments to survivors, doctors' bills, and related matters required a great deal of the Commission's attention for some time after, because no clear-cut policies had previously been developed to keep pace with the growth of the parks and staff.

Another major development during the 1920s, second only in significance to the expanded land acquisitions of this period, was the creation of the Regional Planning Department under jurisdiction of the Park Commission. This was the fulfillment of another of Whitnall's long-range goals, made possible by the enactment in 1923 of several pieces of legislation in Madison giving new authority to the Commission to control planning and zoned development in the rural areas of Milwaukee County. In addition to responsibilities in the areas of highway widening, rural platting, and planned zoning, the new department performed two new and vital functions for the Park Commission. These were supervising the plans and development of the long-talked-of parkway network to follow natural watercourses in the County and providing engineering, landscape, and architectural services for park development. Prior to this, much of the professional design services used by the Commission, aside from the golf courses, was provided by their former colleague, architect Alfred C. Clas, who was hired under contract or served voluntarily. Now the Commission had available a staff of trained engineers and architects to provide the technical expertise and assistance necessary to implement their ambitious objectives. Several members of the planning staff, including Eugene A. Howard and Alfred Boerner, remained affiliated with the park system for many years and made lasting contributions.

An indication of the enthusiasm this development generated for the visionary Charles B. Whitnall was his use of a new identification in his official records for what he now called the "Milwaukee County Park Commission and Rural Planning Board," even before the new department had been officially authorized to begin work. By the summer of 1924 the professionals in the planning department were delivering, on a regular basis, a steady stream of reports, recommendations, and plans for consideration by the Commission at its meetings. The new legislation had greatly enlarged the scope of the Commission's traditional work, but much of this new input from the planners also dealt with the improvement of parks and their facilities. The availability of professional supervision alone allowed for substantial progress to be made in park development, thus avoiding criticism of an earlier period that the park programs could not keep pace with the acquisition of lands.

While the 1920s witnessed major expansion of the park system, the last years of the decade also saw the Commission relieved of its responsibility for airport operation. The experience and skill of the Commission had been important in 1926, when the landing facilities were moved from the Currie Park site to the Hamilton Airport, west of Cudahy, and again in 1928, when the size of the new field was considerably expanded. By then, air traffic in Milwaukee County had grown to such proportions that control of the County airport had become too large and too specialized for the Commission. Legislation enacted in Madison in 1929 transferred administration of the airport to the County Board, through its highway committee, the changeover taking full effect on January 1, 1930. During more than a decade of activity the Commission had handled not only land acquisitions but also all operational details, including leases and rentals to both private and commercial users, so that at the time of transfer the airport was almost self-supporting.

Much of the progress made by the park program in the County during the 1920s resulted from the make-up, talents, and stability of the Commission itself. Early in the decade two of the original Commissioners left the group, Hoyt by retirement in 1921 due to failing health and Currie in 1922 by death. Fred Vogel, appointed in 1917 to succeed Clas, also left in 1921. Their replacements, along with two appointments made in 1919 and 1920, and the continued presence of two original members of the Com-

Notable leaders in municipal park development in Milwaukee County. Clockwise from upper left: Christian Wahl, Charles E. Estabrook, Jerome Drezka, and Charles B. Whitnall.

mission gave the body a sense of stability and familiarity that permitted them to work well together most of the time. Commissioners Kletzsch (1907), Whitnall (1907), Jerome Dretzka (1920), William McGovern (1919), and Nathaniel Greene (1921) continued to serve into the decade of the 1940s. Shorter terms were held by other Commissioners, but, on the whole, turnover within the Commission's ranks was remarkably infrequent for several decades.

A major change did take place within the Commission's structure in 1926 as part of a larger and badly needed reorganization of its operational methods that reflected the only really serious dispute within the Commission's ranks that the historical record reveals. It resulted in the resignation of Charles B. Whitnall as secretary, following a vigorous disagreement on both Commission policy and practice between Whitnall and the then president, William McGovern. McGovern, at the time general manager of the Wisconsin Telephone Company, had been elected Commission president in August 1925. At issue was a decision by the Commission early in 1926 to develop an eighteen-hole golf course in Currie Park on the former airport grounds after the flying facilities had been relocated to the present site at Mitchell Field. Whitnall opposed this move, arguing that the former air field was too small and topographically unsuited for golfing. Beneath the surface may also have been a philosophical problem for Whitnall of too much recreational use of park land interfering with the maintenance of an unspoiled natural setting. After the Commission voted to proceed with the golf project, Whitnall continued his arguments through letters to the Commissioners and the County Board, a procedure to which McGovern strongly objected. Whitnall repeated his arguments at great length in subsequent meetings without success, including one session in July 1926, at which time the Commission also discussed the election of its officers for the coming year. Repeatedly rebuffed by his fellow Commissioners on the Currie Park matter, Whitnall requested that someone else be selected to serve as secretary. In August the issue again surfaced, with McGovern speaking to the Commission (really to Whitnall) about the need for conformity to official decisions. Whitnall responded that his official duties as secretary required him to recognize the Commission's decisions, but they could not keep him from, as he put it, "preaching his gospel." The minutes of this session end with the cryptic note that McGovern and Whitnall "would meet later in the day for another conference."

Whitnall submitted a formal letter of resignation for consideration at a Commission meeting in McGovern's office at the Telephone Company on October 22. Whitnall was not in attendance, and the Commission had no choice but to accept his decision and select Jerome Dretzka as the new secretary. Whitnall continued as a member of the Commission, however.

The Whitnall resignation highlighted several dramatic changes which took place at this time in the Commission's method of operation. Since 1907, and particularly following his selection as secretary in 1919, Whitnall's role in County park affairs had been a commanding one. His philosophy dominated the early plans and programs of the Commission. Commission meetings were delayed when he was late and rescheduled when he occasionally went out of the City. Administratively, his duties were endless, his responsibilities demanding, and his method of carrying them out occasionally irritating to his associates. For example, in June 1925 the Commission took an official position (which Whitnall opposed) on several bills before the legislature in Madison and directed Whitnall to withdraw the measures from consideration. When this was not (or could not be) done and Whitnall failed to notify the Commission, McGovern and Nathaniel Greene (a prominent real estate dealer who was elected vice-president when McGovern became president) became "very much provoked" at the secretary, according to his own minutes. The evangelical zeal with which Whitnall advocated his "gospel" of park planning clashed head on with McGovern's avid support of golfing in the Currie Park incident, and Whitnall felt he could more freely do his preaching after relinquishing the secretary's post. Whitnall's ideas were frequently misunderstood by the public and governmental bodies, but he seemed immune to derision or criticism. One close associate likened him to a cork in water, "push him down in one place and he would come up in another."

Modernization of the administrative structure for the park system was badly needed by this time, and all of the Commissioners, including Whitnall, recognized this. Whitnall had introduced some preliminary changes during December of the previous year to base the 1926 budget on past spending experience and to centralize accounting and purchasing for all park units. Prior to his resignation he also arranged with the County Auditor's office to develop an adequate system of bookkeeping.

As part of the restructuring of administrative practices following Whitnall's resignation, additional innovations were introduced, including a scheduled annual audit of Commission finances and the bonding of staff members. Regular office space was secured for the first time in the Commission's history in rented quarters on Mason Street. Prior to this, much of the administrative activity took place at Whitnall's office in the Commonwealth Savings Bank, while Commission meetings were held most frequently in the quarters of the City Park Board in City Hall and, under McGovern's presidency, in the offices at the Telephone Company. To strengthen the policy-making role of the Commission, McGovern created three standing committees: buildings and grounds, real estate, and judiciary and finance. Significantly, Whitnall was named to the first two but not the third.

Two major personnel changes also occurred in this drastic shakeup of parks administration in the fall of 1926 that were to have long-term implications. First was the election of Jerome Dretzka as secretary to succeed Whitnall. An experienced real estate dealer from Cudahy, Dretzka would continue in this dual capacity as both secretary and Commission member until his retirement in 1956. Dretzka was devoted to the growth and development of a first-class park system for Milwaukee County, but he was also less rigid than Whitnall on certain subjects. Unlike his predecessor, he did not have to carry the philosophical burden of being the parent of the County park movement while executing his official duties. Likeable and effective, Dretzka worked well with the Commission, elected officials, park staff, and the general public in the interests of the County parks.

The second major personnel change to emerge from the 1926 reorganization was the decision to create the position of Park Superintendent. This officer was to have general supervision and direction of all park activities and be responsible directly to the Commission. The only candidate considered for the job was George Hansen, then serving as superintendent of golf activities, who had done an outstanding job in setting up and operating the Grant Park course and then in establishing a similar and even more successful program at Greenfield Park in 1923. In appointing Hansen to this new post, the Commission smoothed out their financial arrangements with him, eliminating the year-end bonus and his earnings from equipment sales and lessons in favor of an annual salary of $6,000.

Throughout much of the 1920s the Park Commission had been engaged in an aggressive land acquisition program, motivated in large part by the desired to purchase suitable park sites before land prices made such action extremely expensive or prohibitive. This view recognized that with the inevitable expansion of residential and commercial development in rural Milwaukee County land values were sure to appreciate. The wisdom behind these efforts is illustrated by one of the few land acquisitions which was not completed. In September 1920 the Commission considered, and rejected, an offer to purchase seventy acres of the so-called Foley tract adjacent to the old airport (Currie Park) for $400 per acre. In 1946 forty acres of the Foley property was finally acquired for $32,000, or twice the price of the 1920 offer!

Despite occasional mishaps such as the Foley case, the County park system had grown to impressive proportions by 1930. After that year the abnormal conditions created by the depression years and the absorption of the City of Milwaukee parks in 1937 tend to obscure or distort the magnitude of growth and expansion during the 1920s. In 1930, two decades after its first land acquisition, the County parks contained a total of 2,173 acres, all but 107 of which were acquired through purchases totalling $1,384,330, or about $670 per acre. In contrast, the City Park Board after its first twenty years of operation had jurisdiction over 823 acres costing a total of $2,039,621, or $2,475 per acre. The City, of course, had been forced to purchase sites much closer to residential centers, where land values were much higher. Yet the foresight of Whitnall and his colleagues to prepare for both the expansion of the central city and the development of the suburbs during the next generation is amply illustrated by these statistics.

In 1930 the Park Commission had sixteen park sites under its jurisdiction, well distributed throughout the County and offering a wide variety of natural and recreational activities. These were:

1. Grant Park (360 acres) — an eighteen-hole golf course with clubhouse, two baseball diamonds, numerous picnic sites, a pavilion with restaurant, a beach with bathing facilities, a tourist camp, and the County nurseries.

2. Greenfield Park (278 acres) — eighteen-hole golf course and clubhouse, picnic grounds, facilities for winter sports, and a log cabin for nature groups. A bathing park and lagoon for boating were under construction.

3. Currie Park (166 acres) — eighteen-hole golf course and clubhouse, and facilities for winter sports. A stone quarry leased to the City of Milwaukee was also located here.

4. Brown Deer Park (364 acres) — eighteen-hole golf course and clubhouse, picnic grounds, bridle paths, playground facilities, a bird refuge, and a large lagoon.

5. Estabrook Park (115 acres) — picnic facilities, a bathing beach, concrete tennis courts, baseball diamonds, bridle paths, and playground facilities.

6. Red Arrow Park (3.5 acres) — playground facilities and open green space in the central city.

7. Sholes Park (40 acres) — now called Jacobus Park — picnic and playground facilities, and parkway route.

8. Blatz Park (95 acres) — part of present Kletzsch Park, featured picnic and playground facilities and accommodation for bathing.

9. Silver Spring Park (80 acres) — present McGovern Park, containing a baseball diamond, lagoon, and picnic facilities.

10. Saveland Park (4 acres) — a neighborhood park, with children's playground, shelter facilities, and a lagoon.

11. Bluff Park (6 acres) — an undeveloped site above the Menomonee Valley slated for parkway development.

12. Hoyt Park (10 acres) — contained playground and recreational facilities then operated by the City of Wauwatosa.

13. Wirth Tract (20 acres) — an undeveloped area adjacent to Currie Park.

14. Hales Corners Tract (606 acres) — later renamed Whitnall Park, it was as yet undeveloped except for some nursery use.

15. Cudahy Tract (7 acres) — an undeveloped area on the lakefront adjacent to Sheridan Park in the City of Cudahy.

16. Wisconsin Avenue Park (20 acres) — picnic and playground facilities.

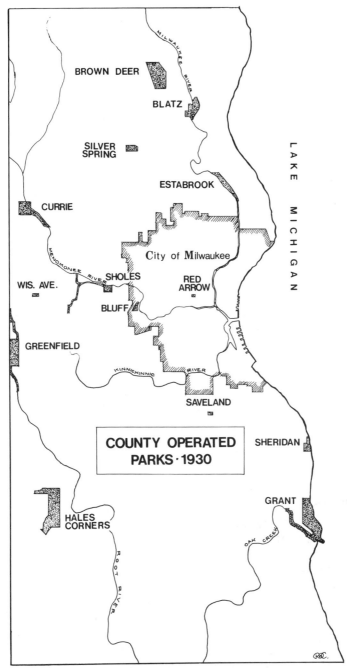

The County park system in 1930. Major parks were well distributed throughout the County, on or near waterways. Parkway development along the stream lines would later link the system together.

In addition to these park facilities, two parkway development projects following the course of the Menomonee River and Oak Creek were under way by 1930.

Although, as noted above, nearly all of the County parks offered a variety of sport and recreational activities, golf was by far the most popular organized attraction and the only one during this era for which reliable user statistics are available. Fourteen thousand golf permits were issued in 1920 for the Grant Park course, the first of the County links to be developed for public use. In 1930 the four eighteen-hole courses at Grant, Currie, Greenfield, and Brown Deer parks issued 363,839 permits, with the first three sites each exceeding one hundred thousand. Golf in the County parks realized profits of over $32,000 that year from user fees and the sale of merchandise which went towards supporting other expenses of the system's operation.

Depression Years and Merger With the City System

The Commission's acquisition program of the 1920s was to bear fruit in the decade which followed. When the effects of the Great Depression were felt throughout the United States, including Milwaukee County, government at various levels embarked on relief programs aimed at providing jobs for millions of unemployed. Public works projects became the focal point of employment efforts by Milwaukee County government in 1931, including substantial appropriations for utilization within the park system. Later, when massive amounts of Federal aid became available to the County, the parks benefited immensely. While the depression era of the 1930s was characterized primarily by economic hardship and human misery, it was also a period during which the parks and their facilities in Milwaukee County were improved far beyond any plan of normal development.

In April 1931 the County Board made the first of a series of substantial appropriations for the employment on park projects of persons then receiving relief or general assistance from the County. This work was severely limited in terms of both hours assigned and wages paid to those employed, but it did generate income for members of the more than 20,000 families serviced by the Department of Outdoor Relief in 1931. Projects included grading work, sewer excavation, bridge construction, installation of curb and gutter, paving, and a great variety of other landscape and construction work in parks and parkways. Nearly $300,000 was appropriated from general funds or transferred from highway accounts in 1931 and 1932 for these purposes, resulting in a great number of permanent and necessary improvements for the park system. Emphasis was also placed on the development of recreational facilities to provide worthwhile outlets for the increased leisure time available to a substantial (and growing) unemployed population.

Again, it was a fortunate legacy of the park system's expansion of the 1920s that an experienced planning department was in place to supervise and coordinate this accelerated park development. Familiar with the needs of the parks, the engineers and architects of the Regional Planning Department responded with more than enough project plans to keep thousands of workers as fully occupied as funding would permit. With the introduction of Federally financed programs into the park system beginning in 1933, the Park Commission was able to submit proposals and plans in remarkably short times to take full advantage of these opportunities. Major construction programs, as well as smaller projects largely to provide work opportunities, were promoted wherever possible with spectacular results. By as early as 1936 park improvements had already been advanced ten to fifteen years ahead of original long-range projections.

All of the available and appropriate Federal relief programs contributed to this effort. The Civil Works Administration and the Federal Emergency Relief Administration made it possible to consolidate overhead utility lines into a central underground system in all major parks. After the Emergency Conservation Works legislation was enacted in March 1933, the first three Civilian Conservation Corps camps were established at Sheridan and Whitnall Parks and on Honey Creek parkway. Later other camps were constructed in Kletzsch and Estabrook Parks and near Blue Mound. Young men from relief households were paid $30 a month ($25 of which went directly to their families) for common labor work directed by park construction superintendents. Officers from the United States Army administered the camps themselves. Much of the CCC labor later was used in parkway development and in river improvement through the construction of dams along the Milwaukee and Menomonee Rivers to aid flood control.

The most productive of the Federal programs was the multifaceted and flexible Works Progress Administration. At least $17,000,000 was received from Washington for WPA projects in the County parks between 1935 and 1941. In addition to major construction and a variety of work programs, WPA funds were used to support recreational and cultural activities of all types. Today, one cannot go into any park area within the system that existed prior to 1930 without seeing evidence of the lasting contribution made by the combined forms of Federal support. A survey and inventory of these physical improvements would be a major, but very revealing, project.

Throughout most of the 1930s very little new park land for the County system was acquired by traditional methods. Most of the land that was added was for parkway development, yet by the close of the decade, acreage in the County system had been increased by nearly 1,500 acres, approximately 40 percent. This seemingly contradictory situation resulted from the transfer, in 1937, of the entire City of Milwaukee park system to the jurisdiction of the County.

As noted earlier, the Milwaukee Park Board, after the initial flurry of purchases of the seven major park sites in 1890-91 (Lake, Kosciuszko, Humboldt, Mitchell, Riverside, Sherman, and Washington Parks) ceased expansion for more than a decade and a half. Then, between 1907 and 1910, six additional tracts were purchased: Gordon, Lincoln, and Kern Parks along the Milwaukee River, Pulaski and Jackson Parks on the south side, and South Shore Park on the lakefront in Bay View. Some boulevard development also occurred, with Layton, Highland, and Sherman being added to Newberry Boulevard as developed roadways within the city. After 1910, expansion of the system remained quite modest, only some 160 acres being added, with most of this located in two large tracts, Wilson Park on the south side (sixty-five acres) and Doctor's Park, a fifty-acre site in the suburb of Fox Point. Doctor's Park was an extreme example of the operation of the 1891 legislation which gave the Park Board authority to locate parks in the City system beyond the City limits.

Two major contributions of the City's park system were the Washington Park Zoo, started initially in 1892 and greatly stimulated by the organization of the Zoological Society in 1910, and the reclamation and development of park acreage from submerged land along the Lake Michigan shoreline. Serious work on this latter project began in 1907 and culminated in the opening of Lincoln Memorial Drive in 1929. Reclamation work was also carried on along the City's south shore, where extensive filling and grading were done.

Throughout most of its history the City's park system was plagued by the lack of adequate financing. This, in part, accounts for its sporadic acquisition program. The substantial acquisitions in 1890-91 and again in 1907-10 were not followed up by sufficient funding for maintenance and operation. The addition of new recreational and amusement programs also failed to receive sustained additional revenue, and new land placed under the Park Board's control, such as the thirteen sites transferred by the Board of Public Works in 1911, carried with them no added support whatsoever. Changes produced by the home rule legislation for the City in 1927 also deprived the Park Board of some of its financial independence and further interfered with park improvement efforts.

The disastrous effect of the Great Depression upon City finances was the severest blow suffered by the Park Board, however. Relief programs provided little real benefit for City parks, being so modest that they barely supported pick-and-shovel and wheelbarrow maintenance work. Improvements to facilities or grounds were totally eliminated after 1933, as the parks, along with other City departments, had to operate under a referendum tax limitation ordinance. Flower beds went unplanted, every other lamp on park drives was turned off, heat and water use was curtailed, and personnel worked reduced hours to provide economy. Yet, as with the County parks, public usage soared. The users of City parks increased from 7,800,000 persons in 1930 to 9,800,000 in 1935, while available income from all sources nosedived over the same period from $2,400,000 to $942,000.

One solution offered to the City's dilemma that received wide support was to turn the municipal park system over to County government. For a number of years supporters of metropolitan government for the Milwaukee area had pointed to the parks as the one area of public services suitable for such transfer. The County's ability to generate funding for park development, while City government could spare little Federal relief aid for such purposes, now made the park transfer a more attractive proposition to many voters than did shifts in fire or police service or the transfer of the museum or library. Under these circumstances a referendum was put to the Milwaukee voters in April 1936 posing these basic questions:

- Should the City parks, along with park employees, be transferred to County government?
- Should the bonded indebtedness of the City parks be paid by the County?
- Should the Board which would administer the transferred parks have a majority of City residents and be appointed by the Mayor and Common Council?

The referendum resulted in a clear-cut directive for the City of Milwaukee to get out of the park business. By more than three-to-one ratio the vote was overwhelming in favor of transferring title of the City parks to the County. The other two propositions were rejected by closer but nevertheless decisive margins. The City would retain its obligation for park bonds and outstanding interest, and jurisdiction over the transferred parks was, in effect, to be given to the County Park Commission without further City involvement.

The transfer formally became effective on November 12, 1936. In all, 1,498 acres of park and parkways at thirty-seven locations were involved, ranging from ward triangles of less than an acre to the nearly 308-acre Lincoln Park. The Washington Park Zoo was included, as was the horticultural garden at Mitchell Park.

In December 1936, representatives of the City Park Board and the County Park Commission assembled at the Republican House Hotel to mark the transfer of the City system to County jurisdiction.

In addition to the sizeable administration problems facing the County Park Commission after a transaction of this size — adjustments in salary and financial practices, absorption of City employees into the County system, and so on — there was the major difficulty involving the neglected condition of many facilities in the former City parks. The few WPA projects being conducted under the City at the time of transfer were of a hand-labor nature, primarily grading and landscape work, due to the absence of fund for materials and equipment. The Park Commission quickly set up new programs for the City facilities totalling several millions of dollars for labor, equipment, and material (County government being obligated to fund a portion of the latter two categories). By the summer of 1937 proposals for work within the City began to flow from the Regional Planning Department with the same regularity as did those for WPA projects in the old County system. Before the Federal government halted approval of new proposals in 1940, nearly $7,000,000 was spent out of WPA funds in the former City parks. This work went a long way toward restoring these facilities to their former usefulness by the time the entrance of the United States in World War II called a halt to all types of park development anywhere in the County.

In addition to the thirty-seven City park sites turned over to the

County in 1936, several suburban municipalities then, or earlier, also transferred park lands to County ownership. These included: Sheridan and Pulaski Parks in Cudahy; Holler Park in the Town of Lake; Hoyt Park in Wauwatosa, and Rawson Park in South Milwaukee. Total Countywide consolidation required an increase in the Park Commission's budget for operation and maintenance to over $600,000 in 1937, an increase in the County tax rate of 56¢ per $1,000 of assessed valuation. Elimination of the park budget in the City dropped the general rate for Milwaukee residents 72¢ per $1,000 for a net saving of sixteen cents. Suburban residents, of course, paid more; and while some complained and threatened legal action, no suits were forthcoming.

The restructuring of a Countywide park system and the improvement of park facilities within the City materially aided the expansion of recreational programs aimed at softening the impact of widespread depression-induced unemployment. Between 1933 and 1936 annual attendance at all forms of County park activities increased by more than one hundred percent, with nine new major programs added or significantly expanded during these years, including community social centers, outdoor pageants and plays, and band concerts. The latter activity was built upon the long tradition of musical programming in public parks, first offered by the City Park Board in the 1890s. Private funding from local businesses and individuals provided the initial support for the first concerts. In 1912 an official Park Board band was organized, which at the peak of its success under the leadership of Joseph Clauder and Hugo Bach, presented seventy-five concerts a year at park sites throughout the city. These offerings had dropped dramatically to only thirteen performances in 1936. Then, with the infusion of WPA support made available through Milwaukee County, the performing arts once again became a major feature of park programming. Highlighting this renaissance was the completion in 1938 of the Blatz Temple of Music in Washington Park. This facility became the setting for the highly successful "Music Under the Stars" concert series, which grew in popularity each year until it attracted a season's record of 80,000 persons by 1945.

The Recreational Department was established in 1935 to provide more fully organized competition for team and individual sports within the park program. New construction projects, made possible by Federal aid, also resulted in badly needed shelter facilities for winter sports so that the number of ice skaters using park rinks grew from 13,000 in 1933 to 127,000 only four years later.

By 1939-40 the outbreak of war in Europe and the start of a preparedness program in the United States rejuvenated the American economy. Employment gradually returned in local industry, reducing the availability of relief manpower for community projects and certain Fed-

The Blatz Temple of Music in Washington Park has been the scene of "Music Under the Stars" programming and other performing arts activities since it was completed in 1938.

eral programs began to be phased out. The WPA authorities in Washington decreed that no new park projects in Milwaukee County would be approved after 1940, and funding made available only to complete those already in progress. Following the attack on Pearl Harbor, the restrictions became more severe. The Park Commission independently decided to halt any new work in the parks, and this decision was reinforced for the duration by Federal directives limiting non-essential activities. For the rest of the war and several years thereafter only necessary maintenance could be carried on.

At the same time, the war years witnessed an expanded use of County parks and an enlarged concept of their place in community life. Gas rationing, tire shortages, and limitations on travel ended long vacation trips and forced Milwaukeeans to seek their outdoor recreation closer to home. The introduction of daylight savings time and round-the-clock work shifts in the community's heavy industry accentuated the need for new methods and schedules of leisure time activities. The concept of parks existing only for summertime and picnic use, which had begun to change during the depression, was now even more substantially altered. There was a growing emphasis on providing recreation and entertainment in the smaller neighborhood parks as well as in the larger outlying facilities. In 1943 eleven million people attended or participated in park activities. The substantial progress made in developing the system during the depression years proved its importance.

During the early years of the war, park personnel received training in

Civilian Defense responsibilities and other useful homefront duties. Their numbers were gradually reduced, however, and labor shortages developed through enlistments in the armed forces, the draft, and departures for better paying jobs in war industries. More than ninety acres of parkland were made available to Milwaukeeans for use as "Victory Gardens." And the varied programs of entertainment and recreation were encouraged and supported by the USO and similar agencies for the benefit of servicemen training at Great Lakes and other nearby installations.

The swimming pool at Kosciuszko Park was one of many park improvements made possible by the WPA program. It was used by neighborhood youngsters even before construction was completed.

Postwar Development Program

With the conclusion of World War II in 1945 Milwaukee County government and, through it, the park system faced major problems. Some reflected immediate community needs, while others were of a more long-range nature. Out of the latter grew the County's postwar public improvement program, which included plans for substantial park expansion, the construction of a war memorial and a sports stadium, and the development of the lakefront. But the most immediate need was for the solution to the critical shortage of housing for ex-servicemen and their families. The

City and County of Milwaukee mutually agreed on a joint approach to this problem, the City undertaking a permanent public housing program, while the County assumed responsibility for temporary measures to alleviate the emergency situation. In December 1946 management of the latter effort, which became known as the Veterans Housing Program, was given to the Park Commission, as the agency then best equipped to handle land acquisition and site development.

To meet the immediate housing need, two types of basic structures were utilized initially: modest-sized mobile or house trailers and fixed prefabricated structures known as Goodyear "Wing Foot Homes." Later, another type of prefab, manufactured by the Harnischfeger Corporation, was used in large numbers in a site at Wilson Park. During the life of the Veterans Housing Program, which extended into the mid-1950s, some 900 trailer homes and nearly 765 prefabricated houses provided living accommodations for 5,000 families. Many of the initial locations used for trailer parks were on park lands. In all, eleven long-term housing sites were developed, five for trailer use and the balance for prefabricated structures.

Reminiscent of its important role in early airport development, the Park Commission served as administrative agency for the Veterans Housing program. The skills of the Regional Planning Department provided valuable technical services, preparing site plans and supervising the installation of necessary utility systems, roads, and public bathing facilities.

As important as this temporary housing program was to the needs of postwar Milwaukee County it did not go unopposed. Some Milwaukeeans strongly objected to government's involvement in what they regarded as the responsibility of the private sector or to the fact that this and other projects were financed by bond issues rather than the usual Milwaukee pay-as-you-go method. One young candidate for the County Board, a veteran of wartime service, narrowly avoided defeat in the 1948 primary election because of his support of the Veterans Housing Program. Today (1987) he holds the office of County Executive.

By 1954 the housing situation had returned to more normal conditions, and the Park Commission recommended that use of the trailer and "Wing Foot" units be discontinued. The County Board approved and this phase of the program was terminated on July 1, 1955. The prefabricated houses at the Wilson Park site continued in use for several years longer.

Another phase of the County's postwar public works program which became the responsibility of the Park Commission to implement was the construction of a community sports stadium. This was regarded as a long-standing need for Milwaukee. In the 1920s consideration was given to such a project as a memorial to World War I servicemen, but nothing resulted from that proposal. During the depression years of the 1930s, when some American cities were channeling Federal relief funds into municipal stadiums, governmental agencies in Milwaukee County chose to focus their construction efforts on other areas. After World War II, however, strong support developed locally for such a project.

Professional baseball was to be the principal beneficiary of the proposed facility. In 1943, '44, and '45 the local Brewers, under the dynamic ownership of Bill Veeck, had won American Association championships while performing at Borchert Field, their ancient and rickety ballpark on the north side. The Green Bay Packers were then playing some of their "home" games in the National Football League in Milwaukee, at Marquette Stadium and State Fair Park, but for this sport, too, a larger modern stadium would be of benefit to the team and its fans. And lurking behind these immediate needs was a growing interest in securing a major league baseball franchise for the city, an impossibility without a new facility.

In January 1946 the County Board of Supervisors referred a resolution on the construction of a municipal stadium to its highway committee, which in turn assigned the matter to the Park Commission for study and recommendations on site, design, and probable costs. This action was a continuation of the tradition, begun with the first County airport and utilized again in the housing program, of calling upon the Commission to serve County government in areas not directly related to the park system.

After eight months of study the Park Commission reported back, recommending that the County erect a new multiple-sport stadium, with a minimum seating capacity of 25,000 (expandable to 60,000), at the so-called Story Quarry site near Bluemound Road and North 44th Street. Costs for the project were then estimated at 1.5 million dollars.

Not everyone in County government or the community was in agreement with the Park Commission's recommended location, however. A number of alternative sites were also proposed, and the County Board finally retained the services of a Cleveland engineering firm to study the various alternatives from the standpoint of location, cost, public transportation and access, and parking. The Osborn Report, dated June 1947, evaluated seven of the best alternatives but did not include one proposal to crowd the stadium into Washington Park. Given the serious concerns being expressed in the mid-1980s about suitability of the site eventually selected, these alternatives merit notice here. In addition to the Park Commission's choice, the Story Quarry location, the others were: the Haymarket site, Fourth and McKinley Streets (north of the expressway from the location of the new Bradley Sports Center); the Vliet Street site, south of Vliet between 47th and 54th Streets (present Milwaukee Public School headquarters); the Lincoln Avenue site, Lincoln and 35th Street;

the Wellauer site, north of Wisconsin Avenue, between 72nd and 76th Streets (the old Bluemound Country Club); State Fair Park, north of the fairgrounds and west of 76th Street; and the Keefe Avenue site, between Keefe and Capitol Drive, west of 60th Street (present Dineen Park).

The Osborn Report favored the Keefe Avenue location as its first choice, stressing that topography and ground conditions would allow for efficient and economical construction of a stadium with abundant parking. The engineers played down its remote and decentralized location and lack of direct transportation access. The second choice of the Osborn report was the Story Quarry site, largely because of its proximity to the center of population.

Totally ignored by the Osborn Report were political considerations from which perspective the Story Quarry site had strong support. This location was the Park Commission's choice. Officials of the City of Milwaukee were on record as favoring its selection and had indicated a willingness to transfer needed land to the County and to carry out essential street improvements for vehicle access.

Debate on the question continued for almost two years. The State Fair location disappeared from serious consideration after representatives of the Fair Board placed impossible conditions on its use for stadium purposes. Commitment to the project was assured, irrespective of the site selected, when the sports facility was included in the County's master plan for public works adopted in 1947, at an estimated cost of 1.6 million dollars. Public enthusiasm was stimulated by the success on the baseball field of the local American Association Brewers, winners of the league postseason playoffs in 1947 and also the Little World Series the same season. They finished in the first division and reached playoffs during the next two years as well, although with less notable success. Their picturesque but archaic ballpark, Borchert Field, lacked sufficient seating and other fan amenities necessary for potential major league status. In view of subsequent developments in the mid-1960s, however, one observation made during the debate over the stadium location and the dream of a big league franchise for Milwaukee deserves notice. In 1947 Supervisor George Hermann raised a warning against the dangers of non-Milwaukee ownership and questioned whether professional baseball was not a business operating in violation of Federal antitrust laws. Shades of the Braves' departure for Atlanta in 1965 and the County's subsequent legal action which followed!

The question of the stadium location was finally settled in January 1949, following some astute political maneuvering by Supervisor Willard "Mike" Lyons. The Story Quarry site, situated in Lyons' supervisory district, became the choice selected by the County. Lining up the necessary votes for Story Quarry in advance of a meeting of the County Board, Lyons deliberately avoided becoming involved in floor debate on the issue. Instead, he allowed supporters of the Haymarket and Keefe Avenue sites to introduce their choices first. Neither was able to attract the necessary affirmative vote. Lyons then obtained a favorable decision for Story Quarry as both a desirable site and also the only one having enough backing for approval by the County Board.

Again, the Park Commission was selected as the agency to carry on the complicated land acquisition program for the stadium and then to supervise its construction. Cooperation with other levels of government was essential in securing the required acreage. An act of Congress and the signature of the President was necessary to transfer a large parcel from the adjacent Veterans Administration grounds. The City of Milwaukee turned over other key parts of the real estate package. The City, then responsible for planning a Milwaukee freeway system, also designated the stadium area as the first segment of the new road network to be constructed so as to provide better access to the ballpark.

Chairman of the Park Commission's stadium committee was William R. McGovern, the president of the Wisconsin Telephone Company and a veteran of more than three decades of service on the Commission. He and his associates moved effectively to complete the involved arrangements under which the County acquired the necessary land. McGovern's business connections and links to high Federal officials proved to be of vital importance. Excavation work began in mid-October 1950, but almost at once the needs of the Korean War threatened to curtail construction. An executive order from Washington banned continuation of projects such as the stadium unless they had been started prior to a specified date. The stadium project met this requirement, but it also helped when one of McGovern's former business associates assisted the County in obtaining a favorable ruling from Washington. Other acquaintances were instrumental in accelerating the delivery of essential construction steel ahead of schedule.

Although the stadium had been promoted with the hope of someday attracting major league baseball to Milwaukee, most Milwaukeeans expected that its tenants for the opening of the 1953 season would be the American Association Brewers, a farm club of the Boston Braves. However, in March 1953 the parent Braves shattered a half-century of fixed major league geography when they obtained National League approval to shift the Boston franchise to Milwaukee. Thus began the glorious "Braves era" at County Stadium, which ended so tragically in 1965 when new (nonresident) ownership again moved the franchise to Atlanta, Georgia.

To accommodate a major league team, the County was required to spend nearly two million dollars to upgrade the stadium almost before its doors were opened. Seating was enlarged within a few years from the

County Stadium as it appeared shortly after opening day, 1953. Note the abbreviated grand-stand, limited bleacher seating around the outfield, and the absence of the surrounding freeway system.

original 26,000 permanent and 10,000 bleacher seats to a capacity of over 44,000 by 1964. Additional expansion in the 1970s, following the arrival of an American League franchise in the form of the new Brewers, has increased the seating to over 56,000.

The excellent facilities at County Stadium and a cooperative attitude of County government materially assisted the return of major league baseball to Milwaukee in 1970, under local ownership and as a result of the diligent efforts of Alan H. Selig and his associates. Now, a decade and a half later the playing facility is again a key factor in the continued success of professional baseball in this community, but from a somewhat different perspective. Questions are being raised about whether the stadium is still adequate to meet the needs of a modern major league franchise. Should it be remodeled and covered with a dome? — or replaced by a new facility? — or sold to the Brewers, with the County withdrawing from stadium operations entirely? Financial difficulties facing both County government and the Brewers in the 1980s have required serious study of these and other considerations. Only time will tell what results will be forthcoming.

Among the major Park Commission projects contained in the County's postwar development program was the establishment of a new zoo. The Washington Park Zoo, or "Zoological Park" as it was officially known, was among the oldest facilities in the system, with some of its buildings dating back to the early years of the twentieth century and, therefore, badly in need of replacement. The location in Washington Park was too small for expansion or for substantial remodeling along the lines of modern zoo design which emphasized the use of natural habitat settings. Strong endorsement and support for a replacement site also came from the Greater Milwaukee Committee as part of its program for civic advancement.

The history of zoo development as part of the local park tradition began shortly after the formation of the City park system. Louis Auer, a member of the first Park Board, and others donated a small deer herd, an eagle, and several bears in 1892-93 to be housed in a barn in Washington (then West) Park. By 1904 the collection had grown to seventy-five birds and animals, special buildings and enclosures were constructed to house them, and the first zoo director, Edward H. Bean, hired to oversee future growth. Prior to 1907, most of the animals and birds on exhibition were native to North America. In that year a monkey cage and sea lion pond were constructed, and the zoo's first major acquisition, an elephant named Countess Heinie, was added. The Countess and a second elephant, Venice, remained popular attractions for more than forty years.

A development of long range significance took place in September 1910, when Washington Park Zoological Society was incorporated for the purpose of increasing public interest and support for the zoo. In 1943 the organization's name was changed to the Zoological Society of Milwaukee

The bear dens at the Washington Park Zoo attracted large crowds of visitors on Sundays and holidays.

County. For more than three-quarters of a century the Society has continued and expanded the early practice of raising private funds for the purchase of animals and other specimens. This policy materially aided the growth of the facility. As a consequence, by 1937 the zoo was literally bursting at the seams.

Relocation was not possible during the depression or until after World War II; but beginning in 1947, the County began acquisition of land for a new zoo in the area south of Bluemound Road and east of Highway 100 in Wauwatosa. The basic purchases of more than 175 acres were completed by 1964. The new site (almost eight times larger than its predecessor) contained both gently rolling and level areas and also sections that were heavily wooded. The design of its facilities emphasized the exhibition of animals and other specimens in their natural settings according to, where possible, continental groupings. Glass partitions on the inside and hidden moats in open areas virtually eliminated the use of bars. Construction of the first building, the monkey house, began in 1958, and other structures were added at regular intervals so that the Washington Park facility was vacated in 1963. Samson, the gorilla who had joined the zoo family in 1950, became a special favorite of visitors to the new location.

During the past twenty-five years, through the combined support of County government and the Zoological Society, the zoo continued its physical development and expansion of educational and scientific services, while remaining one of the most popular attractions in Milwaukee County. Even the introduction of admission charges in 1970, a sharp break with the longstanding tradition of free access, had only a temporary impact upon zoo attendance. An even more radical departure from the past practices occurred in 1980, when administration of the zoo was separated from the park system and turned over to a special board of the Zoological Society. This step reflected the County government's desire to modernize the zoo operation and lessen the burden upon the property tax dollar for cultural activities. It also expressed confidence in the Zoological Society's ability to meet this financial challenge. Creation of an imaginative and aggressive marketing program, combined with the traditional support generated by the Society through gifts and grants, suggests that this confidence was not misplaced.

Still another aspect of Milwaukee County's postwar development program that reflected the steady growth of County involvement in the cultural and recreational life of the community was the construction of a War Memorial facility. While not directly related to park operation or development, the War Memorial was to become an important expression of government support for the performing arts in Milwaukee, an area in which the park system had played a pioneering role.

In the closing years of the Second World War community interest was expressed for the construction of a suitable memorial to the men and women from Milwaukee County who served in the armed forces. The sentiment behind this movement was manifested in the slogan "Which will it be, another flagpole or a living memorial?" By June 1946 supporters from the private sector reached agreement with the County for the cooperative development of a facility that would include a community art gallery, a music hall-theater, and a veterans' center. The 1947 County improvement program committed 1.5 million dollars for land development, while construction costs would be met by a public fund campaign. The project ran into difficulties, however. Only 2.7 million of the original 5 million-dollar funding goal was realized. A bitter debate also broke out over the site for the memorial. There was strong interest in a lakefront location adjacent to Juneau Park, while as late as September 1951 a vocal and politically influential element was campaigning for a more centrally situated site in Washington Park. The County ultimately selected the lakefront property. Utilizing the funds that were on hand, construction was begun in 1955 on a modification of the original concept designed by the distinguished architect Eero Saarinen. The structure was completed two years later. It provided facilities for the Milwaukee Art Center (later renamed the Milwaukee Art Museum), offices for veterans and community groups, and a public meeting hall. The theater-music hall portion was discarded because of the funding shortage.

Theater and musical organizations and their patrons continued to campaign for a new public facility to accommodate their needs. Again a spirited dispute arose over the location. By 1958 there was growing public support for the argument that the proposed music hall did not belong on the lakefront. A downtown location seemed preferable, and finally in late 1960 a location on the east bank of the Milwaukee River near City Hall was agreed upon.

Raising funds for the performing arts center proved to be more successful than the earlier effort, and ultimately 8.8 million dollars in private contributions were secured. Ground was broken in June 1966. At a critical juncture Milwaukee County government contributed an additional two million dollars to meet unexpected construction costs and made completion of the project possible. Dedicated in August 1969 as a memorial to veterans of all wars, the Milwaukee County War Memorial Performing Arts Center, as it was officially known, opened on September 17, 1969.

By the 1980s the Milwaukee County War Memorial had expanded to include four facilities. In addition to the original Saarinen building on the lakefront and Performing Arts Center, the Memorial's Board of Trustees is also responsible for Villa Terrace, a museum of decorative arts administered by the Milwaukee Art Museum, and the Charles Allis Art Museum, transferred by the City of Milwaukee to County jurisdiction in the 1970s. This blending of public and private sector has provided entertainment and cultural benefits for the Milwaukee community through what truly is the "living memorial" envisioned by its early proponents.

Personnel, Policies, and Programs, 1950-1980

In the early 1950s the Park Commission, as beneficiaries of nearly thirteen million dollars of program support authorized by the County's ten-year public improvement package, faced a serious need to restructure its administrative organization. No substantial changes had occurred in the operation of the Commission for many years, while the park system had grown immensely in acreage, activities, employees, and budget. Commission members found it almost impossible to cover the agenda at meetings, there was no time to consider important policy matters, and key administrative staff were overburdened with responsibilities. In 1949 nearly 2,000 individual items of business were handled at thirty-three Commission meetings.

The loss of key personnel also prompted the need for reorganization. In December 1950 George Hansen, parks superintendent for nearly twenty-five years, passed away. Eugene A. Howard, long-time head of the Regional Planning Department, was promoted to County Director of Public Works in 1949 and was no longer available to work closely with the Commission.

A major step toward solving much of the administrative problem was taken by the Commission in 1952 with the creation of a new position of general manager for the park system. Jerome Dretzka, from the perspective of more than three decades of watching the system grow, had recommended such a step two years earlier. He urged that this new office be made responsible for all administrative duties, including many that he had been performing for years in his dual role as executive secretary and Commission member. The first person selected to fill the new general manager's post was Alfred L. Boerner, long-time landscape architect on the Commission staff, who held the position for only a short three-year period before his death in June 1955. Boerner's replacement, appointed early in 1956, was Howard Gregg, another veteran member of the staff who had started as a landscape architect in the Regional Planning Department in 1941. Gregg was to serve as general manager for seventeen years, retiring in 1972. During this time he presided over a remarkable period of growth, physically nearly 5,000 acres were added to the system, new facilities such as the zoo were opened, and programs and services greatly increased.

Boerner Botanical Gardens in Whitnall Park provide a setting for the beauty and diversity of colorful flowers, trees, shrubs and ground cover, for the enjoyment and education of visitors.

On the Commission itself a nucleus of veteran members continued to provide leadership and perspective throughout the 1950s. Commissioners McGovern, Dretzka, and Walter Bender remained active well into the next decade, the first two ultimately serving a total of forty-five and forty-three years respectively, while Bender held the office of president for well over a decade. Two newer members, Richard S. Falk, appointed in 1947, and Paul Pike Pullen, in 1953, continued this tradition of longevity as each remained on the Commission for twenty-five years or more. Pullen's appointment also represented the start of another practice that was eventually regularized by ordinance. He was a member of the County Board of Supervisors at the time he was selected to fill a vacancy on the Commission. Pullen left the County Board in 1955. Subsequently, Supervisors Herbert G. Froemming, Calvin Moody, Clinton Rose, and Daniel Cupertino provided a continuous succession of County Board representation on the Park Commission until the body ceased to exist in 1981. Froemming was originally appointed to the Commission prior to his election to the County Board, however.

The substantial physical growth of the park system after 1950 (it more than doubled its acreage in the next two decades) was accompanied by a corresponding increase in financial support from County government. The nearly five million dollars budgeted for park purposes in 1955 grew to almost thirty-four million by 1978. While revenue sources expanded during this same period, the bulk of the park funding came from the property tax levy. Between 1963 and 1975 the Commission biennial reports disclosed that the levy for management and operations alone increased from 6.3 million dollars to over eighteen million. Funds were appropriated for land acquisition with reasonable regularity during the 1950s and '60s and then tapered off during the decade which followed. As both a substitute and a supplement, State and Federal moneys were also used extensively, particularly in acquiring smaller park sites through HUD "open spaces" and the LAWCON (Land and Water Conservation Act) programs.

This generous level of support enabled the Commission to plan and implement a remarkably diverse series of programs and projects, some expanding existing activities and others pioneering into new areas. The creation of the Mitchell Park "Domes" is one example of this. Like the new zoo facilities, the Horticultural Conservatory erected in the 1960s was dramatically modern in both design and display concepts. Mitchell Park was historically the site of the Conservatory in the old City park system, the first such facility having been erected there in 1898, with substantial reconstruction occurring between 1922 and 1932. Appropriately, the most traditional of the Conservatory's annual presentations, the Christmas show, opened the first of the new dome-shaped facilities in December 1964. The Tropical Dome, highlighted by its twenty-five-foot waterfall, was completed by January 1966, and the Arid Dome was opened to the public a year or so later. One of the most popular facilities in the entire park system, the Conservatory enables visitors to see plants and displays from

In Mitchell Park the horticultural tradition of Milwaukee parks is represented by the older sunken gardens in the foreground and the three modern "Domes" constructed in the 1960s.

all parts of the world and reflects a commitment to provide both enjoyment and education for viewers.

Environmental education was also the focus for the development of the Todd Wehr Nature Center dedicated in June 1974 at Whitnall Park. The center was constructed with funds from the Federal government and the Wehr Foundation and, along with the Boerner Botanical Gardens, gave to Whitnall Park an appropriate emphasis on the study of the natural environment which so interested Charles B. Whitnall.

A less structured form of park education but one which proved very popular with many County residents was begun in 1962 by County Executive John L. Doyne. Responding to a call by President John F. Kennedy for increased physical fitness in America, Doyne began a series of "Treks with the County Exec," which he continued until his retirement from office in 1976. These hikes helped introduce the park system and many of its feature attractions to both participants and those who followed the events through the media.

In the areas of sports and recreation the park system met growing demands for specialized facilities through the development of McKinley Marina on the Lake Michigan shoreline and the Wilson Park recreational complex near the old Veterans Housing site. The marina project involved the reclamation of more than seventy acres through a massive land fill operation and the creation of more than 650 anchoring slips for sailing enthusiasts. Begun in 1959 and its last phase completed in 1979, the marina continued the practice in the County system of linking a natural feature of the local landscape with a growing recreational interest of many Milwaukeeans.

The Wilson Park Recreational Center, begun in the late 1960s, featured an outdoor Olympic-sized swimming pool and an indoor ice skating rink suitable for hockey games, plus traditional recreational facilities. In May 1975 a softball stadium, the first in the park system, was dedicated here.

At many locations throughout the system more modest, but still significant, innovations were being made in response to contemporary recreational needs. In the mid-1960s snowmobiling became popular in the larger parks for owners of private vehicles, and at Brown Deer Park vehicles and trailer sleds were rented under park license. An Alpine ski meet was held in 1966, and tour skiing was first introduced at Whitnall Park the following year. Dretzka Park became the site for a winter sports pavilion when artificial snowmaking equipment and ski tows were installed in January 1969. Snowmaking equipment became available at Currie Park in the mid-1970s, although a ski tow had been in use there as early as 1949. Golf remained ever popular, and the high quality of the park

In 1975, Wilson Park's softball stadium became an important addition to the park system's recreation program. It provided seating for up to 3,600 spectators.

courses was recognized by the selection of the Brown Deer Course as the site of the National Public Links Tournament in 1977. Tennis facilities also became more sophisticated, lighted courts being first introduced in the late 1950s. Many of the system's more than 130 tennis courts are suitable for night play today, a far cry from the early sites in Grant Park sixty years ago where the players had to supply their own nets. The growing interest in physical fitness was also met, in part, through creation of a Countywide network of bicycle trails. The initial section was constructed in Lake Park in 1967, with later expansion along the lakefront, the Milwaukee River, and on the route of an abandoned railroad right-of-way. Symbolically, the park system's seventy-six-mile bicycle trail was completed for the Bicentennial observance in 1976.

In addition to responding to changing and expanding interests of its constituency, the park programs of this period also sought to serve special needs within the community. At Holler Park the summer day camp for the handicapped had been in operation since the depression era of the 1930s. A new bathhouse was erected in 1969 for rehabilitation service provided by the Easter Seal Society, while recreational programming was expanded to year-round offerings. Camp Wil-O-Way, established in Grant Park to serve individuals with emotional and developmental disabilities, proved so successful that a second such facility was created in the late 1970s in

Underwood Parkway. Additional concern for the handicapped prompted the employment of a full-time program director in 1976 and the design in 1978 of a special nature trail for handicapped use in Jacobus Park with substantial support of a private foundation.

Facilities for senior citizen groups and more sophisticated buildings offering a wide range of recreational programs for all ages became an important part of the park system in the 1960s and '70s. In 1961 the parks had only three small senior centers, serving 300 people. Eight years later the number of neighborhood centers had increased sixfold and the users totalled over 55,000. At Washington Park in 1968 the first of a half dozen new, modern structures was dedicated for various leisure-time needs.

Recreational facilities and senior centers, such as this one in Washington Park, represent the park system's efforts to meet the changing program needs of County residents.

Called by various names — Community Centers or Senior/Recreational Centers — these buildings and the activities they offer reflect the growing realization that park programming had taken on new meaning in this era. There was nothing new about their location, however. Reminiscent of the considerations governing the selection of the first City park sites in the 1890s, the new centers reflect the same traditional geographical concerns prevalent nearly a century ago. The Martin Luther King Center, Clinton Rose Senior Center, and McGovern Park Recreation/Senior Center on the north side of the County are balanced by the Kosciuszko Park Community Center, the Wilson Park Senior Center, and the Warnimont Park Recreational/Senior Center on the south side. Only the Washington Park Recreation/Senior Center avoided this pattern, serving the west-central section of Milwaukee County.

The Martin Luther King Center reflects still another important trend in park development during the 1960s and '70s, namely, an effort to increase a park presence in the central city and downtown area of Milwaukee. Land for Martin Luther King Park was acquired by the Park Commission in 1971 from the City of Milwaukee Redevelopment Authority, and Federal funding was instrumental in development of the site and construction of the community center building. Public participation played a significant role in the planning process. The facility was opened in June 1976.

Another central city park created at the same time was Pere Marquette Park, adjacent to the Milwaukee County Historical Center and across the Milwaukee River from the Performing Arts Center. The Historical Center, formerly a bank building, was donated to Milwaukee County in 1965 for use as the museum and research library for the Historical Society. Since the mid-1930s, the Society had quarters in the courthouse. Its links to the Park Commission go back to the same era. In 1937 Supervisor Frederic Heath, the President of the Society, was instrumental in moving the historic Benjamin Church or Kilbourntown House, built in 1846, to Estabrook Park as part of the early development of that area. The park system, Historical Society, and the Colonial Dames of Wisconsin have jointly operated Kilbourntown House since that time.

This involvement by County government in the operation of historic sites and museums, either through the Park Commission or in direct support of community organizations, was enlarged with the use of part of the War Memorial by the Milwaukee Art Museum after 1959 and still further expanded by the County's acquisition of the Milwaukee Public Museum in 1976. The oldest of the community's major museum facilities (first opened in 1894), and also its largest, the Public Museum had been under jurisdiction of the City of Milwaukee prior to its transfer to the County for a purchase price of nearly eleven million dollars. Occupying a facility constructed specifically to house its exhibit and scientific programs and opened to the public in 1964, it is recognized as one of the finest natural history museums in the world and as a cultural and educational asset to the community. Its acquisition and operation by the County is but another reflection of traditional government concern for enriching the quality of life in Milwaukee County.

The cultural aspects of park activities during the postwar decades continued along normal lines. "Music Under the Stars" remained a major feature of this program, offering performances by some of the nation's leading musical talent. The 1957 season, for example, included appearances by Rise Stevens, Richard Tucker, Jerome Hines, and Oscar Levant. By the mid-1960s paid admissions to the concerts dropped off dramatically, only 12,000 attending the series in 1966 and 19,000 in 1967. Yet when two *free* concerts were held during the 4th of July observance in

1966, more than 30,000 Milwaukeeans turned out on two successive evenings to hear Duke Ellington and his orchestra and Leonard Bernstein with the New York Philharmonic. The solution to attendance problems of the annual concert series seemed obvious: offer free admission, with financial support coming from private sponsorship. This was first tried in 1968 with remarkable success. Underwritten by The Journal Company, an extended series of fifteen concerts that year drew audiences totaling 200,000 people. Elsewhere, the Starlight Dome at Humboldt Park was used for drama presented by the Marquette Players, ethnic dancers, band concerts, and similar presentations. The development of a portable stage, or showmobile, brought a variety of offerings to many parks which lacked permanent facilities. When the Humboldt Park Bandshell was destroyed by fire in 1975, it was replaced two years later by an A-frame chalet structure.

The Demise of the Park Commission

On January 1, 1982, after nearly three-quarters of a century of participation in the development of the Milwaukee County park system, the Park Commission as an administrative and policy-making body ceased to exist. Mechanically, its demise was accomplished by provisions of the 1982 Milwaukee County budget, proposed by County Executive William F. O'Donnell and approved by the County Board of Supervisors. This historic step was carried out with no great outpouring of political or media opposition and surprisingly little public protest. It came about because of fundamental changes which had been taking place within County government for more than two decades.

Two developments in particular seem to stand out. The first was the creation of the office of County Executive in 1959 and the shaping of that position into one of leadership rather than merely administering decisions made by others, including boards and commissions which had long held sway in County government. Fundamentally, the traditional role of an appointed body such as the Park Commission was incompatible with the concept of a County Executive responsible for management, policy recommendations, and coordinated administration. In 1962, shortly after he took office as the first County Executive, John L. Doyne proposed a major reorganization of the County administrative structure under which the major boards and commissions "would be abolished in favor of more active County Board participation." Support for such a radical change was not then available, and it was under Doyne's successor, William F. O'Donnell, that effective steps were finally taken to achieve this objective.

The second major factor which contributed significantly to the demise of the Park Commission was a change in the composition and philosophy of the County Board. Increasingly from the late 1960s on, Supervisors elected to office were younger, more "activist" oriented, and they viewed the position as a full-time occupation, or nearly so. Expanding their role in the areas of budget-making and personnel, these County Board members also stressed that elected officials directly responsible to the voters should have the major voice in policy-making. As services provided by County government expanded during this time, staff support for the Board was significantly strengthened, giving members and committees the technical resources necessary to meet increased responsibility.

It should be emphasized that the Park Commission was not a particular target for elimination under these changing circumstances. The issue was more basic and affected other appointive bodies as well. In 1980 the Expressway and Transportation Commission was phased out after twenty-seven years of existence. Two years later the Board of Public Welfare, a County body whose roots went deeper into history than even the Park Commission, ceased to function for the same reason.

A key step in effecting this reorganization was the passage of State legislation in 1978 authorizing Milwaukee County to adopt a cabinet form of government. The County Executive now had the power to appoint the heads of major departments, including parks, subject to confirmation by the County Board. This step represented a clear loss of authority by the Park Commission by sharpening the lines of responsibility within the newly designated Department of Parks, Recreation, and Culture. The park director could not effectively serve two bosses, the County Executive and the Park Commission, and the latter lost out. The removal of the zoo from Park Commission jurisdiction in 1980 was a further weakening of its traditional authority, although other important considerations also influenced that step.

Budget difficulties faced by the County in the early 1980s, particularly in operating departments such as the parks where there was heavy dependence upon property tax funding, also came into play. In the search for new sources of revenue from both within and outside of park operations, greater management flexibility was considered necessary. Elected County officials desired greater involvement in shaping these new policies. This could be best accomplished, they felt, by eliminating the role played by the Park Commission.

Legislative approval necessary for this step was achieved only after some close votes on the floor of the County Board. On November 11, 1981 the Board adopted by a margin of thirteen to eleven the section of the County Executive's budget abolishing the Park Commission. During another session the following day, an effort to rescind the action and reestablish the Commission could not muster sufficient support for immediate consideration, and the proposal was sent to committee. At the December meeting of the Board the measure went through repeated procedural maneuvers, but the final vote sealing the fate of the Commission was twelve to eleven against restoring its role, with two Supervisors excused and not voting. (The two were paired on the question in earlier votes.) Despite this narrow margin the decision produced little public outcry. The average County residents had little or no direct contact with Park Commission members and apparently felt their elected representatives were as fully capable of guiding the affairs of the park system as the Commission had been. The Commissioners met officially for the last time on December 15, 1981, and shortly thereafter the park system, which their predecessors had been so instrumental in establishing, began the observance of its seventy-fifth anniversary.

Observations on the Present and Future

In the brief period since the Commission was relieved of its responsibilities, several important changes have been made in the administrative structure of the park system. Top staff positions have been reorganized in an effort to produce greater efficiency and innovation and also in response to continuing budgetary pressures. A major break with the longstanding tradition followed the retirement of Robert J. Mikula as department director in 1985. Mikula, landscape architect for the park system since 1956, had been named general manager in 1973 upon the retirement of Howard Gregg. Under the cabinet restructuring in 1978 Mikula was appointed to the new position of director of Parks, Recreation and Culture. Outgoing and personable, Mikula served effectively during some of the most difficult years the park system has experienced. He was instrumental in facilitating the organization of a "friends" group, the Park People of Milwaukee County, in 1977 to support and enhance the parks and their programs. This step assumed an added significance after the Commission was terminated. The Park People provide a continuation of active, although modified, citizen involvement in park affairs, in addition to raising private funding for special projects and activities. Selected as Mikula's successor was David F. Schulz, formerly head of the County Department of Administration and the first manager of park affairs to be appointed without a parks background since attorney Charles E. Estabrook handled administrative duties for the Commission prior to World War I.

The choice of Schulz to head the park system was a statement by County officials that new management skills were needed to guide the department through the remainder of the twentieth century. A talented and imaginative professional adminstrator, Schulz reflects the need for balance between professional education and training, management experience, and political "smarts" in dealing with such diverse constituencies as elected officials, public employee unions, and the general citizenry. This break with the long tradition of selecting leadership from among park professionals was accentuated by the choice of a new park director from outside the park system entirely. Promotion from within was a long-standing practice, officially enunciated as early as 1940 by Jerome Dretzka at one of the first sessions of the Park Workers' Short Course. At that time only the ever-prophetic Charles B. Whitnall questioned promotion from within as a fixed policy, observing that it could starve ingenuity and fresh ideas that might be brought to the park system by an outsider.

Among the problems facing the park system in the mid-1980s, that of continued adequate funding seems to be paramount. Tax support has approached near maximum levels. With comparatively little direct State or Federal aid, the parks consumed twenty-eight percent of the County tax levy in 1985. Approximately one-third of budget expenditures is met by user fees and related income, an area that is sure to be targeted for greater attention in the near future. Consideration has been given to increased leasing of park facilities to private operators, including golf courses and concession operations; but as some knowledgeable observers pointed out, this involves the potential for decreased accountability.

Elected officials have stated that unless the County is "mandated to death" by State and Federal programs also dependent upon the tax levy, the parks and other cultural activities will continue to receive County support. For more than seventy-five years County government has been strongly committed to a superior park system, and this tradition will, in all likelihood, be continued. Emphasis may be shifted somewhat, but green space and wooded areas will not be neglected out of a preference for recreational innovations such as the pool slide at Hoyt Park or the massed basketball courts at Meaux Park. Major growth of land holdings, now nearly 15,000 acres, is not envisioned, but neither is the disposal of park acreage, except for parcels surplus to present or future needs.

The historical record over the past 150 years highlights the numerous contributions that made the Milwaukee County park system an important asset, both in terms of the value of land and improvements and also its capacity to enrich the lives of those who use it. Its present character and composition reflect influences such as the foresight of early pioneers, the ethnic traditions of the community, the commitment by government of large sums to finance its growth, the vision and practical skills of citizen leadership, and the professional abilities of staff employees. With this substantial foundation, the park system should be capable of serving, in traditional and new ways, many generations of future Milwaukeeans.

Bibliography

Books

Bruce, William G. *History of Milwaukee City and County.* 3 vols. Chicago: S. J. Clarke Publishing Company, 1922.

Buck, James S. *Milwaukee Under the Charter.* 2 vols. Milwaukee: privately printed, 1884, 1886.

Buck, James S. *Pioneer History of Milwaukee.* 2 vols. Milwaukee: privately printed, 1881, 1890.

Gregory, John G. *History of Milwaukee Wisconsin.* 4 vols. Chicago: S. J. Clarke Publishing Company, 1931.

Illustrated Historical Atlas of Milwaukee County, Wisconsin. Chicago: H. Belden and Co., 1876.

Lurie, Nancy Oestreich. *A Special Style. The Milwaukee Public Museum 1882-1982.* Milwaukee: Milwaukee Public Museum, 1983.

Still, Bayrd. *Milwaukee: The History of a City.* Madison: State Historical Society of Wisconsin, 1948.

Wahl, Christian, "Public Park System of the City." In *History of Milwaukee.* Howard Louis Conard, ed. Chicago: American Biographical Publishing Co., 1985.

Watrous, Jerome A., ed. *Memoirs of Milwaukee County.* 2 vols. Madison, WI: Western History Association, 1909.

Pamphlets

Lewis, Don, et. al., *The Milwaukee County War Memorial Performing Arts Center.* Milwaukee, [1969].

Milwaukee County Park Commission. *Consolidation of Parks Operated by Milwaukee County Park Commission and City of Milwaukee Park Board Effective January 1, 1937.* Milwaukee, 1975 (reprint).

Milwaukee County Park Commission. *Horticultural Conservatory in Mitchell Park.* Milwaukee, [1964].

Milwaukee County Park Commission. *The First Plans For A Parkway System for Milwaukee County.* [Milwaukee, 1924].

Milwaukee County Park Commission. *The Milwaukee County Park System.* Milwaukee, [1963].

Milwaukee County Park Commission. *Your Milwaukee County Parks.* Milwaukee, 1957.

Milwaukee County (Temporary Emergency) Veterans' Housing. Milwaukee, [1948].

Milwaukee County War Memorial. Souvenir brochure. Milwaukee, [1968].

Olmsted, Fredrick Law, and John Nolan. *Report...on Civic Center as Proposed by the Metropolitan Park Commission, City of Milwaukee.* Milwaukee, 1909.

Olson, Frederick I., and Virginia A. Palmer. *Guide to the Milwaukee River.* Milwaukee, 1975.

Which Will It Be? It's Up To You. Promotional brochure, Milwaukee County War Memorial. Milwaukee, [1947].

Whitnall, Charles B., *A Residential Park.* Milwaukee, [c. 1940].

Wittenberger, Avery. *Our County Parks.* Milwaukee, 1972.

—————————. *Parks on Parade.* Milwaukee, 1965.

Articles

Buck, Diane M. "Olmsted's Lake Park." *Milwaukee History* 5 (Autumn 1982):55-64.

Carroon, Robert G. "The Milwaukee Highland Games." *Milwaukee History* 2 (Winter 1979):108-120.

Heath, Frederic. "Lueddemann's-On-The-Lake." *Milwaukee History* 3 (Winter 1980):94-101.

Howard, Eugene A. "Personal Recollections of Milwaukee County Park System, 1924-1960." *Milwaukee History* 5 (Spring-Summer 1982):2-43.

Mueller, Theodore. "Milwaukee's German Heritage." *Historical Messenger* 22 (September 1966):112-119.

Olson, Frederick I. "Milwaukee Makes A Zoo." *Historical Messenger* 13 (June 1957):13-15.

Stover, Frances. "Trotting Races at Cold Spring Park." *Historical Messenger* 10 (June 1954):14-16.

Talsey, Will. "Old Soldiers Home." *Historical Messenger* 15 (June 1959):13-15.

Todd, William J. "Milwaukee's Lincoln Park District: A Look at Three Photomaps." *Milwaukee History* 2 (Autumn 1979):58-64.

Whitford, Philip and Kathryn. "An Ecological History of Milwaukee County." *Historical Messenger* 28 (Summer 1972):46-57.

Zink, Irve. "The Story of Mitchell Park." *Historical Messenger* 10 (December 1954):7-13.

Zinsmeister, Louis A. "A Picnic in Schlitz Park." *Historical Messenger* 9 (September 1953):3-6.

Government Documents

Milwaukee. Board of Park Commissioners of the City of Milwaukee. *Annual Reports, First through Forty-fifth.* 1891-1935.

Milwaukee County. *Manual of the County Government and Rules of Procedure of the Board of Supervisors.* 1919, 1925, 1927, 1931.
Milwaukee County. *Proceedings of the Board of Supervisors of the County of Milwaukee.* For the years 1906 through 1984. The annual volumes of this series contain a wealth of official information on all aspects of park programming. It is particularly helpful for the early years of the Park Commission's existence when other sources are not readily available. Includes a useful index.
Milwaukee County. Board of Supervisors. *Financial Summary for the Decade Ending December 31, 1939.*
Milwaukee County. Park Commission. *Park Workers' Short Course.* Mimeographed. 1940-1942.
　　Later versions of this compilation were titled *Sessions of the Milwaukee County Park Employees Institute.*
Milwaukee County. Park Commission. *Reports.*
　　Over the years this source appears under a variety of titles and in various forms. The first known Park Commission report was prepared in printed form in 1911 (three pages long). In the early 1920s Whitnall wrote at least one typed summary, well illustrated, of a year's activity. *Annual Reports* of the Regional Planning Department were published in 1924 and 1925 containing much information on parkways and parks. From 1926 to 1928 the Park Commission and Regional Planning Department had printed a joint annual report; from 1929 to 1932 it was a biennial statement; and in 1936 a *Quadrennial Report* from the two agencies appeared covering the years 1933 through 1936. A *Quadredecennial Report* was published in 1950 for the period 1937 through 1950. During the 1940s and '50s mimeographed annual and/or biennial reports were also assembled for distribution by the Commission. Then, between 1963 and 1978, the Park Commission issued printed *Biennial Reports* dealing with the highlights of programs and activities of that period.
Milwaukee. Metropolitan Park Commission. *The First Tentative Report of the Metropolitan Park Commission.* 1909.
Wisconsin. *Blue Book of the State of Wisconsin.* 1907, 1913.
Wisconsin. *Laws of Wisconsin, 1907.* (Chapter 250).
――――――――. *Laws of Wisconsin, 1913.* (Chapter 454).

Manuscript Materials

Milwaukee, WI. Milwaukee County Historical Society. Adolph Toellner Papers.
　　Landscape drawings. Includes proposed plans for development of

the Seventh Ward Park (Juneau Park) and the Fourth Ward Park (Carl Zeidler Park), circa 1885. Excellent examples of late 19th-century formal park design.

_____. Frederic Heath Papers.

Park Commission folder, box 7. Contains "Dear Comrade" letters from C. B. Whitnall to Heath, and a copy of the 1926 communication on use of the former airport land in Currie Park, which led to Whitnall's resignation as Secretary of the Park Commission.

_____. Milwaukee County Park Commission Papers.

Archival Collection, 1913-1960. Includes: some records of the City Park Board; files of Eugene A. Howard; minutes of the Park Commission meetings; and a variety of correspondence, internal reports, blueprints and related materials. A very rich and useful body of materials.

_____. Park Files.

Charles B. Whitnall, Report to members of the Milwaukee County Park Commission, [1921]. (Typewritten, with photographs.)

Eugene A. Howard, Recollections on development of Milwaukee County Park System, April 1969. (Typewritten.) Substantial portions of this manuscript were published in *Milwaukee History* 5 (Spring-Summer 1982).

Louis Kammerer, "The Milwaukee Garden," n.d. (Typewritten.)

Marie Whitnall, Biographical sketch of Charles B. Whitnall, [1941]. (Typewritten.) From original published in the Milwaukee Turner magazine, June 1941.

Milwaukee Beer Gardens and Wein Stubes, n.d. (Typewritten.)

Milwaukee County Stadium: Information and Statistics, [1963]. (Typewritten.)

Osborn Engineering Company. Report on Selection of a Stadium Site for County of Milwaukee, Cleveland, Ohio, 1947. (Typewritten, with drawings.)

To the Taxpayers of Milwaukee County, 1951. (Mimeographed.) Arguments supporting location of the War Memorial in Washington Park.

Personal Interviews

Ament, F. Thomas, Chairman of the County Board of Supervisors. Milwaukee, February 21, 1986.

Doyne, John L., former County Executive. Pewaukee, WI. December 26, 1986.

O'Donnell, William F., County Executive and long-time member of the Board of Supervisors. Milwaukee. February 21, 1986.

Miscellaneous Sources

Christian, Marvin L. "The Milwaukee Park Movement: A History of Its Origins and Development." Master's thesis, University of Wisconsin-Milwaukee, 1967.

This study was very useful in explaining the efforts to secure government support for a park system in the City of Milwaukee

Milwaukee County Historical Society. Clipping files, microfilm. For parks, the County Park Commission, and obituary notices.

Old Settlers' Club. Obituaries, 6 vols. Milwaukee County Historical Society.

_____. Memorial Books, 4 vols. Milwaukee County Historical Society.

Travel by Water, Land, and Air: Transportation for Milwaukee County

by Harold M. Mayer _____

Milwaukee County and the City of Milwaukee have served as a transportation focus throughout their entire development. As with all urban areas, the basic functions of the region would be impossible without external transportation connections. On the other hand, the area could not function without means of internal circulation, which makes possible the spatial separation of residences and work-places, as well as the development of clusters, or nodes, of cultural, educational, and recreational activity. Although the combinations of modes of transportation have changed with time, the functions of the external and internal transportation have not. Each period has been characterized by particular combinations of transportation modes. Because external transportation is basic to urbanization, it is necessary, in order to understand the relationships of the area to the rest of the world, to treat each period with its particular combination of transportation modes and relationships, rather than, as is often done, tracing each mode separately. Because of the importance of external transportation, we begin with consideration of the *situation* of the County: its external relationships — the geography of its location.

The Geographic Setting of Milwaukee County Relative to Transportation

Milwaukee County is situated near the western extremity of the "core region" of North America, which extends from the Atlantic seaboard along the southern Great Lakes to Chicago and Milwaukee. In spite of recent more rapid population growth elsewhere, it still contains the continent's greatest concentration of population, economic activity, and transportation. The County is also located within the agricultural "heartland" of the continent near the overlap between the "Corn Belt" to the south and west, and the "Dairy Belt" to the north and west. The proximity of Milwaukee County to both areas, as well as to the urban-industrial core region extending eastward, around the south end of Lake Michigan, is reflected in Milwaukee's role as an interregional transportation gateway. In this role, however, it is overshadowed by proximity of Chicago, the continent's most important interior gateway.

During the early period of settlement, until the coming of railroads into the Midwest in the mid-nineteenth century, Milwaukee's situation north of Chicago on the west shore of Lake Michigan was a favorable one. When the Great Lakes constituted the major axis of movement of settlers and goods between the East and the Midwest, Milwaukee was closer in actual travel time to the eastern seaboard than was Chicago. When the railroads reached Chicago from the East in 1852, the situation was changed: between Milwaukee and the East it was necessary, by overland routes, to pass through Chicago. By 1856, immediately after Milwaukee's rail connection to Chicago and thus to the East, Chicago was the leading railroad center of the continental interior, a status which it never relinquished. On the other hand, the transportation situation of Milwaukee has some advantages, especially in serving the hinterland to the northwest. Its port is nearest to the centers of dairy production, in which Wisconsin leads the nation, and it is situated where it can compete with Chicago for certain other agricultural produce and agricultural-related industries. With opening of the enlarged St. Lawrence Seaway in 1959 Milwaukee regained its advantage over Chicago in that it is a hundred miles closer to the sea by the all-water route.

Within Milwaukee County there are no serious topographic obstacles to transportation: relief is generally favorable, with few steep gradients. Nor are there natural obstacles to external overland transportation.

The three rivers which converge to form Milwaukee's inner harbor are narrow; and, although their lower reaches have been widened and deepened for navigation, their widths did not prevent bridging wherever desired. Flooding is almost never a serious impediment to transportation. On the other hand, absence of significant topographic relief facilitated construction of roads and railroads, while level land favored construction of the County's two airports.

The mouth of the river system constituted the original locus of the Port of Milwaukee, but during the last three decades of the nineteenth century the lower Menomonee valley — known locally as the "Industrial Valley" — became an important part of the port complex, later to decline as conditions changed.

Transportation Before the Beginning of European Settlement

In terms of impact upon the region's present landscape and transportation routes, the native Americans — "Indians" — were significant. Their most important trails, in many instances, are followed by modern streets and highways. Some converge upon the vicinity of the junction of the three rivers, near what is now downtown Milwaukee. These include major diagonal arteries, such as Green Bay Avenue and Fond Du Lac Avenue to

the north and northwest, respectively, Forest Home Avenue to the southwest, and Kinnickinnic Avenue to the southeast. These routes led to the
place the Indians described as "the gathering place of the waters," the site
of downtown Milwaukee.

Milwaukee County and the Pre-Railroad Westward Movement

Waterways provide the easiest routes of travel into regions of sparse
settlement and where roads are lacking or are in primitive condition. The
situation of Milwaukee on Lake Michigan has always been a dominating
factor in the growth and development of the region. At the same time the
convergence of three rivers and the consequent opportunity to develop a
port where, a short distance from their juncture, they enter the lake, were
major considerations in the original European settlement of Milwaukee
County.

Two all-water routes connecting the Great Lakes with the seas constituted the axes of French exploration and of the French colonial empire
in North America. One of these, the St. Lawrence-Great Lakes route,
remains today as a major element connecting the Milwaukee region with
the rest of the world. The other, the Mississippi Basin, with several
connections to Lake Michigan, was also significant in colonial times, and
today is a formidable competitor of the Great Lakes-St. Lawrence route in
providing all-water access to world markets for the produce of Milwaukee's
hinterland.

The immediate area constituting present Milwaukee County was not
an especially strategic locale during the era of French domination. Although the subcontinental drainage divide between the Great Lakes and
the Mississippi Basin is almost imperceptible and easily traversed overland, two major trade routes, both involving short portages across the
divide, bypassed the immediate vicinity of Milwaukee. One was the Lake
Winnebago-Fox River-Wisconsin River route on the north; the other was
the Chicago portage on the south. Although the former is unimportant
today, the latter has two improved navigation connections, for barges,
between the drainage basins: the Chicago Sanitary and Ship Canal, and
the Calumet Sag Channel.

Much of the strategy of the wars between the French and the British in
North America during the eighteenth century revolved around the
struggle for control of the two major water routes — the St. Lawrence-
Great Lakes and the Mississippi and its tributaries. Following the American Revolution, the new nation, expanding westward, sought access to
both strategic water routes. Thus, two streams of settlement emerged,

with the Ohio River the initial route of settlement from the Middle Atlantic region.

The Great Lakes region, including the area which later became Milwaukee County, did not directly benefit from the streams of settlers who moved westward along the Ohio. By the first decade of the nineteenth century there were several urban centers in the Ohio Valley which served as loci for the expanding agricultural frontier. The intervening areas between the Ohio and its tributaries on the one hand and the Great Lakes on the other were slow to be settled. They were not directly accessible by water. Settlement in those areas had to await the coming of railroads in the mid-nineteenth century.

Competition for access to the Great Lakes region on the part of the eastern states and their respective seaports resulted in numerous projects for canals and, later, for railroads. The State of New York completed the Erie Canal from the Hudson River, and thus the Port of New York, to the Great Lakes in 1825. Immediately, the transit time between New York City and Lake Erie was reduced to a small fraction of that previously required, and the cost of moving bulk commodities was reduced by as much as ninety percent. The impact of the Erie Canal on settlement in the Great Lakes region was almost immediate. Population along and beyond the south shore of Lake Erie grew rapidly, and cities such as Cleveland thrived.

Settlement west of Lake Michigan, however, lagged behind that south of Lake Erie by a decade. It awaited the agreement to evacuate the Indians following the end of the Black Hawk War in 1832. Soon thereafter the river mouths along the west shore of the lake rapidly became the sites of villages and then cities. Milwaukee's growth began a few years after that of Chicago; it was platted in 1835 and chartered as a city in 1846. Ever since, it has in many respects lagged behind its formidable rival to the south. Whereas Chicago had a canal across the drainage divide to the Mississippi Basin by 1848, the lack of such a facility directly serving Milwaukee proved to be a handicap.

Milwaukee County's Early Streets and Highways

The present basic street and highway system of Milwaukee County was determined in the late eighteenth and early nineteenth centuries. Characteristic of the Midwest and of other regions of the world settled during the nineteenth century is the rectangularity of the streets and roads. Milwaukee County, in common with the Midwest in general, owes this important characteristic of its landscape and cultural pattern to decisions made by the U.S. Continental Congress in 1785 and 1787, decades before general settlement of the region began.

With the trans-Appalachian westward movement accelerating after the nation became independent, it was obvious that a system of land survey and subdivision was required. The "metes and bounds" system generally used in the East had obvious disadvantages. The decision to avoid settlement patterns, common in many regions of the world, of nucleated villages from which farmers commuted outward to their fields was almost implicit. Individual farms centering in separated farmsteads was more in conformance with the American character. Accordingly it was decided to adopt a rectangular land survey and subdivision pattern. The pattern was established in 1785, and the Northwest Territories Ordinance of 1787 applied it to the area which later became the states of Ohio, Indiana, Illinois, Michigan, and Wisconsin.

In Milwaukee County the effects of the federal land survey are far-reaching. Not only is the transportation network — the streets and high-ways — in a rectangular pattern, but the individual parcels of land are generally rectangular as well. There are several advantages to such rectangularity: it is easy to survey straight lines; utility lines, lacking irregular angles, are easier to install and maintain; cadastral maps and land titles are less ambiguous than under other systems; the coordinates establish orientation and the system of addresses; and the lack of acute angles at intersections increases the safety of vehicular movement. There are, however, some disadvantages to rectangularity. One is the monotony of landscapes and cityscapes which result from straight view lines: it is difficult to take advantage of unique vistas and scenic viewpoints if the streets are always straight. Further, if streets are platted on irregular terrain, the consequent steep gradients may produce excessively rapid runoff, flooding, and erosion. Rectangularity results in unnecessary travel because between most origins and destinations it is necessary to traverse two sides of a triangle rather than the more direct route along the hypotenuse, thus adding considerably to the person-miles or vehicular-miles of travel.

Within southeastern Wisconsin the survey provided for thirty-six-square mile townships. In rural areas the survey townships are generally coincident with the basic local units of government. In Milwaukee County, however, there are no longer any local township governments, since all of the county area is included within its nineteen incorporated municipalities. Within the original townships are mile-square sections. The section boundaries form the basic pattern of roads in rural areas. With the spread of urbanization the section-line roads — and sometimes half-section line roads as well — form the system of preferential or arterial streets. The original surveys reserved a right-of-way thirty-three feet wide along the periphery of each section. Because two rights-of-way associated with contiguous sections adjoin, the typical road or street width is sixty-six feet, unless subsequent widening or narrowing has taken place. The right-of-way width is not due to happenstance; it corresponds to an old English measure, the "chain," which was in use when the survey system was adopted.

Although much of the early traffic to and from Milwaukee County was by lake, overland travel was also common. From the East a common route was along the length of Lake Erie, thence either around Michigan's southern peninsula by lake vessel or — especially in winter — by land across the base of the peninsula between Lakes Erie and Michigan, thence around the southern end of the latter, and northward paralleling the west shore of the lake. This route involved passing through Chicago.

Milwaukee's function as a lake port antedated European settlement in the area. The first sailing ship believed to have visited the area was the *Felicity* in 1779, a small armed sloop of about forty-five tons, built at Detroit in 1773, with a crew of eight.

By late 1834 the three nuclei of Milwaukee were in existence: those founded by Solomon Juneau and his colleagues east of the Milwaukee River, by Byron Kilbourn west of the river, and by George Walker south of the junction of the Milwaukee and Menomonee rivers. Although the rivers formed barriers between the settlements, they furnished access by small craft to all three. Larger lake vessels were excluded from the rivers by the sandbar, about a mile south of the present entrance, which nearly blocked the mouth of the Milwaukee River and thus access to the other two as well. This barrier necessitated transfer of cargo and passengers offshore in the unprotected areas of the lake. Frequent exposure to high winds and waves, particularly from northeast and east, created especially dangerous conditions.

The first cargo pier, situated on the lake shore east of Juneau's settlement, was completed in 1843, but that location provided no protection from offshore. Since 1834 settlers had been urging the federal government to provide funds for a harbor. The first appropriation was made on March 3, 1843 for improvement of the channel across the sandbar. This was followed by another appropriation two years later. Meanwhile, settlement was expanding from the two original nuclei bordering the Milwaukee River a mile north of the entrance. The advantages of a "straight cut" across the bar to the north of the natural entrance became apparent.

The "straight cut" was finally opened in 1857, at the site of the present harbor entrance. Immediately there was a substantial increase in maritime commerce and industrial activity along the Milwaukee River, especially where it bisected the core of the city, and between there and the new entrance. North of the city center, industries dependent upon waterborne commerce proliferated along both banks of the river for about a mile. By that time, however, Milwaukee had railroad access around the lake to and from Chicago and the East.

In contrast to the harbor entrance project which was essential to development of Milwaukee's port, a project to stimulate waterborne commerce to and from the city's hinterland proved to be unnecessary and was abandoned. This was the Milwaukee and Rock River Canal. Railroads made the canal an anachronism shortly after it had gotten under way. It was intended to connect Milwaukee and the Great Lakes with the waterways of the Mississippi basin, just as Chicago's rival canal, begun at about the same time, later proved to be more successful. Milwaukee's canal company was chartered in 1838, and construction started in the following year. Financing proved to be difficult, and Byron Kilbourn, its principal promoter, succeeded in getting a grant from Congress of about 166,000 acres of public land to be sold at not less than $2.50 per acre, the proceeds to be used for canal construction. By 1842 approximately one mile had been built, along the present alignment of Commerce Street parallel to the west bank of the Milwaukee River. Water was diverted into the canal by a dam across the river near the present location of the North Avenue bridge. Although the canal was never completed, the dam was useful in providing water power to many of the industries along the river between the dam site and downtown Milwaukee. A successor dam occupies the site now, marking the upstream limit of the estuary, the water level of which is the same as that of Lake Michigan, and marking for many years the head of navigation on the river.

Railroad Developments During the Nineteenth Century

Overland connections to Milwaukee's hinterland were primitive at first, but need for improvement was soon evident. During the 1840s several plank roads led inland. These were generally provided by private capital, under franchise from the State, with tolls charged for their use. The name of one of them — Watertown Plank Road — survives in the name of a contemporary highway. In addition to private vehicles on these roads, there was also common-carrier service by stagecoach. One company, Frink & Walker, the "Greyhound" of its day, eventually operated several thousand miles of scheduled services, including routes from Milwaukee to Chicago and thence to Detroit.

Railroads rapidly replaced the plank roads and aborted the canal. Many prominent Milwaukeeans, including Kilbourn, Juneau, and Alexander Mitchell were among the promoters of Milwaukee's first railroad, the Milwaukie & Mississippi. It was incorporated on February 11, 1847 as the Milwaukie & Waukesha Rail Road Company. The latter name was changed to the former on February 1, 1850 in order to reflect the western goal of the line. In spite of the prominence of its sponsors, funding proved difficult. Farmers along the route mortgaged their properties in return for shares in the company. The first rails were laid on September 12, 1850. On February 25, 1851 the first train operated between Milwaukee and Waukesha, a distance of 20.7 miles. Thus began the system which later became the Chicago, Milwaukee & St. Paul, later the Chicago, Milwaukee, St. Paul & Pacific, then the Milwaukee Road, and finally on January 1, 1986 part of the Soo Line following a merger.

MILWAUKIE & MISSISSIPPI RAILROAD.
Byron Kilbourn. Pres., Milwaukie. Wm. Taintor, Sec.. Milwaukie. Wis.

Miles	Fares.	MILWAUKE WAUKESHA	1st Tr'n	2d Trn		Miles	Fares.	WAUKESHA MILWAUKE	1st Tr'n	2d Trn
		TRAINS LEAVE	AM.	PM.				TRAINS LEAVE	AM.	P.M.
		Milwaukie....	7 15	3 15				Waukesha....	10 00	6 00
5	15	Wauwatosa....	7 30	3 30		3	10	Plank Road ..	10 09	6 09
10	30	Elm Grove....	7 45	3 45		6	20	Powers' Mill..	10 18	6 18
14	40	Powers' Mill..	7 57	3 57		10	30	Elm Grove....	10 30	6 30
17	45	Plank Road...	8 06	4 00		15	45	Wauwatosa....	10 45	6 45
20	50	Waukesha....	8 15	4 15		20	50	Milwaukie....	11 00	7 00

All Steamers on the Lake touch at Milwaukie.
Stages run from Waukesha to different points in the vicinity.

A timetable of Milwaukee's first railroad, dated June, 1851. Trains operated the twenty miles between Milwaukee and Waukesha twice daily.

The schedule of passenger trains on Milwaukee's first railroad in 1851 provided two daily trains in each direction between Milwaukee and Waukesha with a running time of one hour. That the line was a link with other carriers is demonstrated by the published timetable which stated that "all steamers on the lake touch at Milwaukie" and "stages run from Waukesha to different points in the vicinity." Three years later, in 1854 the line was opened to Madison, and it reached the Mississippi at Prairie du Chien in 1857.

The financial crash of 1857 resulted in foreclosure of many farm mortgages which had provided an important part of the financing for the railroad and brought the company to bankruptcy on May 9, 1859. After a series of corporate changes and mergers, Alexander Mitchell took over control of the railroad companies. In 1867 some were reorganized as the Milwaukee & St. Paul; by that time it had reached the Twin Cities.

Along with several additional lines in Wisconsin, including some to the north, northwest, and west of Milwaukee, a line — the second to connect the two cities — was completed between Milwaukee and Chicago in the spring of 1873. The first had been built closer to the shore of Lake Michigan, as two railroads, connecting at the Illinois-Wisconsin border, in 1855; in 1863 the two end-to-end lines were consolidated, after which through passenger and freight trains were operated. The line became part of the Chicago & North Western System in 1883, and later a second North Western line was built between Milwaukee and Chicago, bypassing the shoreline communities.

The railroads and the port together made Milwaukee an important gateway, with interchange of freight and passengers taking place at numerous terminals along the Milwaukee River and the lake shore north of the harbor entrance. Later, in the 1870s and subsequently, when the lower Menomonee Valley was developed as an industrial and port area, railroad lines, yards, and industrial trackage were constructed there, including facilities for rail-water interchange. Bulk commodities, including agricultural produce such as wheat and corn brought to the waterfronts by rail, moved directly or after storage and processing into the holds of lake vessels. Shipments of wheat from Milwaukee amounted to 95.5 thousand bushels in 1845, passed ten million in the 1860s and reached 22.7 million in 1875. Subsequently with the movement of wheat production westward from Wisconsin the traffic declined to less than 900 thousand bushels by 1920. Some of the wheat was milled in Milwaukee; shipments of flour peaked at 4.4 million barrels in the mid-1880s. Manufactured goods moved east from Milwaukee by either rail or lake vessel. Many companies operated package freighters, some carrying passengers as well, between Milwaukee and other lake ports as far east as Buffalo, while others competed with railroads connecting Milwaukee with other ports on the west shore of Lake Michigan, including Chicago. Others offered cross-lake services to Michigan ports, there connecting with eastern railroads. Costs for waterborne transit were generally considerably less than for all-rail movement. Some lake carriers offered joint rail-water rates, and some were actually owned and operated by the railroads until the practice was prohibited by the Panama Canal Act.

Inbound waterborne cargoes consisted of lumber from the upper lakes region and coal from Lake Erie ports. During the late nineteenth century Milwaukee received by water much of the lumber produced in northern Wisconsin and the upper peninsula of Michigan; but as the forests were depleted there, the traffic virtually ended early in the twentieth century. On the other hand, coal was an essential commodity for the railroads and other users, and Milwaukee was the leading Great Lakes port for receipt of coal until the 1950s. The waterways of the lower Menomonee Valley were lined with coal terminals, and much of the coal was moved to inland destinations by rail. The port's coal traffic increased steadily during the late nineteenth and early twentieth century; between 1910 and 1920 the annual volume ranged between four and five million tons.

Internal Transportation Within Milwaukee County: Nineteenth Century

Movement of people and goods within Milwaukee County during the nineteenth century was generally slow and inconvenient. Trips, consequently, were short. Urban areas, including Milwaukee itself, were therefore compact and developed at high density. Except for a small amount of commuting by steam railroad during the latter half of the century, mechanical power was not adopted for internal movement until near the end of the century, when the street railways were electrified.

Section-line roads, which were graded as settlement proceeded, provided access between the outlying settlements within the County on the one hand and Milwaukee on the other, as well as between the scattered farmsteads and the growing number of small communities which became trade centers for the agricultural areas. Other roads, mainly diagonals, focused on Milwaukee. Among the latter, the Chicago and Green Bay Road was especially significant. As mid-century approached, public funds were scarce, and private financing of road improvements became necessary. During the 1840s some roads were operated as turnpikes. The Watertown Plank Road, for example, was built not only to facilitate travel between Milwaukee and its westerly environs but also to improve access to Madison, the State capital. Prior to its construction a travel time of as much as ten days between Milwaukee and Madison was not uncommon. Fallen trees and flooded streams imposed formidable obstacles, and in many places swamps made transit extremely difficult. Where poor drainage and soft ground impeded movement, transverse planks were laid. Construction of the road was begun in 1847 and completed in 1855, but its importance was soon diminished as the railroads were extended into Milwaukee's hinterland.

Major streams imposed constraints upon overland travel. In some instances fording was possible, but bridges were built where traffic demanded. Notable among the bridges were those crossing the three rivers separating the three core settlements of Juneautown, Kilbourntown, and Walker's Point, which now constitute the core of Milwaukee. The narrow Menomonee River separating Kilbourntown and Walker's Point was not a formidable obstacle, although the poorly drained lowland of the valley, nearly a mile wide, added to the expense of grading and draining the approaches to the several low-level bridges spanning the river and, later, the several canals within the valley.

More critical, and much more in the public eye during the early years of settlement, was bridging of the Milwaukee River, especially where it separated Juneautown from Kilbourntown. In the platting of the two settlements during the early 1830s it was deliberately arranged that the street grids on either side of the river did not match. Competition between the settlements was intense. Business and other interests west of the river, led by Byron Kilbourn, opposed bridging the river which they believed would improve access to the rival settlement across the stream. Also, it was believed that bridges would obstruct navigation on the river.

The first bridge across the river in what is now downtown Milwaukee was begun as late as the spring of 1840. Built at County expense, it was completed in the summer of 1841, connecting Chestnut Street (now Juneau) on the west with Division Street on the east. In 1842 the first of a consecutive series of bridges connected what is now Wisconsin Avenue on the two sides of the river. Other bridges soon followed. Because the alignment of the east-west streets on the two sides of the river did not coincide, the bridges had to be built on a skew, with an S-shaped street alignment resulting. Succeeding bridges, to the present, have the same nonlinear alignment.

Rivalry between the two early settlements flared up on May 8, 1845, when the west-siders removed two of the bridges. The dispute continued for several days, during which physical confrontations resulted in some injuries. A compromise was finally reached late in the year. One of the long-term results was that the dispute called attention to the need for unification of the several governmental units. This was accomplished with the charter establishing the City of Milwaukee on January 31, 1846.

Improvement of the streets began soon after platting of the settlements. Originally, property owners were responsible for half the cost of sidewalks upon which their properties fronted, and male residents of ages twenty-one to sixty were required to work two days per week on the roads, streets, and alleys, or pay two dollars. By 1842 most of the work was done under contract. Many of the streets in what is now downtown Milwaukee were paved by mid-century. On the streets, travel was on foot or by horse-drawn vehicles. As a result, the urban areas continued to be compact and crowded.

Early public transportation between urban centers was provided by stagecoaches operating on public roads and, where possible, on the turnpikes, including the plank roads. Within the urban settlements, there were for-hire hacks and omnibuses, the former operating on demand without fixed routes and the latter on more-or-less scheduled intervals on regular routes. These vehicles, uncomfortable as they rattled over the irregular pavements or on poorly paved or unpaved roads and streets, would frequently bog down. Travel took place generally only when absolutely necessary.

The Union Depot located at the foot of Reed Street, now South Second Street, south of the Menomonee River. This terminal was in use between 1866 and 1886. In the left foreground is an "omnibus," typical of that which carried passengers and baggage between the depot, steamer docks, and hotels.

The earliest common carriers of passengers in Milwaukee County were the omnibuses. They were essentially an intracity version of the stagecoach. By the late 1840s such vehicles were common in Milwaukee. They were used typically to connect the steamboat docks and later the railroad depots with hotels, although gradually they evolved into the basic mode of public transportation. In June 1851 the Milwaukee Common Council franchised three operators of public omnibuses. For two decades omnibuses constituted the basic public transportation in Milwaukee and other portions of the county. By the mid-1870s the spread of street railway lines made omnibus transportation almost obsolete. Three-quarters of a century later the process was reversed when the motor bus replaced the electric trolley car.

In several eastern cities, notably New York and Baltimore, horse-drawn railway cars operated on the streets as early as 1832. They were, however, extensions of and associated with intercity steam railroads. The idea of putting horse-drawn vehicles on rails spread rather slowly during the 1830s and '40s. After 1850 the number of cities with horse-drawn street railways spread exponentially; by the end of the decade most major American cities had initiated street railway service. The innovation reached Milwaukee later than in many cities. On September 4, 1859 George Walker, the founder of Walker's Point, and others organized the River and Lakeshore City Railway Company, with a capital stock of fifty thousand dollars, and they obtained a franchise. By the following May the initial line was ready, and on May 27, 1860 the first two cars, built in Philadelphia, were unloaded from the brig *D. Ferguson*. Three days later Milwaukee's first horse-drawn street railway service began.

The street railway franchises generally required the operating company to maintain rails flush with the street pavement and to be responsible for the pavements between and adjacent to the rails. The result was greatly reduced friction, a smoother ride and considerably less effort on the part of the horses. Speed, of course, was much greater than possible with the omnibuses. As the street railways expanded, the cities expanded peripherally, and the daily trips between home and work were extended over ever-increasing distances.

Public and private local transportation in Milwaukee about 1885. The three horsedrawn modes shown include a streetcar, carriage, and dray (truck).

The initially franchised company was soon augmented by other franchised operators. The Milwaukee City Railway was organized in March, 1865 by five prominent Milwaukeeans: John Plankinton, Fred Layton, Samuel Marshall, Charles Ilsley, and W.S. Johnson, with capital stock initially at $100,000. The company was authorized to place tracks wherever it wished. One of its first actions was to absorb the original horsecar operator, the River and Lake Shore City Railway Company, which was in financial difficulties. By 1880 the company had thirty-two cars, 280 horses, over fourteen miles of routes, and it employed 250 persons. Another operator was the Cream City Railroad Company, which served the East Side of the city as well as Bay View, where the Illinois Steel Company rolling mills were located. The West Side Railway Company, like the Cream City, was franchised in 1874. It operated on Wisconsin and Grand Avenues with a double-track line. Other lines were subsequently opened, and by 1881 the West Side company had ten miles of routes.

Many of the horsecar lines, as well as some of the early electric trolley lines, were closely related to real estate developments and land speculation. Promoters sought to benefit from the improved accessibility provided by the street railways, especially on and beyond the peripheries of the then built-up areas, as well as profits from the street railways themselves.

Unlike many other urbanized areas of the United States during the late nineteenth century, Milwaukee County never included cable-operated street railways among its transportation facilities. One company, however, was organized to build and operate a cable line on Milwaukee's West Side; but before construction began, the company's franchise, in October 1889, was changed to permit the company to adopt the newly-developed electric trolley car.

The electric trolley car came into general use in the late 1880s. In general, its beginnings and subsequent development in Milwaukee County paralleled similar developments elsewhere. Horsecar lines were electrified, extensions to and beyond the urban peripheries were built, and new lines were added, in some instances paralleling the existing horsecar routes. On and beyond the edge of the urbanized areas, the new trolley lines, like their predecessors, the horsecar lines, were associated with real estate developments. In order to develop holiday and weekend traffic, the street railway promoters commonly developed resorts and amusement parks along or at the outer ends of the lines. In Milwaukee County, as elsewhere, separate entrepreneurs and corporations received franchises, constructed and extended lines, and merged into unified systems.

The Milwaukee Common Council, concerned with a diversity of proposals for street railway franchises, appointed a committee in August 1889 to inspect the systems in operation in several eastern cities. On October 14,

1889 the Council passed an ordinance authorizing three companies —
Cream City, the Milwaukee Cable Railway (shortly reorganized as the
Milwaukee Electric Railway Company), and the West Side Railway Company — to provide an electric system consisting of overhead wires, using
the rails to complete the electric circuit. Milwaukee's first electric trolley
line was opened on April 3, 1890, when the West Side company operated
the first of an order of nineteen cars on two round trips from Twelfth and
Wells Streets to 34th Street. Other electric lines soon followed. The several
franchised companies which operated horsecar lines were in intense competition for the securing of rights to electrify and to extend their systems.
One group, dominated by John A. Hinsey and Charles Pfister, controlled
most of the lines on Milwaukee's East and South Sides, while another,
controlled by Henry Clay Payne and with financial support from Henry
Villard, the principal builder of the Northern Pacific Railway, was strongest on the city's West Side.

Villard organized the Edison Illuminating Company of Milwaukee in
1889. Control and subsequent electrification of the street railways constituted an excellent complement to the power operations because, although electric power demand was at maximum during the night, the
electric street railways could furnish an outlet for power during the
otherwise times of light demand, during daytime. To accomplish this,
Villard organized the Milwaukee Street Railway Company and induced
many prominent Milwaukeeans to invest in the company or its parent, the
North American Company. Villard's Northern Pacific Railway collapsed
as a result — and partly as a cause — of the financial panic of 1893-94,
leaving the street railway company as Villard's principal holding. Financial difficulties beset the company, and in 1894 more tracks were removed
than added. Several suburbs, development of which was promoted on
promise of street railway extensions, were left without transit access.

On January 29, 1896 foreclosure of the Milwaukee Street Railway
took place, and the properties were sold to a group which them formed the
Milwaukee Electric Railway & Light Company, the "TM". On February 1,
it received the transit and power properties, the former including over one
hundred miles of trackage and 310 cars.

Operation and expansion of the street railway system was not without
difficulties. A strike which attracted nationwide attention and which was
accompanied by violence lasted for four years beginning in April 1896.

As the twentieth century opened, the TM operated lines which blank-
eted the city of Milwaukee and extended into several of the nearby
suburbs. On the city's East Side the principal route was northward from
downtown on Jackson Street, east on Ogden Avenue, northeast on Far-
well, and northward on Glen Avenue (now Downer Avenue) to Capitol
Drive in Shorewood, with a branch to Lake Park, which had been laid out

A streetcar heads east on the trestle which spanned the Menomonee Valley and paralleled the Wisconsin Avenue viaduct. Milwaukee County Stadium is visible at upper left.

by Frederick Law Olmsted in 1895. A second line paralleled the east bank of the Milwaukee River on a series of streets to North Avenue, east on Brady Street, north on Murray to Park Place, and northward on Oakland Avenue, ending in Whitefish Bay. On the West Side a series of lines furnished dense coverage; among the longer routes was one which followed North Third Street and Green Bay Avenue to Keefe Avenue. The longest northwesterly route zigzagged to a terminal at Western Avenue (now 35th Street) and Villard Avenue in what was then North Milwaukee. There were two long West Side lines: one on Walnut Street to Western Avenue and out Pabst Avenue (now Lloyd Street) ending west of 73rd Street; the other on Grand Avenue (now West Wisconsin Avenue) to Eleventh Street and west on Wells Street, ending at the County Institution grounds in Wauwatosa. This line was noteworthy because it crossed the Menomonee Valley on a famous double-track steel viaduct, 2,085 feet long and ninety feet above the valley floor. The Wells Street line was the last to be abandoned, in 1956, because of the presence of the viaduct and the franchise which prevented use of the structure by buses. The viaduct was removed in 1961-62.

South of the Menomonee Valley the principal streetcar route in 1900 to the west extended along National and Greenfield Avenues, through what is now West Allis, thence westward as a single-track line with passing sidings to Waukesha Beach on Pewaukee Lake.

Several east-west lines on the Southwest Side, in additon to the National Avenue line, included those on Washington Street, Greenfield Avenue, and Mitchell Street, the latter extending southwestward on Forest Home Avenue, terminating at Layton Park (31st Street). On the South Side a line crossed the Kinnickinnic River, passed through what later became Cudahy, and continued as a single track to South Milwaukee.

Thus, even as soon as a decade after the first electric street railway was opened, Milwaukee County's system served not only nearly all built-up portions of the city but also a number of suburban communities. In addition, closely related to the street railway system, the beginnings were made toward what later became an extensive system of interurban electric railways radiating from downtown Milwaukee.

The growth of the street railway system during the last four decades of the nineteenth century had profound impact in shaping the expansion and physical pattern of settlement in Milwaukee County. Prior to that time, separation of workplace and residence was much less common than subsequently. Those who did commute did so only for relatively short distances, except for the rare instances in which suburban train services were available as an adjunct to the intercity services of the steam railroads. With the advent of the horsecar, and to a much greater degree in the 1890s with spread of the electric trolley car, separation of work and residence locations became increasingly common. However, the route pattern of the street railways favored downtown Milwaukee, where most of the lines converged. Many industrial areas, such as the lower Menomonee Valley, were not directly accessible by streetcar.

The street railways were major influences in shaping the characteristics of residential neighborhoods and communities during the period of large-scale in-migration late in the nineteenth century. Older immigrant groups, notably those of Germanic origin, had less need than the newcomers, such as the Poles and others from eastern Europe, to cluster in ethnic neighborhoods. Distance of the daily journey to work varied with ethnicity; thus the street railways served, in a sense, as instruments of economic homogenization or ethnic, social, and spatial segregation. It has been found that the length and direction of the journey to work — in large part by street railway — in the late nineteenth century, was related to occupational status as well as to ethnicity. Persons in higher-status occupations tended to live farther from their work than did those of lower economic status, but economic status was also related to ethnicity. Rising affluence tended to increase the total demand for mass transportation; at the same time that the street railways facilitated access to more and more of the urbanized portion of the County, the socioeconomic and ethnic differences in commuting patterns tended to become less pronounced.

As the twentieth century began, the County benefited from many extensions and improvements to its external transportation linkages as well as to its internal mass transit. Steam railroads, interurban electric railways, and improved roads facilitated the movement of people and goods between Milwaukee County and its hinterland areas in all landward directions, while the Port of Milwaukee was increasingly important as a locus of interregional movement.

The Early Twentieth Century:
Era of Railroad Dominance

The period between the beginning of the twentieth century and World War II was marked by the dominance of railroad transportation for overland intercity and interregional movement of people and goods. Toward the end of that period, competitive modes of transportation — highways and, later, air transportation — challenged the railroads' dominance. Milwaukee County was a major node in the rail network of the Midwest. Then as now, however, it had to compete with Chicago, the dominant railroad center of North America, less than a hundred miles to the south. Both of the major railroad systems serving Milwaukee County had their principal gateway connections in Chicago. Both were regional systems; neither of them extended beyond the Midwest to any coastal ports. Both, nevertheless, were extremely important to the Milwaukee area in that they brought agricultural produce and a wide variety of other freight to Milwaukee, thus constituting the basis of many of the area's most important manufacturing industries, as well as distributing the industrial products to regional and national markets. Rates and services of all except a few relatively unimportant private railroads in the nation were brought under federal regulation by the Interstate Commerce Act of 1887; not until 1980 were they freed from much of such regulation and enabled to compete more effectively with other transportation modes.

Most important of the railroads serving Milwaukee County in the late nineteenth and early twentieth century was the Chicago, Milwaukee & St. Paul system. From a modest beginning in 1851, the system had expanded by 1900 to one virtually blanketing the Midwest from a line westward from Chicago to the western edge of the corn belt and into the spring wheat belt of the Dakotas. It linked Milwaukee with gateways where it connected with other railroads at Chicago, Omaha, Kansas City, Minneapolis-St. Paul, and Duluth. During the 1890s the nature of the railroad's traffic changed; whereas in 1894 grain constituted 32 percent of the traffic, a few years later the percentage had declined to 23 percent, even though the tonnage of grain that it moved had doubled. Diversification of its traffic mix was taking place; the proportion of agricultural products and of manufactures increased rapidly. The railroad was a major employer of significance to the local economy of Milwaukee County, and it was the County's most important carrier serving its many industrial establishments.

Soon after dredging and filling of the lower Menomonee Valley took place in the 1870s and '80s, the railroad established its principal maintenance shops and repair facilities for the entire system in the valley. Until well past the middle of the twentieth century these facilities constituted one of the County's principal employers. When the brief era of high-speed streamlined passenger trains occurred following introduction of the Milwaukee Road's famous fleet of *Hiawathas* in 1935, the rolling stock was constructed in the Milwaukee shops. For decades, major repairs to locomotives as well as freight and passenger cars were made in the Milwaukee facilities. In addition, the lower Menomonee Valley was the site of the railroad's principal freight classification yard serving the region's industrial complex and hinterland. The Valley area, in proximity to downtown

Northeast view of the lower Menomonee Valley in 1966. The shops of the Milwaukee Road are in the foreground.

Milwaukee, attracted many industries, with employment in the thousands. The railroad, furthermore, was an important consumer of coal until dieselization took place after the middle of the twentieth century. The railroad was one of the principal reasons for the importance of the Port of Milwaukee in receipts of waterborne coal.

The Milwaukee Road was never among the nation's strongest railroads. Until the early twentieth century it was handicapped by not reaching for the important coastal regions and ports by which it could participate effectively in overseas traffic without turning it over to connecting railroads at inland gateways.

Alexander Mitchell, the leading figure in the railroad's expansion, was its president until his death in 1887. Almost immediately thereafter the road was faced with a series of difficult problems: adjustment to conditions imposed by the newly-adopted Interstate Commerce Act, frequent labor strife, and a struggle among competing interests for control of the company. Most serious was the competition of other railroads to the northwest of Chicago and Milwaukee. As a regional system its rates constituted a handicap, because the fourth section of the Interstate Commerce Act prohibited higher rates for short hauls than for longer ones. Its rivals were extending westward, capturing much of the traffic of the northern Great Plains. East of the Twin Cities, the Milwaukee Road — then more commonly known as the "St. Paul" — faced competition from several other systems in the Twin Cities-Chicago corridor. The problem came to a head when a group including J.P. Morgan and James J. Hill gained control of the Chicago, Burlington & Quincy, a railroad whose Twin-Cities-Chicago main line bypassed Milwaukee along the Mississippi River. The same group controlled the two main railroads west of the Twin Cities, the Northern Pacific and the Great Northern, both of which reached to the Pacific Northwest, connecting there with company-owned transpacific steamships. With connecting rival lines at the Twin Cities providing through service to the Chicago gateway under unified control and consequently unwilling to "short-haul" themselves by turning traffic over to the Chicago, Milwaukee & St. Paul at the Twin Cities, the latter railroad was forced to take a radical step, which, in retrospect, was a major cause of its undoing decades later.

In 1905 the Milwaukee Road decided to build westward to Puget Sound. Although the selected route closely paralleled that of the two earlier rivals — the right-of-way was actually in sight of the Northern Pacific for much of the distance — the decision appeared to be a matter of survival. The first trains operated over the new line between Chicago and Seattle-Tacoma in 1909. Numerous branch lines followed, to tap the wheat areas of the Dakotas and the Palouse region of eastern Washington, the mineral areas of the northwestern mountains, and the forest areas of the

Northwest. In 1912 another momentous decision was made: to electrify the mountain portions of the railroad.

The rivalry among the railroads and consequent electrification of the Milwaukee Road had significant impact on Milwaukee County, for the fortunes of the company contributed both directly and indirectly to the County's economic base in terms of employment, purchases, and industrial attraction. The westerly extension, however, did not ultimately enable the company to survive. Unexpected costs of land acquisition and construction, failure of the northwest economy to continue its boom, and concomitant leveling off of growth of the region's lumber and mining industries, the formidable competition of the two rival parallel railroads, and, finally, diversion of much of the anticipated transcontinental traffic through the newly-completed Panama Canal, all combined to place the Milwaukee Road in an untenable financial position. On March 18, 1925 it was placed under receivership, to be reorganized as the Chicago, Milwaukee, St. Paul & Pacific on March 11, 1927.

During its entire existence the Milwaukee Road was one of the two leading carriers of freight in Milwaukee County. It was also an important passenger carrier. It had one of the three principal lines between Chicago and the Pacific Northwest. In 1935, to compete with its rivals' streamliners, the *Burlington Zephyrs* and the Chicago & North Western's *400* fleet, the Milwaukee Road initiated a fleet of *Hiawathas* between Chicago, Milwaukee, and the Twin Cities as well as to other points in the northern and northwestern hinterland. Much of the rolling stock was built in the Milwaukee shops located in the lower Menomonee Valley, and the equipment was maintained and repaired there.

The Chicago & North Western has been, and is, an important competitor of the Milwaukee Road in serving Milwaukee County and its midwestern hinterland. Unlike the Milwaukee Road, the main line of the North Western does not pass through the County but stretches directly west from Chicago to the Omaha-Council Bluffs gateway and to Fremont, Nebraska, west of the Missouri River, connecting there with the Union Pacific, forming the "Overland Route" to the Pacific coast. The North Western, however, also has two parallel lines between Chicago and Milwaukee. The first was the original connection between the two cities in 1855. A second line, farther inland from the Lake Michigan shore, was later built as an exclusively freight route, connecting in Chicago with the system's main east-west line as well as with all other railroads serving the Chicago gateway.

Beginning in the late 1850s the North Western system added numerous routes north and west of Milwaukee, somewhat parallel to those of the Milwaukee Road: to Minneapolis-St. Paul and Duluth-Superior, to Green

Bay and northern Wisconsin as well as to Michigan's Upper Peninsula, and to many other points north, northwest, and west.

The North Western's lake shore line passes through the South Side of Milwaukee, where freight movements use an east-west line to and from the Butler Yard, while passenger trains formerly continued crossing the lower Milwaukee River on a swing bridge and entered the passenger depot on the lakefront at the foot of Wisconsin Avenue, the city's principal downtown street. Trains continued north or northwestward on a double-track line along the lakefront at the foot of the morainic bluffs and then swung inland parallel to the east bank of the Milwaukee River through Shorewood. This route was eliminated in 1965 with the move of the passenger service to the new Union Station shared with the Milwaukee Road, and the former right-of-way was converted into a bicycle trail.

*The Chicago and North Western Railway depot at the foot of Wisconsin Avenue looking southward from Juneau Park. The train is the **Twin Cities 400** which operated from 1935 until abandonment of passenger service through Milwaukee's depot in 1965.*

The North Western, like its two competitors in the Chicago-Twin Cities market, initiated a high-speed passenger train in 1935. It was named the *400*, because the schedule called for 400 minutes over the 400 miles between the two terminals. Other *400s* followed; as late as the early 1960s they were familiar sights passing through Juneau Park on Milwaukee's East Side lakefront.

Milwaukee County in the Interurban Era, 1905 To 1963

During the first half of the twentieth century Milwaukee County was served by several interurban electric railways which centered in downtown Milwaukee and provided commuter service to many suburban areas and satellite cities within the County and southeastern Wisconsin. One important line also connected Milwaukee with Chicago.

The interurban electric railways were closely associated with the electric street railways and generally were complementary to the urban streetcar systems. Nationally, they developed just before the dominance of automobile and highway transportation. They combined some of the physical characteristics of steam railroads and other burgeoning urban rail transit systems. Typically the tracks of the interurbans were laid in city streets, sometimes shared with local streetcars; in rural areas the tracks were either alongside the roads or on private rights-of-way. Cars were heavier than those of the street railways but generally lighter than the steam railroad cars. Electric power, and especially the development of multiple-unit control which enabled several cars to be operated as a train with the number of motors proportionate to train length, enabled the stops to be more closely spaced than was possible with steam trains, but without significantly increasing overall transit times. Thus stations could be closer together; and urban development, as in some portions of Milwaukee County, could be more or less continuous along the rail axes, whereas with steam commuter service urbanization was more typically clustered around the train stops.

The expansion and decline of interurban lines in the Milwaukee region more or less followed that of such lines in the nation as a whole. The first interurban electric railway in the United States was initiated in 1889. The peak year was 1916, when 15,500 miles of routes were in operation. The automobile eventually doomed the interurbans. Abandonments were numerous in the 1930s, but no new lines were built after 1927. Some of the remaining lines were converted into standard freight railroads, but the last true interurban in the nation ceased operation in January 1963; significantly, it was the Chicago, North Shore and Milwaukee.

Milwaukee County was served by two interurban systems: the Milwaukee Electric Railway and Light Company's system (the "TM") and the North Shore Line. The former system in its heyday was comprised of 198 miles of routes. They centered, after 1905, in a terminal at the Public Service building (now Wisconsin Electric) on the south side of Michigan Street between Second and Third Streets in downtown Milwaukee. This terminal was one of the busiest electric interurban terminals in the nation.

The TM interurban system originated as an extension of Milwaukee's street railway system. When the Milwaukee Electric Railway and Light

Company was established in 1896, it planned to develop as a system in part by accretion. Most of its routes were built by separate companies which were later absorbed. It began by acquiring the twelve-mile Milwaukee-Wauwatosa line, built in 1895; it was extended to Waukesha in 1898. Meanwhile, the company built a line southward through Racine to Kenosha, which it reached in June 1897. Other lines followed: through Hales Corners to East Troy in 1907, from Waukesha westward to Oconomowoc and Watertown in 1908, and to Burlington, as a branch of the East Troy line, in 1909. Other extensions were planned but never built. An independent company, the Milwaukee Northern, constructed an interurban line northward from Milwaukee through Port Washington to Sheboygan between 1905 and 1908; this was absorbed by the TM in 1928.

Many improvements were made by the TM long after building of new lines ceased. Sections of lines on city streets were converted to private rights-of-way, and some were double-tracked. With the advent of buses the company coordinated its services with those of bus lines, thereby eliminating the need for some of the proposed extensions.

The western lines were provided in the 1920s with a seven-mile private right-of-way into Milwaukee. In places this was triple and quadruple-tracked, constituting, in part, a high-density rapid transit line. Parts of that line now form the route of Interstate Highway 94 in the lower Menomonee Valley.

The automobile and the depression following the crash of 1929 eventually proved fatal to the TM system. Its first abandonments were in 1938 and 1939, when the Burlington and East Troy lines were cut back to Hales Corners, and several other portions of the system were eliminated before World War II. The last section was ended on June 30, 1951, following a fatal collision on Labor Day of 1950.

The Chicago, North Shore and Milwaukee (the "North Shore Line") was the second, and in some ways the more important, of the two interurban systems which served Milwaukee and Milwaukee County. It began as a street railway in Waukegan and North Chicago, Illinois, in 1895. In 1899 the line was opened through the north shore suburbs of Chicago between Waukegan and Evanston. In 1907 it was extended northward to Milwaukee, entering the city on a right-of-way paralleling South Sixth Street. On the city's South Side the tracks were in the street, shared with the company's local streetcar line, operated in order to maintain the franchise. It entered downtown Milwaukee on the newly built Sixth Street viaduct across the lower Menomonee Valley.

The North Shore Line carried heavy traffic to and from Fort Sheridan and Great Lakes naval station during both World Wars. Military personnel used the line heavily for recreation trips into Milwaukee as well as Chicago.

The North Shore Line updated service between Chicago and Milwaukee in 1941 with two
"Electroliners." The streamlined, air-conditioned interurban trains operated five times daily
at under two hours, including all stops.

Direct entrance into Chicago was obtained over the North Side elevated railway in 1919. Thus Milwaukee and Chicago were connected by a
third railway company, competing with the Milwaukee Road and the
North Western. The North Shore Line had the advantage of local stops on
the south side of Milwaukee and on the north side of Chicago.

On June 6, 1926, the North Shore Line opened a newly built heavy-
duty double-track line through the Skokie Valley in Illinois, bypassing the
built-up shoreline suburbs between Waukegan and Evanston and substantially reducing transit time between Milwaukee and Chicago to two
hours including intermediate stops. Service then was hourly in each
direction. Some trains had dining cars; others had parlor-observation cars.
The line had the reputation of being America's fastest interurban, with
trains reaching speeds of over eighty-five miles per hour.

Like many other interurbans, the North Shore Line operated a package freight service which provided a minor part of its revenues. Part of the
operation consisted of containers, with overnight door-to-door pickup and
delivery in Milwaukee and Chicago; this was one of the earliest "piggyback" operations by any railroad. Another innovation was the provision
in 1941 of streamlined air-conditioned interurban train service between
Milwaukee, Racine, Kenosha, and Chicago. Two "Electroliner" trains
provided five daily round trips with overall times of under two hours

including intermediate stops. It would have been faster but for the need to move the trains over the elevated railway on Chicago's North Side between local trains, and with numerous sharp curves there.

The North Shore Line could not compete with the parallel train service of the North Western and the Milwaukee Road, both of which not only operated Milwaukee-Chicago trains but also local commuter trains out of Chicago. For many years there were fifty daily weekday trains on the three railroads in each direction between the two cities. Growth of automobile traffic, in addition to competition from the two standard railroads and ultimately intercity buses, diluted the North Shore Line's passenger traffic. In 1955 the Shore Line route, which carried only local Chicago suburban traffic since opening of the parallel Skokie Valley line, was abandoned, and early in 1963 the last Skokie Valley route train departed, thus ending for Milwaukee, and for the nation, the era of the interurban electric railway as a transportation mode.

The Port of Milwaukee and its Pre-Seaway Traffic

During the last half of the nineteenth century and until World War II the Port of Milwaukee was essentially a Great Lakes port, although there were from time to time a few direct all-water transits between Milwaukee and overseas by small vessels able to pass through the series of Canadian canals which preceeded the opening of the present enlarged St. Lawrence Seaway in 1959.

With the opening of the "straight cut" in 1857 the principal focus of the port was along the Milwaukee River from the new entrance channel, through the downtown area as far as the dam near North Avenue, which marked the head of navigation. Along both banks of the river for over a mile from the entrance there were numerous multistory warehouse and loft buildings, some of which received and shipped waterborne package freight directly across the adjacent wharves. There were also freight sheds, open areas for bulk commodities, and "heavy" manufacturing and distributing industrial establishments. North and south of the downtown area direct water access attracted many industries: lumber mills and storage yards receiving timber and logs from the upper lakes, metalworking establishments using lake transportation for receipt of coal, machinery, and other goods and shipping their products to other Great Lakes ports, leather tanneries receiving tanbark from the upper lakes forests and hides from the numerous stockyards in Milwaukee, Chicago and elsewhere, and many other types of industrial and commercial establishments. Passenger and package freight vessels, alongside the river wharves, connected Milwaukee with other ports on both sides of Lake Michigan as well as with more distant ports on the other Great Lakes.

As lake traffic grew and vessels became larger, it became evident that expansion of waterfrontage devoted to port use and to port-associated industries was needed. In the 1870s and 1880s extensive dredging of the lower Menomonee River and of new canals associated with it took place.

The Milwaukee River warehouse district south of downtown. The sailing vessel and steam tug are typical of the late 19th century. The schooners often carried lumber, hides, and other commodities to the many industries along the Milwaukee River north of the downtown area.

The spoil was deposited behind bulkheads to form landfill upon which were subsequently located many of Milwaukee's major industries. By the early twentieth century the lower valley was the locus of a major part of the port's activity. The Chicago, Milwaukee & St. Paul Railroad's principal freight yards and shops were located on an extensive site in the valley. The railroad, along with other industries, received coal by lake boat; for many years Milwaukee was the leading coal-receiving port on the lakes. On the other hand, beginning with the 1880s the port's bulk commodity traffic did not measure up to that of some of the other lake ports, notably Chicago, because, with one exception, there were no large primary iron and steel

View of the Milwaukee River downtown looking north from Clybourn Street. The passenger and freight vessels in the foreground are typical of the Goodrich fleet of that period; Goodrich liners connected Milwaukee and other Lake Michigan ports for nearly eighty years. Milwaukee City Hall and the Pabst Building are in the background, left to right.

plants in the city. Consequently iron ore, coal, and limestone receipts did not constitute important parts of the port's traffic.

On the other hand, the agricultural hinterland of Milwaukee County produced a large volume of waterborne shipments through Milwaukee. During the 1880s Milwaukee ranked high among the wheat-shipping ports of the world. Much of it moved through the lakes to eastern lake ports, notably Buffalo, which developed a large flour-milling industry rivaling that of Minneapolis-St. Paul. Some of the wheat was transshipped from there and other eastern lake ports by rail, or through the New York State Barge Canal system for east coast destinations, while some was transshipped overseas. Grain elevators were conspicuous along Milwaukee's river frontages.

Although bulk commodities, especially grain and coal, constituted most of the port's tonnage, package freight, consisting mainly of manufactured goods, contributed much high-value traffic. Package freight vessels connected Milwaukee with many ports on all of the Great Lakes and in many instances competed with the railroad by offering lower "differential" rates. Some also carried passengers. Commercial travelers and tourists patronized them in large numbers. Notable among the services at Milwaukee were those of the Goodrich Line, which operated for eighty years until put out of business by the Great Depression following the crash of 1929. This line offered all-year service between Milwaukee and Chicago as well as northward along the west shore of the lake. Several passenger-package freight lines crossed the lake from Milwaukee to western Michigan ports such as Muskegon and Ludington; they developed a significant movement of fruit into Milwaukee. Until recently there was a commercial establishment on the Milwaukee River called the "Fruit Boat."

Operations of the package freighters were largely curtailed as a result of the Panama Canal Act, which prohibited railroads from engaging in competitive water transportation. Some of the lake lines had been controlled by railroads, and others offered joint rail-water through rates. Some, however, managed to survive until World War II. A few passenger vessels operated until the late 1960s, when more stringent safety regulations made continued operation economically impracticable.

Two of the passenger vessels which served Milwaukee were especially well known. One was the *Lady Elgin,* a side-wheel steamer which sank in 1860 off Wilmette, Illinois with heavy loss of life. Another, more for-

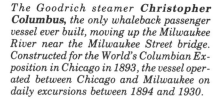

*The Goodrich steamer **Christopher Columbus,** the only whaleback passenger vessel ever built, moving up the Milwaukee River near the Milwaukee Street bridge. Constructed for the World's Columbian Exposition in Chicago in 1893, the vessel operated between Chicago and Milwaukee on daily excursions between 1894 and 1930.*

tunate, was the *Christopher Columbus,* the only whaleback passenger ship ever built. Designed originally to serve the World's Columbian Exposition in Chicago in 1893, in 1894 it was chartered by the Goodrich Line, which operated it in daily summer excursion trips between Chicago and Milwaukee until 1930, when obsolescence and economic conditions caught up with it. During its nearly four decades it brought hundreds of thousands of visitors to Milwaukee.

As lake bulk freighters became much larger, the depths in the Milwaukee River and the lower Menomonee River, together with the narrowly restrictive channels and numerous movable bridges, indicated need for a more adequate port, preferably with easier access from Lake Michigan and with more extensive land areas for terminals and port-associated industrial establishments. Traffic at the port had grown from 2.36 million tons in 1890 to 7.74 million in 1910 and 8.64 million in 1913, after which it fluctuated within a narrow range for many years, peaking in 1929 at 8.56 million tons. The ideal port site was behind the federal offshore breakwater south of the river entrance. The area was actually a peninsula called Jones Island between the pre-1857 river mouth and the newer artificial entrance, bordered on the west by the lower Kinnickinnic River. The "island" was occupied by people, mainly commercial fisherman who came from the Baltic coast of Poland. At the south end was the iron and steel plant, Milwaukee's only major one, which was forced to close in 1929 because of obsolescence and difficult economic conditions.

Milwaukee's first local port agency was created in 1909; in 1920 the City, under State authorization, organized the Board of Harbor Commissioners. The residents of Jones Island were relocated on the mainland to the west, and acquisition of the port site proceeded. The lower Kinnickinnic River was dredged and widened, the land area was extended by fill, and a complex of port terminals was constructed. Eventually these consisted of piers and slips for general cargo on the lake shore, a "heavy lift" wharf and backup area on the Inner Harbor, numerous warehouses and transit sheds, a liquid cargo pier, two slips for cross-lake railroad car ferries, a complex of about twenty miles of railroad trackage served by Milwaukee's two railroads, and sites for port-related industries.

With these facilities becoming available, much of the port traffic shifted from the rivers. A series of federal projects provided channels through the harbor entrance and in the Inner Harbor between Jones Island and the mainland sufficient to accommodate the larger lake vessels, and, later, for the "salties" able to travel through the St. Lawrence Seaway. The project depth is twenty-seven feet, the same as that in the Seaway and the Great Lakes connecting channels.

For many years a substantial part of the waterborne traffic of the Port of Milwaukee consisted of cross-lake movements to and from western Michigan ports. Because the lake constitutes a barrier at right angles to the main transportation axis of the northeastern United States, the major alternative for traffic between the hinterland of Milwaukee County and the east is the circuitous route around the southern end of the lake, involving the congested and time-consuming movement through metropolitan Chicago.

Almost from the beginning of settlement in southeastern Wisconsin, passengers and freight were carried across the lake by several lines of steamboats. This service continued until the 1970s in various forms. The last was by the famous *Milwaukee Clipper* from 1941 until 1970 between Milwaukee and Muskegon. During the summers it carried passengers and tourist automobiles, and during the other nine months it carried, except during World War II, newly manufactured automobiles in both directions between assembly plants and over-the-road haulers on both sides of the lake. The company also operated for several years a converted wartime landing craft, the *Highway 16*, which also carried new automobiles in both directions.

More important, however, were the railroad car ferries. The Port of Milwaukee handled more railroad ferry traffic in most years than did any

*The **Milwaukee Clipper** entering Milwaukee harbor. This vessel operated between Milwaukee and Muskegon, Michigan from 1941 until 1970.*

other lake port. Between the two World Wars the ferry traffic averaged between 25 and 35 percent of all the port's lake cargo tonnage. It was carried on two routes: that of the Grand Trunk Western Railway to Grand Haven and later to Muskegon and that of the Pere Marquette (later the Chesapeake & Ohio or "Chessie") to Ludington. The Ludington route was begun in 1897 and the Grand Trunk in 1906.

The ferries carried up to twenty-six freight cars each, loading through stern ramps to tracks on the main deck. The Grand Trunk ferries did not carry highway vehicles but had accommodations for sixteen passengers, while the Pere Marquette ("Chessie") vessels carried automobiles, alternatively with railroad cars, and had accommodations for several hundred passengers, with staterooms, bars, and dining rooms. The ferries operated year-round. They were built as ice-breakers and to withstand winter storms; although there were several casualties through the years, the most notable one being the sinking of the Grand Trunk ferry *Milwaukee* in the fall of 1929 with loss of all of the crew, there were no passengers.

The railroad ferries were important links in the rail network. They provided access for two eastern railroads into Milwaukee, where interline connections were made with western lines, in addition to enabling Milwaukee area shippers to avoid the congestion and delays of the Chicago gateway. They gave metropolitan Milwaukee rate parity with Chicago on movements to and from the east.

Eventually technology spelled the end of the railroad ferries. Both railroads, with extensive networks in Michigan, also had heavily built main lines into Chicago, on which they could operate trains of over 100 cars. By the early 1980s the ferries were gone from Milwaukee; the only ferry across Lake Michigan remaining in 1986 is a single vessel between Kewaunee, Wisconsin and Ludington, Michigan.

With the decline of railroad ferry service there were attempts on both sides of the lake to initiate a more modern cross-lake service from Milwaukee. Various proposals were made during the early 1980s, and by mid-1986 there was a prospect of a publicly subsidized passenger-auto ferry, using a converted former railroad vessel to begin seasonal operations by the summer of 1987.

Modern Highways in Milwaukee County

As the twentieth century began, Milwaukee County's network of roads and streets consisted essentially of the rectangular grid established as a result of the Northwest Ordinance of 1787, and a series of diagonal roads converging on the main urban nodes, mainly downtown Milwaukee.

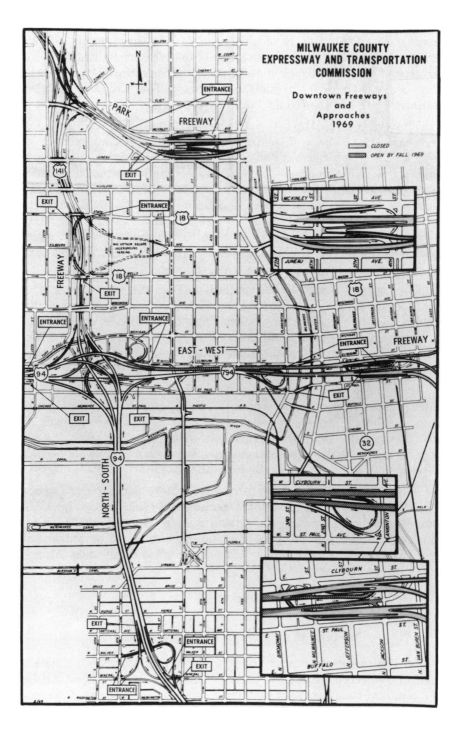

MILWAUKEE COUNTY
EXPRESSWAY AND TRANSPORTATION
COMMISSION

Downtown Freeways
and
Approaches
1969

In many instances street railway tracks occupied the main streets in Milwaukee and some suburban communities; all had been electrified by 1900. Within the following years long ribbons of commercial establishments proliferated along these arterials while at some of the major intersections higher-density concentrations of retail and service establishments, attracted by streetcar access from four or more directions, tended to develop. In rural areas, "farm to market" roads, generally unpaved, were common. Intercity travel by road was nearly non-existent. As rural areas became urbanized, subdivisions were platted in the familiar rectangular pattern, with typical urban blocks of about five acres.

Milwaukee County benefited from the several programs of Federal and State aid for highway construction and improvement as the numbers of motor vehicles increased. Beginning in 1916, a series of federal acts provided highway funds for the States and through them to counties and local governments. Milwaukee County took advantage of these opportunities, and many of its arterial routes were improved, some, after the 1920s, with four or more lanes. But this was not sufficient; the number of motor vehicles increased faster than the capacity of the roads to handle them. In many instances the proliferation of highway-oriented businesses with direct access to the arterial roads and streets caused extreme congestion.

During the 1930s Germany built a network of *autobahnen* primarily in anticipation of military action, and Italy constructed *autostrade* for the same reason. These were "superhighways" for high-speed heavy-volume movement. They provided complete freedom from intersecting traffic, medial separation of the two directional movements to avoid head-on collision, and long-radius horizontal and vertical curves permitting constant speeds. At the New York World's Fair in 1939 General Motors, in an elaborate series of exhibits, presented the concept of "motorways," modeled after the German and Italian prototypes. The exhibits were viewed by millions of people.

The Federal Highway Act of 1938 authorized the Bureau of Public Roads to recommend to Congress a program for superhighways "not exceeding three in number." The report was transmitted on April 27, 1939. In April 1941 President Roosevelt appointed a National Interregional Highway Committee to investigate the need for a nationwide system of modern roads. The report, reinforced by the wartime demonstration of the

A central portion of Milwaukee's expressway system. Most of the construction was completed during the 1960s.

utility of domestic highway transportation and for the anticipated need for a vast postwar program of public works to mitigate the expected unemployment, was submitted to Congress on January 12, 1944. In August, 1947, the general pattern of routes was approved, but no further action was taken. With the resumption of motor vehicle production and the renewed availability of fuel after the war, the need for a new system of highways was evident. Eight years after submission of the inter-regional highway report, during the summer of 1952, President Eisenhower, in a radio and television address to the nation, urged action on the previously recommended Interstate system. The problem remained, however, of how to obtain the many billions of dollars that the system would cost. A short time after the Presidential address General Motors again stepped into the picture, by announcing a prize contest for the best solution. The first prize winner was Robert Moses, the famous New York "power broker" who earlier had been responsible for the parkway systems on Long Island and in Westchester County.

The program was initiated by the Federal-Aid Highway Act of 1956 and the associated Highway Revenue Act. They provided for a "National System of Interstate and Defense Highways" consisting of 41,000 miles of superhighways, later increased to 42,500 miles. The Act provided for 90 percent Federal funding of land acquisition and construction by means of a trust fund for which taxes on motor fuel, tires, and other items were imposed. Estimated cost of the system, in 1956 dollars, was 27 billion, making it the most expensive public works program up to the time. Subsequently, inflation, unexpected land and relocation costs, especially in urban areas, and additions to the system, have resulted in costs of over 100 billion dollars. By 1986 the system was nearly completed except in some urban areas where changing traffic conditions and local objections, especially because of environmental considerations, delayed or prevented construction. Some of the more expensive and questionable portions have been "demapped" — eliminated from the system prior to construction — or were aborted before completion. In Milwaukee County there are notable examples of both.

The Interstate system constitutes a prototype for other major express highways, built to Interstate standards. Examples are Highway 15 in the southwestern part of the County and Highway 45 to the northwest.

Milwaukee County began its portions of the Interstate system somewhat later than did many other metropolitan areas. The major elements, locally called "freeways," were essentially completed by 1969. Within the County, the principal portions are: I-94 from downtown Milwaukee southward to Chicago and westward to Madison; I-43, a reconstruction of former Highway 141 northward to Green Bay, and the southern and western portions of a partial circumferential route constituting I-894. In

The Marquette interchange at the southwest corner of downtown Milwaukee. This is the intersection of Interstates 94 South, 94 West, 43 North, and 794 East.

the mid-1980s there were several uncompleted and aborted portions of the Interstate system and associated freeways within the County, and some portions have been demapped. The original plan called for an inner circumferential loop surrounding downtown Milwaukee. I-43 constitutes the western unit of the loop, and I-794, with an elevated viaduct and a low-level fixed bridge across the Milwaukee River, the southern link. The northern link is incomplete, with ramps connecting to city streets east of a low-level fixed bridge across the river. At the southwestern corner of the loop is the Marquette interchange, one of the most complex in the entire nationwide system.

The eastern portion of the loop was planned as a freeway through a part of the Milwaukee County Park System's lakefront complex. As a result of opposition for environmental reasons, the final resolution was construction of a conventional dual surface highway — Lincoln Memorial Drive — on a former Chicago & North Western Railway right-of-way through Juneau Park.

The northern part of the lakefront loop was originally planned to swing inland to a link with the now-aborted Park Freeway, which, in turn, was to extend westward to an interchange with Highways 41 and 45, planned, but not finally built, as part of the system. A wide strip of land was acquired, scores of residential properties were purchased, residents were forced to relocate, and, after many years of controversy, the link was demapped. In the mid-1980s much of the vacated land was still vacant, although some construction of housing and other buildings was under way.

Another route which was not built, and was demapped, was to have been an Interstate freeway southward, close to the Lake Michigan shore parallel to and east of I-94, toward Chicago. As part of this route a high-level bridge, the Hoan Memorial Bridge, was built together with a long viaduct extending the length of Jones Island. There is no connection at the southern end except through ordinary narrow city streets. The bridge spans the entrance to the rivers and Inner Harbor by means of a graceful steel arch which won many engineering and architectural awards, but the route carries only a small fraction of the traffic that was intended. The demapping of the proposed Interstate freeway beyond the southern end is, of course, largely responsible. Several alternative connections were proposed, but by mid-1986 no decision had been made. Among them was a causeway lakeward of the present shore, a wide surface avenue along or parallel to the Chicago & North Western right-of-way, and a conventional road partly through the lakefront County parks. All such proposals met with strong objections from residents of nearby areas.

At the north end of the bridge an equally controversial series of issues attracted public attention for nearly two decades. These were related to connections between the north end of the bridge route, the lakefront portion of the inner loop, and I-794, the viaduct bordering the southern portion of downtown Milwaukee. Associated with the controversy was inability of many interests — Federal, State, City, County, and private — to decide upon future land uses near the proposed connection. The design for the connection among the several roads was finally decided in 1984, and the connecting ramps were opened late in 1985.

The latest portion of the freeway system within the County to be opened is the Airport Spur, a short stretch connecting I-94 South with the General Mitchell International Airport terminal complex. This link was opened in 1978.

The freeway system within the County has had major impact upon travel to, from, and within the County. Its existence relieves some of the city streets and rural highways of substantial traffic which otherwise would have caused unacceptable congestion. Also, the freeways are used by express buses of the Milwaukee County Transit System. In recent years, however, with the increase in suburban employment, "freeway flyer" use has leveled off, in large part because the bus routes are primarily oriented to the downtown area.

The Milwaukee County government is responsible for operation, maintenance, and policing of the Interstate system within the County.

Air Transportation Within Milwaukee County

Milwaukee County owns and operates two civil airports: General Mitchell International Airport, the only air carrier airport in southeastern Wisconsin with scheduled service and an important center for both general and military aviation, and the Lawrence J. Timmerman Airport, a general aviation facility in northwestern Milwaukee.

In 1919 the first airport in the County was established at Currie Park, on the County's western edge south of Capitol Drive. It was one of the first publicly owned airports in the nation. But advances in aviation soon made it unsatisfactory. In 1925 the Federal government adopted a policy of advertising for bids by private interests to operate airmail routes. One of the proposed routes was to connect Chicago and the Twin Cities. As a result of local lobbying, Milwaukee was designated as an intermediate stop. This was the incentive for the County Board to recommend a site for an adequate airport. Fortunately, a private airport existed within the County. Thomas F. Hamilton had established, after World War I, a pro-

A Hamilton metal monoplane at the Milwaukee County Airport about 1927, originally Hamilton Field.

peller manufacturing business; the Hamilton propeller achieved fame during the war and was in demand for civil aircraft later. To accommodate his customers' aircraft he had purchased fifty-six acres just south of the city in 1920. On October 5, 1926 the County Board appropriated $150,000 to purchase Hamilton Field. On January 7, 1927 the field was renamed Milwaukee County Airport. Almost immediately improvements were initiated; they included better drainage, fuel tanks, and improved lighting. Scheduled service was initiated by Northwest Airways, predecessor of the present Northwest Orient Airlines, on July 5, 1927, with stops by three-passenger Stinson aircraft between Chicago and the Twin Cities.

Hamilton's propeller business was expanded, when he decided to manufacture metal aircraft at a plant on Milwaukee's South Side. From the plant parts were trucked to the airport and assembled there. The planes were single-engine high-wing monoplanes with cabins for six passengers and two pilots. Northwest Airways bought nine of them. The plant was closed down, however, in 1930, and the planes were thereafter serviced in Wichita, Kansas, which subsequently became a major center for manufacture of general aviation aircraft.

The Milwaukee County Airport was used during the winter months as an alternate to Milwaukee harbor, serving as the western terminal for a scheduled service across Lake Michigan using amphibian aircraft. A service began on September 1929 to Grand Rapids, Michigan. An advertisement in January 1930 featured a connection with Michigan Central trains at Grand Rapids to New York and other eastern points: "Avoid the Lake Michigan detour! Trains stop beside planes at Grand Rapids." The planes carried six passengers between Milwaukee and Grand Rapids for a fare of eighteen dollars. On two of the three daily round trips intermediate stops were made at Muskegon. The operation, by Kohler Aviation, was absorbed into Pennsylvania Airlines, which, eventually after several successive mergers, became part of United Airlines in 1961.

Following a series of scandals, the scheduled airlines of the nation were brought under Federal regulation in 1938, and reorganization of the previously operating companies took place. On May 4, 1938 a Federal WPA project was authorized for construction of a new terminal at the County Airport. It was opened on July 1, 1940. By that time the famous Douglas DC-3, a twenty-one-passenger twin-engine aircraft introduced in 1936 had become the standard of the major scheduled airlines.

During the period immediately before entry of the United States into World War II Milwaukee's scheduled air service included routes by Northwest Airlines through Milwaukee to Chicago, to Seattle and Portland on the west coast, to Winnipeg, and to many intermediate cities, and by Pennsylvania-Central Airlines to many points in the northeastern United States. By that time, however, Chicago's Municipal Airport (now

Midway) had become the overwhelmingly dominant hub of the nation's airline network, and many points were accessible to Milwaukee only through Chicago.

On March 17, 1941 the Milwaukee County Airport was re-named General Mitchell Field in honor of the grandson of Alexander Mitchell, who was prominent in Milwaukee's early transportation developments. General Mitchell demonstrated the potential importance of military air power in 1921 by sinking captured German warships with aerial bombing.

The Army Air Force leased a portion of Mitchell Field in 1942 for training pilots for the Air Transport Command. A number of C-47 aircraft were based at the field. For a short time a camp for German prisoners of war was operated at the field. The Army terminated its lease on February 5, 1948.

During the years following the war, commercial air transportation developed rapidly. Planes were larger and with much longer range. Between 1945 and 1955 aircraft in scheduled service tripled, the average number of seats per plane increased from nineteen to fifty-one, average speed from 155 to 208 miles per hour, route miles from 49 thousand to 79 thousand, and the number of passengers in the nation from 6.58 million to over 38 million. The Mitchell Field terminal building opened in 1940 was clearly inadequate. The field had been expanded, runways lengthened, and modern navigation facilities installed, in part with Federal aid. Planning for a new terminal began soon after the war's end, and on May 9, 1950 a contract was let for site preparation. The site for the new terminal was on the west side of the field, seven miles south of downtown Milwaukee. Construction proceeded slowly because the extent of Federal aid was less than expected. The building, which forms the nucleus of the present terminal complex, was opened on June 19, 1955.

Meanwhile, several military aviation groups continued to be based at the airport with facilities on the east side and in the southwest corner of the field.

In 1959 two events occurred which vitally affected the subsequent status of commercial airline activity at Mitchell Field. One was the introduction of jet-powered aircraft. The other was opening of Chicago-O'Hare International Airport only seventy miles from Mitchell Field.

Major airlines rapidly replaced their propeller-driven aircraft with jets, which were much larger and nearly twice as fast as well as being more economical to operate. Airports had to expand to accommodate them and the greatly increased passenger, cargo, and mail loads which they made possible. When the County acquired the airport in 1927, there were two cinder runways 2,000 and 1,700 feet long. With each new generation of aircraft improved runways were provided. In 1958 extension of the northeast-southwest runway on a viaduct over Howell Avenue was authorized, and it was completed in 1964. By the mid-1980s Mitchell Field had five runways, two of which were capable of handling the largest commercial aircraft in service, the Boeing 747. One of the runways is 9,690 feet long; another is 8,011 feet.

Traffic at Mitchell Field increased from 752 thousand passengers in 1960 to 1.76 million in 1970 and just under 3.3 million in 1980. Some decreases in air travel accompanied the business recession of the early 1980s; in 1984 passenger traffic at Mitchell Field was down to 2.537 million, a decrease of nearly 12 percent from the previous year. With improved business conditions in 1985 air passenger traffic increased considerably.

The terminal complex at General Mitchell Field in 1967. Since that time considerable expansion has occurred, and the airport expressway spur now connects the area with Interstate 94.

Milwaukee's status as an airline hub has been constrained by proximity to Chicago, with the world's busiest airport less than one and one-half hour's drive from Milwaukee and only a few minutes by air from Mitchell Field. The Federal Aviation Authority classifies Milwaukee as a "medium air carrier hub"; in typical recent years it ranked about thirty-fifth in the nation, a position far below the population rank of the metropolitan area.

Federal regulation of the routes and fares of the nation's domestic airlines ended with the Airline Deregulation Act of 1978. The effects on Milwaukee's airline traffic have been somewhat negative. Among the results of deregulation have been the proliferation of airlines, some of which did not survive, expansion of some of the larger ones by merger, growth of the "hub and spoke" route-patterns focusing on a few large hubs with direct service by large aircraft producing economies of scale on the highest-density routes and the substitution of shorter-distance flights by smaller aircraft and smaller operators between major hubs and the lesser ones. Milwaukee's situation in the shadow of Chicago has been exacerbated as a result of deregulation. Mitchell Field has fewer long-distance direct and nonstop flights than would otherwise be the case, resulting in more circuitous routes and connections with attendant delays and inconvenience than prior to deregulation. On the other hand, the proliferation of airlines has resulted in more options for travelers and shippers, but generally by use of connecting rather than direct flights. Many of the connecting flights are by smaller planes of the major airlines and others by "commuter" airlines. The latter connect at larger hubs such as Chicago, Detroit, and Minneapolis. Nevertheless, the number of schedules serving Milwaukee doubled in the postderegulation years to 1986, although many with smaller planes. To many destinations Milwaukee is on a spoke rather than being a hub.

During the early 1980s Republic Airlines was the dominant carrier at Mitchell Field. It was formed by merger of three regional airlines. Milwaukee was a secondary hub for Republic, with more flights at Mitchell Field than any other airline. In postmerger modification of its route pattern in 1985 it designated Minneapolis, Memphis, and Detroit as its hubs, and the number of scheduled flights at Milwaukee was reduced to fewer than half of the previous number. In 1986 a prospective merger of Republic with Northwest, Milwaukee's second-most-important airline, took place.

No major airline has ever used Milwaukee as a principal hub. One small airline, Midwest Express, an expansion of an in-house operation of Kimberly-Clark based in Appleton, Wisconsin, converted into a common carrier in 1985, with its scheduled operations radiating from Milwaukee. A crash of one of its three DC-9s with loss of thirty-two lives on takeoff from Mitchell Field in September 1985 was the first major airline accident at that airport, but it did not prevent Midwest from expanding its route pattern during the following months from Milwaukee to other cities; in 1986 it operated to Appleton, Atlanta, Dallas-Fort Worth, Boston, Washington D.C., and Madison. It is the only airline with Milwaukee as its principal hub.

Although many air cargo carriers have substantial Milwaukee business and maintain offices and stations in Milwaukee County, it is estimated that 75 to 80 percent of the area's air freight is trucked to and from Chicago's airports. On the other hand, several carriers of small air shipments, including Federal Express, Emery, and United Parcel Service, began direct air operations at Mitchell Field during the early to middle 1980s.

In spite of dominance of Chicago as an air carrier hub, the long-range trend of Milwaukee's air traffic demanded expansion and improvement of its only air carrier airport. Ground access to Mitchell Field was improved in 1978 with opening of the Airport Spur freeway connecting a short distance west of the airport with I-94, and by construction of a 3,700 stall parking structure as part of the terminal complex. An International Arrivals Building, opened in 1974, has never been effectively used as it failed to generate international flights in competition with O'Hare. A massive expansion of Mitchell Field's terminal built around and including portions of the 1955 terminal building was completed in 1985, and a new control tower was opened soon thereafter.

The number of aircraft, aircraft movements, and licensed pilots in general aviation in Milwaukee County, as elsewhere, far exceeds the number in commercial air carrier service. General aviation includes all aviation activities other than scheduled air carriers and military aviation.

General aviation within the County is carried on both at Mitchell Field and at the County's other airport, Timmerman, which is a general aviation facility without scheduled service. At Mitchell Field there are two FBOs, fixed base operators offering aircraft and engine maintenance, instruction, sales, and charter flights. There are several hangars used by corporate aircraft. With the deregulation of commercial airlines and development of hub-and-spoke patterns, many business organizations found it more convenient to operate their own planes or to use charter services for personal travel and in some instances for cargo between points not adequately served by the regular airlines.

The Lawrence J. Timmerman Airport, owned, like Mitchell Field, by Milwaukee County, is a general aviation field in the northwestern part of the City of Milwaukee. Formerly known as Curtiss-Wright Field, it was originally privately owned and run by a fixed-base operator. The County bought the airport in 1947 and subsequently named it for a member of the County Board and its onetime chairman who was an aviation enthusiast. At the time of its purchase by the County it embraced 130 acres and included a main building built in 1932. It was later expanded to 435 acres, including clear zones. The first of two paved runways was built in 1951. Timmerman Airport did not handle jet aircraft until 1981 because of the fear of neighbors that they would create excessive noise. Tests indicated that one of the corporate jets, a Cessna Citation, caused less noise than some of the propeller-driven aircraft based on the field; as a result Timmerman's first jet was permitted to base there.

Comprehensive regional airport planning has produced several reports looking toward the end of the twentieth century. The regional planning agency — the Southeastern Wisconsin Regional Planning Commission (SEWRPC) — concluded that, while some additional facilities may be needed for general aviation in the future within its seven-county area, expanded facilities at Mitchell Field would be adequate for commercial air carrier service into the next century. It thus will remain as the only air carrier airport in southeastern Wisconsin.

Milwaukee County and its vicinity have been an important center of aviation experimentation and innovation since the early years of the twentieth century. In 1953 Timmerman Airport was the site of the first convention of the newly founded Experimental Aircraft Association, at which time forty planes, mostly antiques, arrived at the field. The organization grew rapidly; by the mid-1960s more than 10,000 aircraft and over 300,000 people attended the annual event, well beyond Timmerman's capacity. Meanwhile, the EAA established at Hales Corners near the southwestern corner of Milwaukee County a museum of antique and experimental aircraft which became internationally known. Small aircraft could be flown in at nearby Hales Corners Airport.

It soon became evident that a more adequate location was needed, both for the museum and for the annual "fly-in" which attracted thousands of aircraft and hundreds of thousands of spectators. In 1970 the EAA decided to locate in Oshkosh, Wisconsin, and in the early 1980s a permanent museum was opened there. The annual fly-in has become the world's largest annual aviation event.

The Port of Milwaukee and the St. Lawrence Seaway

The role of the Port of Milwaukee and the character of its traffic were transformed as a result of opening of the enlarged St. Lawrence Seaway in 1959. The Seaway did not represent creation of a new route between the Great Lakes and the oceans but, rather, the fourth in a successive series of improvements of a route largely provided by nature. The latest pre-Seaway system between Lake Ontario and tidewater in the lower St. Lawrence was a series of canals with fourteen-foot depth paralleling the St. Lawrence River in the hundred miles above Montreal and circumventing its rapids. By 1896 the system was available to small vessels: lake-type vessels could move about 3,000 tons through the canals and small ocean-going ships — "salties" — up to 1,600 tons, topping off to ocean draft at Montreal or other lower St. Lawrence ports. An occasional commercial ship carried cargo directly between Great Lakes ports, including Milwaukee, and overseas, but most of the overseas traffic was transshipped in the lower St. Lawrence.

Following World War II several European shipping companies, aware that the enlarged Seaway would probably be built, pioneered the direct route between the Great Lakes and northwestern Europe on the one hand and Mediterranean and Caribbean ports on the other. These vessels were limited in size by dimensions of the then-existing St. Lawrence canal system, with twenty-seven locks in the hundred miles above Montreal, and with maximum draft of fourteen feet. In 1933 the first scheduled cargo liner service between the lakes and overseas was begun by the Norwegian Fjell Line. By 1939 it was joined by several other companies, using vessels specially designed for the service and able to transit the canals and locks. Many called regularly at Milwaukee as well as other lake ports. World War II caused temporary suspension of these services.

Beginning in 1946, the operations were resumed, in large part with modern new vessels, some of which were designed to be "jumboized" — cut in two and lengthened if or when the proposed Seaway were to become a reality. Milwaukee saw many such vessels.

The enlarged Seaway was authorized by the Canadian Parliament in 1951 and by the U.S. Congress in 1954. In April 1959 the route was opened to commercial traffic, with dedication ceremonies in June. The liner companies which had initiated the direct overseas services quickly brought in much larger vessels. Direct overseas traffic at Milwaukee increased from 12.9 thousand tons in 1951 to 51 thousand in 1958, the last pre-Seaway year. In 1959 the direct overseas traffic at the port increased to 177 thousand tons, and it reached 685 thousand in 1961. During the sixties tonnage fluctuated but reached one million tons in 1970 and 1.13 million in 1973. Following the fuel crisis of that year and depressed international trade conditions, overseas direct traffic at Milwaukee declined to 553 thousand tons in 1974. Subsequently in each year it has been considerably below its former peaks.

In anticipation of the Seaway, the Harbor Commission developed at Jones Island several general cargo breakbulk piers and terminals and a "heavy lift" wharf equipped with cranes to transfer heavy and bulky machinery and other cargoes. These facilities are among the most efficient of any in the Great Lakes. Much of the credit is attributed to the dynamic port director, Harry Brockel, who resigned in 1968 to become associated with the University of Wisconsin-Milwaukee's Center for Great Lakes Studies until his death. Brockel acquired an international reputation for the development and operation of Milwaukee's port. Also considered a factor favoring the port's overseas traffic was the high quality of its labor relations, which enabled it to secure many shipments which otherwise would have moved through the Port of Chicago or coastal ports.

Total traffic at Milwaukee's port, including not only the public facilities at Jones Island and the Inner Harbor but also the numerous private terminals, was considerably greater than the direct overseas traffic each year. Between 1946 and 1961 it generally fluctuated from seven to nine million tons annually, but in 1962 it declined precipitously, to 6.7 million tons, and in subsequent years it continued to fall, reaching a low of 2.9 million tons in 1974.

*Coal being discharged in the lower Milwaukee River from the **Harry L. Findlay**, a vessel which operated under that name between 1933 and 1965.*

The decline in total port tonnage resulted from changes in the nature of the traffic. Coal, which was a dominant component, declined as local demand lessened: the railroads no longer used coal as a locomotive fuel, coal for domestic heating gave way to oil, gas, and electricity, and the decline of many so-called "smoke-stack" industries also reduced demand. The electric utility company serving Milwaukee County and nearby areas developed nuclear power and also received increasing quantities of coal directly by unit train. Although a new coal-fired plant on the lake shore at Oak Creek in southern Milwaukee County was served by a private harbor which for a while received Illinois coal by lake vessel from South Chicago, the plant later shifted to unit trains from Wyoming and central Illinois.

With the reduction in lakeborne bulk cargo traffic, the proportion of direct overseas imports and exports to total port traffic increased; whereas in 1961 overseas tonnage constituted 10.6 percent of the port's total, by 1979 it was 41 percent.

The economic recession of the early 1980s played havoc with Milwaukee's waterborne traffic, as with that of most ports around the world. Great Lakes ports were especially vulnerable because of long-range changes in the economic base of the region. The unfavorable trade balance resulting in large part from the high value of the U.S. dollar and the inability of American manufacturers to compete with lower costs abroad hit the Great Lakes region especially hard. Much of the activity of the region was in "heavy" manufacturing, especially of motor vehicles and machinery, and in the production of metals consumed in those industries. Smaller automobiles meant less demand for metals. In the late 1970s and early '80s Milwaukee County and its immediate hinterland lost much of its former production of durable goods, inputs to which, in turn, involved transport of bulk commodities suitable to waterborne movement.

The major proportion of the Port of Milwaukee's export traffic consists of agricultural produce. Grain — especially corn — but also wheat, barley, and soybeans, moves through the port. Two waterfront grain elevators are largely responsible; both are privately owned and operated. One, the Cargill elevator, is in the lower Menomonee Valley, unreachable by the larger lake vessels because of shallow channel and sharp turns. In recent years it has seen only an occasional smaller ship. The other, the Continental elevator, handles most of the port's grain exports. These fluctuate in accordance with changes in worldwide demand and government policies, such as those relative to exports to the Soviet Union and the "Food for Peace" — Public Law 480 — program for government-aid exports to lesser-developed countries. In addition to grain, much of the government-aid traffic consists of a variety of products, such as powdered milk, handled as breakbulk cargo at the public piers on Jones Island.

A significant part of Milwaukee's port traffic consists of "heavy lift" and "project" cargoes. These consist of machinery and other items which are too heavy or bulky to move overland to or from coastal ports. Milwaukee has a heavy lift wharf equipped with cranes capable of moving up to 300 tons to and from ships alongside.

During the early 1980s it became evident that the port's future depended upon a series of emerging conditions not anticipated earlier. It became clear that the conditions favoring the peak traffic of a decade and more earlier were not likely to recur. Durable goods manufacturing, responsible for much of the traffic earlier, had become less important in the Milwaukee region. Service activities do not create significant port traffic.

Less permanent, perhaps, are the nation's international trade imbalance and the relative increase in transpacific compared with transatlantic trade. These developments have been generally unfavorable to Great Lakes and Seaway traffic volumes.

Physical characteristics of the Seaway became increasingly constraining as the size of ships increased worldwide. The standard twenty-seven-foot depth of the Seaway and connecting Great Lakes channels, together with the dimensions of the Seaway and Welland Canal locks, limits the size of ocean-going ships able to enter the Great Lakes. Another limitation of the Seaway is its vulnerability to blockage due to accidents in the narrow channels and at the fifteen locks between Lake Michigan and tidewater. One blockage late in the 1984 season and two late in 1985 shut off the route for many days. Fortunately, the obstructions were cleared up in sufficient time to prevent any of the "salties" from being landlocked in the lakes over the winter, but the vulnerability remains.

Seasonal closure is a serious disadvantage especially to time-sensitive general cargo. Although it may be feasible to extend the open season by a few weeks, it is not practicable to keep the Seaway open year-round.

Changes in the technology of both water and land transportation are proving to be generally unfavorable for traffic of the Seaway, the Great Lakes, and the lake ports, including Milwaukee. Containerization, railroad piggybacking, and the intercity express highways, including the Interstates, together with the many railroad mergers and consequent economies of scale of railroad operations, particularly since the Staggers Act of 1980, enabled railroads to achieve greater flexibility in rate-making; all tended to improve the competitive position of highway and rail transportation relative to all-water routes between the Great Lakes and coastal ports. Within the ports, economies of scale, in part the result of these developments, have demanded the concentration of traffic at fewer but larger and more efficient ports where capital investment in more adequate harbor improvements and terminals can be justified. In general, the Great Lakes ports, including Milwaukee, are handicapped by these developments.

Lack of a consistent national merchant marine policy is also proving to be disadvantageous to the Port of Milwaukee. The U.S.-flag merchant marine has been declining relative to those of other nations ever since the end of World War II. Very few American-registered vessels enter the lakes through the Seaway; high costs and lack of adequate subsidy policy have resulted in scarcity of American ocean-going ships able to transit the Seaway. Container and roll-on-roll-off vessels, in which private American companies pioneered, are generally too large to serve the Great Lakes-direct overseas traffic. In 1985 and 1986 only two U.S. companies operated scheduled overseas liner services in the lakes; each scheduled Milwaukee

calls approximately monthly during the navigation season. Military cargoes and government-assisted cargoes, including the "Food for Peace"
shipments, involve preference for U.S.-flag ships. Most such cargoes originating in the Great Lakes region move through coastal ports because of
the scarcity of U.S.-flag ocean-going ships available for lakes-overseas
movement. Of particular concern in the mid-1980s is the inconsistent
policy on the one hand of mandatory preference for U.S. ships and on the
other hand of the legal requirement that P.L. 480 cargoes be routed to
produce the "lowest landed cost" at overseas destinations. For many such
cargoes, movement through the lakes and the Seaway meets the cost
requirement, but movement is inhibited because of unavailability of
American ships. In 1986 Milwaukee and other Great Lakes interests
brought suit against the Federal government to resolve this issue.

It is considered very unlikely that traffic through the Port of Milwaukee in the foreseeable future can approach the peak levels of the late
1960s and early '70s, but the port can serve some of the more specialized
needs of agricultural, commercial, and industrial activities of the Milwaukee region and its hinterland.

Milwaukee County's Transit System in the Twentieth Century

In recent decades Milwaukee County's basic mode of internal personal
transportation, as in all metropolitan areas of the nation, changed from
mass transit to the private automobile. Nevertheless, mass transit remains as an essential element of the County's infrastructure.

By 1900 the street railways within the County had been completely
electrified. Between then and the period of World War I the trolley car was
the most important element in influencing the direction and character of
urban growth and expansion within the County. The automobile was still
a novelty and essentially a pleasure vehicle for the affluent. Streetcars,
however, were overcrowded, especially during the morning and afternoon
peak periods. Following an investigation, the Wisconsin Railroad Commission in 1913 ordered that "during the maximum half hour of any rush
period there shall be supplied an average of at least 67 seats for every 100
passengers demanding transportation in a given direction at any point of
the line."

With mass production of automobiles shortly thereafter, they became
available at prices which many people could afford, and street railway
ridership declined rapidly. By 1915 the headway between streetcars was
increased from five minutes to thirty minutes. World War I, however,
arrested the downward trend. Increased demand was met by purchase of
additional cars, initiation of multiple-unit operation in which cars were
coupled into two-car trains, and skip-stops limited to eight per mile were

introduced. To save fuel, temperature in the cars was reduced to 45 degrees F; it was estimated that this saved a million tons of coal annually in addition to reducing the cost of operation.

On April 17, 1920 the first buses were introduced by the transit system on Mitchell Street, where the prospective traffic did not seem to justify extension of the trolley line. Soon thereafter bus routes which served as extensions and feeders to the trolley lines proliferated. The system-wide fare structure, with transfers, was applied to the bus routes, and at many of the transfer points turnouts and shelters were provided.

A separate type of bus operation was begun by the transit system under the name Wisconsin Motor Bus Lines in April 1921, at higher fare than the rest of the system and serving primarily the more affluent areas. Whereas the feeder buses were painted orange, the Wisconsin Motor Bus Lines were distinguished by the "Green" buses. Transfers were issued only between the Green bus routes and not with the other routes of the system. Some Green buses had seating on their roofs, but the upper decks soon had to be enclosed because of weather conditions during most of the year. The Green routes were merged into the general system in the 1950s, and the buses which served them lost their separate identity.

The demise of the street railways was portended in 1926, when the first replacement of trolley cars by buses took place. It was on Lisbon Avenue between Washington Park and Wanderers Rest Cemetery. Five years later buses replaced streetcars on the outer portion of the Oakland Avenue line from Silver Spring to Fox Point. The "bustitution" of the street railways thereafter proceeded rapidly. Following a strike in 1934 with rioting and interruption of transit service, the company decided to convert all of the remaining streetcar lines to operation with free-wheeling rubber-tired vehicles.

The trolley bus, sometimes known as the trackless trolley, was introduced to Milwaukee as replacement for the North Avenue streetcars in 1936. These vehicles had several advantages over both the streetcar and the bus. They could pull up to the curb for loading and discharge, had the flexibility of maneuvering through traffic, were almost noiseless, and, although requiring overhead transmission lines, eliminated the need for trackage. On the other hand, they could not, unlike buses, detour away from their normal routes because of the need for wires. In 1937 the 35th Street line was converted to trolley bus, and in 1938 conversion of the Holton-Mitchell line brought the first trolley buses into downtown Milwaukee.

With entrance of the United States into World War II and consequent rationing of motor fuel and tires and the ending of civilian auto production, further elimination of streetcar lines was prohibited. After the war, the

Scene on West Wisconsin Avenue looking east near 5th Street in the late 1940s. The streetcar is typical of those serving Milwaukee from the 1930s until final abandonment of street railroads in the 1950s. Note the bus stop in the foreground.

policy of replacing the street railway lines was continued. Sale of the system by the Wisconsin Electric Power Company to a new corporation, the Milwaukee and Suburban Transport Corporation, effective January 1, 1953, did not result in any change in the policy. By the end of 1957 only one streetcar line remained. The last scheduled operation was on March 2, 1958. Trolley buses, however, continued to operate until the last route, on National Avenue, was converted to bus operation in 1965. Since then Milwaukee County's transit system has been one of the most extensive all-bus systems in the United States.

After World War II ridership on Milwaukee County's transit system declined almost continuously. In 1950 the system had 214.4 million revenue passengers, but in 1975 there were only 48.7 million, a decline during the quarter-century of 77 percent. It was even more precipitous than that of the nation as a whole, which was 59.5 percent during the same period.

The main reason for the decline was the increased ownership and use of automobiles. In 1950, when automobiles were first generally available after the war, there were 172 thousand, or one per 4.45 persons, registered in Milwaukee County. By 1970, when the County's freeway system was nearly completed, there were over 406 thousand automobiles, or 2.6 per person in the County.

During the past few decades nearly all of the major urban and metropolitan transit systems in the United States which had been under private ownership were transferred to public agencies. Except for a few suburban bus routes which remain in private hands, Milwaukee County's transit system followed the national trend. On July 1, 1975 the Milwaukee and Suburban Transit Corporation ("The Transport Company") sold its properties to Milwaukee County for 13 million dollars. The County contracted with the Transport Company to operate the system, with the same personnel. This arrangement continues to the present, with the system publicly owned and privately operated. Several important reasons made the change in ownership inevitable. As with nearly all urban and metropolitan transit systems, escalating costs and declining ridership made it impossible for private transit systems to be profitable. Public subsidies for mass transit became almost ubiquitous. A Federal agency — UMTA, the Urban Mass Transit Administration — was created to administer subsidies by the Federal government amounting to up to 80 percent of the costs of improvement and operation. Private transit companies were not eligible for such assistance. Because many of the Transport Company's buses were approaching the end of their useful lives, replacement and modernization were necessary.

During the first year of Milwaukee County ownership, 1976, the County Transit System carried 46.2 million riders. Ridership increased to a peak of 67 million in 1980. This was far below the earlier volumes, however, which were over 200 million in the early postwar years.

In 1985 the system handled 56.6 million revenue passengers, a five percent decrease from the 59.6 million of the preceding year. Over 60 percent of the decrease, however, was the result of a change in the policy relative to student riders, which required middle school students to travel in the yellow school buses rather than, as previously, on the County transit system.

In 1985 the system had 580 buses, of which 500 were in service during peak hours. The buses operated on sixty-four routes, and on an average day they carried 65 thousand revenue passengers, or about 20 million per year.

Even before transfer of the bus system from private to County ownership, the system initiated a number of special routes and services. Temporary routes have long been operated at times of special events, such as sports contests and festivals. Also, charter services contribute to the revenues. Of special importance are the "Freeway Flyers" and the "U-Bus" operations.

The Freeway Flyers are the nearest approach to rapid transit in metropolitan Milwaukee. They consist, as the name indicates, of express bus operation on portions of the County's seventy-mile freeway system. The first Freeway Flyer was begun on March 1, 1964 with six daily trips between the parking lot of an outlying shopping center and downtown Milwaukee. As both demand and the freeway system expanded, additional routes were added. At the outer terminal of each route is a "park and ride" facility, consisting either of a dedicated parking area adjacent to a freeway access, or a shopping center parking lot, the excess capacity of which is used during the day.

Between 1980 and 1984, partly as a result of the business recession, use of the Freeway Flyer buses declined each year, but the downward trend was reversed with a slight increase in 1985, during which year the service accounted for 1.47 million passengers.

Another special service of the County Transit System is the U-Bus operation. The University of Wisconsin-Milwaukee, located in the city's northeast area three miles from downtown, is the region's second-largest generator of personal travel. It is basically a commuter institution with over 26 thousand students and a large staff. Parking spaces on the campus are limited, and cars park on the neighborhood streets, causing inconvenience to the residents. To mitigate this condition as far as possible, the university contracted with the transit system to operate several bus routes with subsidized fares from "park and ride" lots in outlying portions of the County to the campus.

There has been some interest in augmenting the transit system by one or more "light rail" lines. These would be essentially modern versions of the street railway, but at least partly on separate rights-of-way. But population densities in Milwaukee County appear to be insufficient to justify the capital investment in such facilities, and the objections of residents in the neighborhoods through which the lines would pass may be formidable. With the policy of reduced Federal expenditures current in the mid-1980s and with consequent increased pressures on State, County, and local budgets to meet other needs, there is very slight prospect of light rail construction in metropolitan Milwaukee in the near future.

Intermodalism, Deregulation, and Milwaukee County's Railroads In the Late Twentieth Century

During World War II the nation's railroads handled over 70 percent of the ton-miles of domestic freight within the United States. Although the volume approximated that of the war years by the late 1960s, the railroads' share of the national total moved by all transportation modes had declined to 40.8 percent in 1969 and to 39.8 percent in 1970. During the following decade the total railroad freight volume fluctuated within a narrow range slightly above the 1970 volume, but the railroads did not share in the total increase by all modes. By the early 1980s the railroads' share varied between 35 and 37 percent annually, even though the ton-miles exceeded the 1944 wartime peak. The commodity mix, however, was significantly different, with increases in bulk commodities, especially coal and grain, and declines in high-revenue freight, including manufactures. The railroads no longer moved less-than-carload freight except as TOFC (trailer on flatcar) or containerized traffic. On the other hand, motor trucks increased their volume of intercity freight by more than ten-fold between 1939 and the mid-1980s. Milwaukee County's freight carriers reflected these trends.

In 1979, before the business recession reduced railroad shipments, metropolitan Milwaukee originated 78 thousand carloads of railroad freight and terminated 95 thousand carloads. It was estimated that the area's rail shippers and consignees accounted for over half of the manufacturing employment, and that over 1.8 thousand people were employed by railroads within the area.

Intermodalism refers to the integration of two or more modes of transportation in freight movement between origin and destination; more specifically, use of motor trucks for part of the movement, mostly for pickup and delivery in terminal areas, and of rail TOFC for the line-haul over longer distances without break-of-bulk en route. In many instances trucks move the shipments by highway for as much as several hundred miles before loading the trailers or containers onto rail cars. Typically, Milwaukee County shipments would move by highway to the Chicago terminal district for loading aboard rail cars, thereby avoiding the delays of all-rail movement through the Chicago terminal complex.

Although the Chicago, North Shore & Milwaukee Railroad pioneered overnight container movement of freight during the twenties, general adoption of TOFC and COFC (containers on flatcar) did not become common until the late 1950s, when the Interstate Commerce Commission authorized tariffs for such intermodal movements. In order to meet the competition of highway trucks, which move over 60 percent of the nation's traffic in manufactured goods, the railroads have, especially since 1980 where permitted, acquired ownership or financial interest in highway carriers. Railroads, in turn, have largely replaced their former freight terminals, typically located in central city areas or near the outlying classification yards, with intermodal "ramps" where the trailers and containers are transferred between truck and rail.

In Milwaukee County, the Milwaukee Road established an intermodal ramp facility on its property in the lower Menomonee Valley, a short distance from downtown. During the early 1980s it loaded and unloaded trailers and containers to and from approximately fifty rail cars per day. The North Western's piggyback facility was established at its National Avenue yard, just west of the Inner Harbor and south of the Milwaukee River; it handled from twenty to eighty trailers per day. The Soo Line, not entering Milwaukee County directly until its takeover of the Milwaukee Road, operated a piggyback interchange on its former main line in suburban Waukesha but closed it early in 1986, moving the highway-rail interchange to the port area on Jones Island.

Intermodal rail traffic originating and terminating in Milwaukee County has been influenced by proximity to metropolitan Chicago, the dominant rail node of the continent. Trailers and containers can be trucked over the Interstate highway to and from Chicago more expeditiously than they can be moved there by rail, even aside from the delays to all-rail movements within the Chicago area.

Beginning with deregulation of air cargo in 1977, the Federal government has pursued a policy of reducing or eliminating regulation of domestic interstate transportation. The Staggers Act in 1980 largely deregulated the railroads, for the first time in a century. The railroads were then able to act more freely in response to economic forces, to meet more effectively the competition of alternative transportation modes. They were also permitted in most instances to become multimodal organizations. Milwaukee area shippers benefited by having an increased number of options in routing of freight. Also, large shippers, for the first time in a century, were able to enter into negotiated rates with the carriers, and several Milwaukee county industries took advantage of such negotiated rates.

Even before the Staggers Act, the U.S. railroads were freed from many of the former restrictions against abandoning unprofitable routes and services. In some instances where shippers had alternative highway transportation, abandonments took place; in other instances changes in location of industries made continuation of rail service redundant. Where a major railroad abandoned service over a lightly used and unprofitable route, the line could be continued by conversion into a separate "short line" with connection to a larger railroad but insuring, at least for a while, continued rail service to establishments on the line. Milwaukee County saw one such conversion. A route of the Milwaukee Road from its North Milwaukee yard to Horicon and other points northwest of the metropolitan area became an independent short line, the Wisconsin & Southern. Prior to the Soo-Milwaukee Road merger, this line had furnished the entrance of the Soo Line into Milwaukee by means of trackage rights. The merger permitted the Soo Line to enter Milwaukee directly over the former Milwaukee Road tracks.

Several other railroad lines were abandoned or greatly reduced in importance within Milwaukee County. One was the former northerly main line of the Chicago & North Western, from the passenger depot which stood at the foot of Wisconsin Avenue in Milwaukee northward along the lakefront and the east side of the Milwaukee River. The line was abandoned when the passenger depot was closed in 1965, when the North Western joined the Milwaukee Road in the new Union passenger station. Finally, all North Western passenger service at Milwaukee ended with creation of Amtrak in 1971. The former North Western right-of-way from the lakefront depot site northward through the city's East Side and the village of Shorewood was in part converted into a bicycle and hiking trail under County auspices, with a single track remaining for part of the distance. It provides an infrequent freight service for several remaining industries from the railroad's Butler Yard northwest of the County.

Another redundant local rail line is the so-called "beer line" of the former Milwaukee Road paralleling the west bank of the Milwaukee River. This line lost nearly all of its traffic with the closing of the Schlitz brewery.

During recent years the railroad map of the United States changed rapidly, in part as the result of mergers among many of the larger railroad systems. The Chicago & North Western, one of the two principal railroads serving Milwaukee County, had, during the past several decades, not only abandoned many of its economically marginal and unprofitable lines but also had taken over several important regional railroads by means of merger. These extended the territory accessible to Milwaukee County by single-carrier movements. Also, by constructing a line into the Powder River basin in Wyoming, it could compete with a rival in securing low-sulfur coal traffic, some of which moves to the electric plants of the Milwaukee region by unit trains.

The former Milwaukee Road, on the other hand, became bankrupt in 1977 and gave up over half its route mileage. With abandonment of its line west of Minnesota to the Pacific Northwest it converted from a "transcontinental" railroad to a much smaller regional system.

Nearly eight years of studies, hearings, and litigation ensued relative to the reorganization and prospective future of the railroad. It was clear that industries in the Milwaukee area could be assured of competitive railroad service only if the Milwaukee Road could be restored to health and that it was possible by merger with a stronger railroad. But which one?

In order to determine the stand that Milwaukee area interests should take relative to a prospective merger, the mayor of Milwaukee appointed an Urban Transportation Study group consisting of representatives of business, academia, and the several railroads. The group strongly recommended opposition to merger of the Milwaukee Road with the Chicago & North Western on the grounds that the Milwaukee area would be dominated by a single railroad without effective rail competition.

The Soo Line has a main line passing through Waukesha County, a short distance west of Milwaukee County. It served the same territory as the truncated Milwaukee Road; both had lines passing through the Milwaukee metropolitan area between Chicago and Minneapolis - St. Paul. Merger of the two would eliminate some duplication of routes and facilities and at the same time create a stronger competitor for the North Western.

The final consummation of the Soo-Milwaukee Road merger took place on January 1, 1986, with the absorption of the Milwaukee Road into the Soo Line Railroad. The Soo Line, in turn, is 56 percent owned, and thus controlled by, the Canadian Pacific.

Although Milwaukee County industries are assured of continuation of effective competitive railroad service, some aspects of the merger are negative, insofar as the County is concerned. Railroad employment in the County is substantially reduced. Much of the operation of the merged railroad system is moved from Milwaukee upstate in Wisconsin, primarily to Stevens Point, and to Chicago. Further reduction of railroad facilities and employment in Milwaukee's lower Menomonee Valley, once a thriving railroad complex, became inevitable. This creates major problems for Milwaukee in prospective reuse of increasing areas of redundant and derelict former railroad sites. Perhaps of equal importance, the Milwaukee Road as such no longer exists, and the Milwaukee name disappeared from the logo and name of the merged railroad. For the first time since 1851 the name "Milwaukee" is not a part of any railroad's name; this absence is symbolic of Milwaukee's reduced role as a railroad center.

On the other hand, some additional through freight traffic is being rerouted through Milwaukee County. The merged railroad chose the former Milwaukee Road's main line through the city of Milwaukee as its principal Chicago-Twin Cities lines, diverting most through freight trains from the former main line of the Soo, which passes through Waukesha County.

For years following World War II Milwaukee enjoyed excellent passenger train service to Chicago, the Twin Cities, Madison, and other midwestern points via both the Milwaukee Road and the North Western. Frequent trains connected Milwaukee with Chicago. As elsewhere, Milwaukee's passenger train schedules declined both in numbers and in quality during the past few decades. From about 10,000 intercity trains per day in 1929 the number decreased to about 300 by 1971. Although the passenger equipment of both of Milwaukee's two railroads was generally in good shape and some of it relatively new, patronage fell off rapidly. Growth of the Interstate highway system encouraged intercity automobile travel. Airlines, including short-distance commuter lines, were rapidly expanding. The car-rental business was growing, and air travelers could arrange to have a car awaiting their arrival at almost any airport. The intercity buses offered formidable competition to the railroads, especially for travel between points less than a few hundred miles apart. The high-density corridors radiating from Milwaukee County, such as those to Chicago, Madison, and Green Bay, were especially suitable for bus travel. The Greyhound Corporation, which began as a local operator in northern Minnesota in the 1920s, expanded nationwide until it operated 60 percent of all scheduled intercity bus services in the nation. In Milwaukee it utilized a new terminal on Wisconsin Avenue, and in Chicago its terminal was in the Loop. Both were more centrally located than were the railroad depots in the respective cities. Because buses are smaller units than trains, they could offer more frequent service and could adjust their schedules more rapidly to fluctuations in demand than could railroads.

Other intercity bus companies proliferated, often in competition with Greyhound. Among those serving Milwaukee County were the Wisconsin Coach Lines, Wisconsin-Michigan Coaches, and the popular Badger Coaches connecting Milwaukee with Madison, the state capital and university community. Three bus lines, including Greyhound, have direct services between Milwaukee and O'Hare airport, thereby reinforcing the competitive position of O'Hare relative to Milwaukee County's Mitchell International Airport.

As a result of declining railroad passenger traffic, the Interstate Commerce Commission was authorized by the Railroad Passenger Service Act of 1970 to "prescribe regulations for the adequacy of intercity passenger train service." In 1971 the National Railroad Passenger Corporation (Amtrak) was created to take over most of the remaining intercity railroad passenger services. The railroads were given the option of joining or not joining the new public corporation. If they chose to join, they were relieved of responsibility for continuing any of their own intercity passenger trains but were required to operate, for compensation, any trains that Amtrak chose to use on their routes. Both the Milwaukee Road and the North Western joined Amtrak. Since both had passenger services between Chicago, Milwaukee, the Twin Cities, and beyond, Amtrak had to decide whether to provide service over either or both the railroads. It decided to discontinue all passenger trains serving Milwaukee, except those to Chicago and the Twin Cities. It further chose to use the Milwaukee Road's main line between those points rather than the North Western's, because the former line, having previously received substantial federal aid for roadbed and track rehabilitation, was in better condition. Since the formation of Amtrak all passenger trains serving Milwaukee have been re-equipped, and the quality and reliability of the service have been considerably improved.

The same cannot be said about schedule frequency. In 1973 Amtrak had seven daily trains in each direction between Milwaukee and Chicago. This was substantially fewer than the fifty on three railroads two decades earlier. Two of Amtrak's trains stopped in Milwaukee en route between Chicago, the Twin Cities, and Seattle. In subsequent years the service was reduced to as few as three trains between Milwaukee and Chicago and one tri-weekly train to the Twin Cities and Seattle. In early 1986 the Milwaukee service consisted of four daily trains each way Milwaukee-Chicago, one of which served the Twin Cities and Seattle. There were, however, serious gaps in the schedules, such as the absence of any southbound train after mid-afternoon, or northbound from Chicago after early evening, thereby greatly reducing the utility of Amtrak for round-trip business or social travel between the two cities.

The Federal policy in the mid-1980s to achieve a balanced budget, in part by reducing government services, has been a cloud over Amtrak, making realistic planning for the future impossible. In 1986 there was a serious threat to continuation of Amtrak. If it were to terminate, Milwaukee County would have no railroad passenger service whatever.

Conclusion

Development and evolution of Milwaukee County during the century and one-half since its beginning have been, as with all areas, dependent upon the nature and availability of both external and internal transportation. External transportation made possible the specialized economic roles that the County played, and is playing, relative to the State, the Midwest, the nation, and the world. Its manufactured goods and the agricultural produce and resources of its hinterland are distributed worldwide, and it receives inputs from all parts of the United States and the rest of the world. All of it must be transported within the County.

Within Milwaukee County movement of people and goods is served by a reasonably adequate set of multimodal transportation systems which have facilitated the spread of the urbanized area and have been a major force in the evolution of the metropolitan area, characterized by low population density and freedom from congestion in comparison with most large contemporary American urban areas.

Throughout its evolution Milwaukee County has had to meet the competition as a transportation node of its much larger neighbor less than one hundred miles to the south. Because of location on the west side of Lake Michigan, it has always been in the shadow of Chicago. All land travel to the south and east and some to the west must pass through or around the Chicago metropolitan area at the south end of the lake. Except for air transportation, Lake Michigan constitutes a barrier between Milwaukee County and the eastern core region of the continent; there are, in 1986, no regular crosslake services. Even by air, the "intervening opportunity" of the world's busiest civil airport a few minutes by air from Milwaukee County dominates its air traffic potential.

Nevertheless, Milwaukee and Milwaukee County have developed their own characteristic milieu and ambience. With a changing economic base in the late twentieth century, the area has changing transportation requirements. Planning and coordination of its transportation facilities and services are indispensable prerequisites to renewed and continued health and prosperity of the metropolitan area of which Milwaukee County is the core and heart.

Selected Bibliography

Ballert, Albert G., "The Lake Michigan Car-ferry Service," *Papers of the Michigan Academy of Science, Arts and Letters* 36 (1950): 379-385.

Barton-Aschmann Associates, Inc., *Milwaukee Area Transit Plan,* prepared for the County of Milwaukee, Wisconsin Expressway and Transportation Commission. Chicago, June, 1971.

Canfield, Joseph M., *T M, The Milwaukee Electric Railway & Light Company.* Chicago: Central Electric Railfans Association, Inc., 1972.

Cary, John W., *The Organization and History of the Chicago, Milwaukee and St. Paul Railway Company.* Milwaukee, n.d., ca. 1893.

Chicago and North Western Railway Company, *Yesterday and Today, A History of the Chicago and North Western Railway System.* Chicago, 1905 and 1910 (two editions).

Flint, Henry W., *The Railroads of the United States; Their History and Statistics.* Philadelphia: John E. Potter and Co., 1868.

Foeste, Joan, "The Changing Role of the Commuter Airplane in Meeting the Demand for Air Service at Wisconsin Communities in the Post Deregulation Period." Master's thesis, University of Wisconsin-Milwaukee Department of Geography, December 1982.

General Mitchell Field: A Record of Progress; 50th Anniversary, 1926-1976. Milwaukee: Ken Cook International, 1976.

Goals for Greater Milwaukee: Deciding Our Future. Milwaukee: Goals for Greater Milwaukee 2000, Inc., n.d., ca. 1984.

Hamming, Edward, *The Port of Milwaukee.* Research Paper No. 26. Chicago: The University of Chicago Department of Geography, December 1952.

Heilmann, Ronald L., Harold M. Mayer, and Eric Schenker, *Great Lakes Transportation in the Eighties.* Madison: University of Wisconsin Sea Grant Institute, 1986.

Hilton, George W., and John F. Due, *The Electric Interurban Railways in America.* Stanford, Cal.: Stanford University Press, 1960.

Horner and Shifrin, *Airport Plan, Milwaukee County, Wisconsin.* Milwaukee County Board of Supervisors, March 1945.

Howard, D.H., "Construction of the Skokie Valley Line," *Journal of the Western Society of Engineers* 32 (June 1927):82-194.

Kuhm, Herbert W., "When Milwaukee's Streetcars Were Horse-Drawn," *Milwaukee History* 2 (Summer 1979):30-37.

Kuhm, Herbert W., "The Whaleback Era and the S.S. *Christopher Columbus,*" *Milwaukee History* 5 (Winter 1982):101-108.

Mayer, Harold M., "By Rail Across Lake Michigan," *Trains* 2 (September 1942):14-20.

Mayer, Harold M., "Wisconsin's Great Lakes Ports: Background and Future Alternatives," for the Wisconsin Department of Transportation, Division of Planning. Milwaukee: The University of Wisconsin Center for Great Lake Studies, July 1975.

Mayer, Jonathan D., "The Journey to Work: Ethnicity and Occupation in Milwaukee, 1860-1900," Ph.D. dissertation, University of Michigan Department of Geography, 1977.

McShane, Clay, *Technology and Reform: Street Railways and the Growth of Milwaukee, 1887-1900.* Madison: The State Historical Society of Wisconsin, 1974.

Middleton, William D., *North Shore; America's Fastest Interurban.* San Francisco, Cal.: Golden West Books, 1964.

Milwaukee Board of Harbor Commissioners, "The Milwaukee Harbor Project," Milwaukee, 1936.

Milwaukee Department of City Development, *The Milwaukee Railroad Operations Study,* 1983.

Mueller, Paul S., "Locational Behavior of Manufacturing Establishments in the Milwaukee SMSA, 1947-1979." M.A. thesis, University of Wisconsin-Milwaukee Department of Geography, May 1980.

Newman, Donald, *Headlights & Markers: A Pictorial History of Public Transportation in Milwaukee.* Milwaukee: University of Wisconsin-Milwaukee, 1982.

"The North Western's New Line to Milwaukee," *Railway Gazette* 39 (August 11, 1905):128-129.

Origin-Destination Traffic Survey of the Milwaukee Metropolitan Area. A Study Conducted by State Highway Commission of Wisconsin and Local Government Units in Cooperation with the U.S. Public Roads Administration. Milwaukee, 1946.

Quaife, Milo, *Lake Michigan.* The American Lake Series. Indianapolis: The Bobbs-Merrill Company, 1944.

Richards, Curtis William, *Differential Traffic Changes on Transit Routes in Milwaukee, 1950 to 1975.* Milwaukee: The University of Wisconsin-Milwaukee Center for Urban Transportation Studies, 1977.

Schenker, Eric, *The Port of Milwaukee: An Economic Review.* Madison: The University of Wisconsin Press, 1967.

"Second Generation Regional Airport Plan Ready for Public Review," *Southeastern Wisconsin Regional Planning Commission Newsletter* 26 (September-October 1986).

Simon, Roger David, "The Expansion of an Industrial City: Milwaukee, 1880-1910." Ph.D. dissertation, University of Wisconsin (Madison) Department of History, 1971.

Southeastern Wisconsin Regional Planning Commission, *A Jurisdictional Highway System Plan for Milwaukee County, Wisconsin.* Waukesha, 1969.

Southeastern Wisconsin Regional Planning Commission, *A Regional Land Use Plan for Southeastern Wisconsin - 2000.* Waukesha, 1975.

Southeastern Wisconsin Regional Planning Commission, *Milwaukee Area Alternative Primary Transit System Plan Preparation, Test, and Evaluation.* Waukesha, 1982.

Southeastern Wisconsin Regional Planning Commission, *A Primary Transit System Plan for the Milwaukee Area.* Waukesha, 1982.

Southeastern Wisconsin Regional Planning Commission, *Transit-Related Socioeconomic, Land Use, and Transportation Conditions and Trends in the Milwaukee Area.* Waukesha, 1980.

Still, Bayrd, *Milwaukee: The History of a City.* Madison: The State Historical Society of Wisconsin, 1948; second printing, 1965.

Temkin, Barry, "Oats and Iron: Horse Drawn Transportation in Milwaukee, 1850-1890." Bachelor's thesis, University of Wisconsin (Madison) Department of History, 1970.

Thaller, Michael, "Structure and Process in Railroad Network Development Under Competition: The Case of the Granger Railroads." Ph.D. dissertation, University of Wisconsin-Milwaukee Department of Geography, 1973.

Uber, Harvey A., *Environmental Factors in the Development of Wisconsin.* Milwaukee: Marquette University Press, 1937.

U.S. Army Corps of Engineers, *The Port of Milwaukee, Wisconsin,* prepared by the Water Resources Center Port Series, No. 47, revised 1984. (Also earlier editions). Washington: U.S. Government Printing Office, 1984.

U.S. Army Corps of Engineers, *Transportation on the Great Lakes.* Transportation Series, No. 1, revised 1937. (Also earlier editions). Washington: U.S. Government Printing Office, 1937.

U.S. Army Corps of Engineers, *Waterborne Commerce of the United States, Part 3, Waterways and Harbors, Great Lakes.* New Orleans: District Engineers, U.S. Army Engineer District. Annual.

Whitebeck, Ray Hughes, *The Geography and Economic Development of Southeastern Wisconsin.* Madison: Wisconsin Geological and Natural History Survey, 1921.

General Bibliography

A major objective of this volume of six essays on selected aspects of the history of Milwaukee County is to move the focus of historical research and writing away from its previous narrow concentration on the City of Milwaukee and toward a broader view of Milwaukee County and even of the larger metropolitan area surrounding the City of Milwaukee. This is not to suggest that the earlier emphasis on the City was misplaced — the City remains central to any study of southeastern Wisconsin — but rather that it is long overdue for us to recognize the growing role of County government and of the many suburbs, both within and outside Milwaukee County.

In furtherance of this objective, this bibliographical essay is intended to provide guidance to the general reader and the scholar alike who want to know more about Milwaukee County history and who will conclude that the footnotes and bibliographical notes to the individual essays are too narrowly focused for their needs. This essay deliberately avoids covering the City of Milwaukee because the task is so enormous; we desperately need a competent and up-to-date bibliography for the City (and the County and metropolian area as well), but meanwhile those interested may consult Still (pp. 601-610), Anderson and Olson (p. 222), Byron Anderson, and Fleckner and Mallach, all noted below.

Most histories of Milwaukee deal with the city and pay little specific attention to the County or fail to distinguish the City from the rest of the County. This is true of A. C. Wheeler, James S. Buck, Rudolph A. Koss, Howard L. Conard, John Goadby Gregory's 1931 volumes, H. Russell Austin, Bayrd Still, and Robert W. Wells. More attention to the County is found in Frank A. Flower, *History of Milwaukee, Wisconsin, from Prehistoric Times to the Present date* (1881); Jerome A. Watrous, editor, *Memoirs of Milwaukee County* (1909); William George Bruce, *History of Milwaukee, City and County* (1922); Joseph Schafer, *Four Wisconsin Counties: Prairie and Forest* (1927), and Gregory, *Southeastern Wisconsin: A History of Old Milwaukee County* (1932). George J. Lankevich, compiler and editor, *Milwaukee: A Chronological and Documentary History, 1673-1977* (1977), though prone to error, is unique. The Writers' Program of the WPA produced a never-published typescript "History of Milwaukee," dated 1947, which is available in several area libraries. Harry H. Anderson and Frederick I. Olson, *Milwaukee: At the Gathering of the Waters* (1981, 1984) is the most recent general history; its relatively short text is augmented by forty-two sketches of area institutions, both business and non-business. The most scholarly history, Bayrd Still, *Milwaukee: The History of a City* (1948, reissued 1965), is seriously out of date.

The records and governing proceedings of the City and County of

Milwaukee and of the several suburbs are extensive but rarely organized in true archival form or readily available. A guide to some of these records is John A. Fleckner and Stanley A. Mallach, editors, *Guide to Historical Resources in Milwaukee Area Archives* (1976). Printed reports of these governments are generally available, although not always complete, in the offices of the various governments or their departments, as well as in major area libraries, especially the Milwaukee Public Library and the University of Wisconsin - Milwaukee Golda Meir Library, as well as in the Milwaukee County Historical Society.

Background and basic data, including statistics, may be found in the decennial federal and state censuses, the *Wisconsin Blue Books* (1853, annual 1959-82, thereafter biennial), H. Yuan Tien, editor, *Milwaukee Metropolitan Fact Book 1940, 1950, and 1960* (1962), Frances Beverstock and Robert P. Stuckert, editors, *Metropolitan Milwaukee Fact Book: 1970* (1972), and the records and reports of the City Club (now defunct), the Citizens' Governmental Research Bureau (especially its *Bulletins*), and the Southeastern Wisconsin Regional Planning Commission. City directories for Milwaukee since 1847-48 and for the larger suburbs in the twentieth century are invaluable. Legislative data up to 1942 were assembled by the Wisconsin Historical Records Survey in *Origins and Legislative History of County Boundaries in Wisconsin* (1942) and *County Government in Wisconsin* (3 volumes, 1942).

Also generally useful are Ray Hughes Whitbeck, *The Geography and Development of Southeastern Wisconsin* (1921); *Milwaukee History,* the quarterly of the Milwaukee County Historical Society, indexed (since 1978; formerly *Historical Messenger*); Index to the *Milwaukee Sentinel,* 1837-1890, at the Milwaukee Public Library; Byron Anderson, *A Bibliography of Masters Theses and Doctoral Dissertations on Milwaukee Topics* (1981); Donald E. Oehlerts, compiler, *Guide to Wisconsin Newspapers, 1833-1957* (1958); and George F. Breitbach, sponsor, *Manual of Duties of All Elected and Appointed County Officials and Commissions,* a snapshot in 1937 of Milwaukee County government.

The physical appearance of an earlier era, the latter 1800s, may be found in the twelve listings for Milwaukee communities in Elizabeth Singer Maule, *Bird's Eye Views of Wisconsin Communities: A Preliminary Checklist* (1977). For maps, illustrations, and data a century ago see H. Belden and Co., *Illustrated Historical Atlas of Milwaukee County, Wisconsin* (1876). The earlier built environment is also featured in Richard W. E. Perrin, *Milwaukee Landmarks* (revised 1979); Landscape Research, *Built in Milwaukee, An Architectural View of the City* (1981); *Guide to Milwaukee County Landmarks* (1981, with 1984 update); and H. Russell Zimmermann, *The Heritage Guidebook: Landmarks and Historical Sites in Southeastern Wisconsin* (1976).

General Bibliography

Anderson, Byron. *A Bibliography of Masters Theses and Doctoral Dissertations on Milwaukee Topics.* Madison: State Historical Society of Wisconsin, 1981.

Anderson, Harry H., and Frederick I. Olson. *Milwaukee: At the Gathering of the Waters.* Tulsa: Continental Heritage Press, 1981.

Beverstock, Frances, and Robert P. Stuckert, eds. *Metropolitan Fact Book: 1970.* Milwaukee: University of Wisconsin-Milwaukee, 1972.

Breitbach, George F. *Manual of Duties of All Elected and Appointed County Officials and Commissions.* Milwaukee: Milwaukee County Clerk's Office, 1937.

Bruce, William George. *History of Milwaukee, City and County.* 3 vols. Chicago: S. J. Clarke, 1922.

Fleckner, John A., and Stanley Mallach, eds. *Guide to Historical Resources in Milwaukee Area Archives.* Milwaukee: Milwaukee Area Archives Group, 1976.

[Flower, Frank A.] *History of Milwaukee, Wisconsin, From Prehistoric Times to the Present Date.* Chicago: Western Historical Co., 1881.

Guide to Milwaukee County Landmarks. Milwaukee: Milwaukee County Historical Society, 1981, rev. 1984.

Gregory, John Goadby. *Southeastern Wisconsin: A History of Old Milwaukee County.* Chicago: S. J. Clarke, 1932.

H. Belden Co., *Illustrated Historical Atlas of Milwaukee County, Wisconsin.* Chicago: H. Belden & Co., 1876.

"History of Milwaukee." WPA unpublished typescript #4. Milwaukee, 1947.

Landscape Research Associates. *Built in Milwaukee: An Architectural View of the City.* Milwaukee: Department of City Development, 1981.

Lankevich, George J., ed. *Milwaukee: A Chronological and Documentary History, 1673-1977.* Dobbs Ferry, N. Y. Oceana Publication, Inc., 1977.

Maule, Elizabeth Singer. *Bird's Eye Views of Wisconsin Communities: A Preliminary Checklist.* Madison: State Historical Society of Wisconsin, 1977.

Oehlerts, Donald D., compiler. *Guide to Wisconsin Newspapers, 1833-1957.* Madison: State Historical Society of Wisconsin, 1958.

Perrin, Richard W. E. *Milwaukee Landmarks.* Milwaukee: Milwaukee Public Museum, revised edition, 1979.

Schafer, Joseph. *Four Wisconsin Counties; Prairie and Forest.* Madison: State Historical Society of Wisconsin, 1927.

Still, Bayrd. *Milwaukee: The History of a City.* Madison: State Historical Society of Wisconsin, 1948.

Tien, H. Yuan, ed. *Milwaukee Metropolitan Fact Book, 1940-1950, and 1960.* Madison: University of Wisconsin Press, 1962.

Watrous, Jerome A., ed. *Memories of Milwaukee County*. 2 vols. Madison: Western Historical Association, 1909.

Wisconsin Blue Books. 1853, annual 1859-82, thereafter biennial. Madison: Legislative Reference Bureau, 1853-Present.

Wisconsin Historical Records Survey. *County Government in Wisconsin*. 3 vols. Madison, 1942.

―――――――――――. *Origins and Legislative History of County Boundaries in Wisconsin*. Madison, 1942.

Whitbeck, Ray Hughes. *The Geography and Development of Southeastern Wisconsin*. Madison: State of Wisconsin, 1921.

Zimmermann, H. Russell. *The Heritage Guidebook: Landmarks and Historical Sites in Southeastern Wisconsin*. Milwaukee: Heritage Wisconsin Corporation, 1976.

Photographic and Illustration Credits

City of Milwaukee, Engineering Department:
67.
Kalmbach Publishing Co.:
331.
Milwaukee County Administration:
205 top.
Milwaukee County Board:
134, 136, 176, 310, 364.
Milwaukee County Department of Parks, Recreation and Culture:
296, 313.
Milwaukee County Executive:
125, 131.
Milwaukee County Graphic Reproduction:
359, 369.
Milwaukee County Historical Society:
6, 20, 25, 26, 28, 29, 32, 35, 36, 38, 39, 41, 44, 46, 52, 61, 65, 90, 94, 95, 98 all, 102, 106, 109, 112, 117 bottom, 128, 149, 156, 166, 174, 183, 186, 200, 203, 207, 208, 212, 214, 215, 220, 222 all, 224, 227, 259, 261, 263, 268, 270, 282, 284, 286 all, 298, 299, 304, 305, 309, 335, 336, 339, 342, 345, 348, 350, 351, 354, 356, 361, 374.
Milwaukee County School of Nursing:
205 bottom.
Milwaukee County Sheriff's Department:
179, 180.
Milwaukee Journal:
151, 154, 157, 160, 165, 168, 219, 235, 312.
Milwaukee Public Library, Local History Room:
117 top, 119, 352.
Richard Hyrnewicki:
frontispiece, dust jacket.
Robert W. Cassidy:
291.

Notes on Authors

Frederick I. Olson, Professor Emeritus of History, University of Wisconsin-Milwaukee, took all of his degrees at Harvard University. A former president of the Milwaukee County Historical Society, he serves on numerous boards and committees relating to state and local history, and he has written and lectured extensively in these fields. Recently, with Harry H. Anderson, he wrote *Milwaukee: At the Gathering of the Waters.*

Donald B. Vogel holds degrees from St. Lawrence University (B. A.), San Jose State College (M. A.), and State University (Ph. D.). He is Professor of Governmental Affairs, at the University of Wisconsin-Milwaukee, specializing in public administration. He is co-author of *Milwaukee: A Contemporary Urban Profile.*

Karel D. Bicha has a bachelor's degree from the University of Wisconsin-Madison and a doctorate from the University of Minnesota in 1963. Professor of History at Marquette University, he specializes in American history and is the author of several studies on ethnic groups.

Steven M. Avella is Assistant Professor of History at St. Francis Seminary, with degrees from Dominican College, Franciscan School of Theology, and the University of Notre Dame. He is currently at work on a study of Catholic social and intellectual life in Wisconsin.

Harry H. Anderson, Executive Director of the Milwaukee County Historical Society, has degrees from Concordia College and the University of South Dakota and additional graduate work at Northwestern University. He is co-author of a history of Milwaukee, has edited the Frank-Kerler letters, and has written many articles relating to Milwaukee and western history.

Harold M. Mayer has a Ph. D. from the University of Chicago and currently serves as Professor of Geography at the University of Wisconsin-Milwaukee with specializations in transportation and urban geography. He has taught at the University of Chicago and Kent State University and was a city planner in Chicago and Philadelphia. He has written extensively on city planning, transportation, and urban geography.

Ralph M. Aderman, who has a Ph. D. in American literature from the University of Wisconsin-Madison, is Professor Emeritus of English at the University of Wisconsin-Milwaukee. He has collected and edited the letters of Washington Irving and J. K. Paulding as well as several collections of essays. Since 1956 he has edited *Milwaukee History* and its predecessor, the *Historical Messenger.*